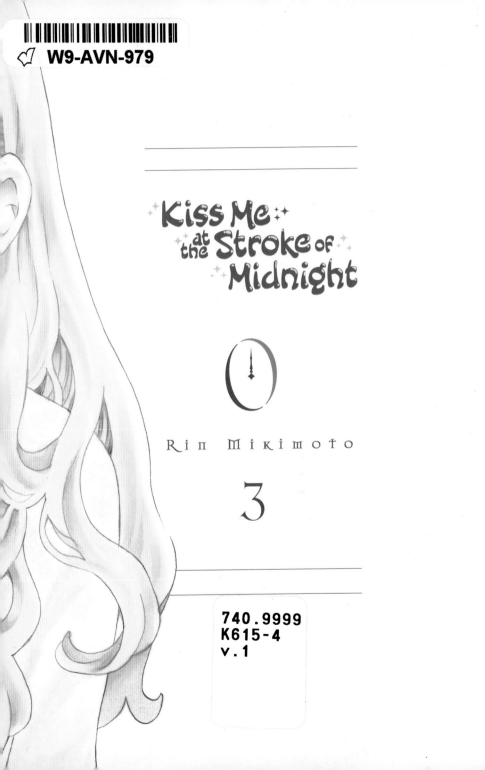

Kiss Me at the Stroke of Midnight

Rin Mikimoto

3

Contents

STORY.8

I Call Dibs

004

STORY.9

She's Really Cute

049

STORY.10

If You Want It So Badly, Then Do It with Me

091

Simultaneous Compilation
"Love's Reach" Special Chapter

The Genius Girl's Happy Wedding

134

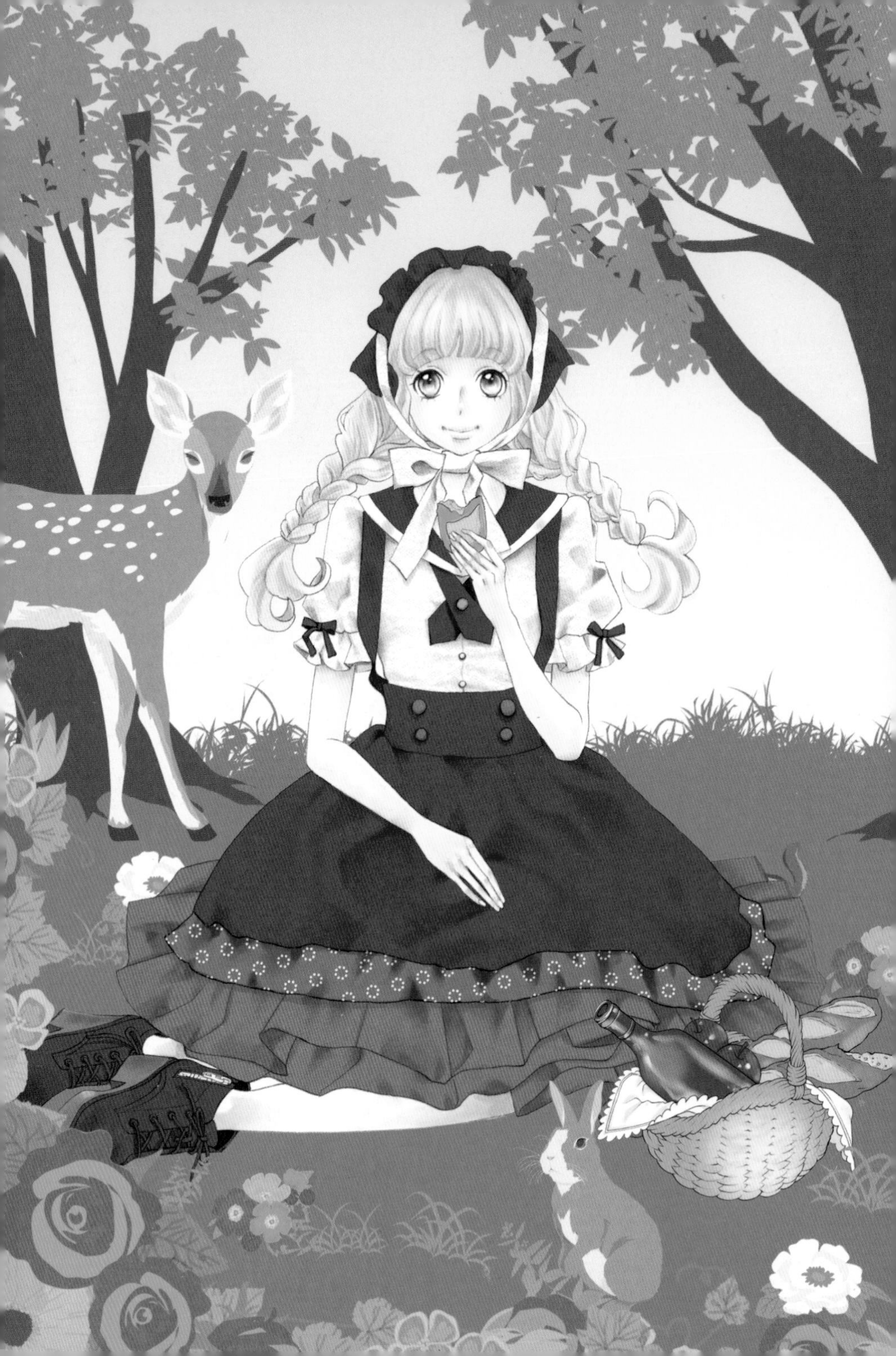

Kiss Me
at the Stroke of
Midnight

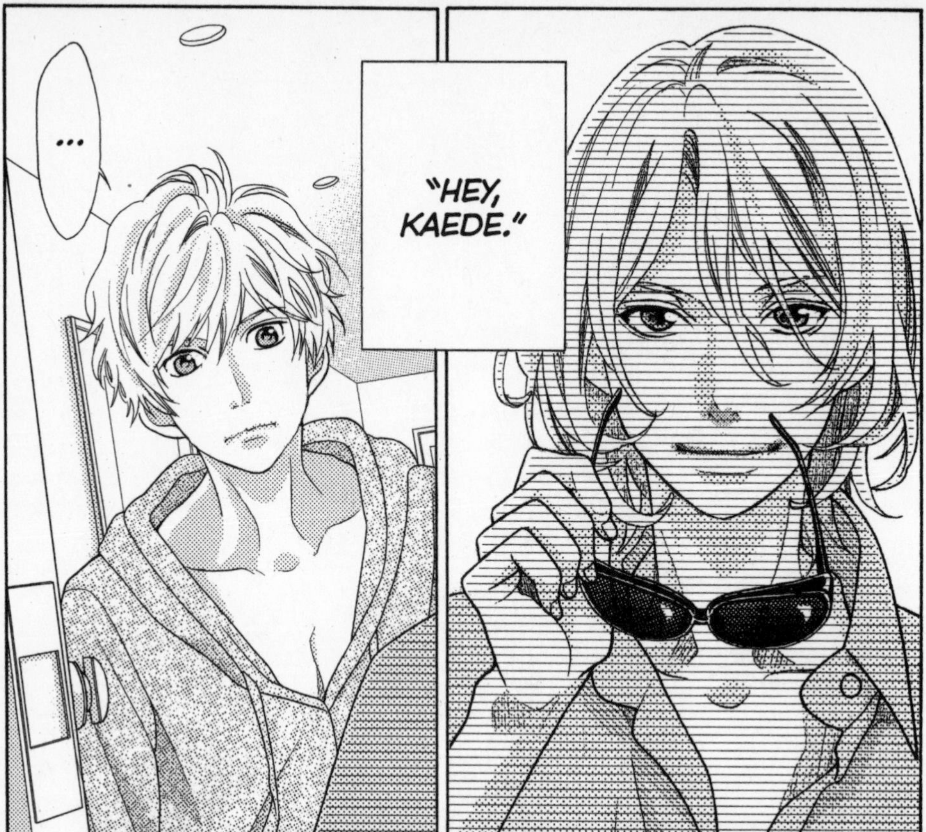
"HEY, KAEDE."
...

STORY&CAST

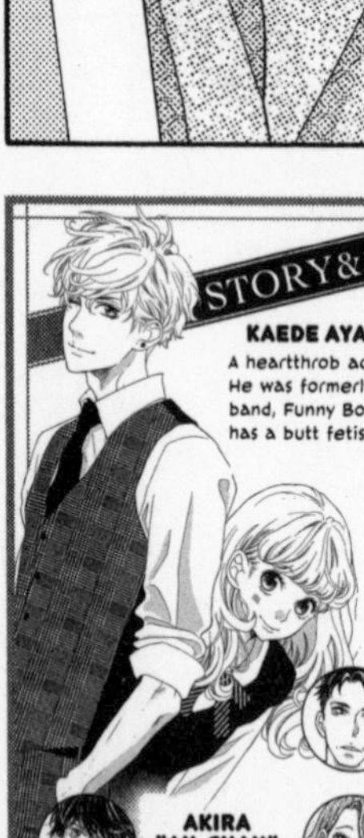

KAEDE AYASE
A heartthrob actor who's a real prince! He was formerly a member of the boy band, Funny Bone. His secret is that he has a butt fetish.

HINANA "NANA" HANAZAWA
A high school girl with an overly serious personality. Her secret is that she wants to fall in love with a prince from a fairy tale.

SHIGE-CHAN
Kaede's manager. He struggles to keep Kaede in check.

AKIRA "AH-CHAN"
Hinana's childhood friend. He's in a band.

HIKARU "RUN-CHAN"
Hinana's childhood friend. She's the vice president of the student council.

Kiss Me at the Stroke of Midnight

Hinana, a high school girl, dreams of a fairy-tale romance with a prince. And when she meets the famous heartthrob, Kaede, her dream becomes a reality...! After getting an unexpectedly low grade on a quiz, Hinana decides to study extra hard and refrain from thinking about Kaede all the time...but after getting an invitation from Kaede, she ends up going to his place! Hinana continues her studying even at Kaede's, but seeing Kaede asleep and defenseless makes her heart pound like crazy! To Kaede's surprise, he discovers that Hinana may not be as innocent as she appears. But just when the two of them were happily flirting, Kaede's former Funny Bone bandmate Mitsuki shows up...!

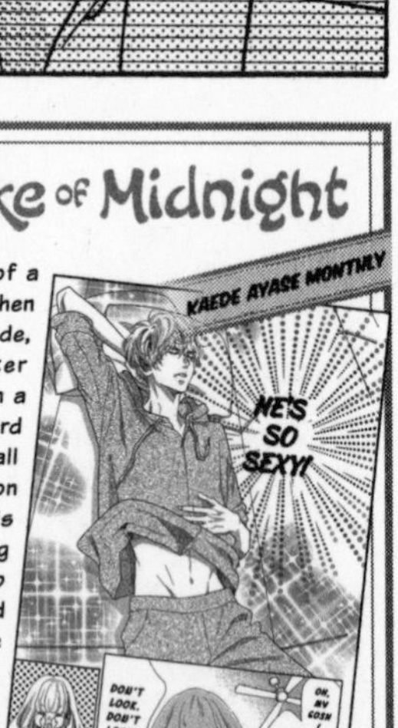
KAEDE AYASE MONTHLY
HE'S SO SEXY!
DON'T LOOK. DON'T LOOK.
OH, MY GOSH! HIS STOMACH! HIS ABS!
HIGHLIGHTS

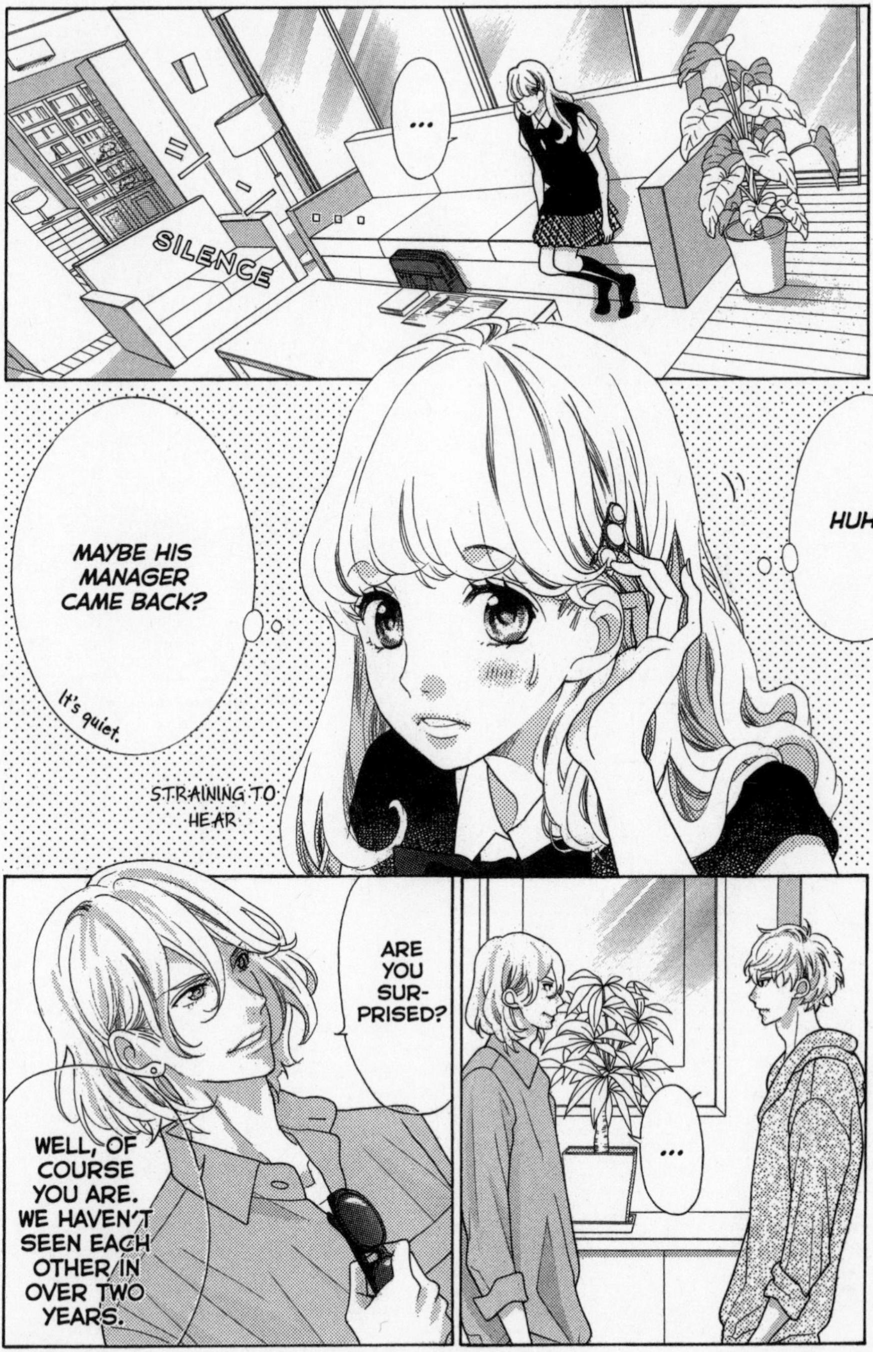
...
SILENCE
HUH?
MAYBE HIS MANAGER CAME BACK?
It's quiet.
STRAINING TO HEAR
...
ARE YOU SUR-PRISED?
WELL, OF COURSE YOU ARE. WE HAVEN'T SEEN EACH OTHER IN OVER TWO YEARS.

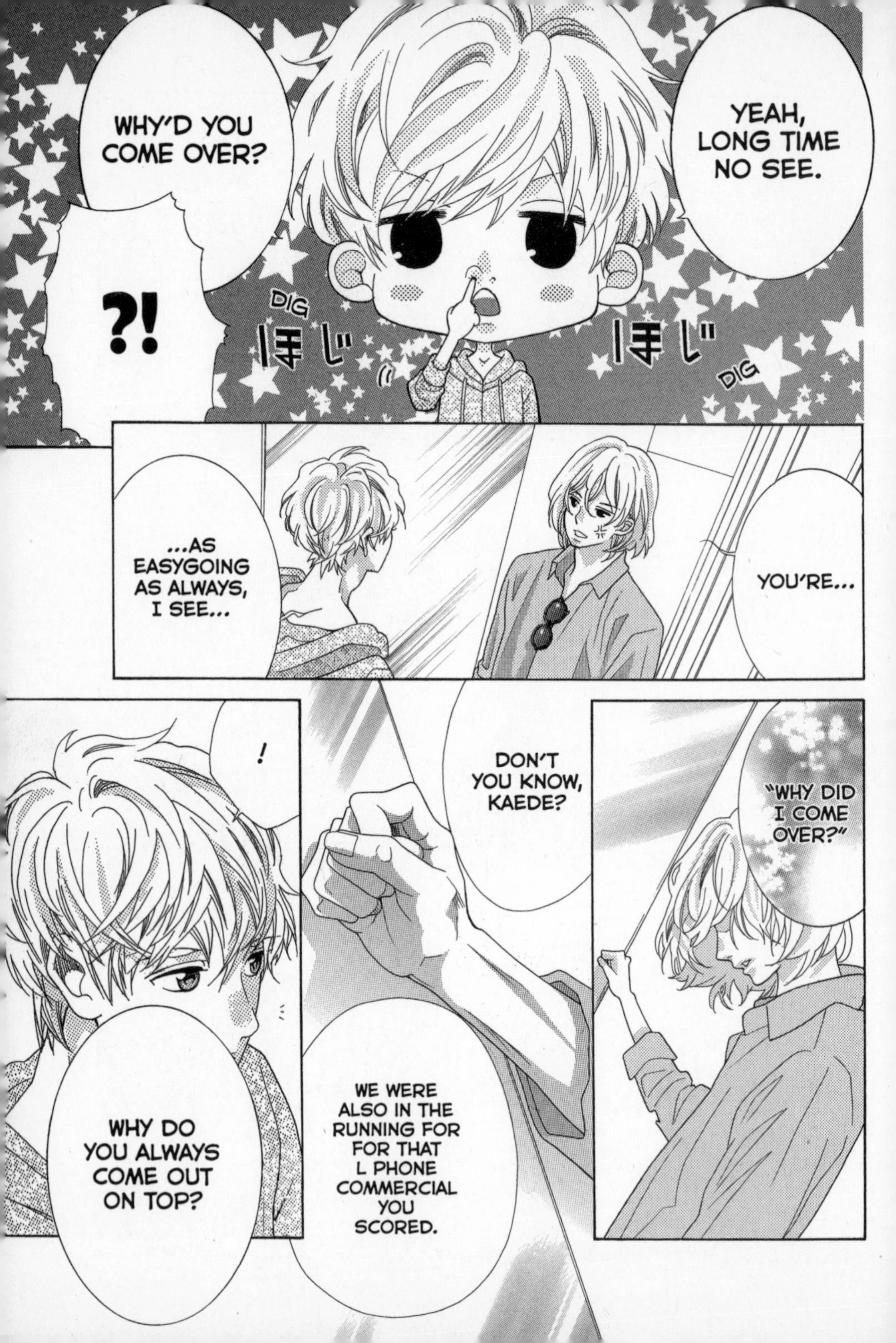
YEAH, LONG TIME NO SEE.
WHY'D YOU COME OVER?
ほじ
DIG
ほじ
DIG
?!
YOU'RE...
...AS EASYGOING AS ALWAYS, I SEE...
"WHY DID I COME OVER?"
DON'T YOU KNOW, KAEDE?
WE WERE ALSO IN THE RUNNING FOR FOR THAT L PHONE COMMERCIAL YOU SCORED.
!
WHY DO YOU ALWAYS COME OUT ON TOP?

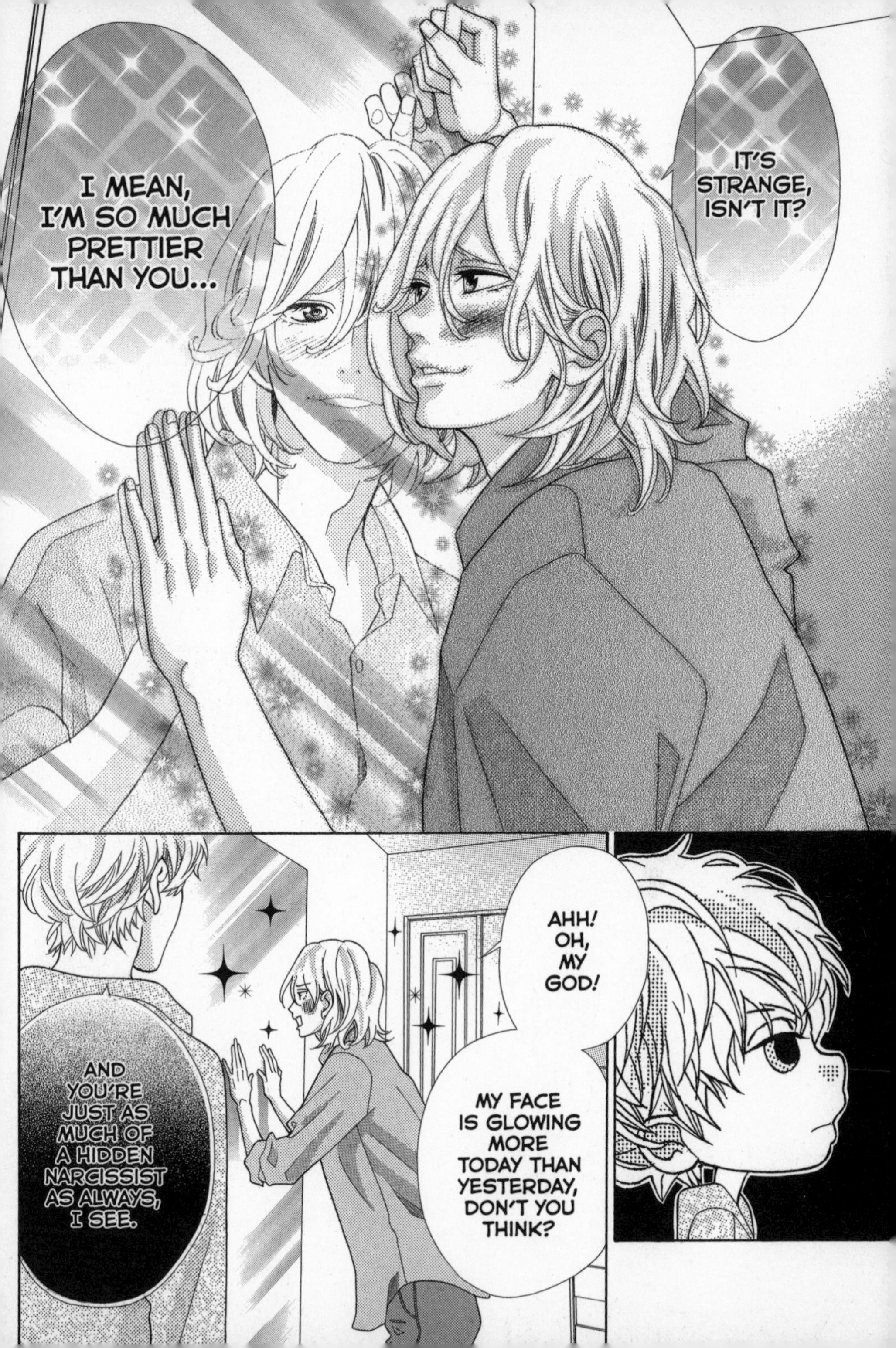
IT'S STRANGE, ISN'T IT?
I MEAN, I'M SO MUCH PRETTIER THAN YOU...
AHH! OH, MY GOD!
MY FACE IS GLOWING MORE TODAY THAN YESTERDAY, DON'T YOU THINK?
AND YOU'RE JUST AS MUCH OF A HIDDEN NARCISSIST AS ALWAYS, I SEE.

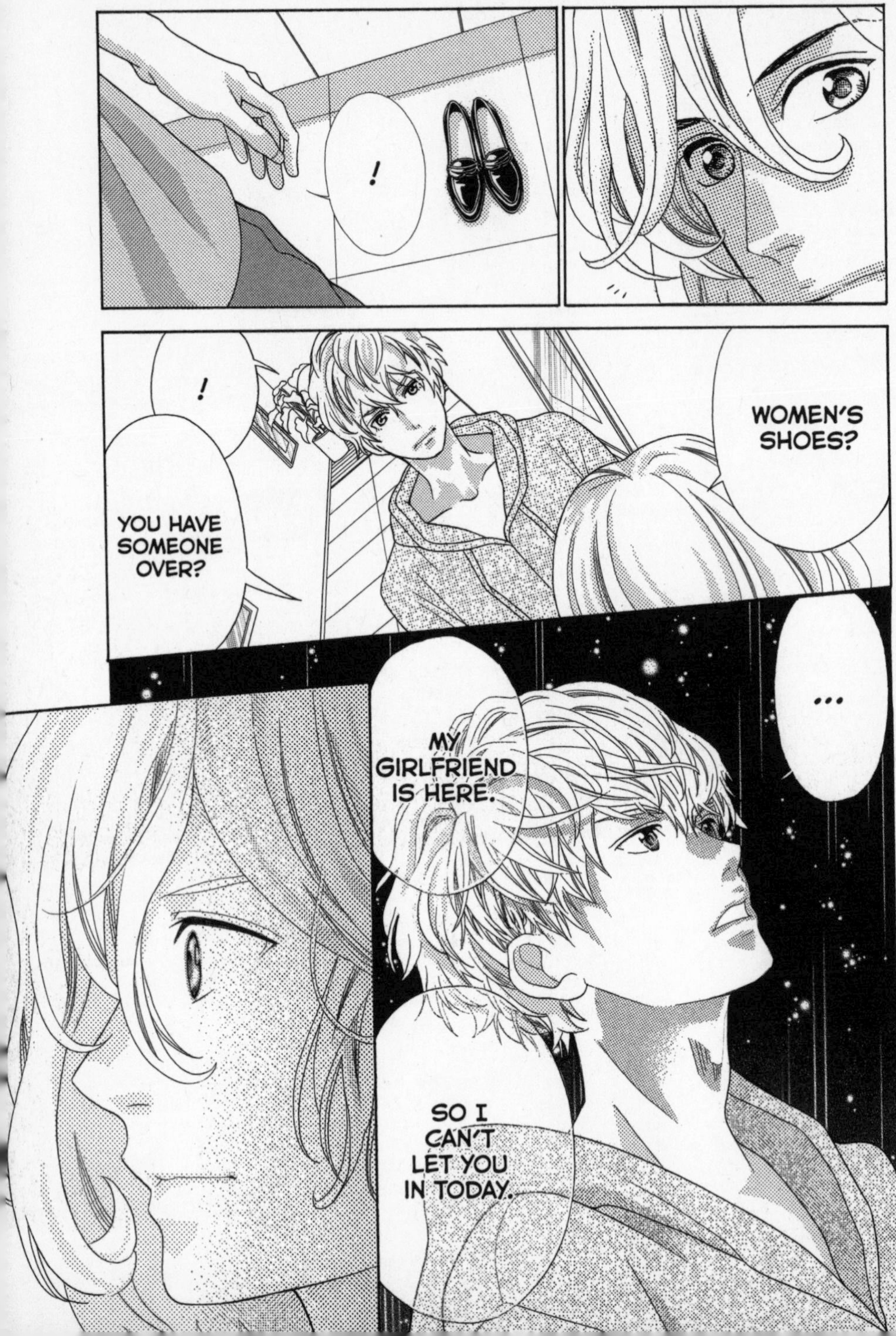
!
WOMEN'S SHOES?
!
YOU HAVE SOMEONE OVER?
...
MY GIRLFRIEND IS HERE.
SO I CAN'T LET YOU IN TODAY.

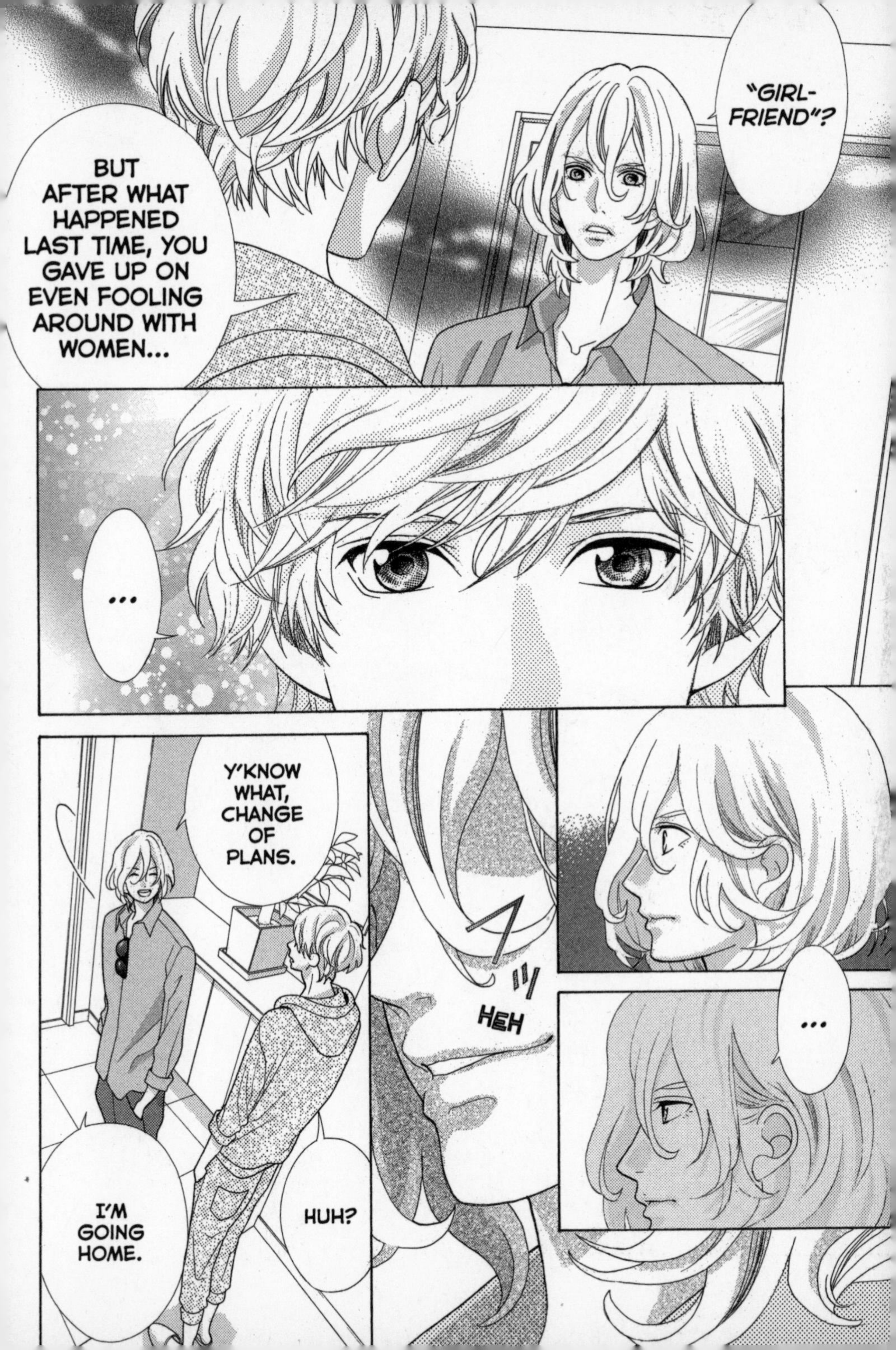
"GIRL-FRIEND"?
BUT AFTER WHAT HAPPENED LAST TIME, YOU GAVE UP ON EVEN FOOLING AROUND WITH WOMEN...
...
...
HEH
Y'KNOW WHAT, CHANGE OF PLANS.
HUH?
I'M GOING HOME.

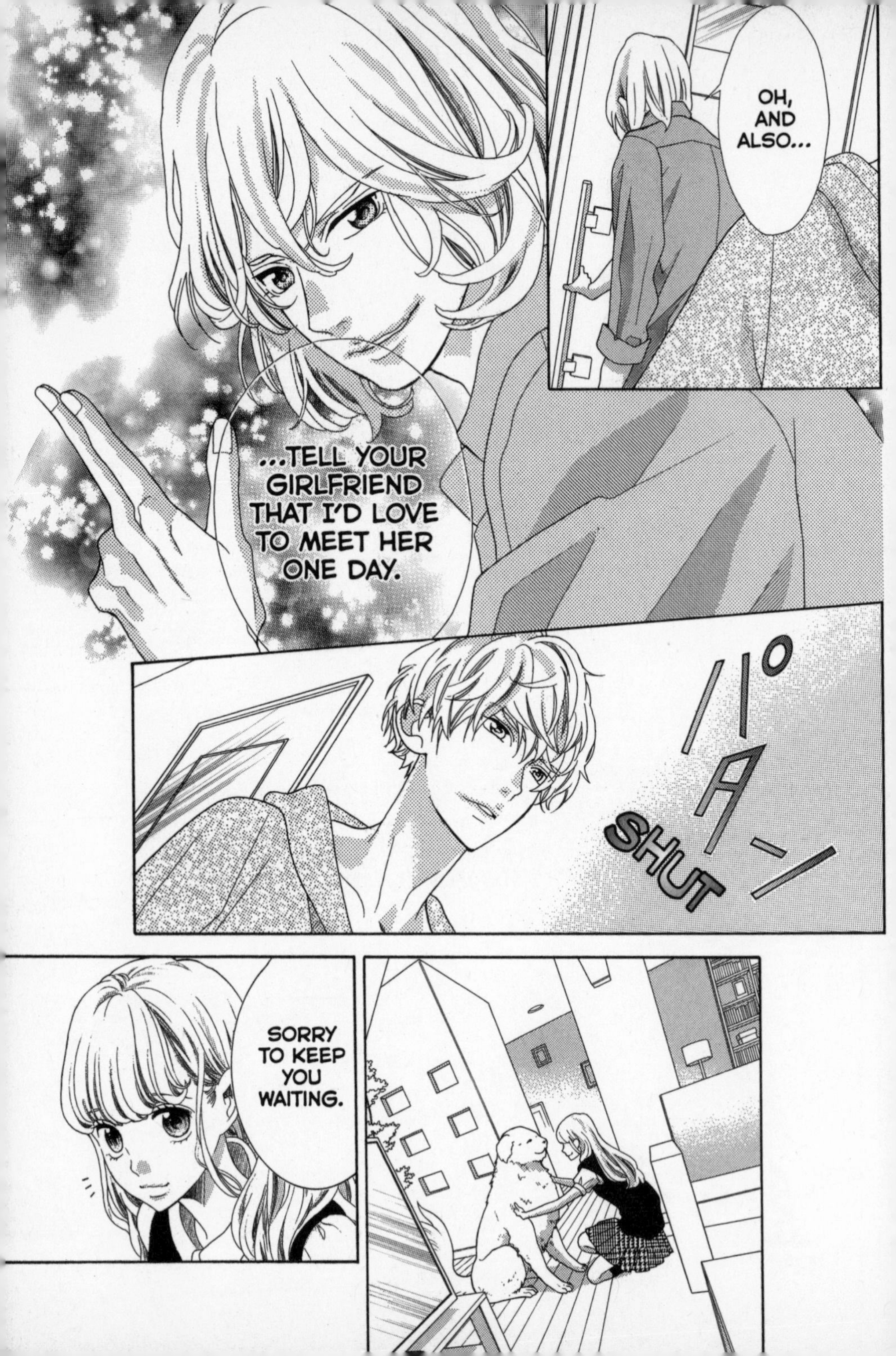
OH, AND ALSO...
...TELL YOUR GIRLFRIEND THAT I'D LOVE TO MEET HER ONE DAY.
SHUT
SORRY TO KEEP YOU WAITING.

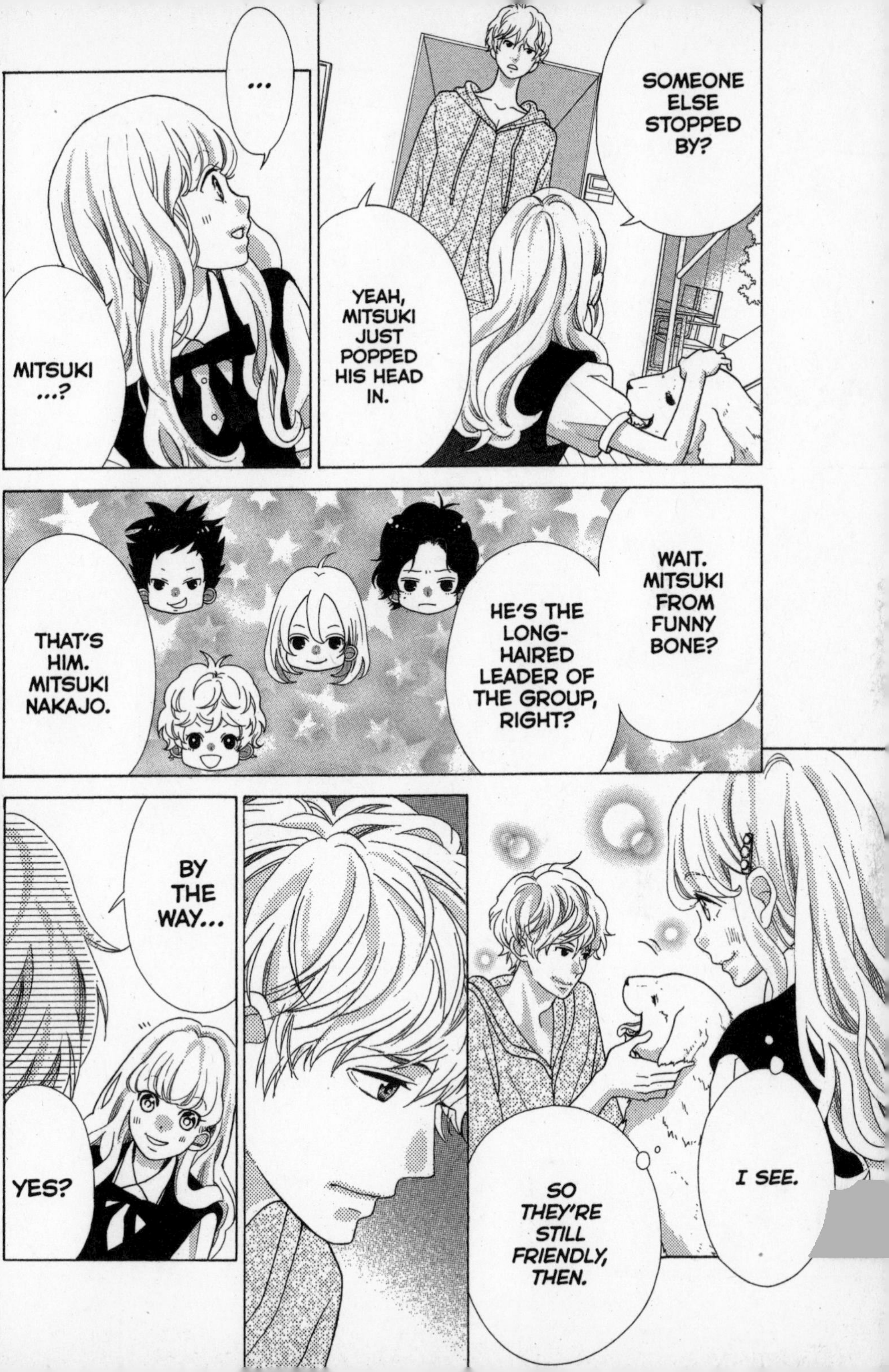
SOMEONE ELSE STOPPED BY?
YEAH, MITSUKI JUST POPPED HIS HEAD IN.
...
MITSUKI ...?
WAIT. MITSUKI FROM FUNNY BONE?
HE'S THE LONG-HAIRED LEADER OF THE GROUP, RIGHT?
THAT'S HIM. MITSUKI NAKAJO.
I SEE.
SO THEY'RE STILL FRIENDLY, THEN.
BY THE WAY...
YES?

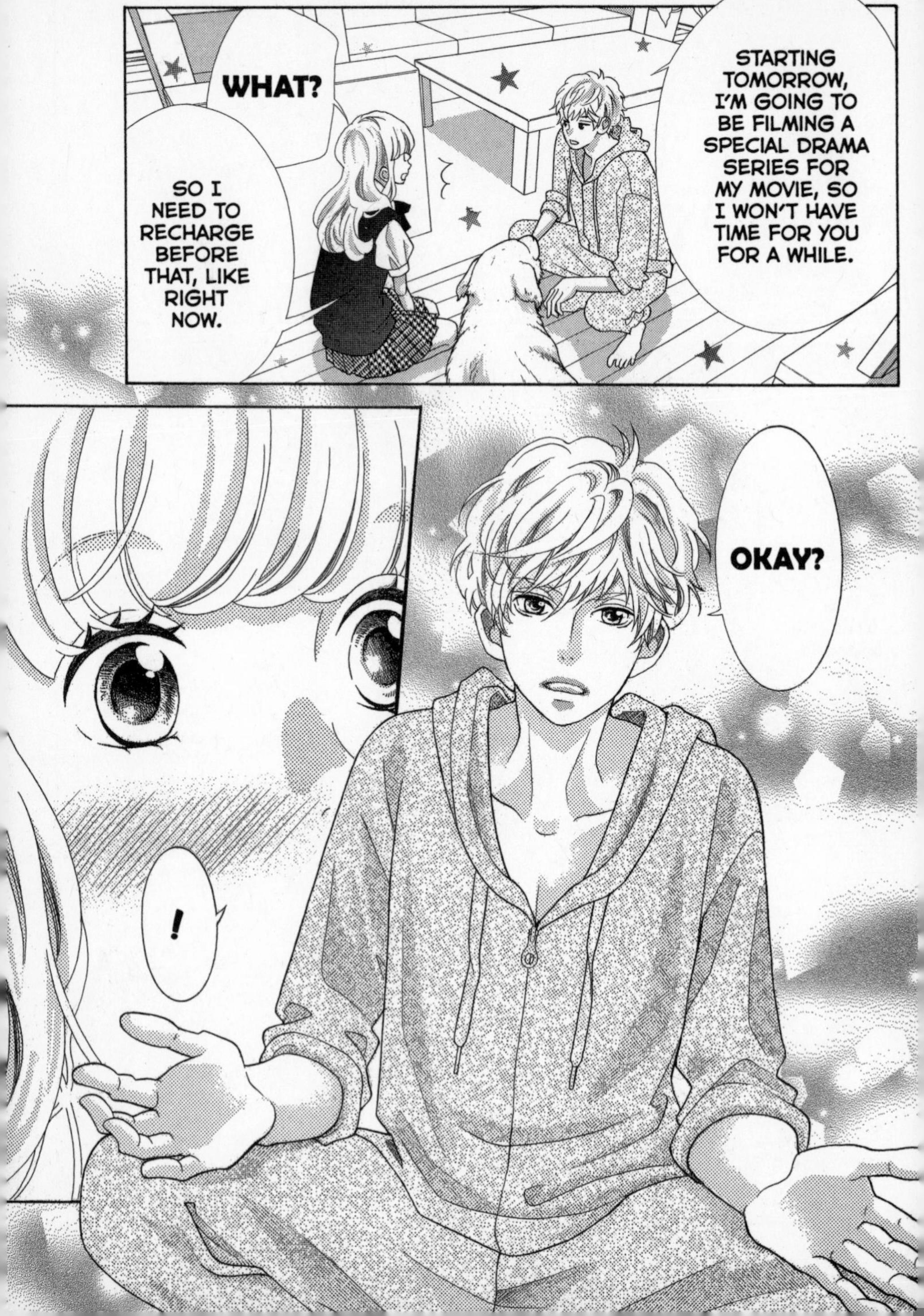
STARTING TOMORROW, I'M GOING TO BE FILMING A SPECIAL DRAMA SERIES FOR MY MOVIE, SO I WON'T HAVE TIME FOR YOU FOR A WHILE.
WHAT?
SO I NEED TO RECHARGE BEFORE THAT, LIKE RIGHT NOW.
OKAY?
!

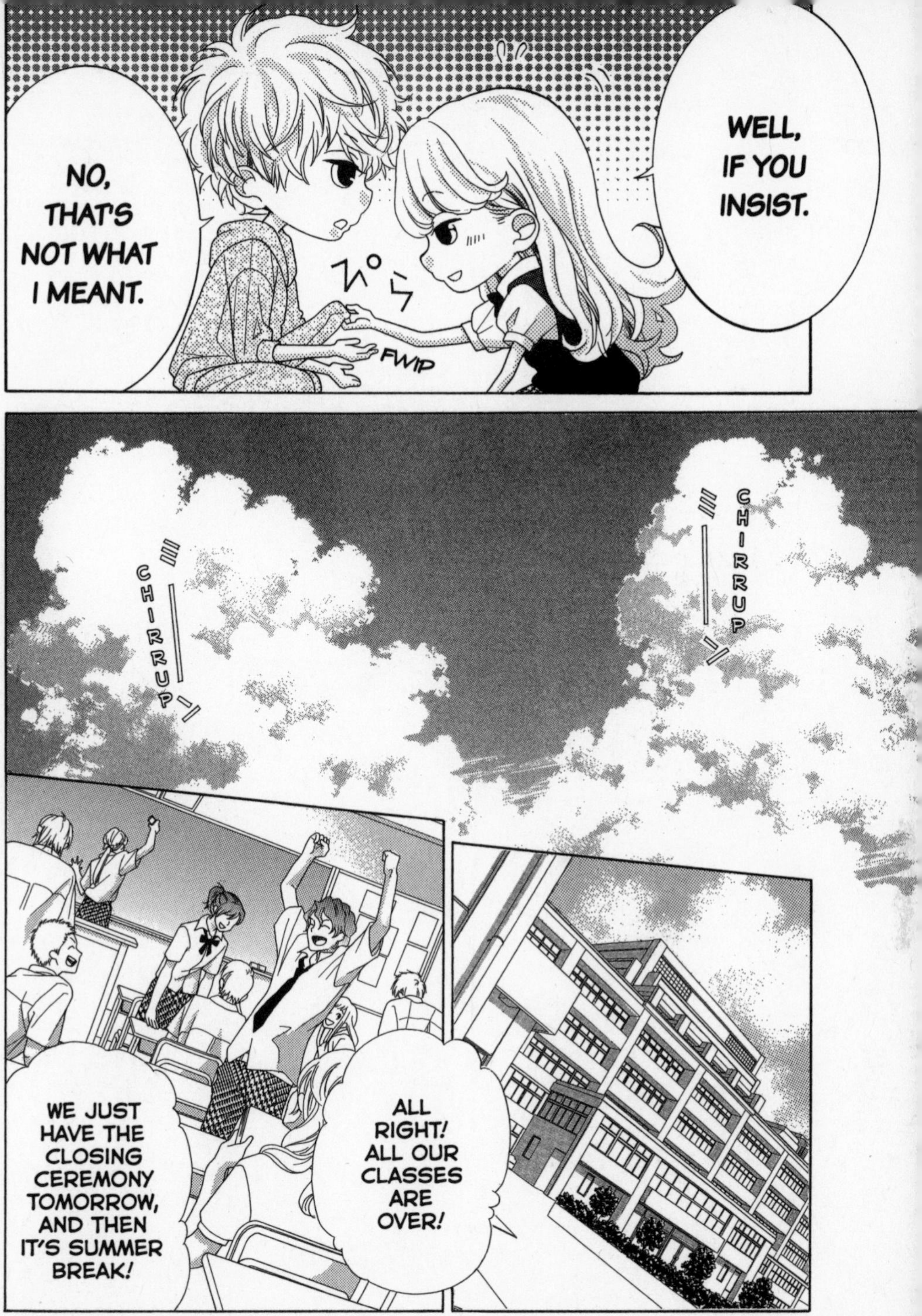
WELL, IF YOU INSIST.
NO, THAT'S NOT WHAT I MEANT.
FWIP
CHIRRUP
CHIRRUP
ALL RIGHT! ALL OUR CLASSES ARE OVER!
WE JUST HAVE THE CLOSING CEREMONY TOMORROW, AND THEN IT'S SUMMER BREAK!

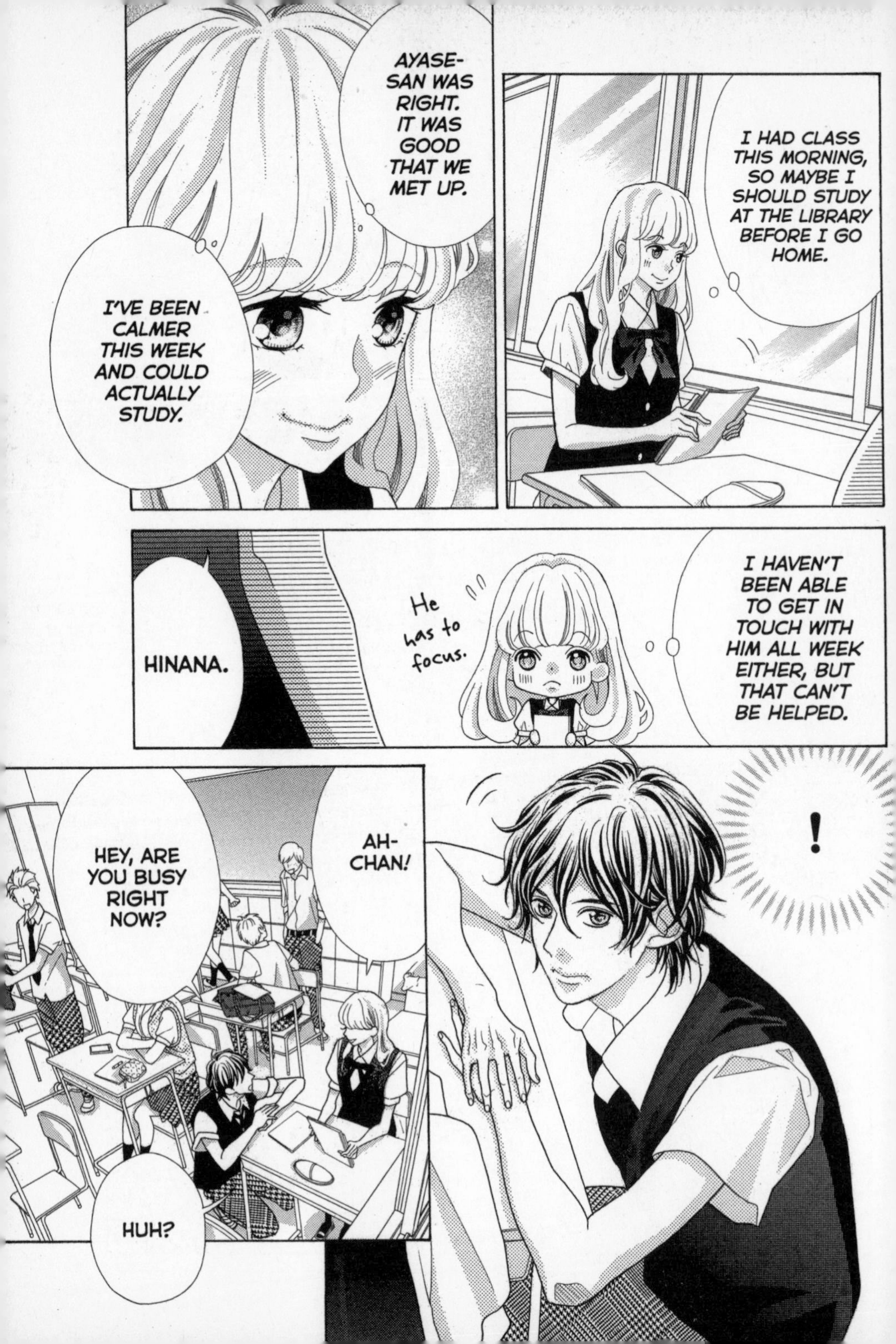
I HAD CLASS THIS MORNING, SO MAYBE I SHOULD STUDY AT THE LIBRARY BEFORE I GO HOME.
AYASE-SAN WAS RIGHT. IT WAS GOOD THAT WE MET UP.
I'VE BEEN CALMER THIS WEEK AND COULD ACTUALLY STUDY.
I HAVEN'T BEEN ABLE TO GET IN TOUCH WITH HIM ALL WEEK EITHER, BUT THAT CAN'T BE HELPED.
He has to focus.
HINANA.
!
AH-CHAN!
HEY, ARE YOU BUSY RIGHT NOW?
HUH?

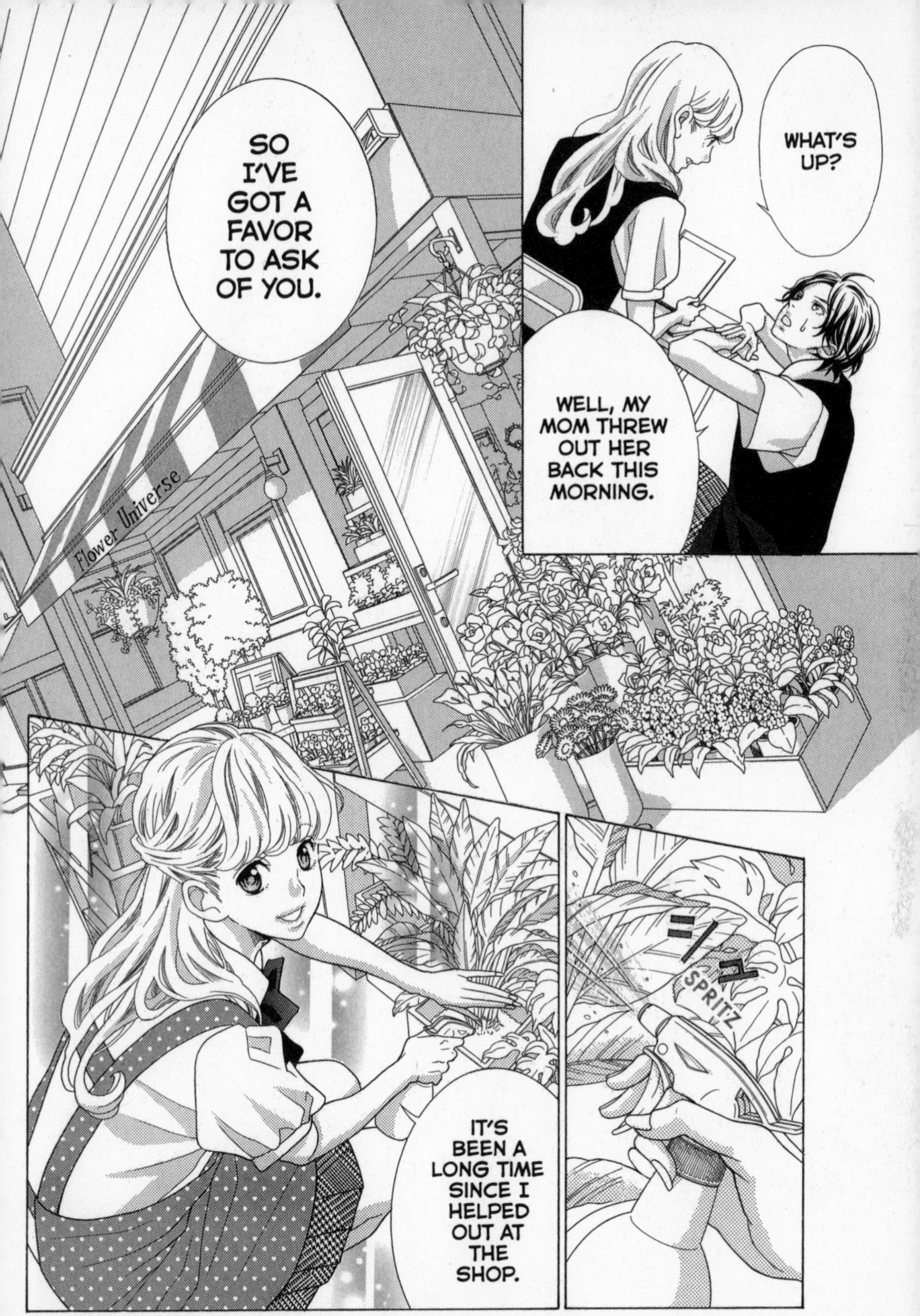
WHAT'S UP?
WELL, MY MOM THREW OUT HER BACK THIS MORNING.
SO I'VE GOT A FAVOR TO ASK OF YOU.
Flower Universe
SPRITZ
IT'S BEEN A LONG TIME SINCE I HELPED OUT AT THE SHOP.

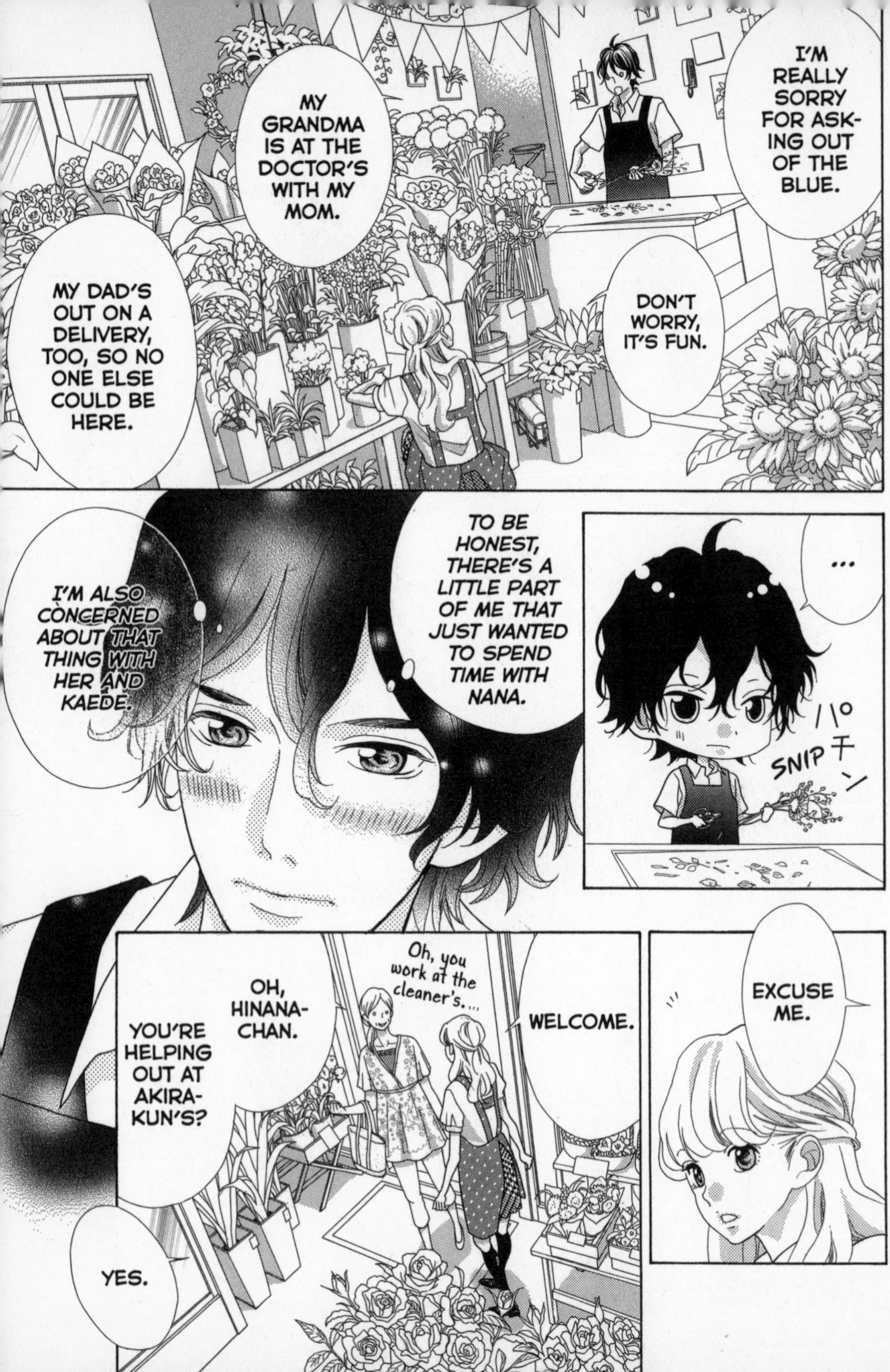
I'M REALLY SORRY FOR ASKING OUT OF THE BLUE.
MY GRANDMA IS AT THE DOCTOR'S WITH MY MOM.
MY DAD'S OUT ON A DELIVERY, TOO, SO NO ONE ELSE COULD BE HERE.
DON'T WORRY, IT'S FUN.
...
パチン
SNIP
TO BE HONEST, THERE'S A LITTLE PART OF ME THAT JUST WANTED TO SPEND TIME WITH NANA.
I'M ALSO CONCERNED ABOUT THAT THING WITH HER AND KAEDE.
EXCUSE ME.
WELCOME.
Oh, you work at the cleaner's....
OH, HINANA-CHAN.
YOU'RE HELPING OUT AT AKIRA-KUN'S?
YES.

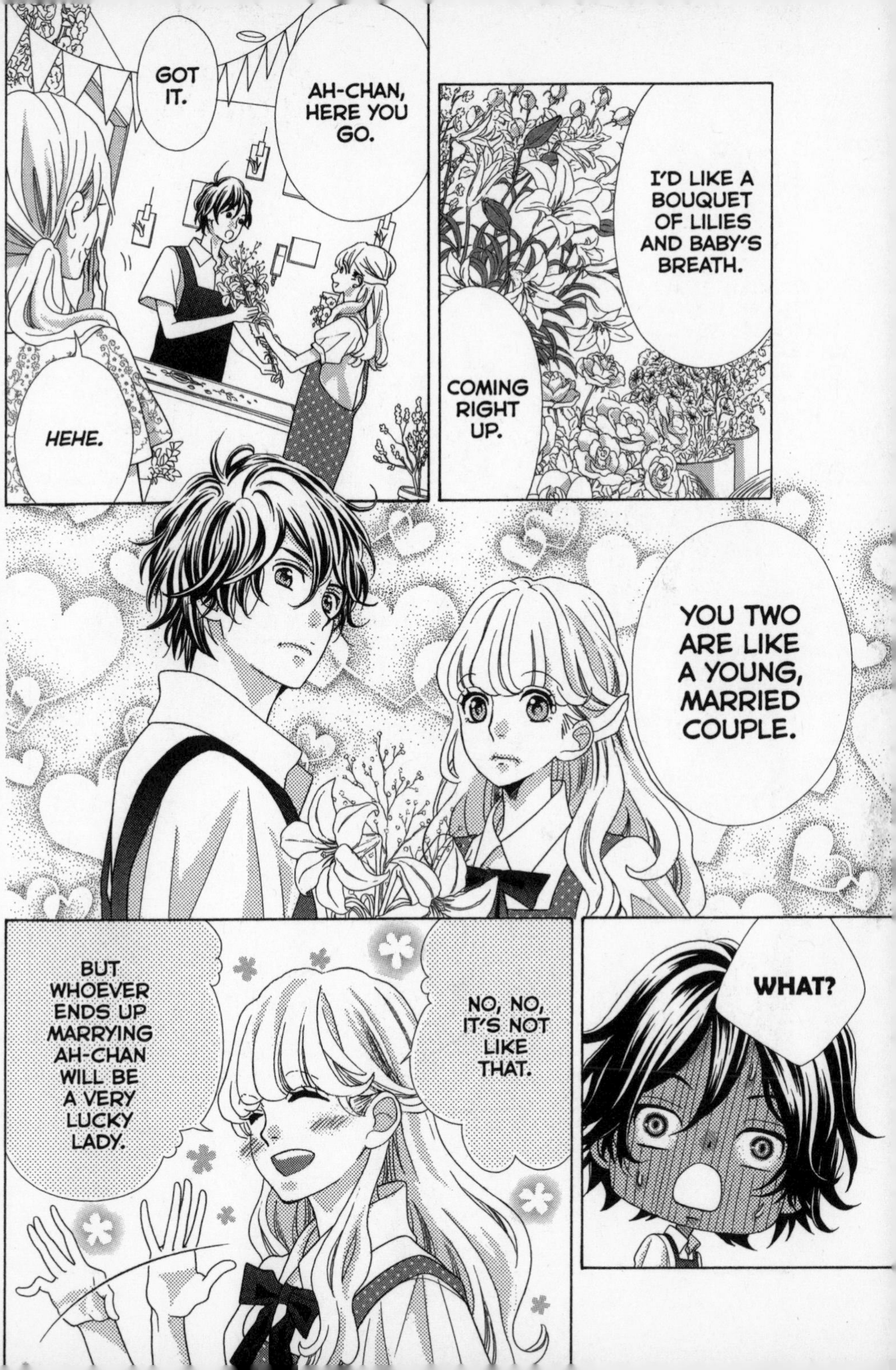
I'D LIKE A BOUQUET OF LILIES AND BABY'S BREATH.
COMING RIGHT UP.
AH-CHAN, HERE YOU GO.
GOT IT.
HEHE.
YOU TWO ARE LIKE A YOUNG, MARRIED COUPLE.
WHAT?
NO, NO, IT'S NOT LIKE THAT.
BUT WHOEVER ENDS UP MARRYING AH-CHAN WILL BE A VERY LUCKY LADY.

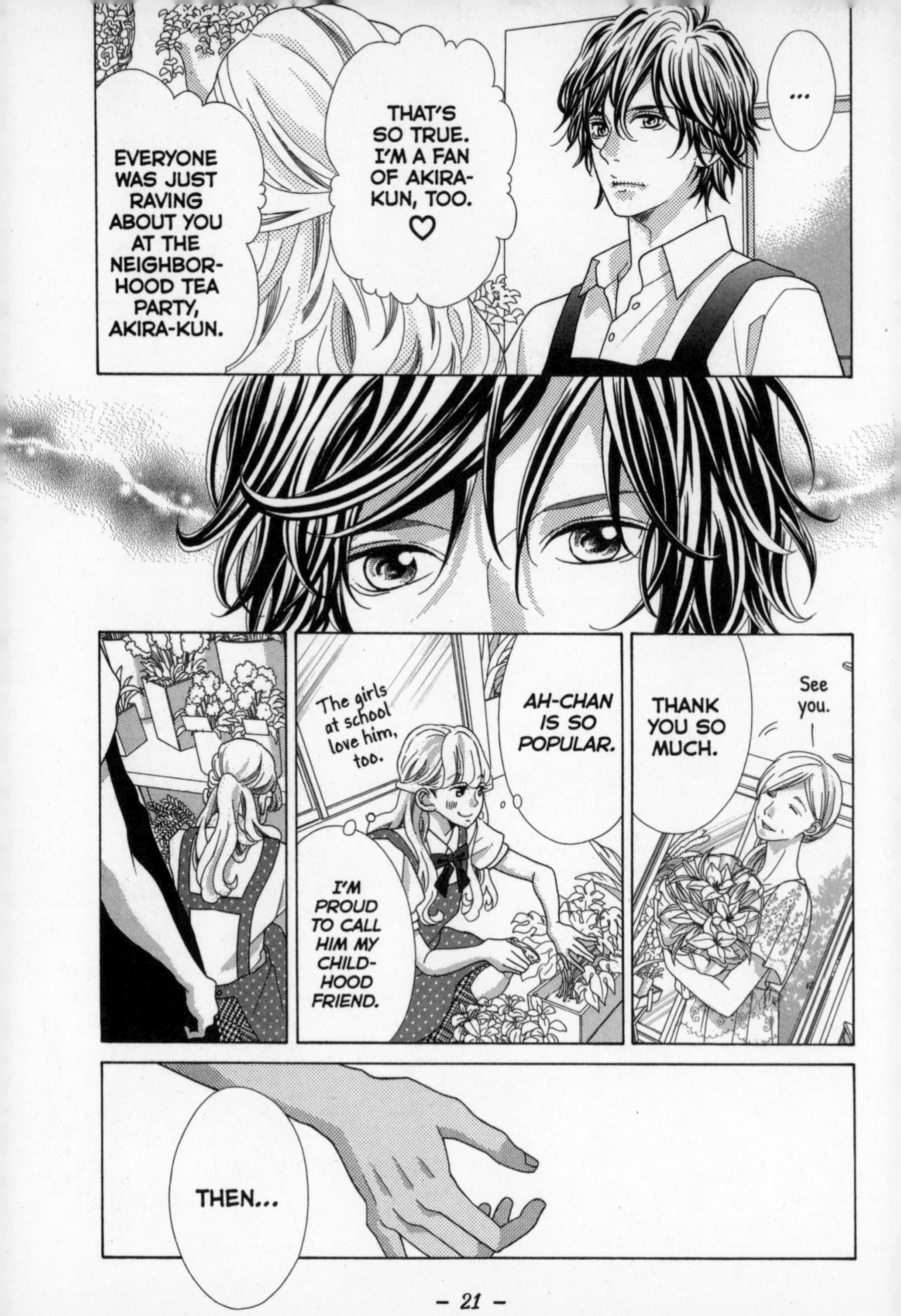
...
THAT'S SO TRUE. I'M A FAN OF AKIRA-KUN, TOO. ♡
EVERYONE WAS JUST RAVING ABOUT YOU AT THE NEIGHBOR-HOOD TEA PARTY, AKIRA-KUN.
See you.
THANK YOU SO MUCH.
AH-CHAN IS SO POPULAR.
The girls at school love him, too.
I'M PROUD TO CALL HIM MY CHILD-HOOD FRIEND.
THEN...

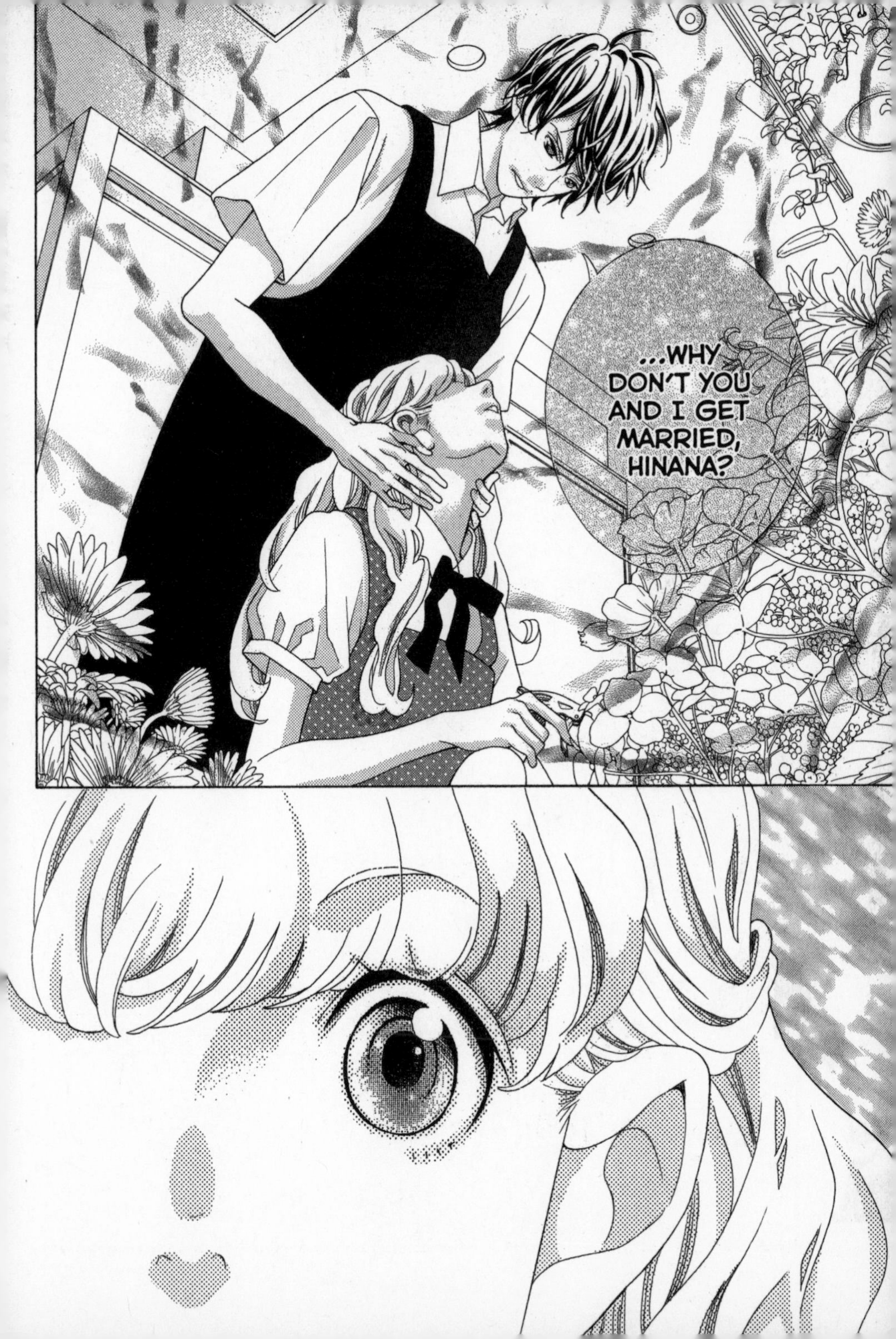
...WHY DON'T YOU AND I GET MARRIED, HINANA?

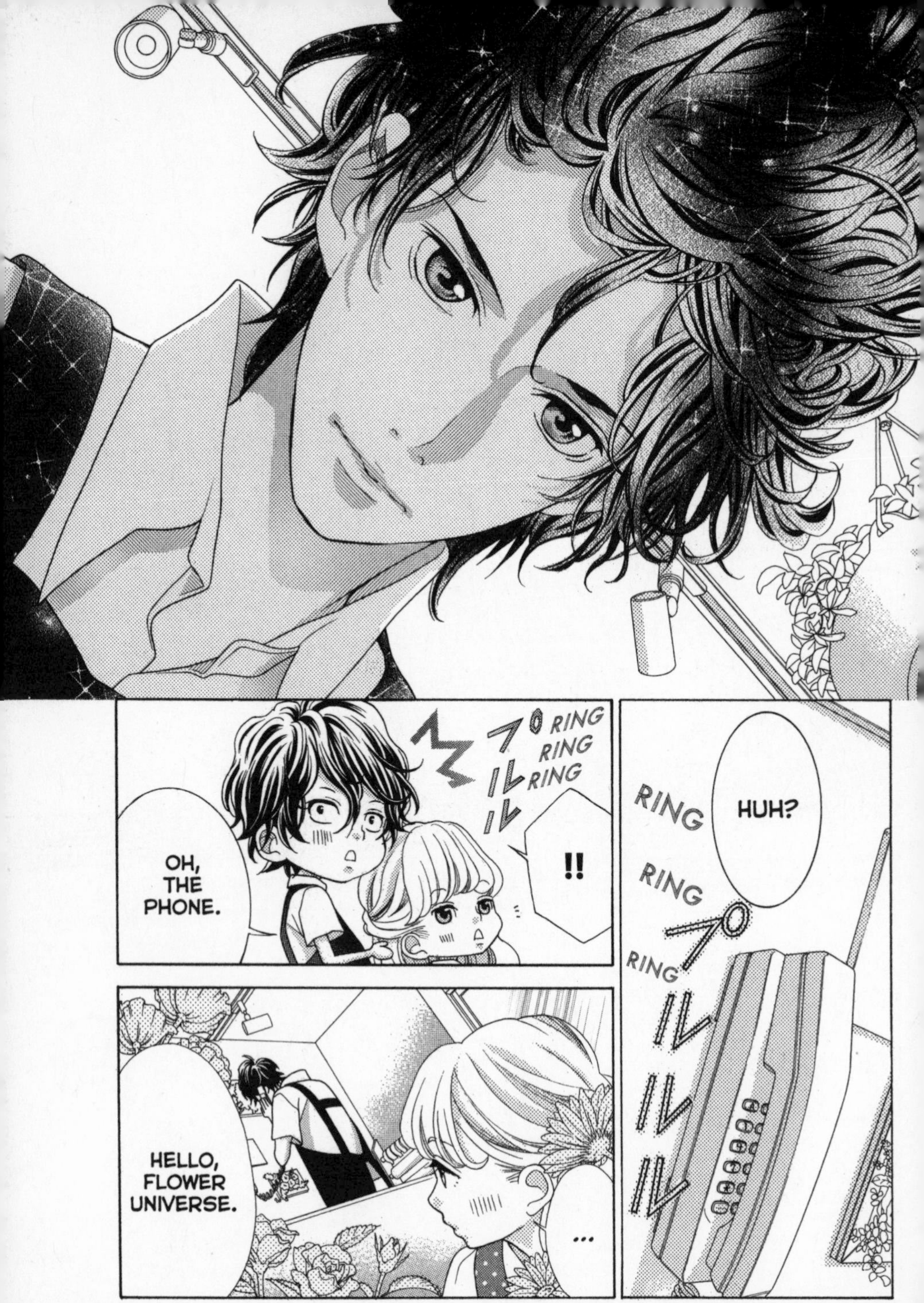
HUH?
RING
RING
RING
RING
RING
RING
!!
OH, THE PHONE.
...
HELLO, FLOWER UNIVERSE.

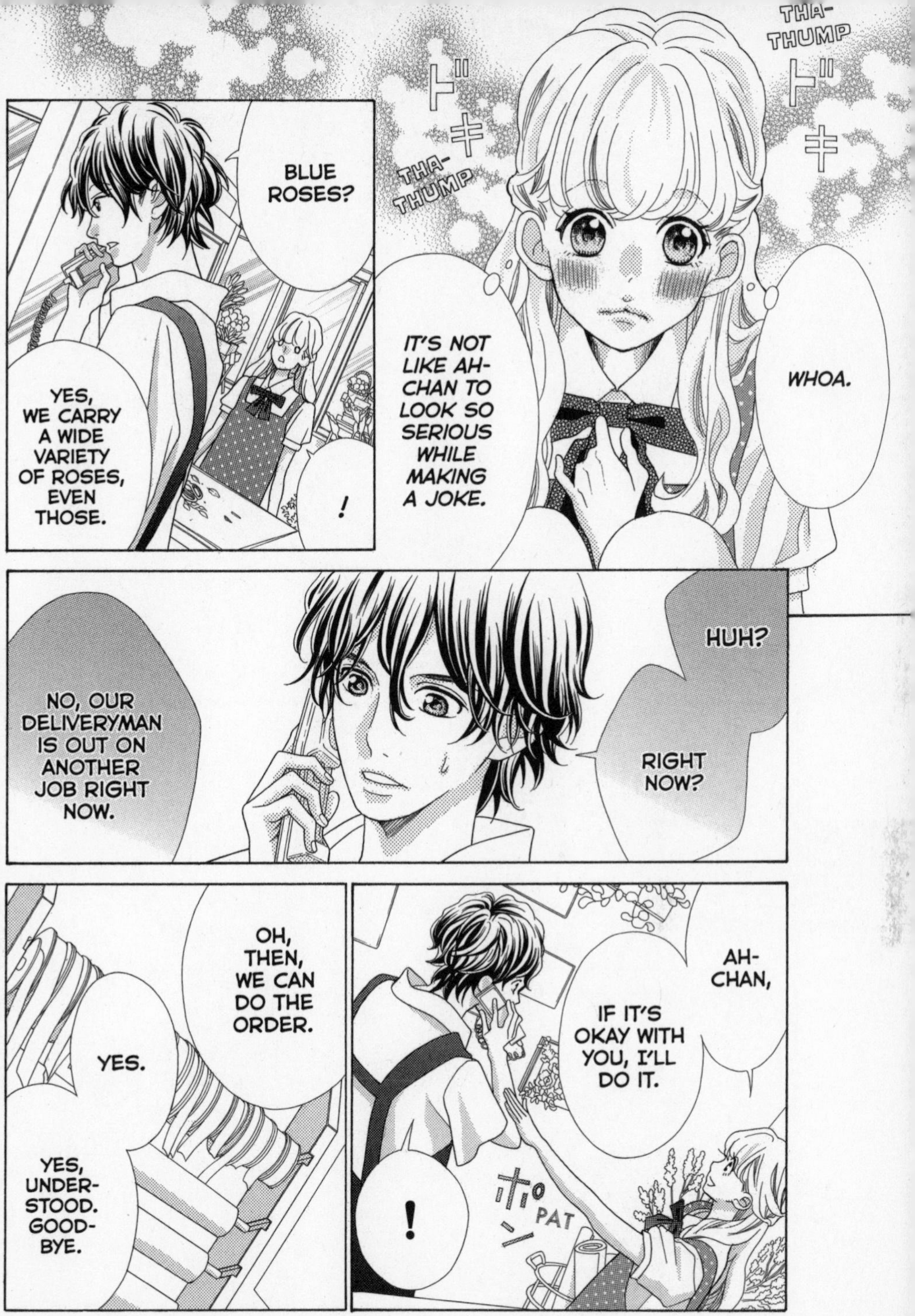
THA-THUMP
ドキ
THA-THUMP
ドキ
WHOA.
IT'S NOT LIKE AH-CHAN TO LOOK SO SERIOUS WHILE MAKING A JOKE.
BLUE ROSES?
!
YES, WE CARRY A WIDE VARIETY OF ROSES, EVEN THOSE.
HUH?
RIGHT NOW?
NO, OUR DELIVERYMAN IS OUT ON ANOTHER JOB RIGHT NOW.
AH-CHAN,
IF IT'S OKAY WITH YOU, I'LL DO IT.
ポン
PAT
!
OH, THEN, WE CAN DO THE ORDER.
YES.
YES, UNDERSTOOD. GOOD-BYE.

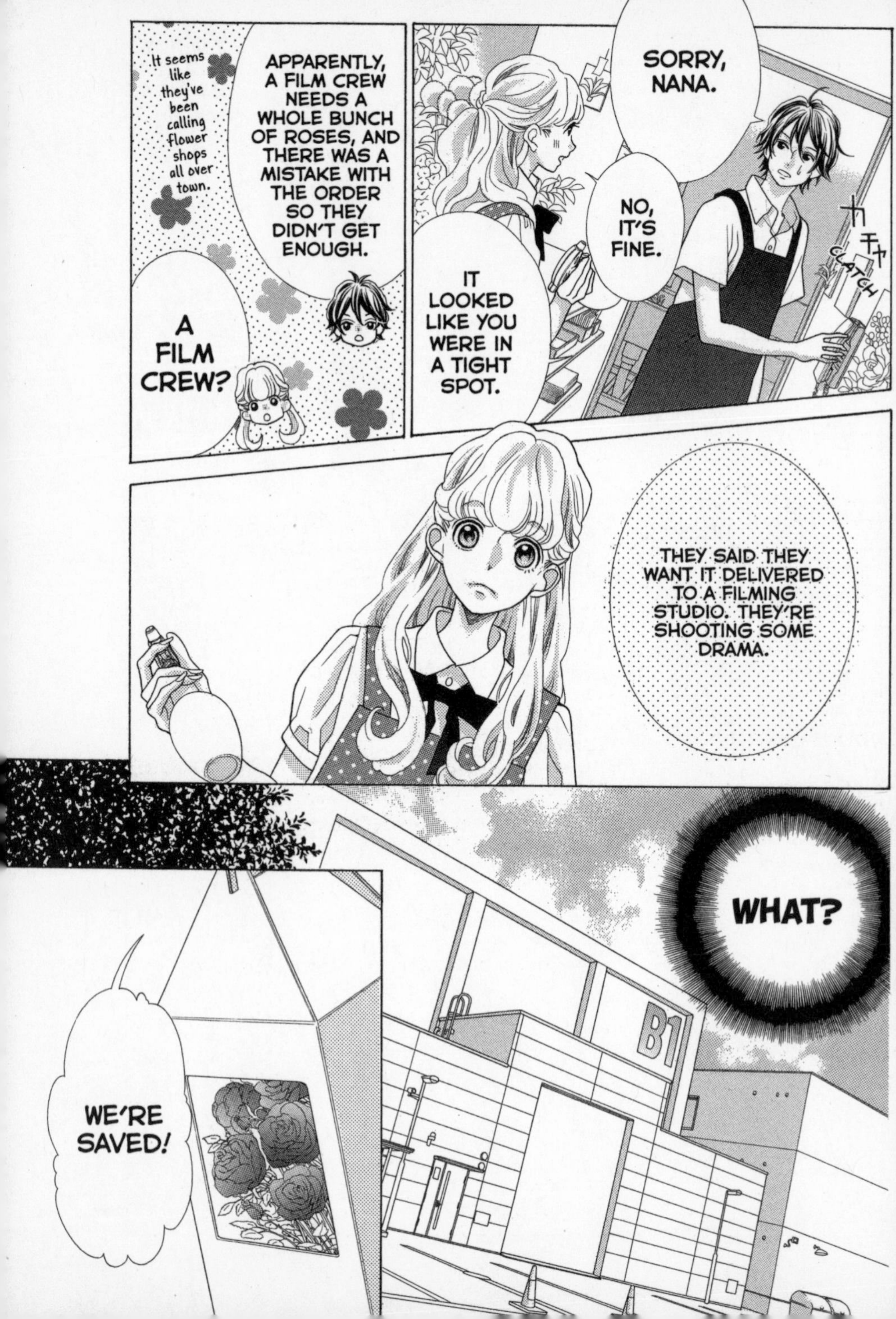
SORRY, NANA.
カチャ
CLATCH
NO, IT'S FINE.
IT LOOKED LIKE YOU WERE IN A TIGHT SPOT.
APPARENTLY, A FILM CREW NEEDS A WHOLE BUNCH OF ROSES, AND THERE WAS A MISTAKE WITH THE ORDER SO THEY DIDN'T GET ENOUGH.
It seems like they've been calling flower shops all over town.
A FILM CREW?
THEY SAID THEY WANT IT DELIVERED TO A FILMING STUDIO. THEY'RE SHOOTING SOME DRAMA.
WHAT?
B1
WE'RE SAVED!

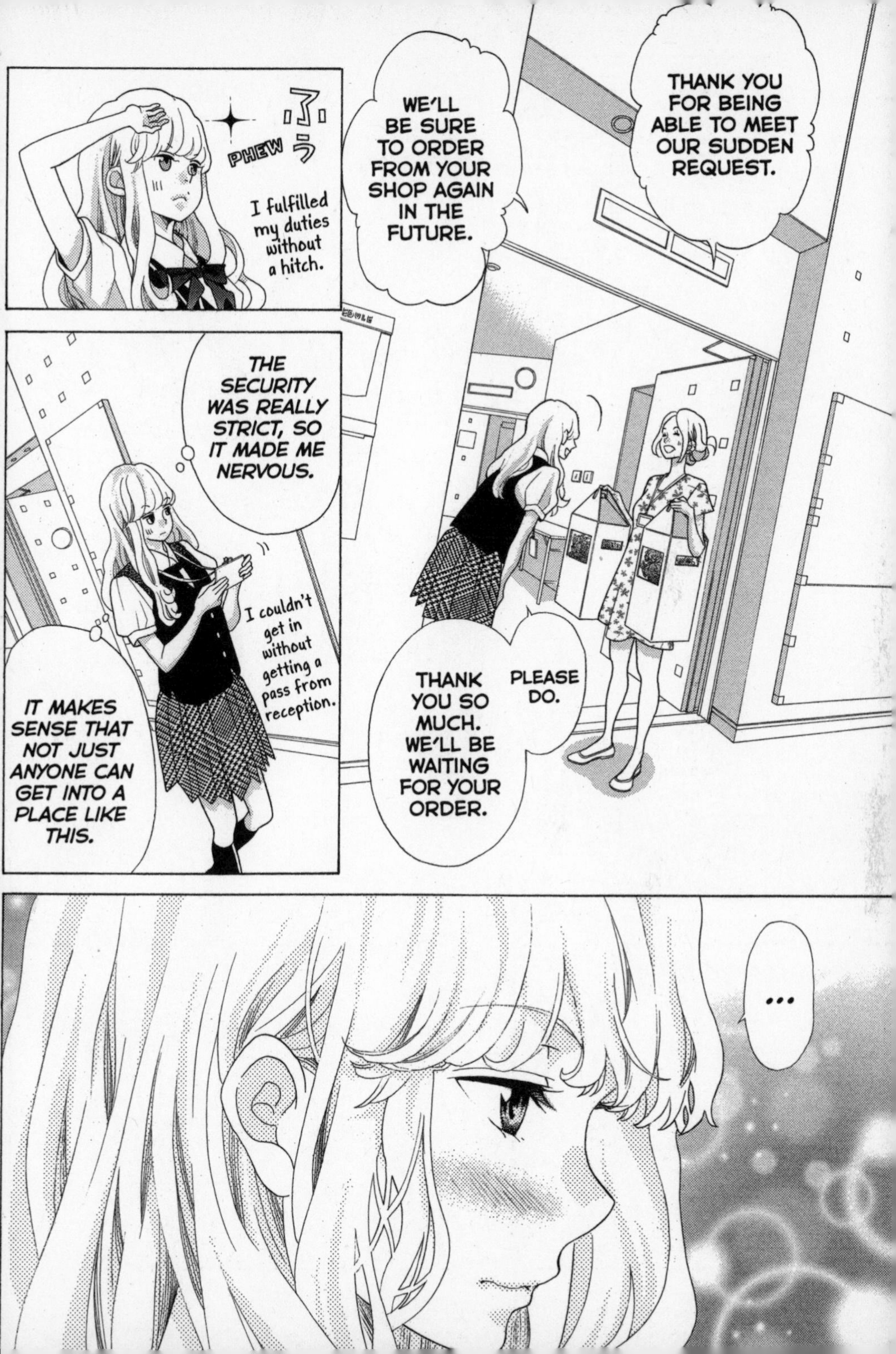
THANK YOU FOR BEING ABLE TO MEET OUR SUDDEN REQUEST.
WE'LL BE SURE TO ORDER FROM YOUR SHOP AGAIN IN THE FUTURE.
PLEASE DO.
THANK YOU SO MUCH. WE'LL BE WAITING FOR YOUR ORDER.
ふう
PHEW
I fulfilled my duties without a hitch.
THE SECURITY WAS REALLY STRICT, SO IT MADE ME NERVOUS.
I couldn't get in without getting a pass from reception.
IT MAKES SENSE THAT NOT JUST ANYONE CAN GET INTO A PLACE LIKE THIS.
...

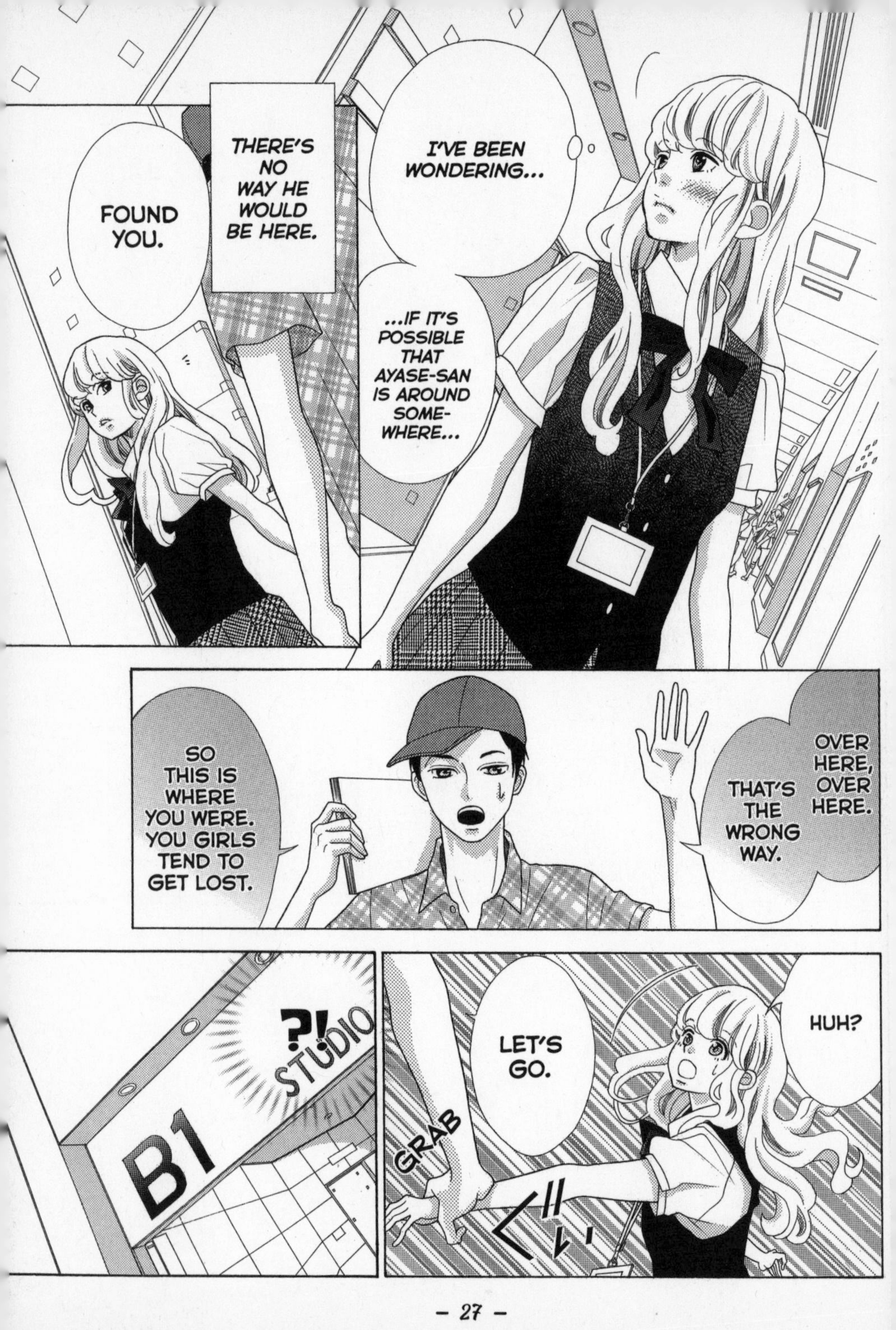
I'VE BEEN WONDERING...
...IF IT'S POSSIBLE THAT AYASE-SAN IS AROUND SOME-WHERE...
THERE'S NO WAY HE WOULD BE HERE.
FOUND YOU.
OVER HERE, OVER HERE.
THAT'S THE WRONG WAY.
SO THIS IS WHERE YOU WERE. YOU GIRLS TEND TO GET LOST.
HUH?
LET'S GO.
GRAB
?!
STUDIO
B1

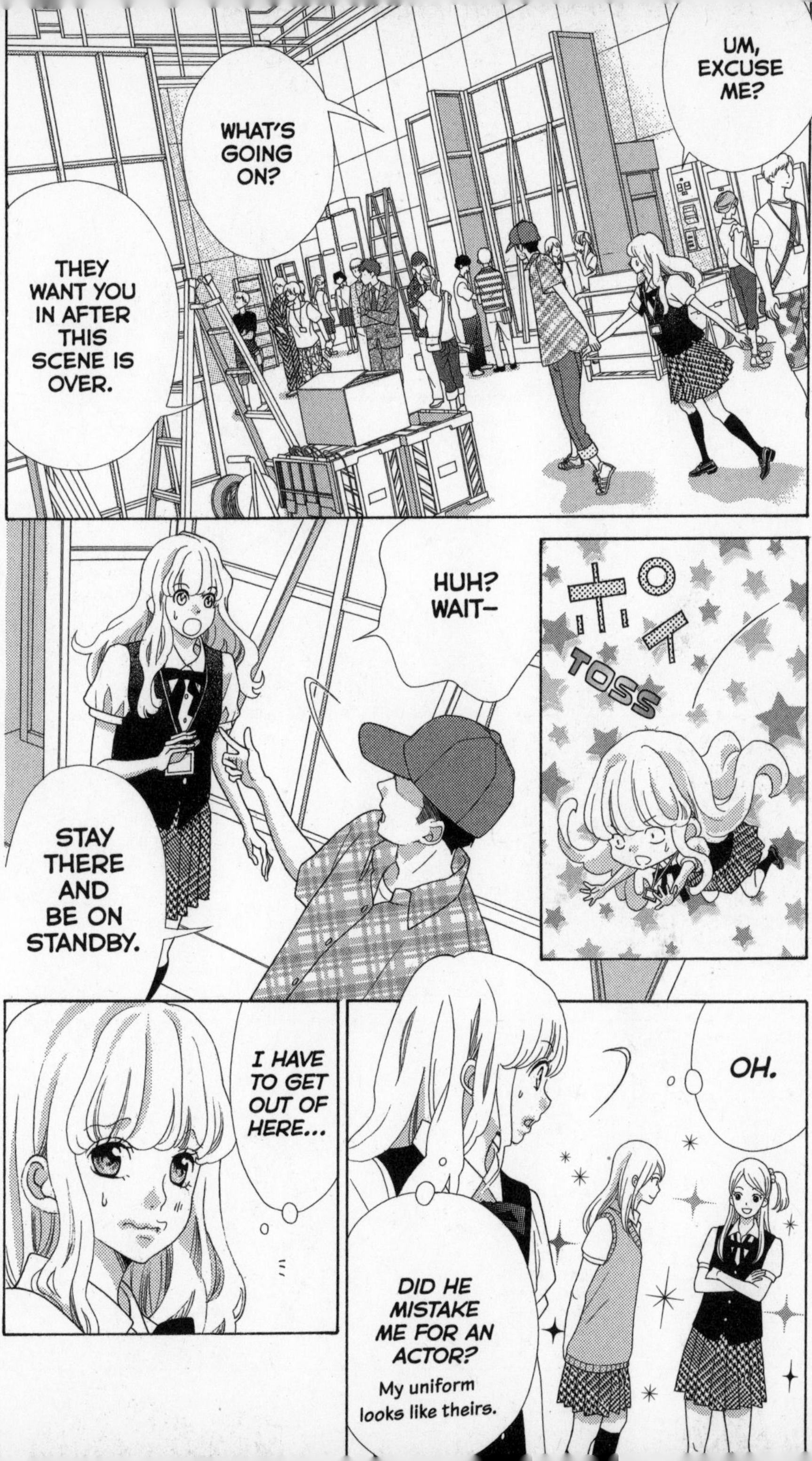
UM, EXCUSE ME?
WHAT'S GOING ON?
THEY WANT YOU IN AFTER THIS SCENE IS OVER.
TOSS
HUH? WAIT–
STAY THERE AND BE ON STANDBY.
OH.
DID HE MISTAKE ME FOR AN ACTOR?
My uniform looks like theirs.
I HAVE TO GET OUT OF HERE...

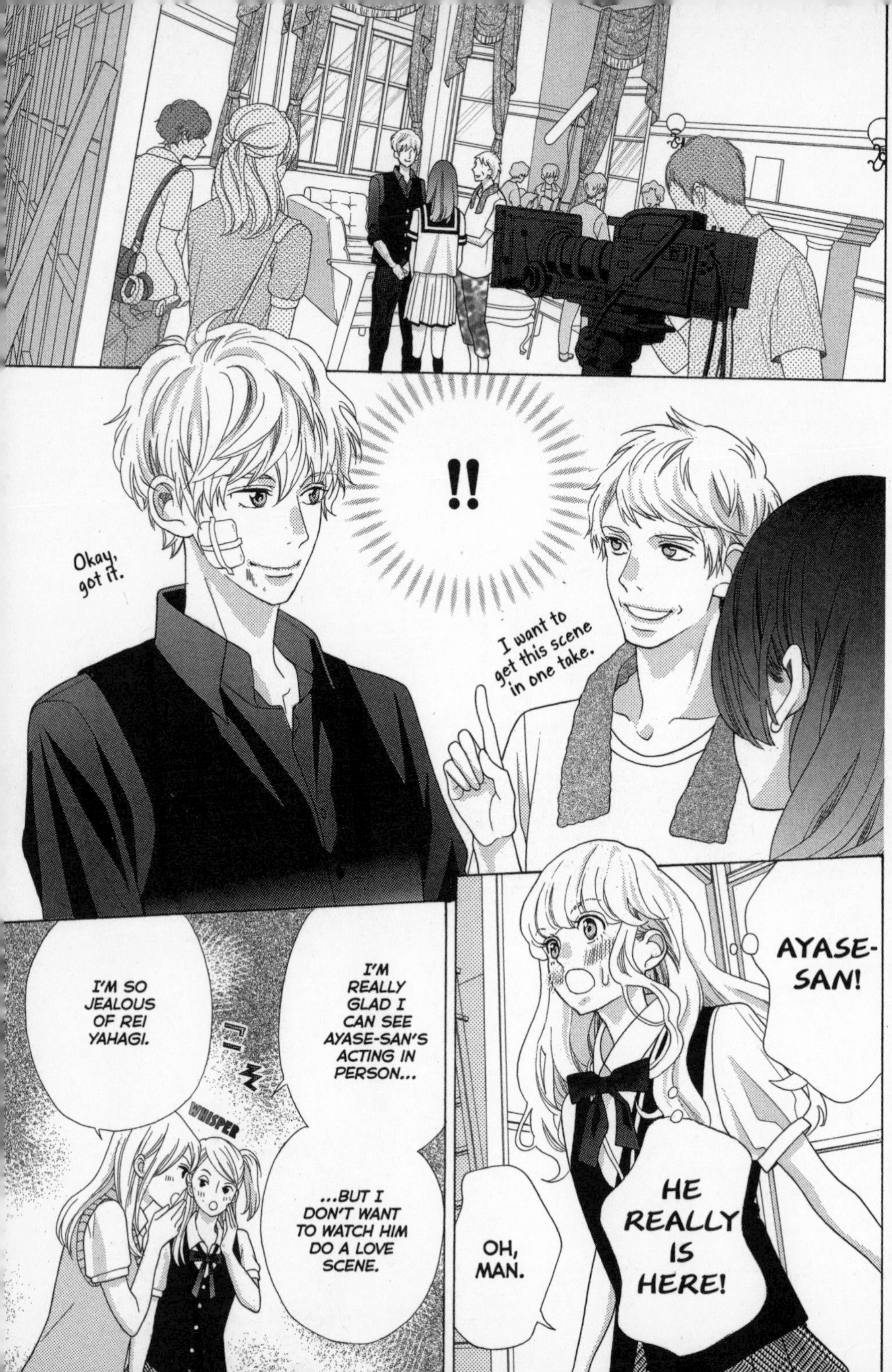
I want to get this scene in one take.
!!
Okay, got it.
AYASE-SAN!
HE REALLY IS HERE!
OH, MAN.
I'M REALLY GLAD I CAN SEE AYASE-SAN'S ACTING IN PERSON...
...BUT I DON'T WANT TO WATCH HIM DO A LOVE SCENE.
I'M SO JEALOUS OF REI YAHAGI.
WHISPER

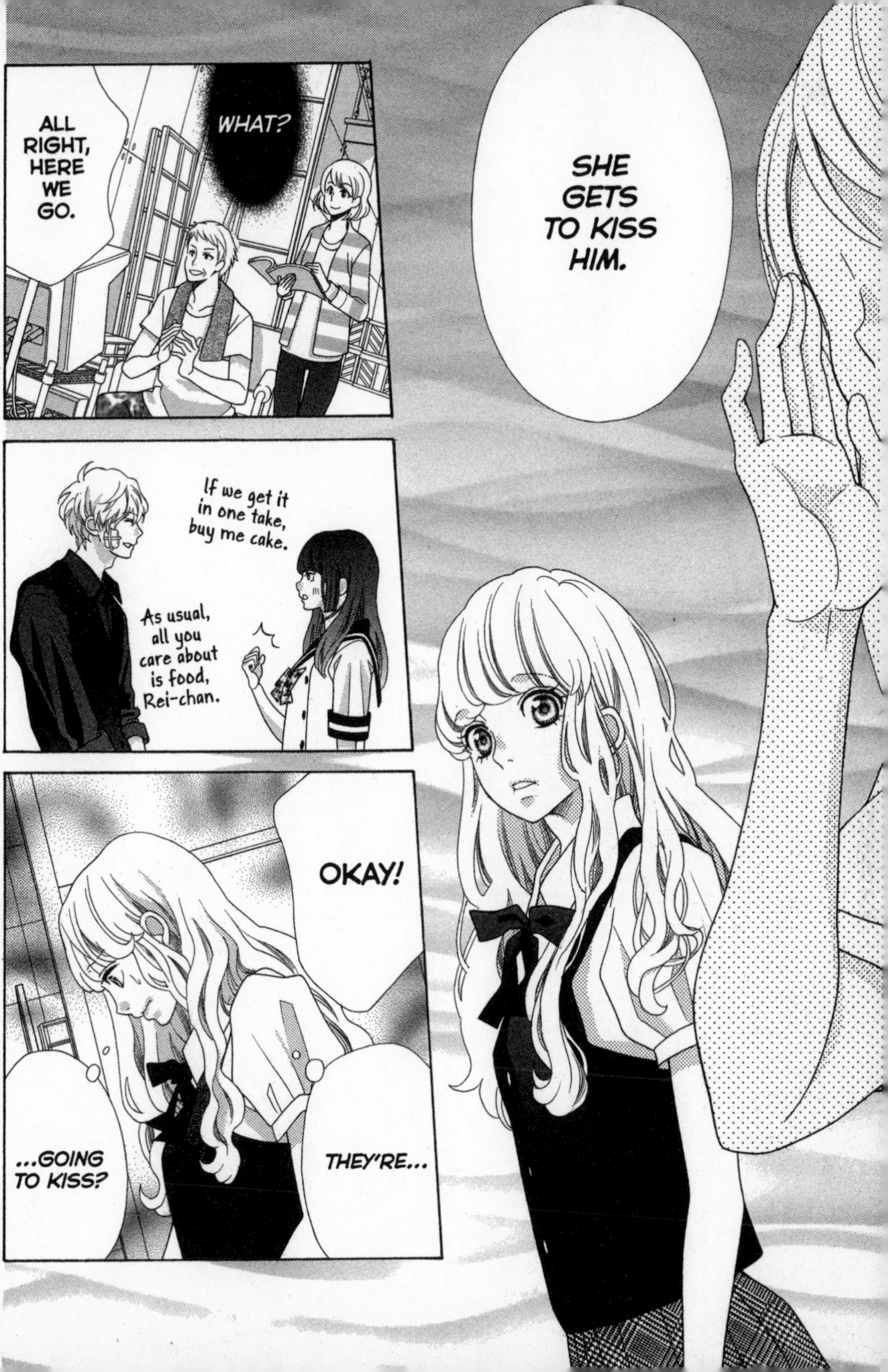
SHE GETS TO KISS HIM.
WHAT?
ALL RIGHT, HERE WE GO.
If we get it in one take, buy me cake.
As usual, all you care about is food, Rei-chan.
OKAY!
THEY'RE...
...GOING TO KISS?

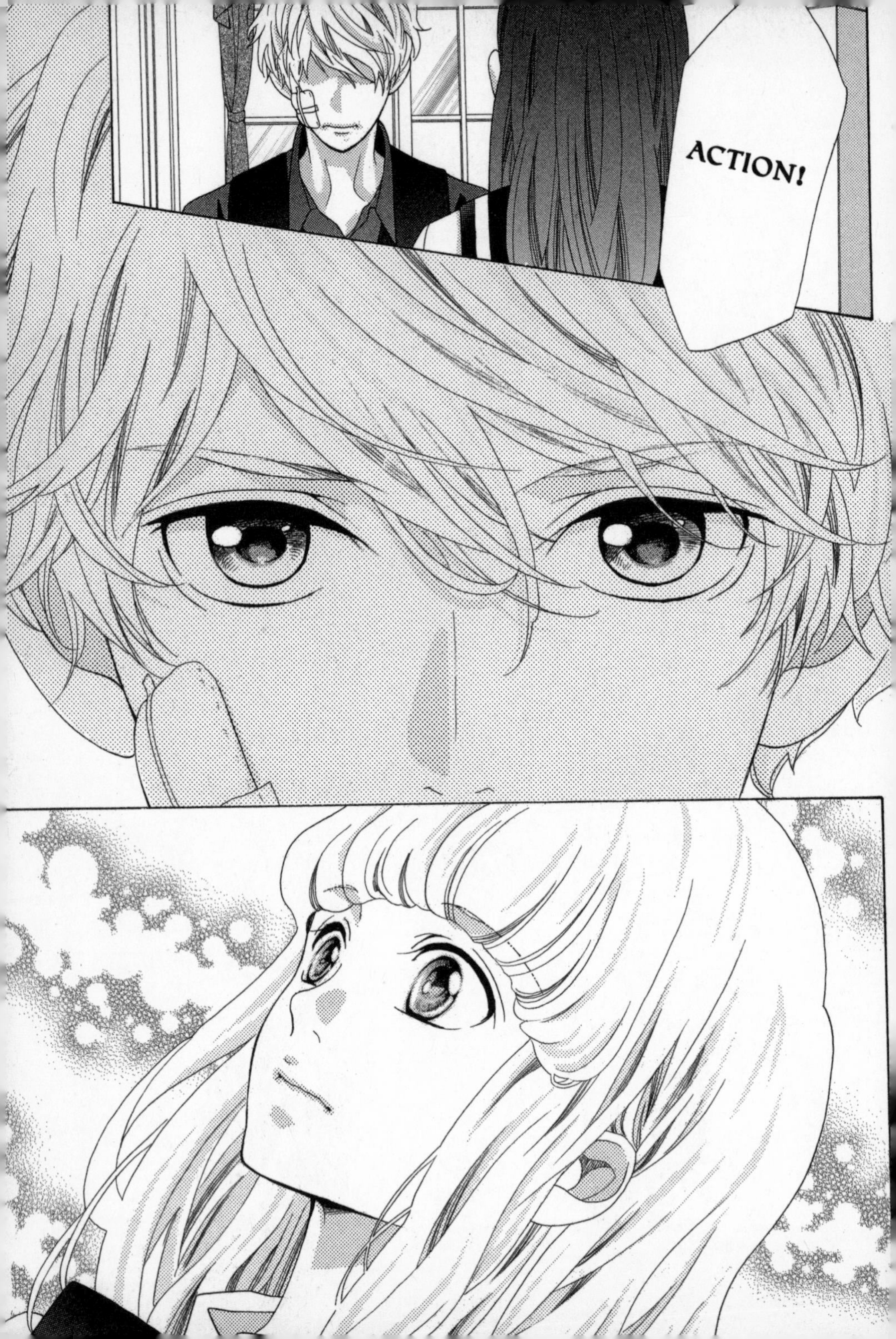
ACTION!

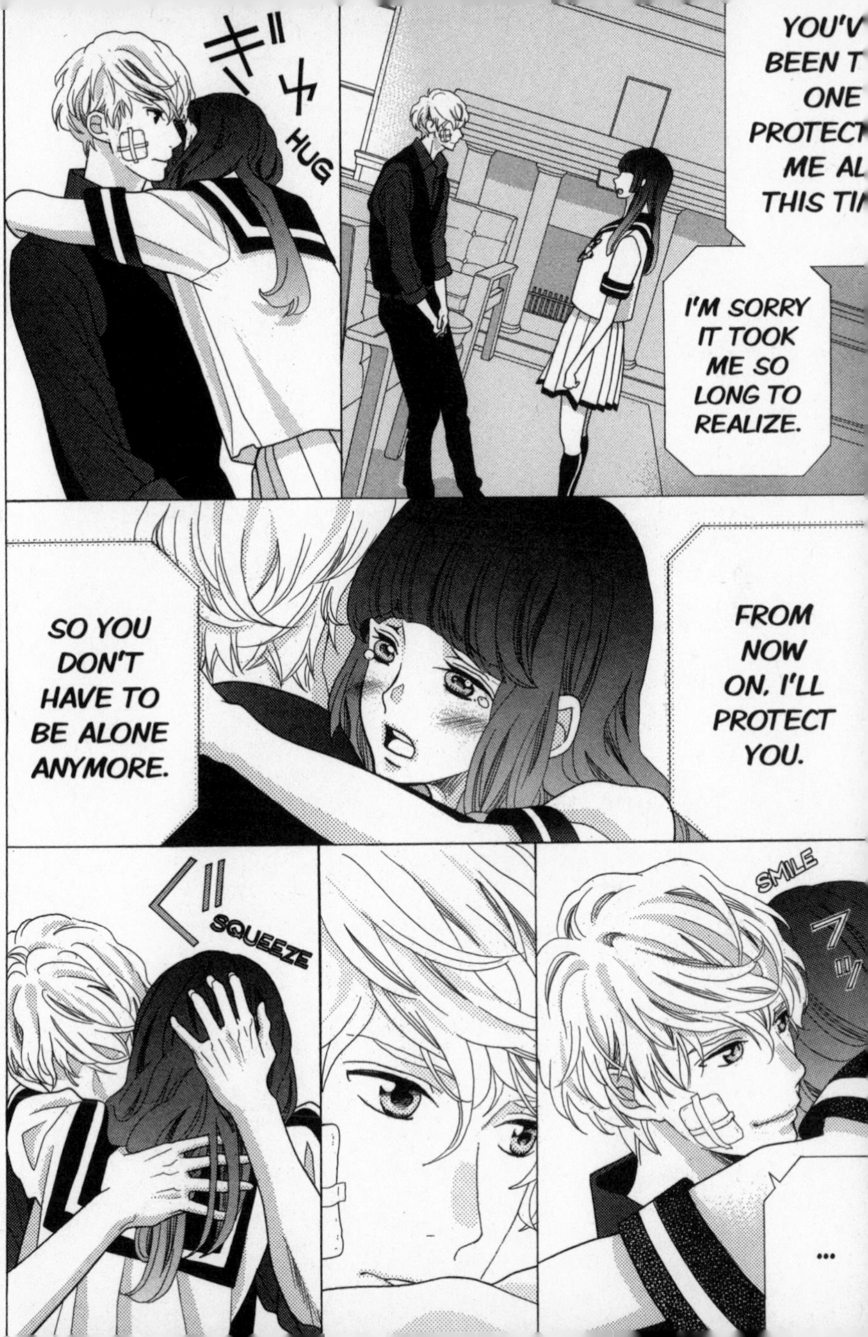
YOU'V BEEN T ONE PROTECT ME AL THIS TI
I'M SORRY IT TOOK ME SO LONG TO REALIZE.
ギュ
HUG
FROM NOW ON, I'LL PROTECT YOU.
SO YOU DON'T HAVE TO BE ALONE ANYMORE.
SMILE
フッ
...
ぐっ
SQUEEZE

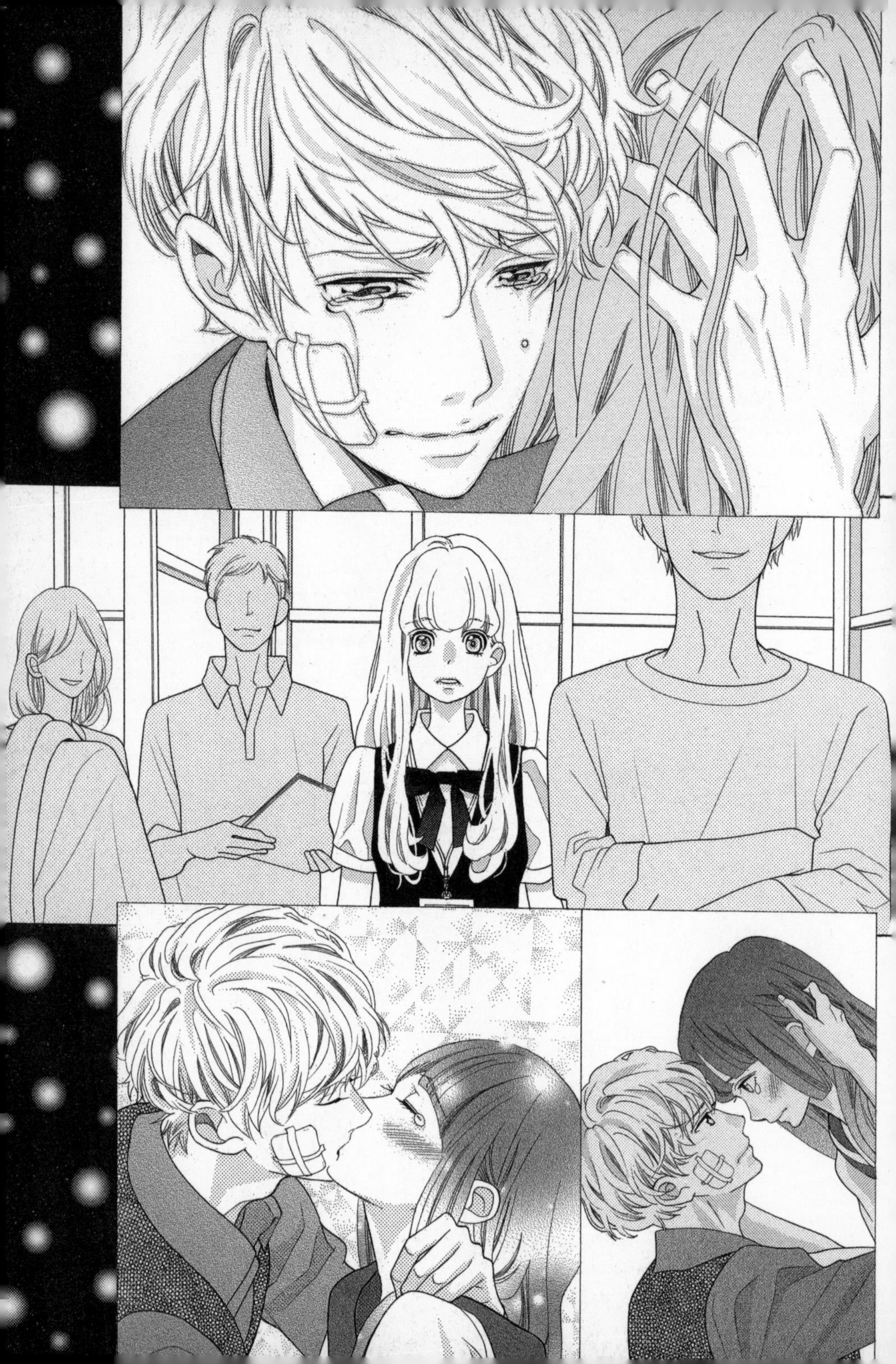

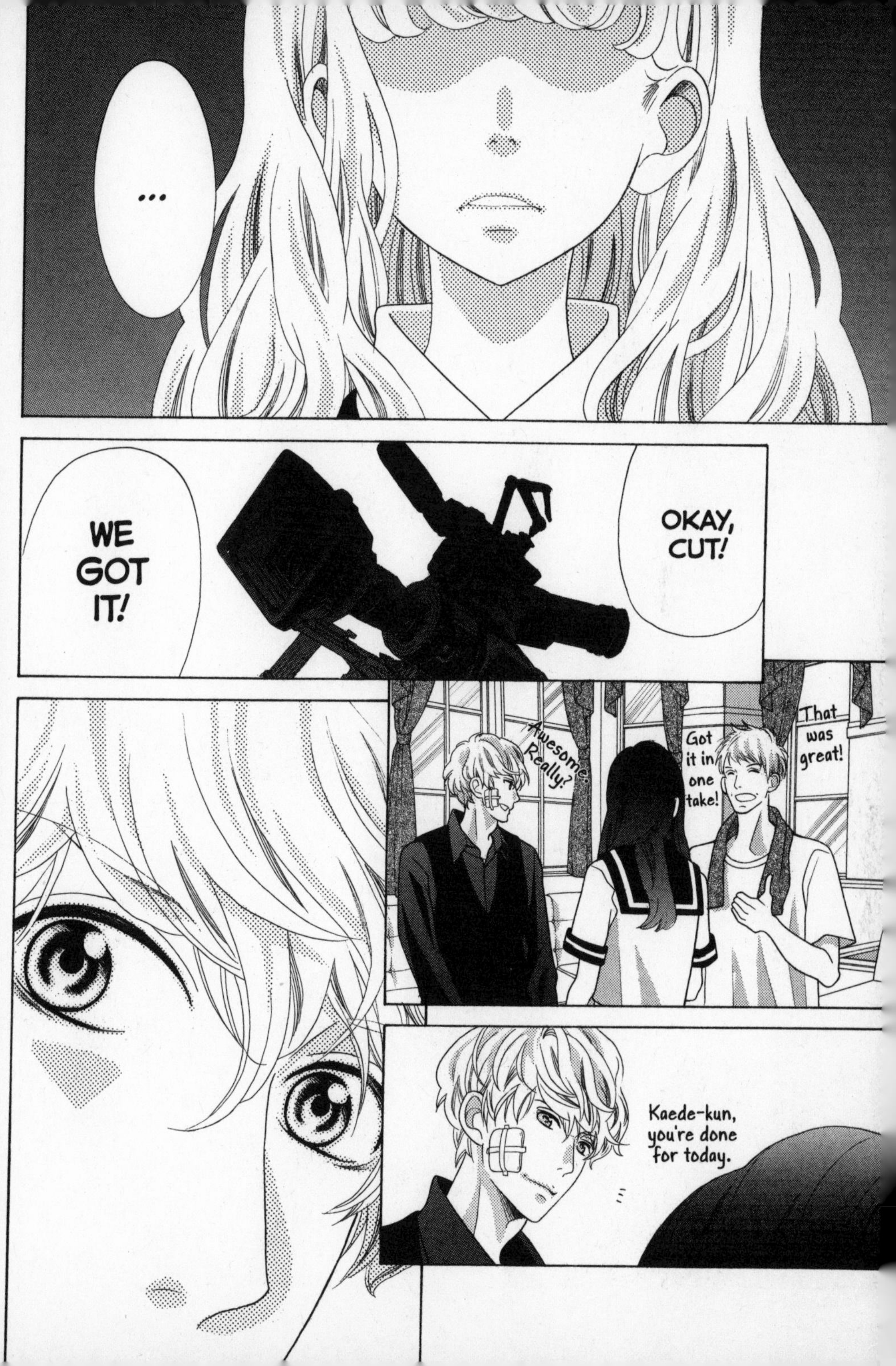
...
OKAY, CUT!
WE GOT IT!
That was great!
Got it in one take!
Awesome. Really?
Kaede-kun, you're done for today.

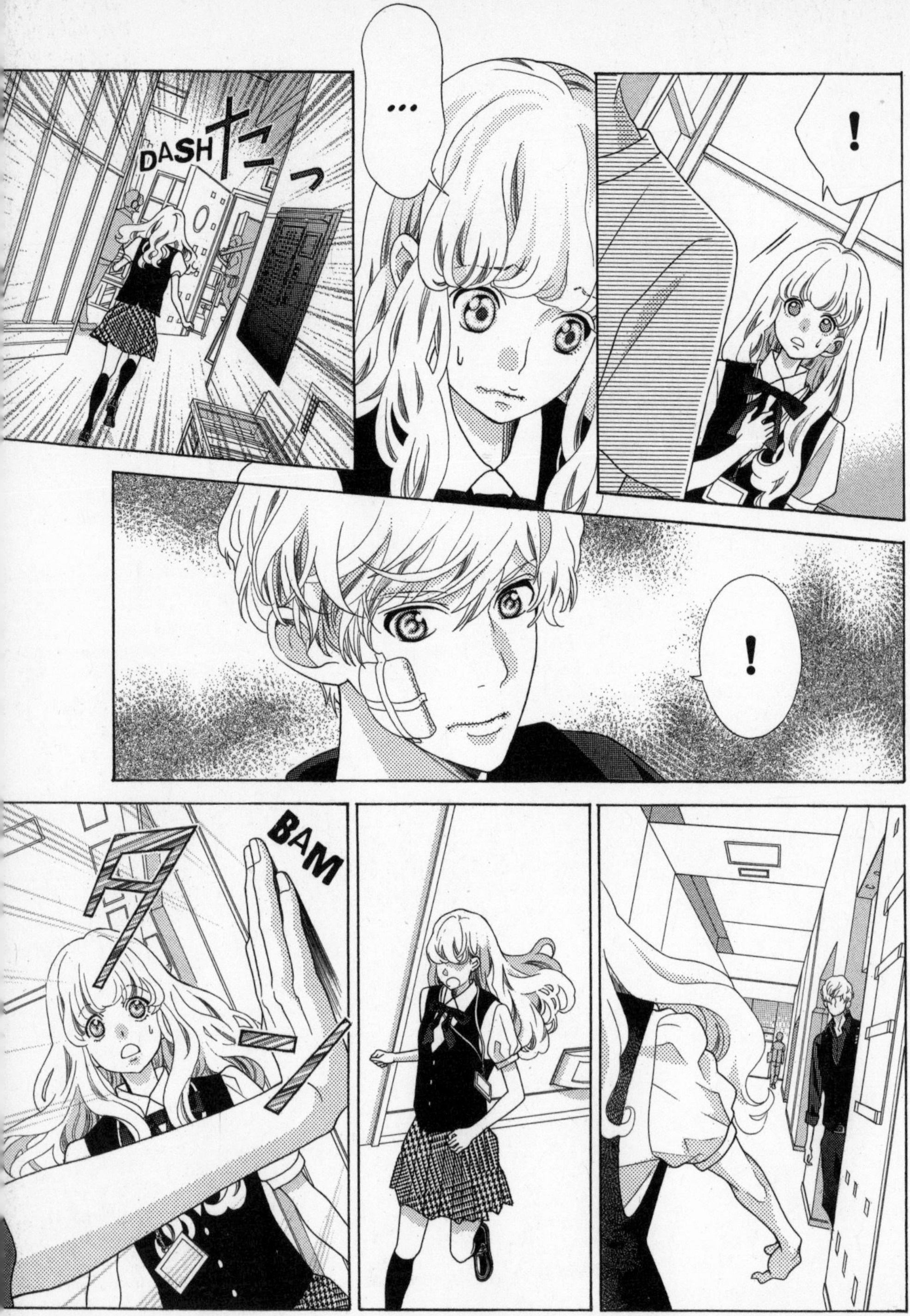
!
...
DASH
!
BAM

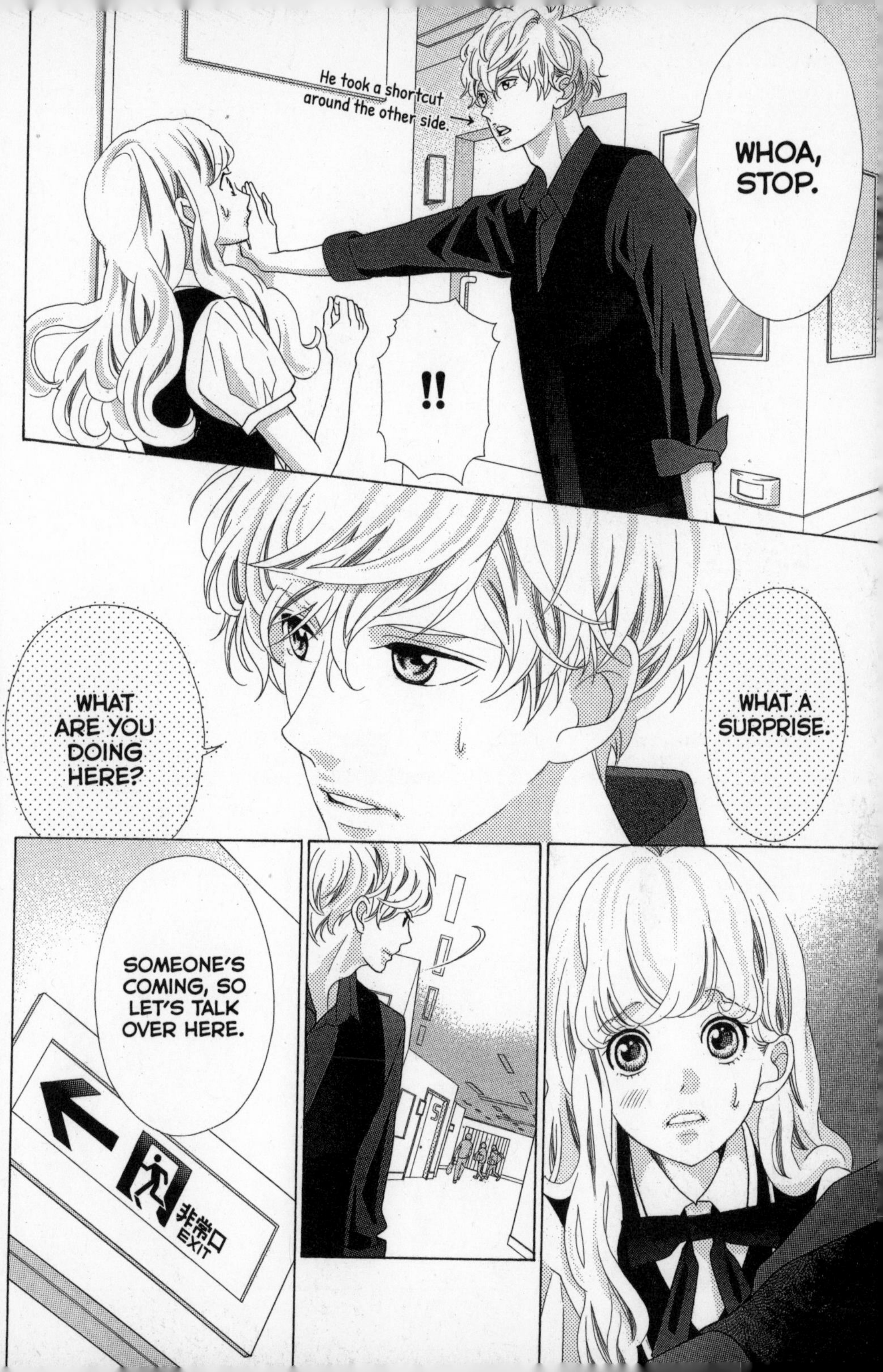
WHOA, STOP.
He took a shortcut around the other side.
!!
WHAT A SURPRISE.
WHAT ARE YOU DOING HERE?
SOMEONE'S COMING, SO LET'S TALK OVER HERE.
非常口
EXIT

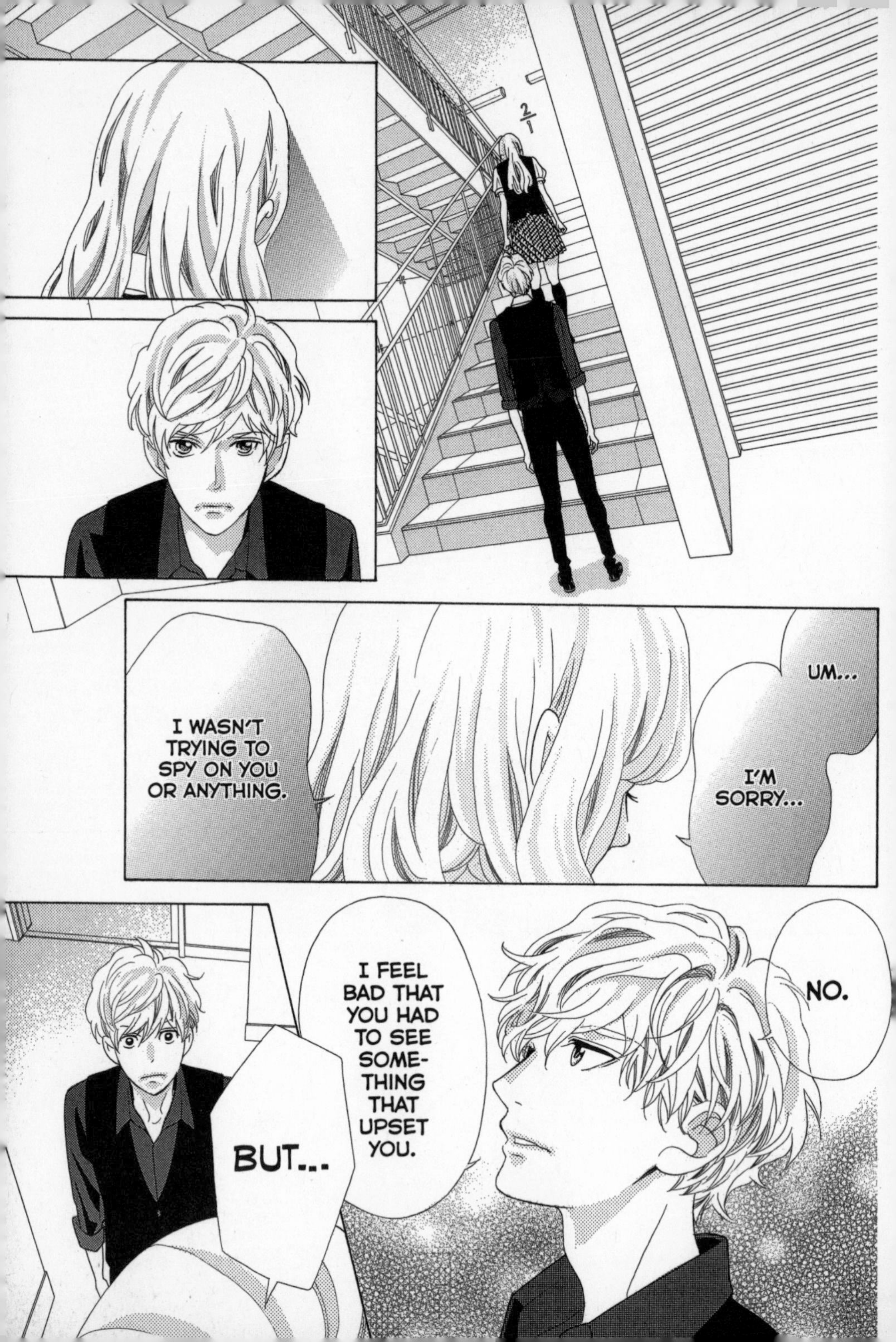
UM...
I'M SORRY...
I WASN'T TRYING TO SPY ON YOU OR ANYTHING.
NO.
I FEEL BAD THAT YOU HAD TO SEE SOME-THING THAT UPSET YOU.
BUT...

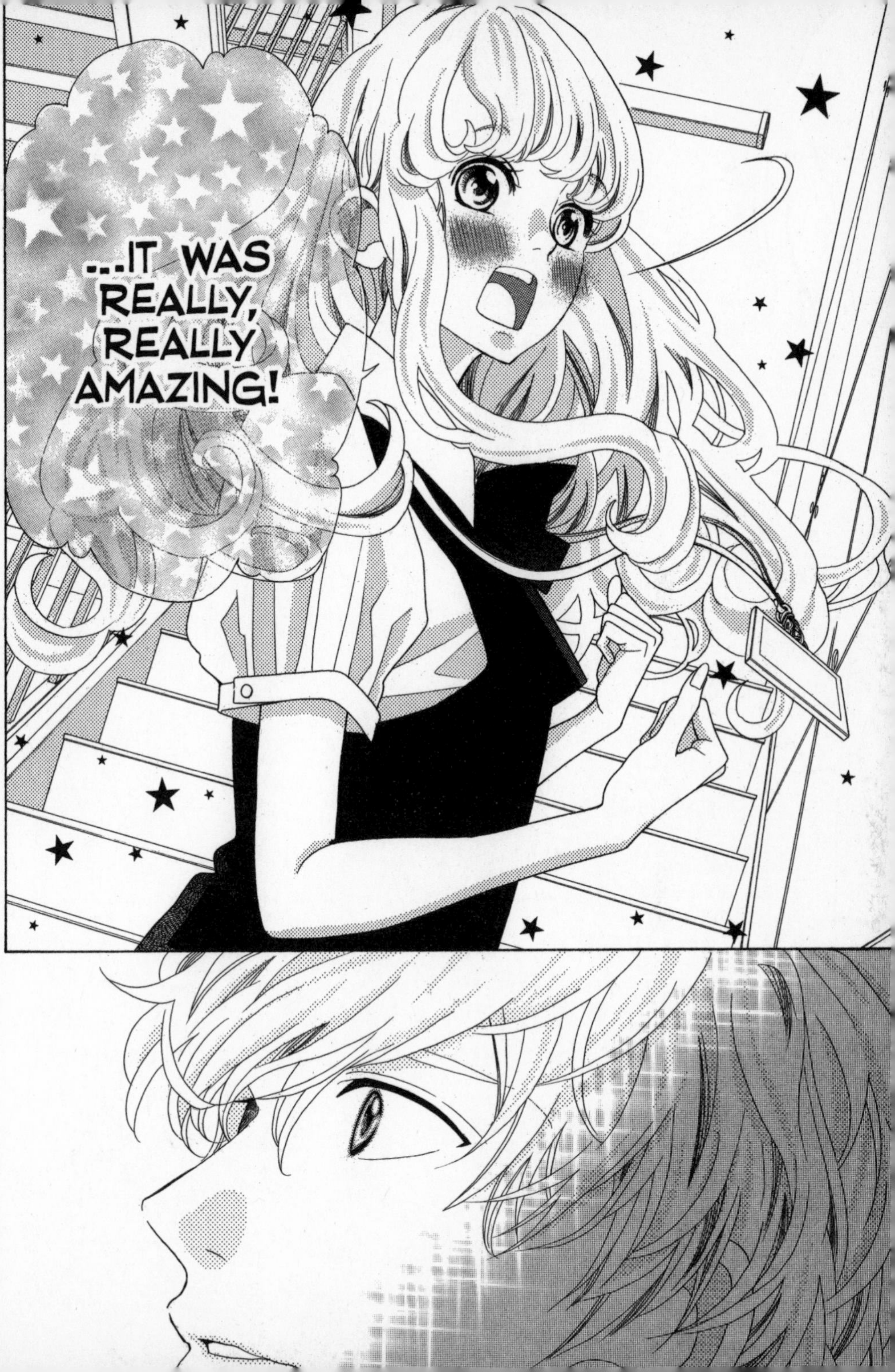
...IT WAS REALLY, REALLY AMAZING!

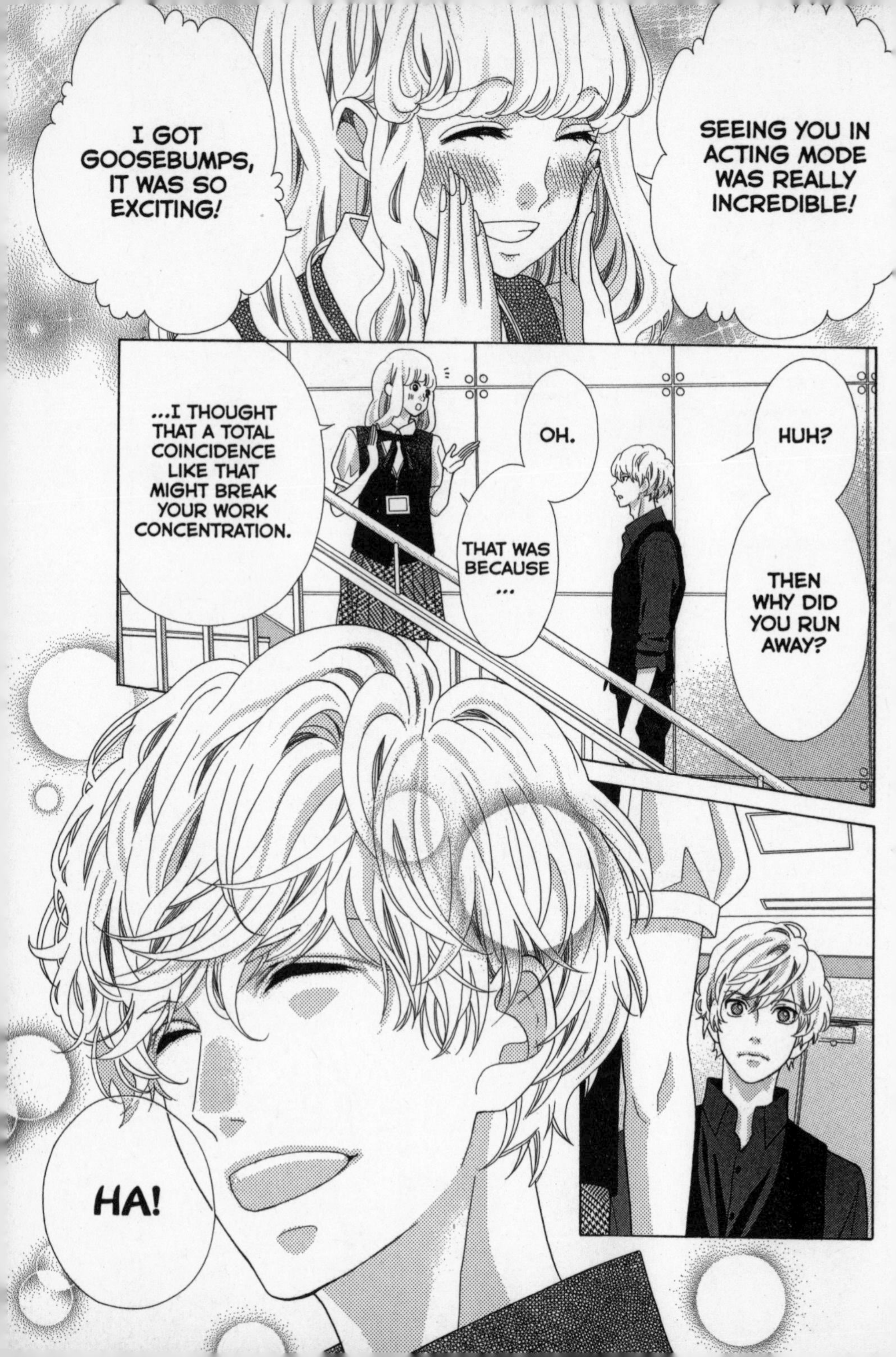
SEEING YOU IN ACTING MODE WAS REALLY INCREDIBLE!
I GOT GOOSEBUMPS, IT WAS SO EXCITING!
HUH?
THEN WHY DID YOU RUN AWAY?
OH.
THAT WAS BECAUSE ...
...I THOUGHT THAT A TOTAL COINCIDENCE LIKE THAT MIGHT BREAK YOUR WORK CONCENTRATION.
HA!

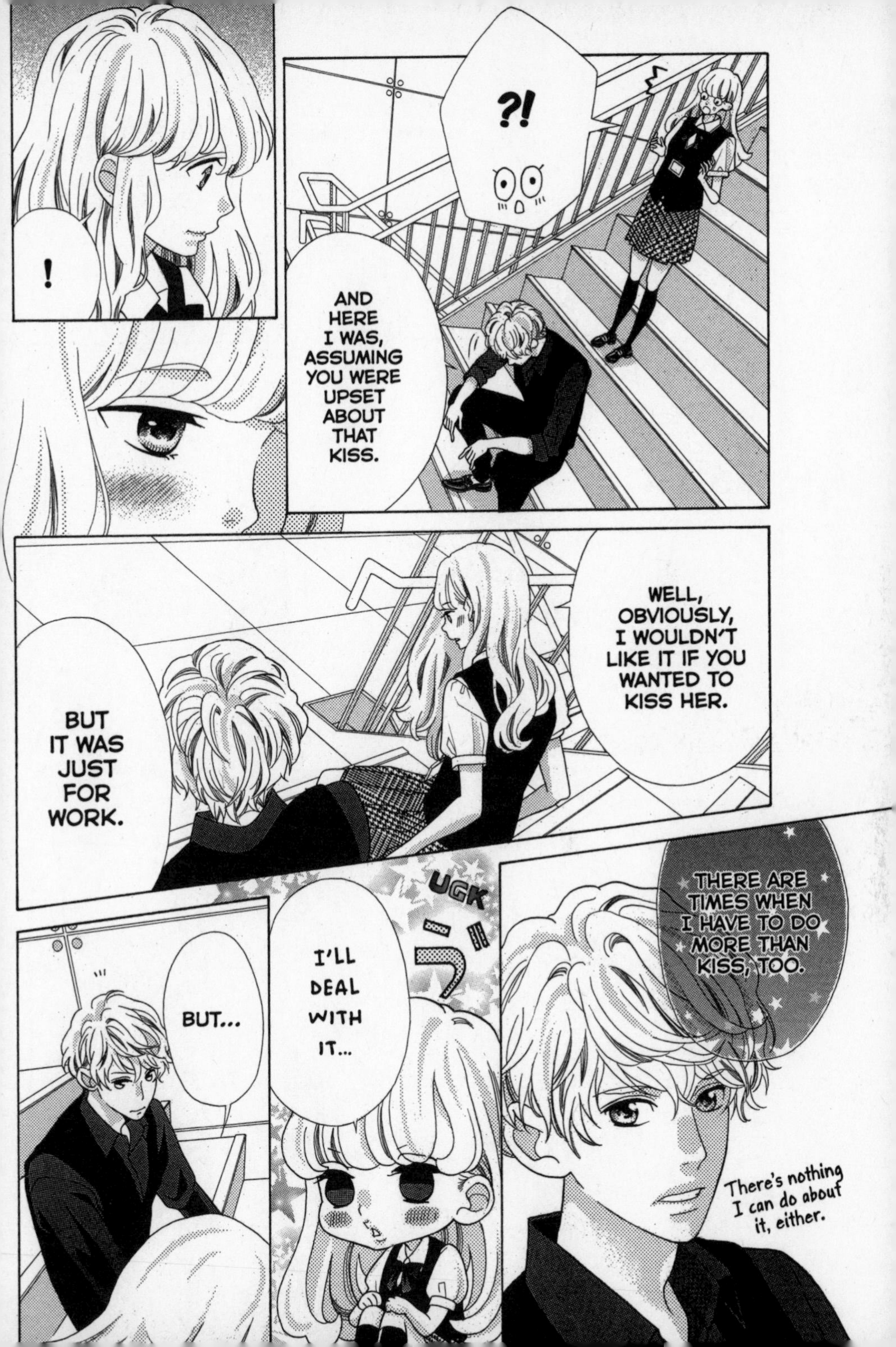
?!
AND HERE I WAS, ASSUMING YOU WERE UPSET ABOUT THAT KISS.
!
WELL, OBVIOUSLY, I WOULDN'T LIKE IT IF YOU WANTED TO KISS HER.
BUT IT WAS JUST FOR WORK.
THERE ARE TIMES WHEN I HAVE TO DO MORE THAN KISS, TOO.
There's nothing I can do about it, either.
UGK
I'LL DEAL WITH IT...
BUT...

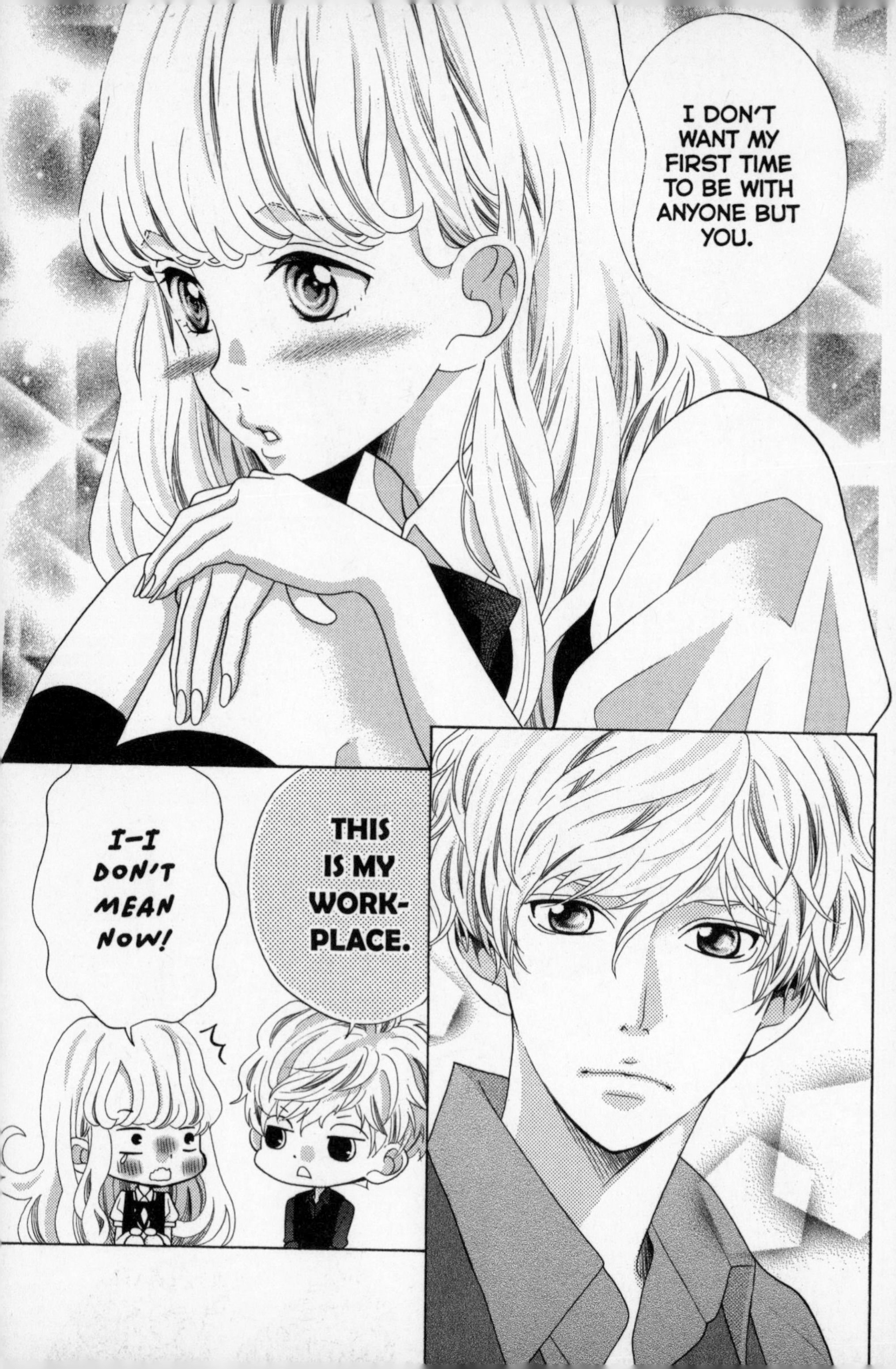
I DON'T WANT MY FIRST TIME TO BE WITH ANYONE BUT YOU.
THIS IS MY WORK-PLACE.
I-I DON'T MEAN NOW!

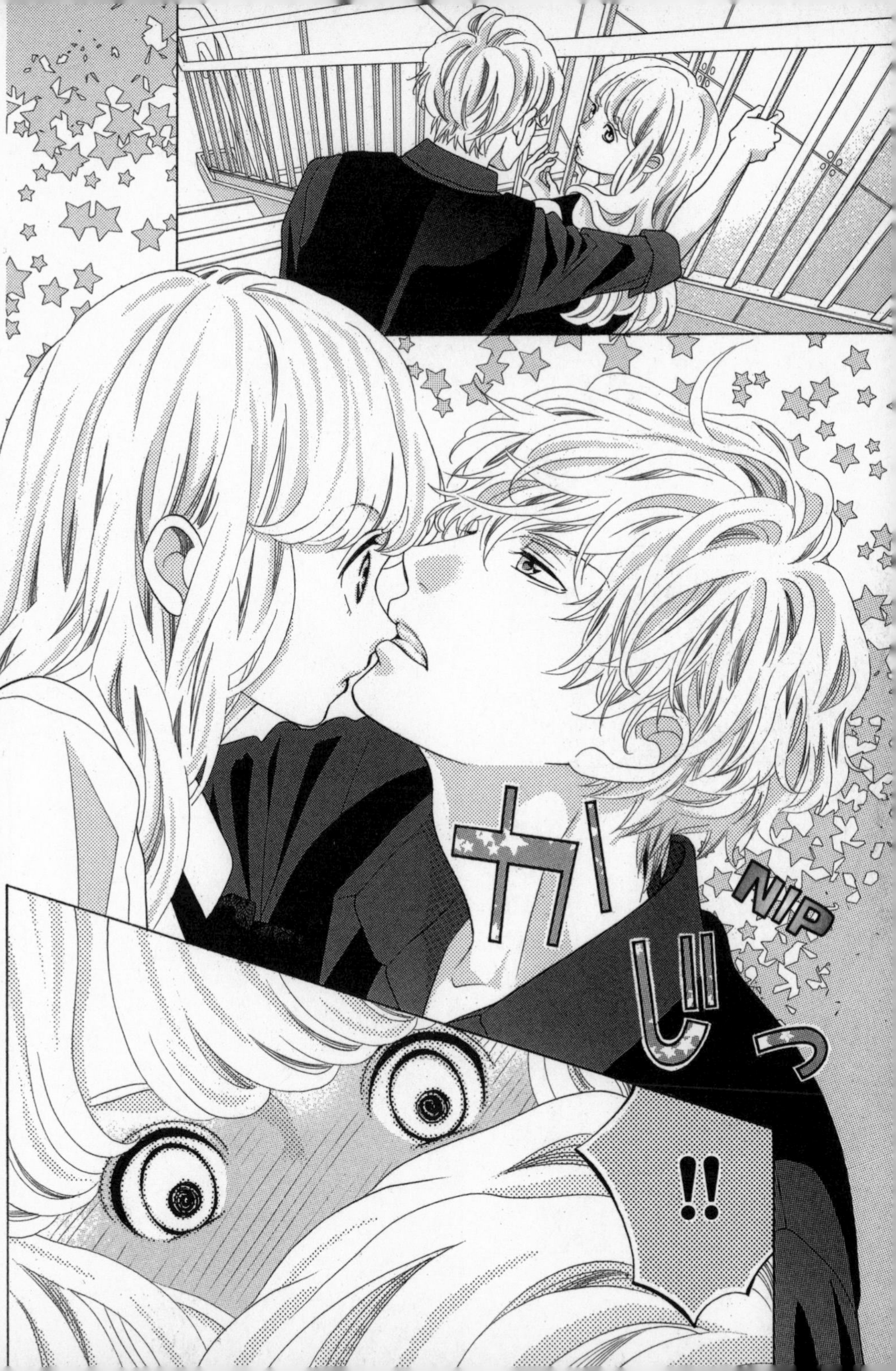
カリ
NIP
じっ
!!

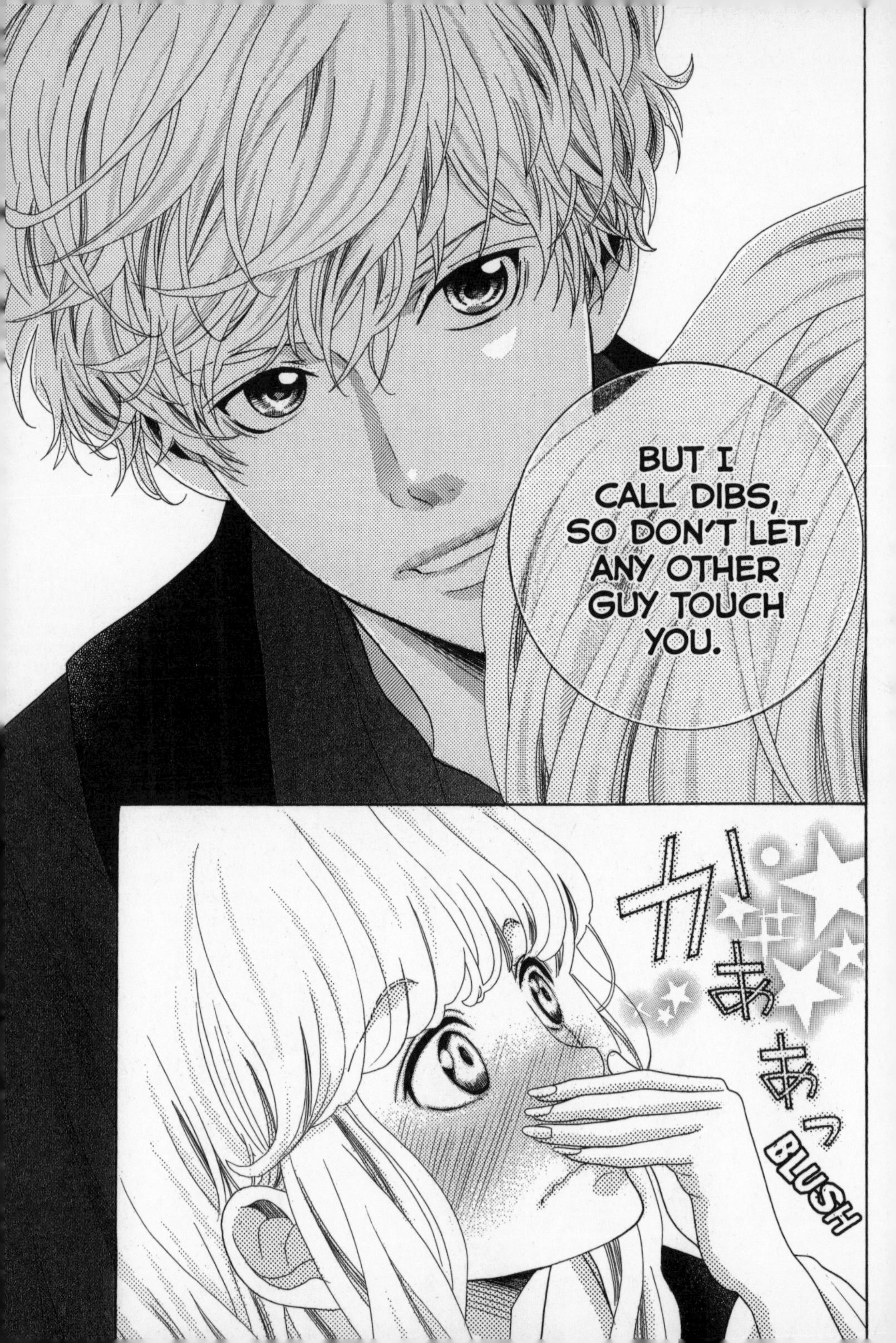
BUT I CALL DIBS, SO DON'T LET ANY OTHER GUY TOUCH YOU.
カーあぁっ
BLUSH

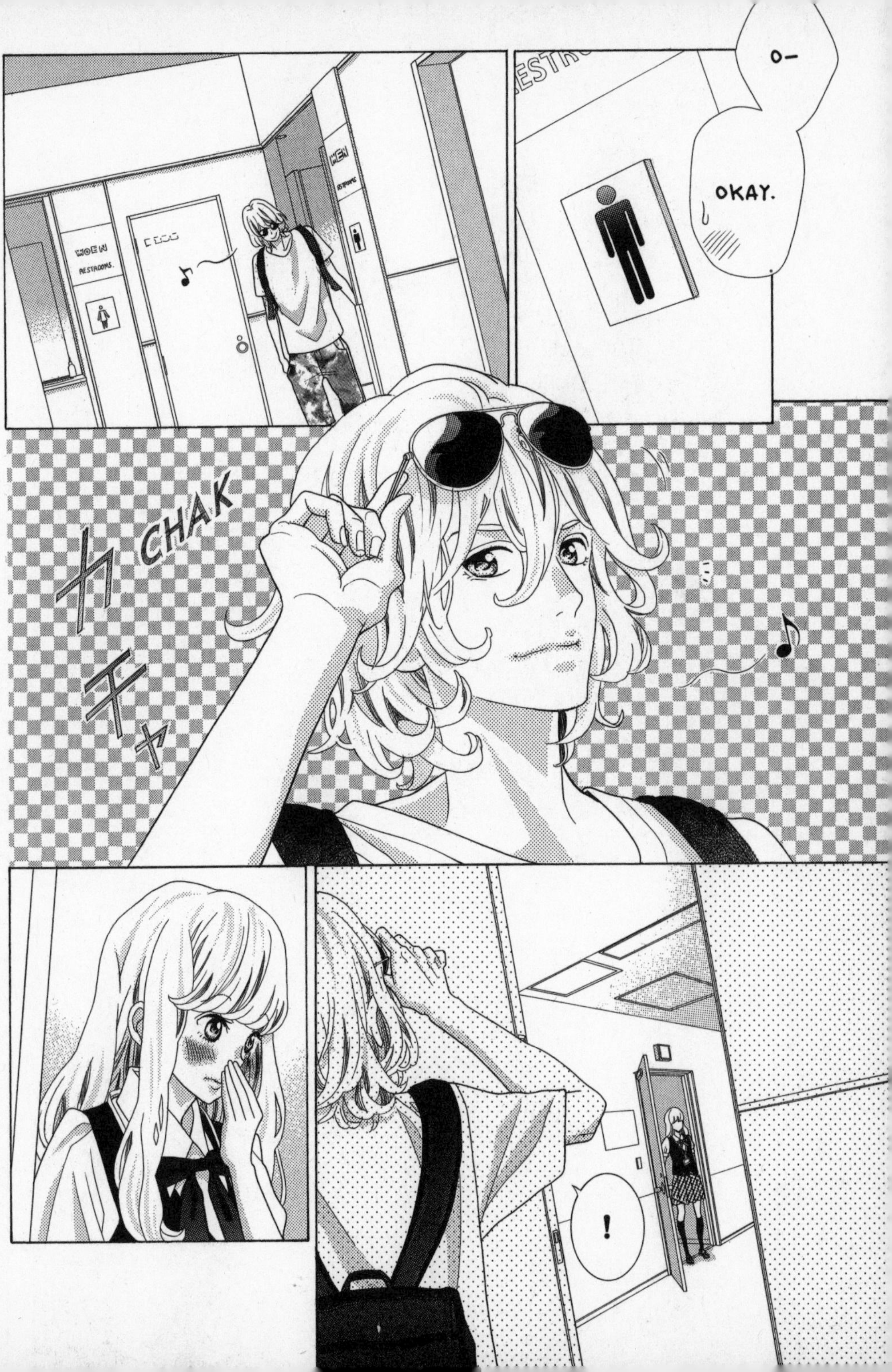
O–
OKAY.
CHAK
!

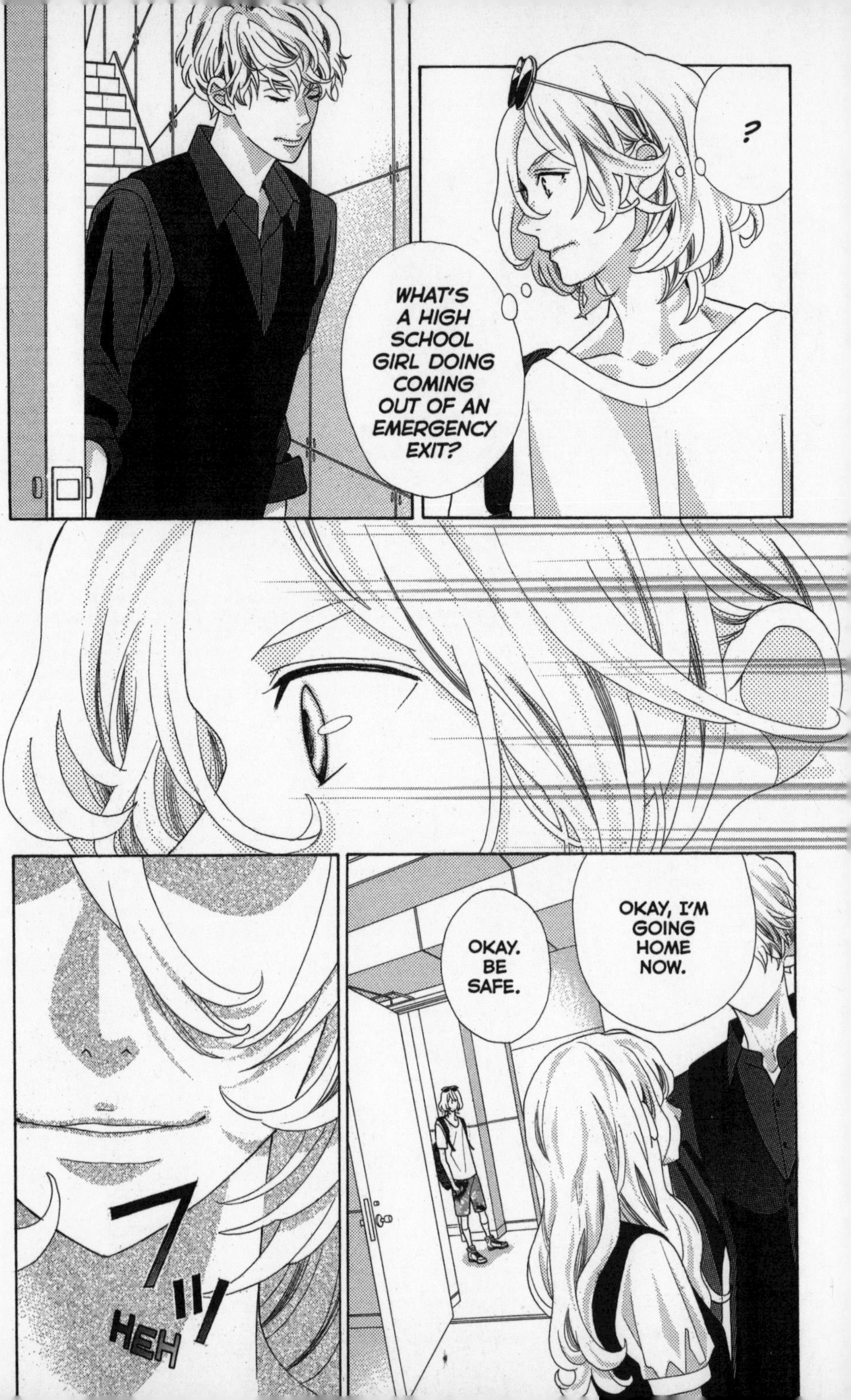
?
WHAT'S A HIGH SCHOOL GIRL DOING COMING OUT OF AN EMERGENCY EXIT?
OKAY, I'M GOING HOME NOW.
OKAY. BE SAFE.
HEH

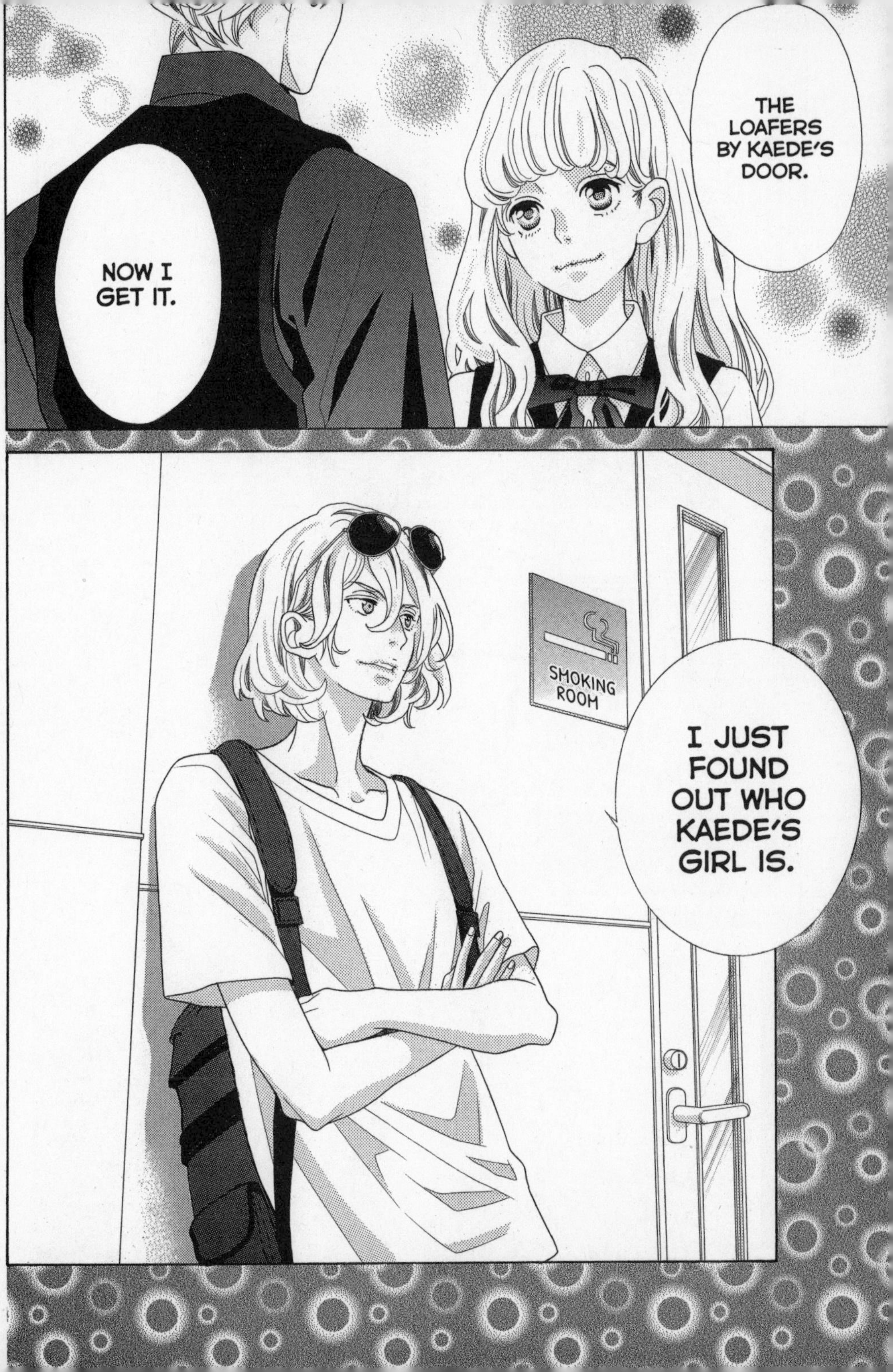
THE LOAFERS BY KAEDE'S DOOR.
NOW I GET IT.
SMOKING ROOM
I JUST FOUND OUT WHO KAEDE'S GIRL IS.

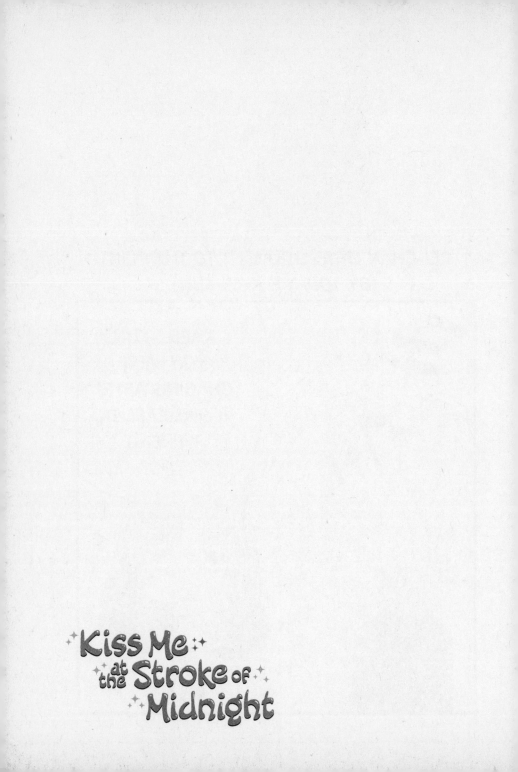

Kiss Me at the Stroke of Midnight

REI-CHAN GETS STRAIGHT TO THE POINT
(BY TODAY'S KIRA-KUN)

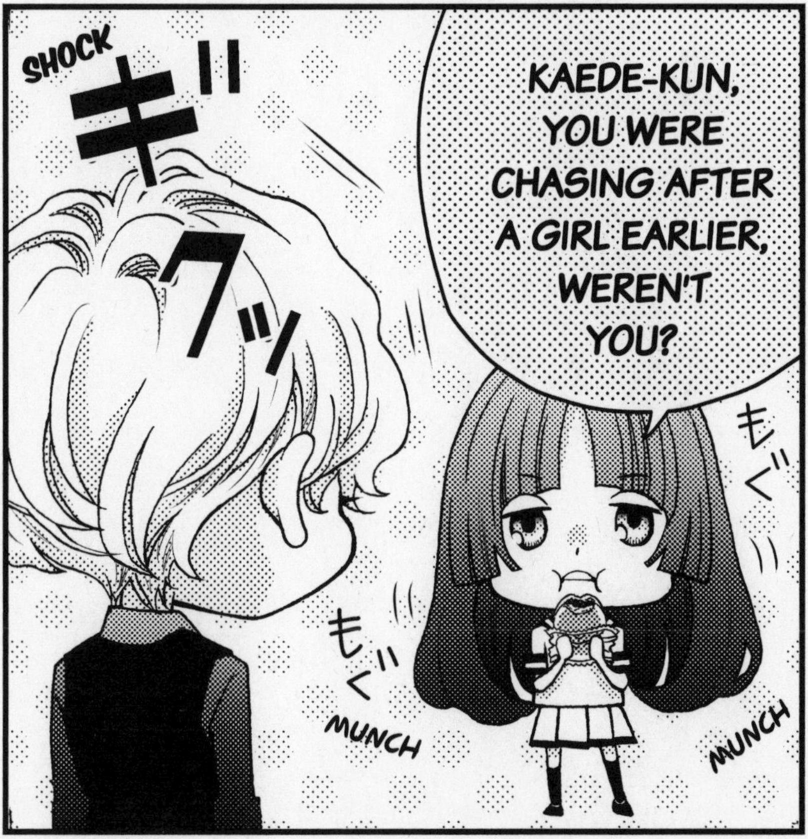
KAEDE-KUN, YOU WERE CHASING AFTER A GIRL EARLIER, WEREN'T YOU?
もぐ
MUNCH
SHOCK
もぐ
MUNCH

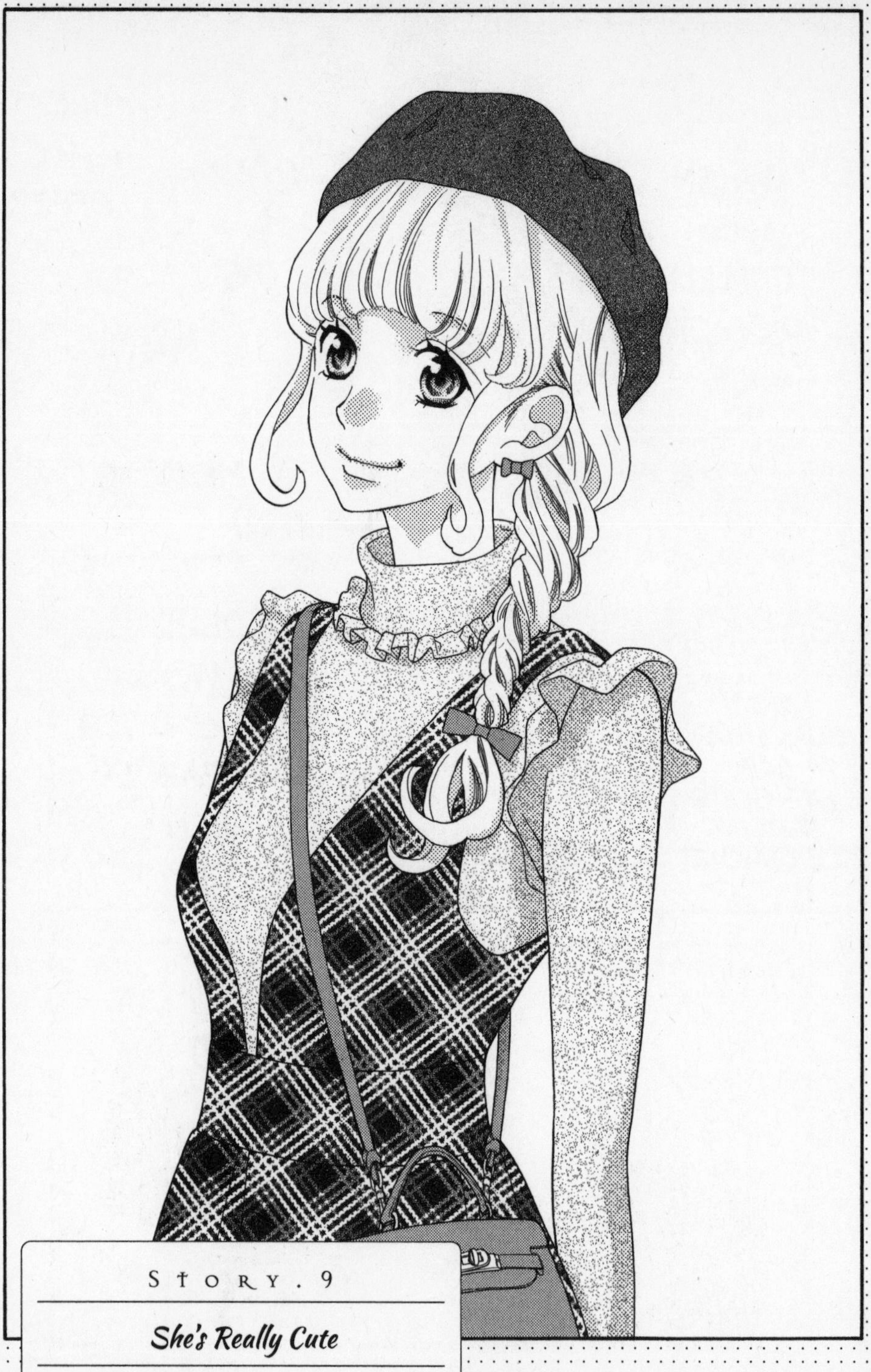

STORY . 9

She's Really Cute

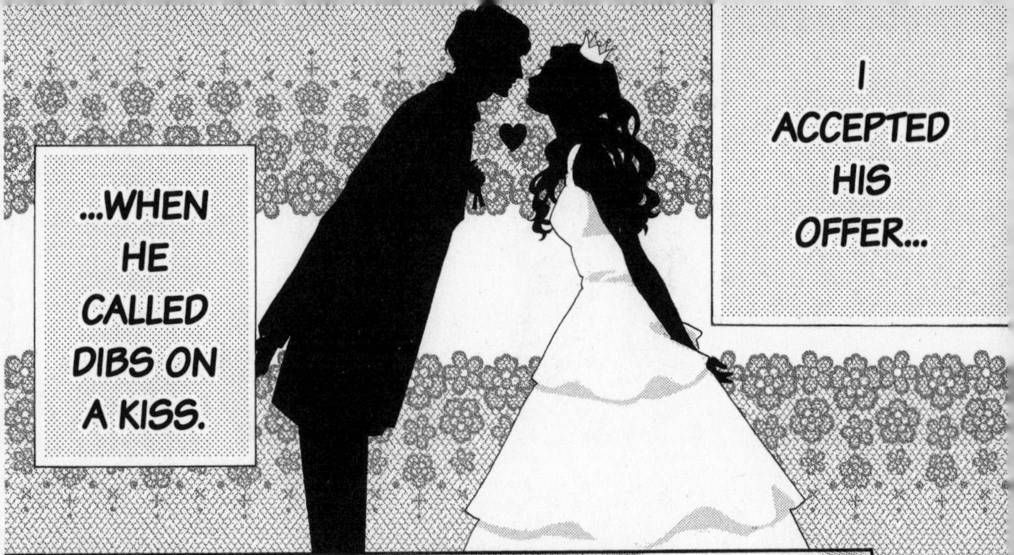
I ACCEPTED HIS OFFER...
...WHEN HE CALLED DIBS ON A KISS.

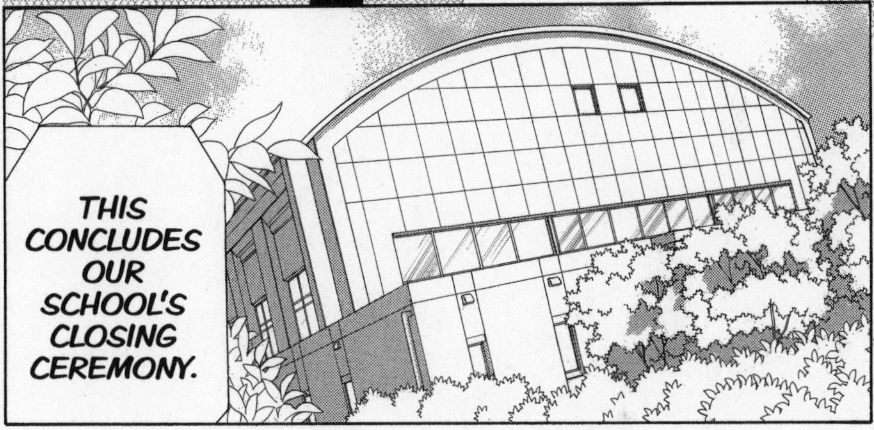
THIS CONCLUDES OUR SCHOOL'S CLOSING CEREMONY.

Kiss Me at the Stroke of Midnight

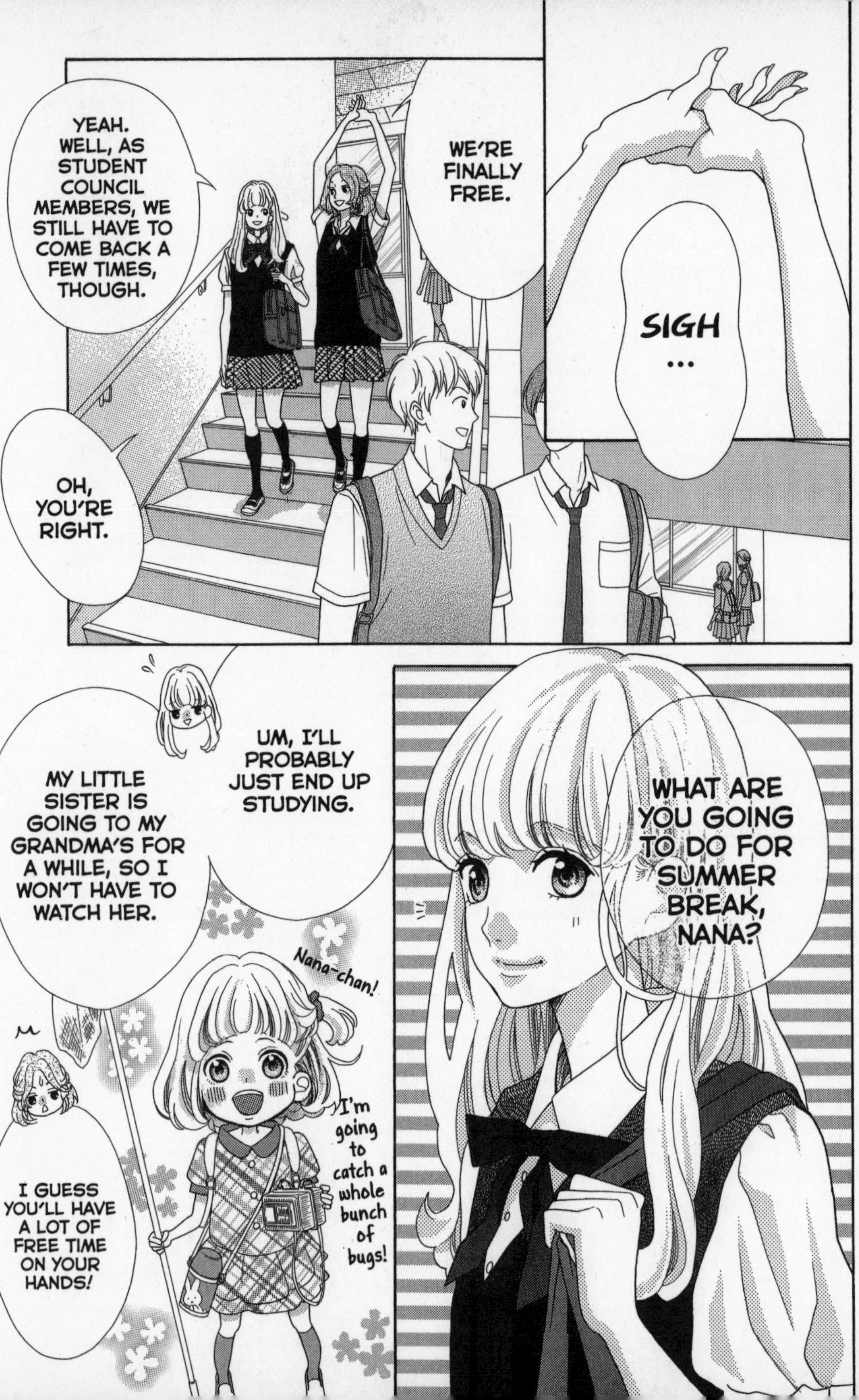
SIGH ...
WE'RE FINALLY FREE.
YEAH. WELL, AS STUDENT COUNCIL MEMBERS, WE STILL HAVE TO COME BACK A FEW TIMES, THOUGH.
OH, YOU'RE RIGHT.
WHAT ARE YOU GOING TO DO FOR SUMMER BREAK, NANA?
UM, I'LL PROBABLY JUST END UP STUDYING.
MY LITTLE SISTER IS GOING TO MY GRANDMA'S FOR A WHILE, SO I WON'T HAVE TO WATCH HER.
Nana-chan!
I'm going to catch a whole bunch of bugs!
I GUESS YOU'LL HAVE A LOT OF FREE TIME ON YOUR HANDS!

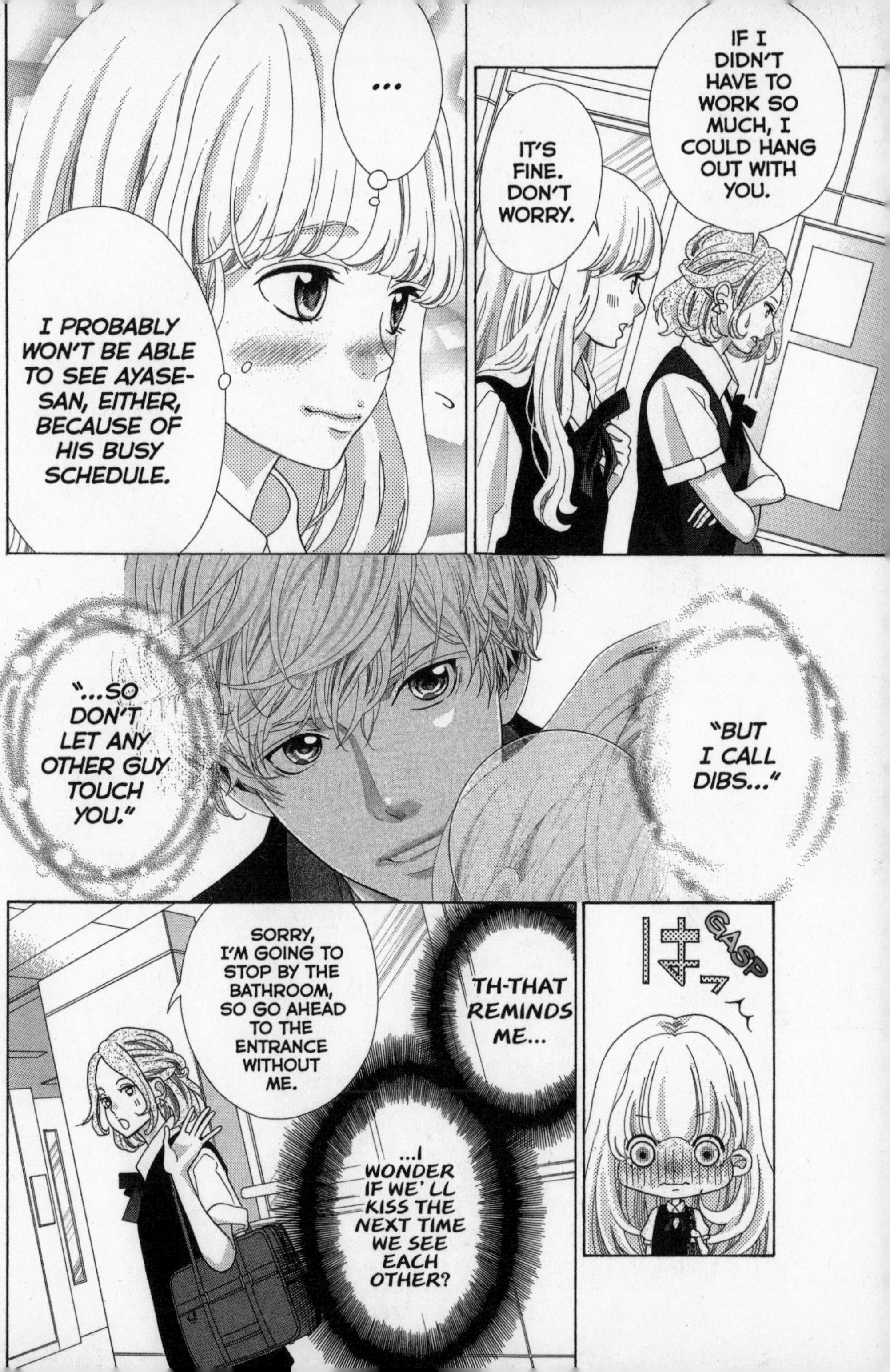
IF I DIDN'T HAVE TO WORK SO MUCH, I COULD HANG OUT WITH YOU.
IT'S FINE. DON'T WORRY.
...
I PROBABLY WON'T BE ABLE TO SEE AYASE-SAN, EITHER, BECAUSE OF HIS BUSY SCHEDULE.
"BUT I CALL DIBS..."
"...SO DON'T LET ANY OTHER GUY TOUCH YOU."
はッ
GASP
SORRY, I'M GOING TO STOP BY THE BATHROOM, SO GO AHEAD TO THE ENTRANCE WITHOUT ME.
TH-THAT REMINDS ME...
...I WONDER IF WE'LL KISS THE NEXT TIME WE SEE EACH OTHER?

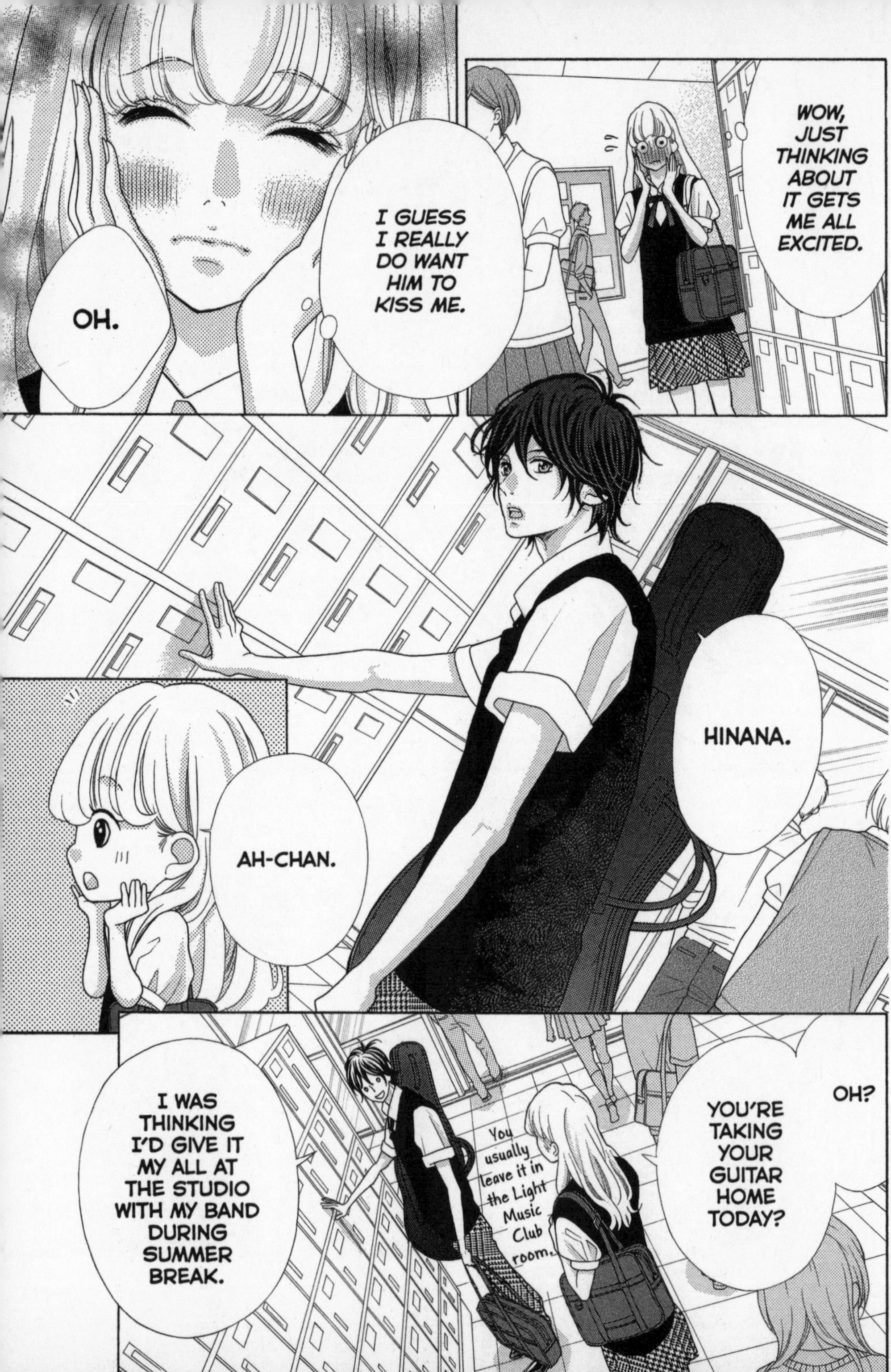
WOW, JUST THINKING ABOUT IT GETS ME ALL EXCITED.
I GUESS I REALLY DO WANT HIM TO KISS ME.
OH.
HINANA.
AH-CHAN.
OH?
YOU'RE TAKING YOUR GUITAR HOME TODAY?
You usually leave it in the Light Music Club room.
I WAS THINKING I'D GIVE IT MY ALL AT THE STUDIO WITH MY BAND DURING SUMMER BREAK.

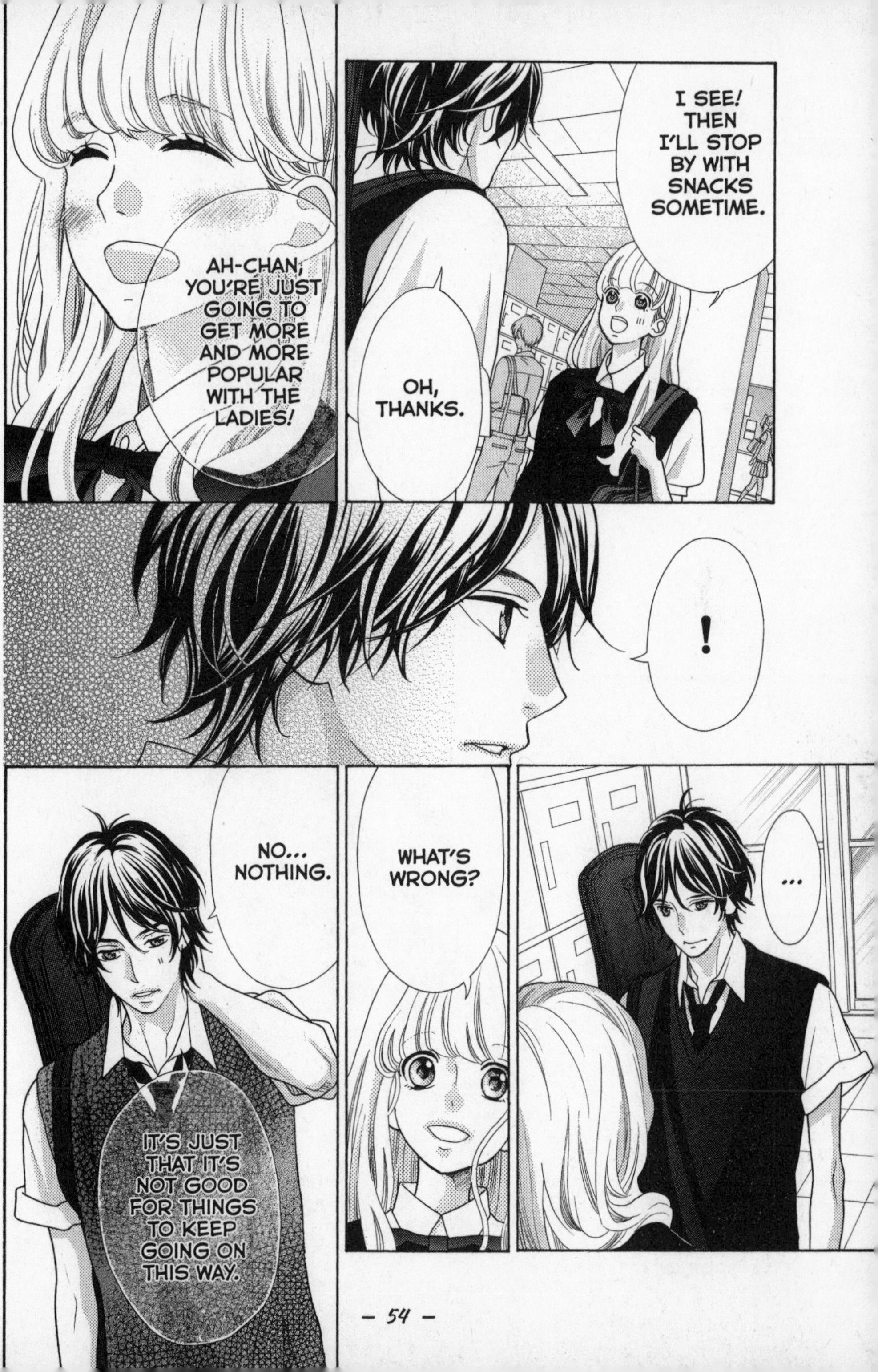
I SEE! THEN I'LL STOP BY WITH SNACKS SOMETIME.
OH, THANKS.
AH-CHAN, YOU'RE JUST GOING TO GET MORE AND MORE POPULAR WITH THE LADIES!
!
...
WHAT'S WRONG?
NO... NOTHING.
IT'S JUST THAT IT'S NOT GOOD FOR THINGS TO KEEP GOING ON THIS WAY.

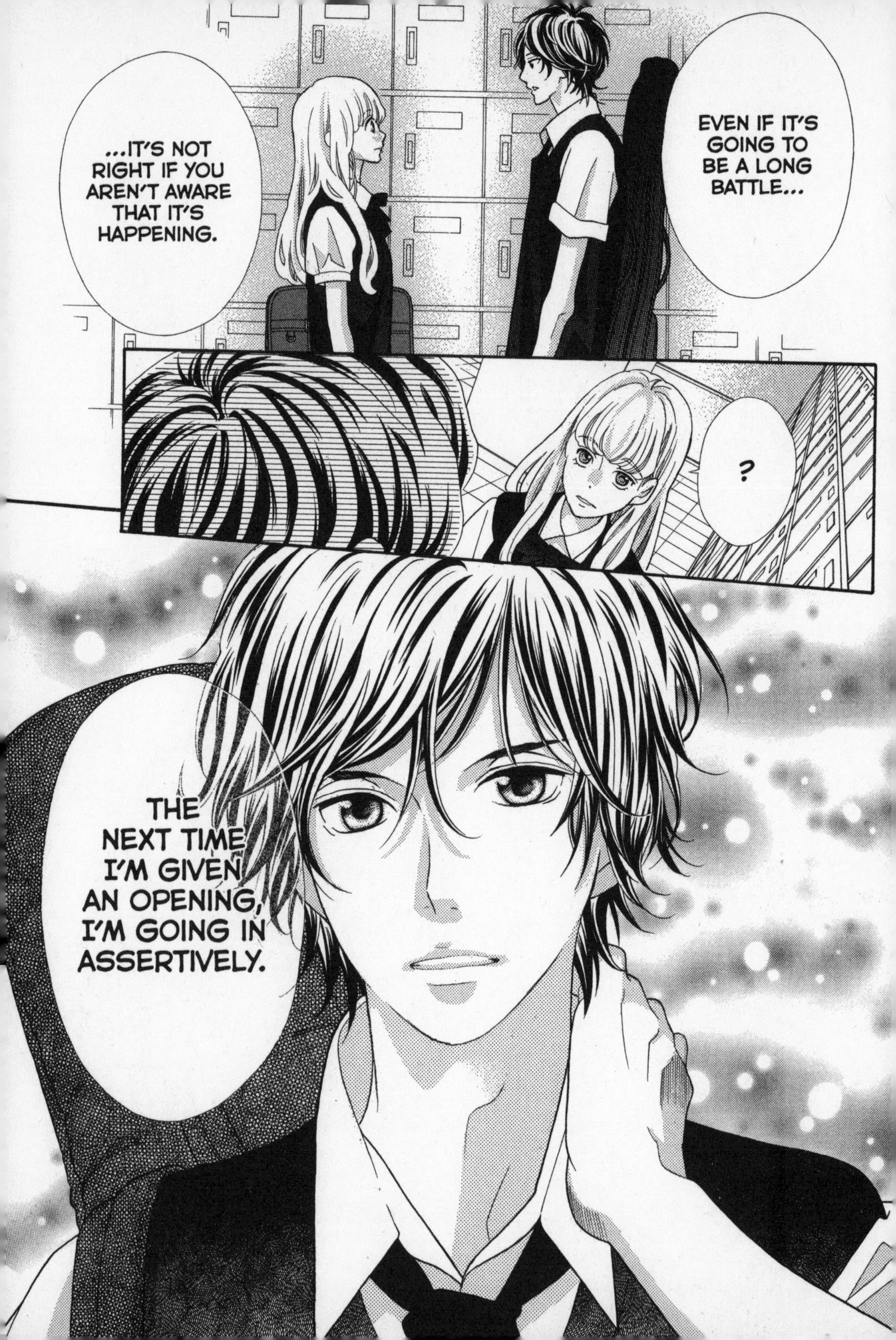
EVEN IF IT'S GOING TO BE A LONG BATTLE...
...IT'S NOT RIGHT IF YOU AREN'T AWARE THAT IT'S HAPPENING.
?
THE NEXT TIME I'M GIVEN AN OPENING, I'M GOING IN ASSERTIVELY.

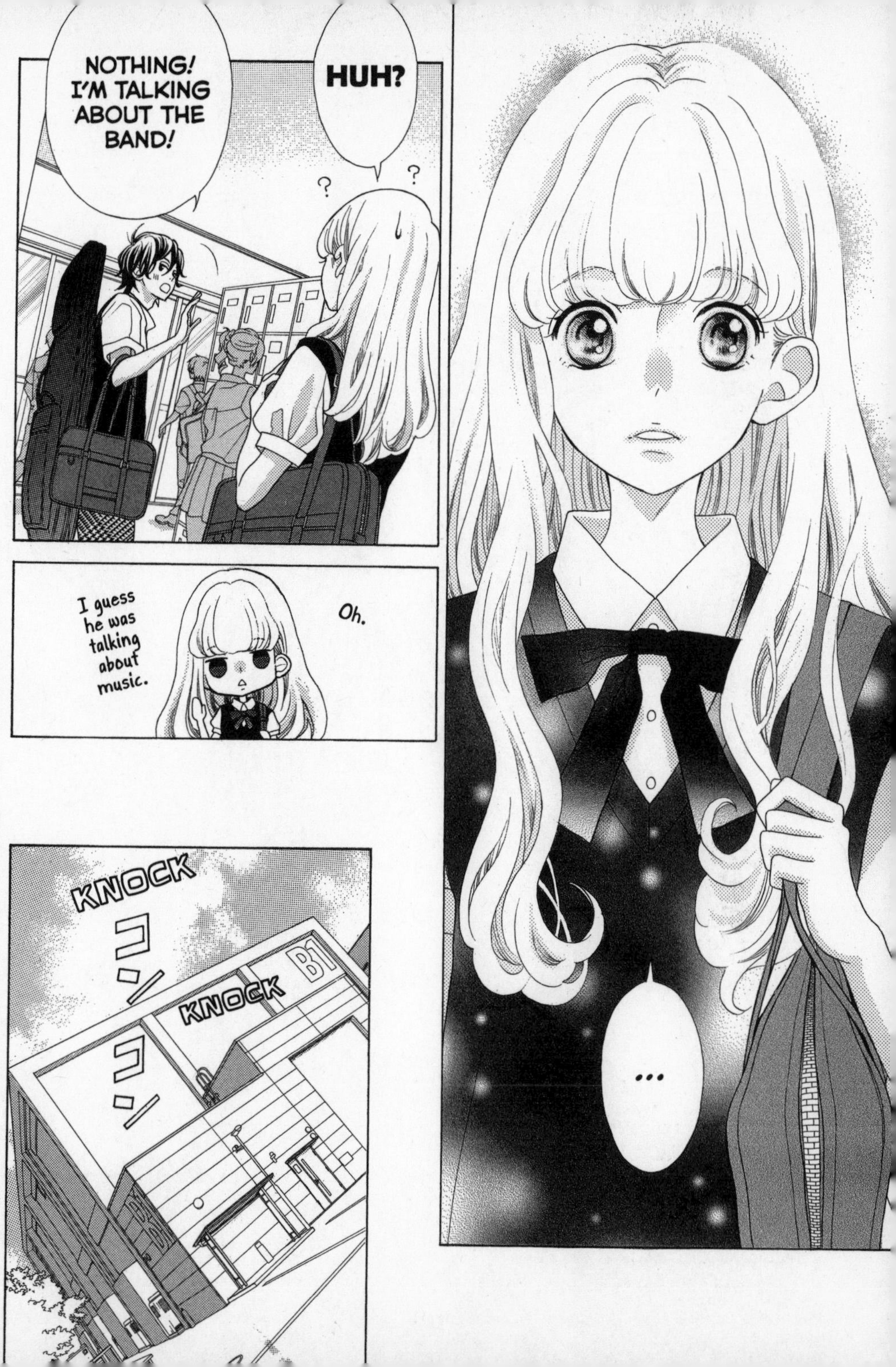
...
HUH?
NOTHING! I'M TALKING ABOUT THE BAND!
Oh.
I guess he was talking about music.
KNOCK
KNOCK

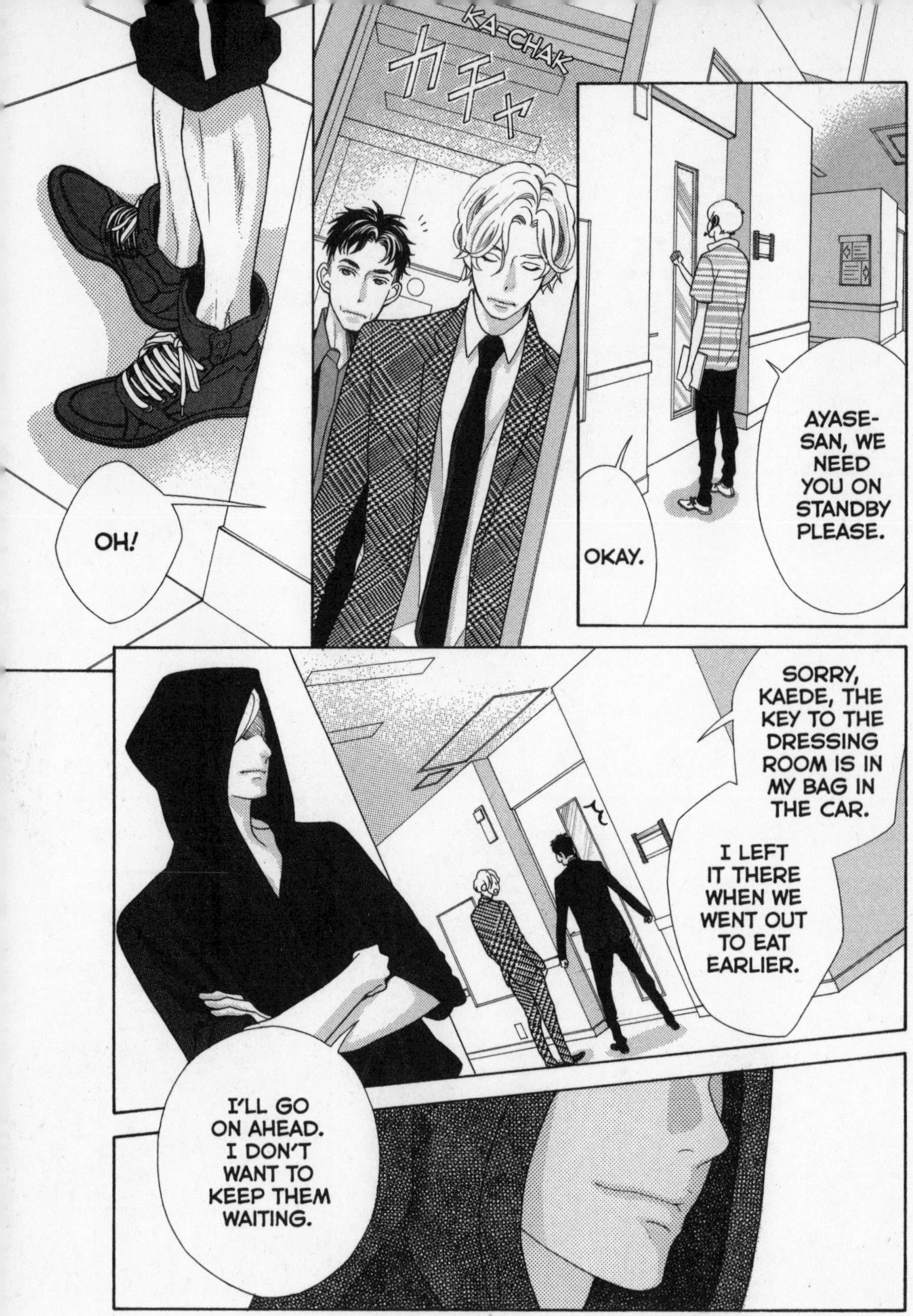
AYASE-SAN, WE NEED YOU ON STANDBY PLEASE.
OKAY.
カチャ
KA-CHAK
OH!
SORRY, KAEDE, THE KEY TO THE DRESSING ROOM IS IN MY BAG IN THE CAR.
I LEFT IT THERE WHEN WE WENT OUT TO EAT EARLIER.
I'LL GO ON AHEAD. I DON'T WANT TO KEEP THEM WAITING.

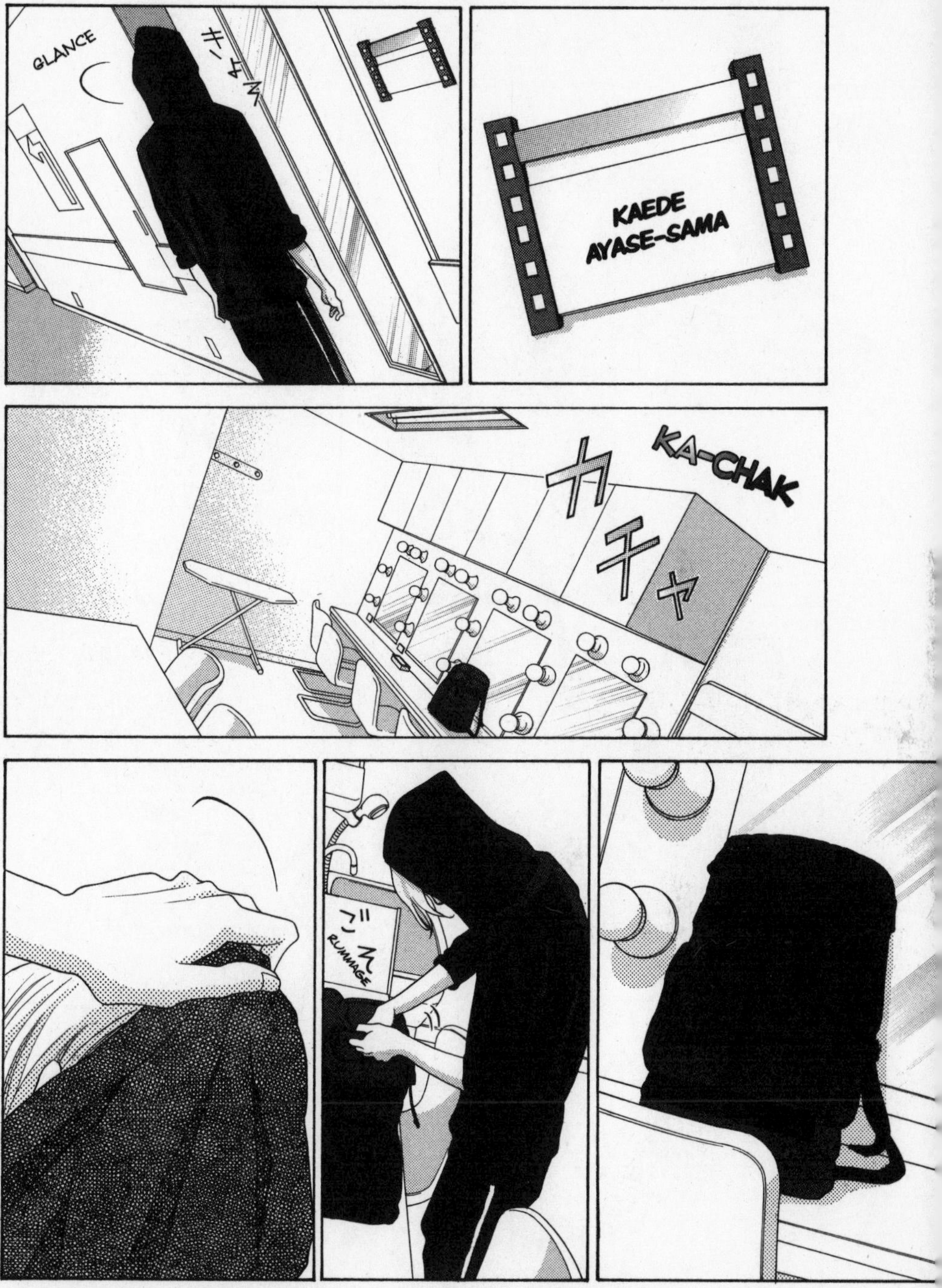
KAEDE
AYASE-SAMA
GLANCE
KA-CHAK
カチャ
RUMMAGE

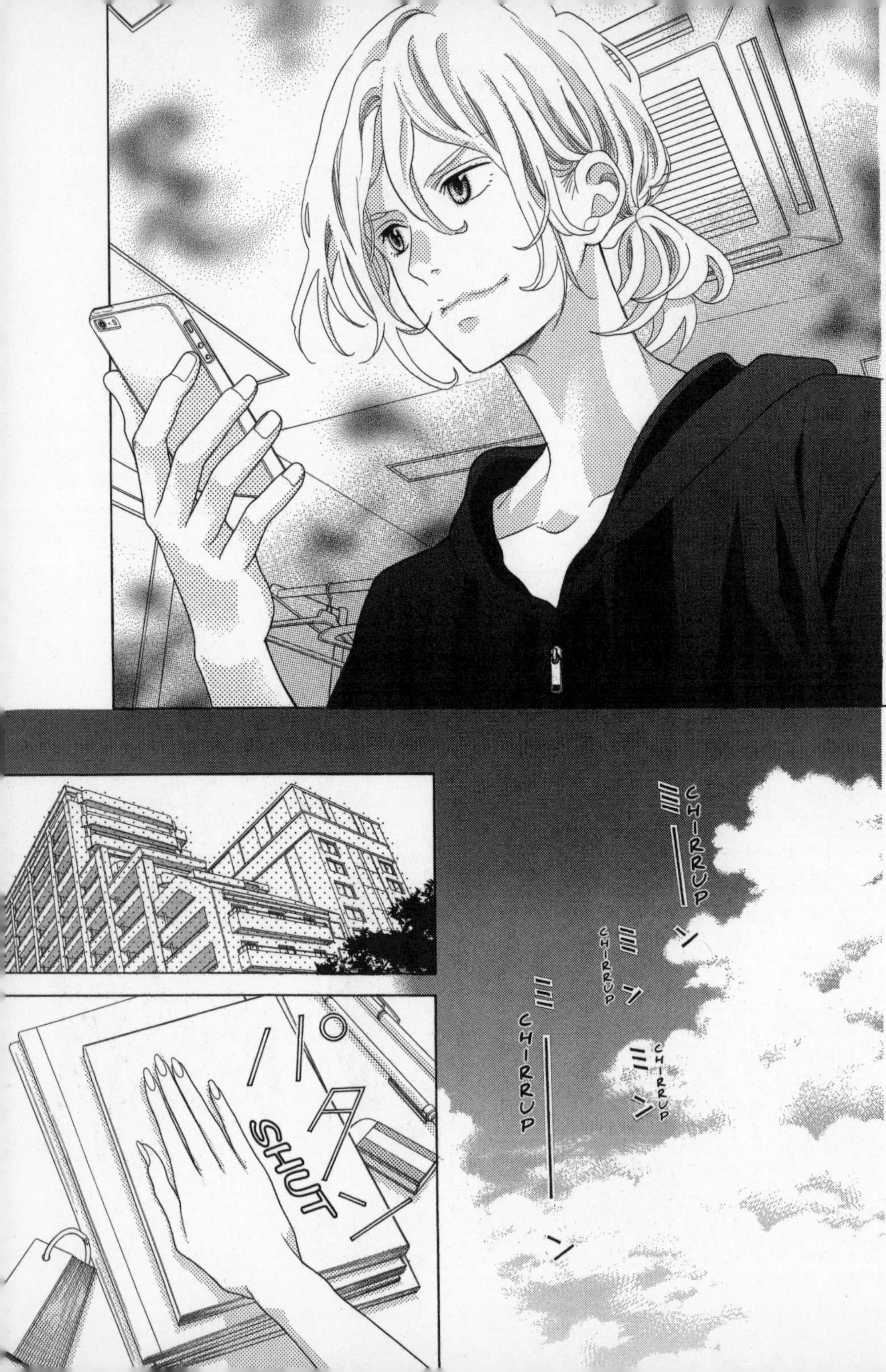

ミーーン
CHIRRUP
ミン
CHIRRUP
ミーーーン
CHIRRUP
ミン
CHIRRUP
パターン
SHUT

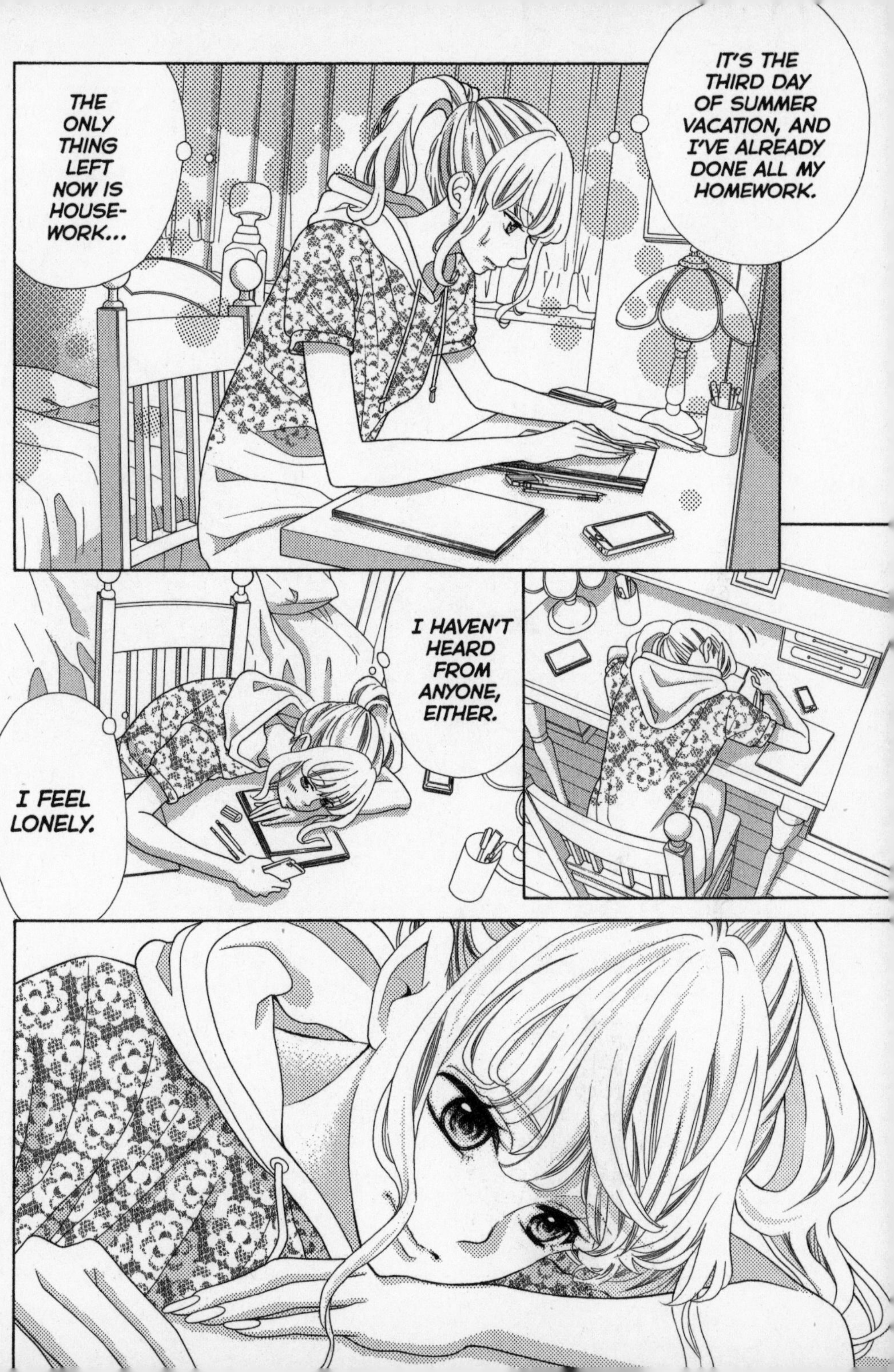
IT'S THE THIRD DAY OF SUMMER VACATION, AND I'VE ALREADY DONE ALL MY HOMEWORK.
THE ONLY THING LEFT NOW IS HOUSE-WORK...
I HAVEN'T HEARD FROM ANYONE, EITHER.
I FEEL LONELY.

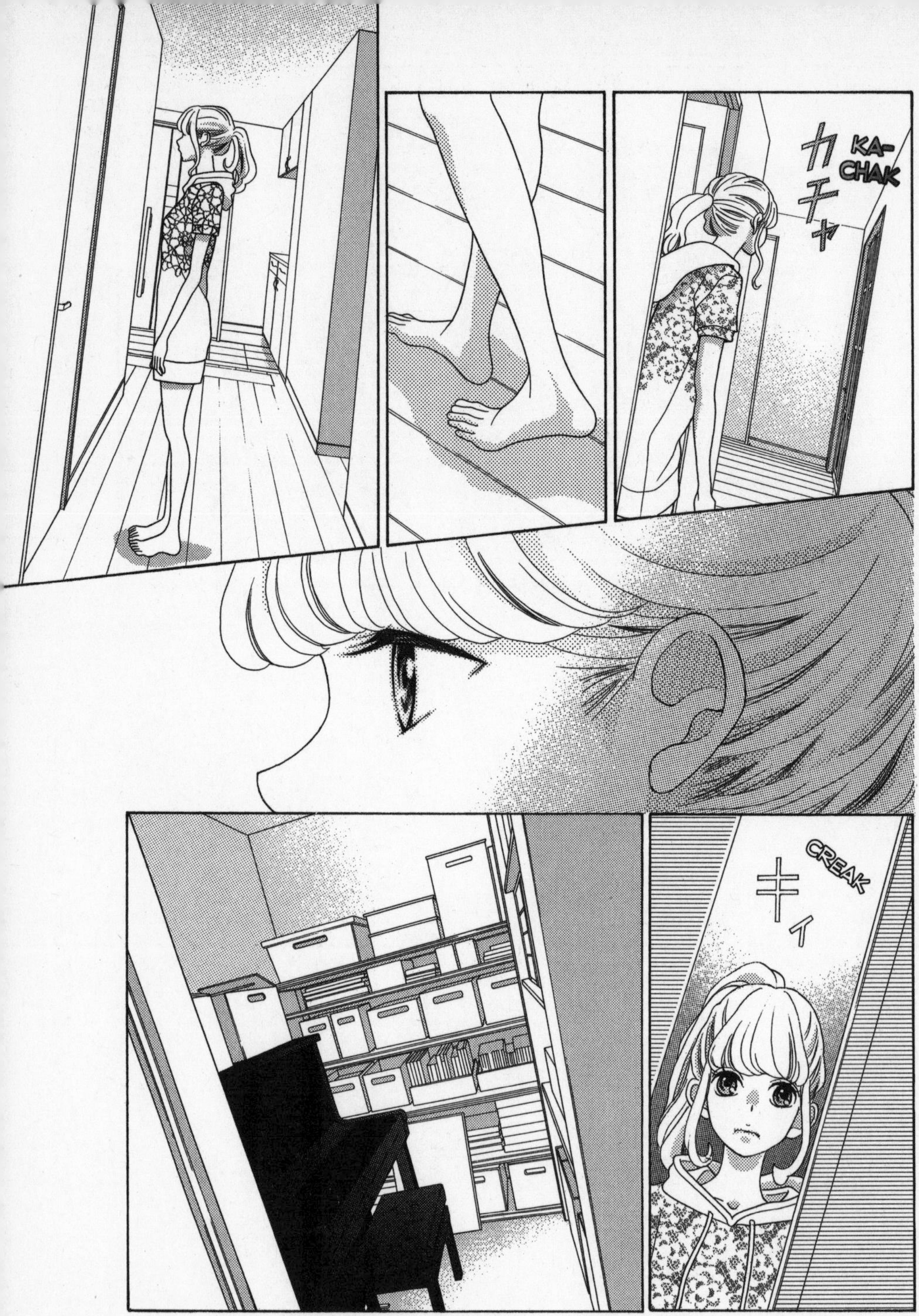
KA-CHAK
カチャ
CREAK
キイ

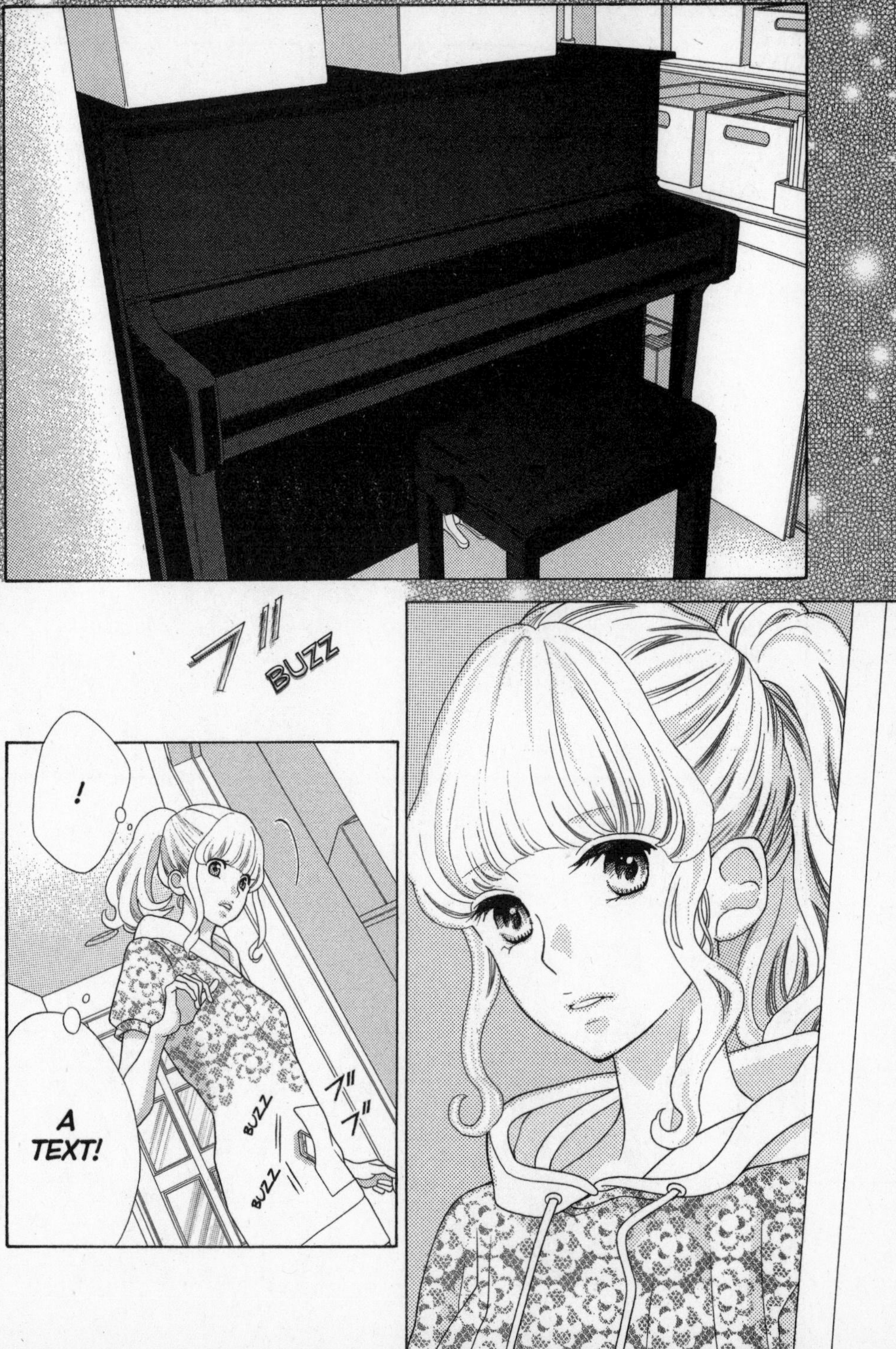
ブ
BUZZ
!
A TEXT!
ブ
BUZZ
ブ
BUZZ

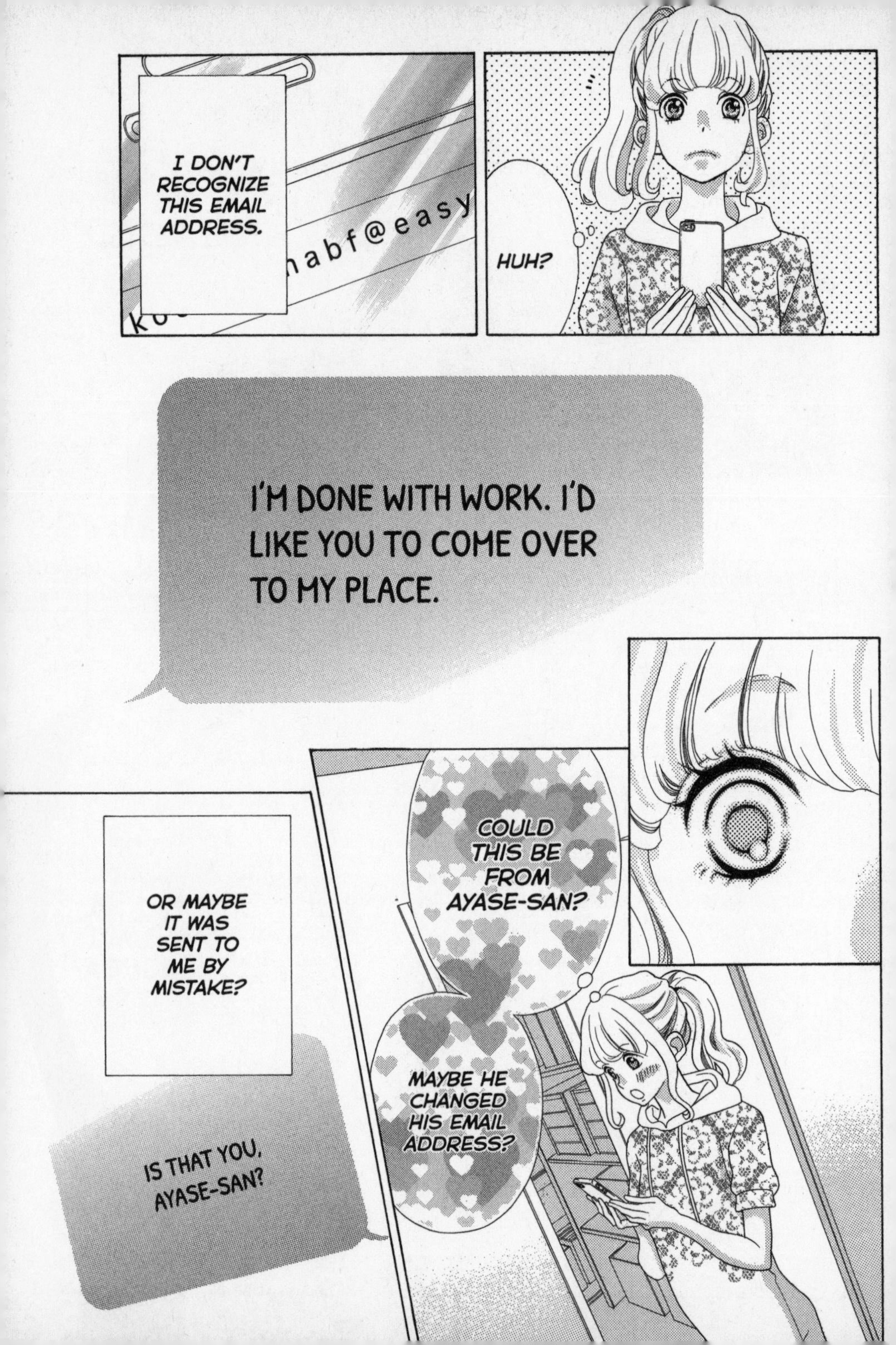

…
HUH?
I DON'T RECOGNIZE THIS EMAIL ADDRESS.
habf@easy
I'M DONE WITH WORK. I'D LIKE YOU TO COME OVER TO MY PLACE.
COULD THIS BE FROM AYASE-SAN?
MAYBE HE CHANGED HIS EMAIL ADDRESS?
OR MAYBE IT WAS SENT TO ME BY MISTAKE?
IS THAT YOU, AYASE-SAN?

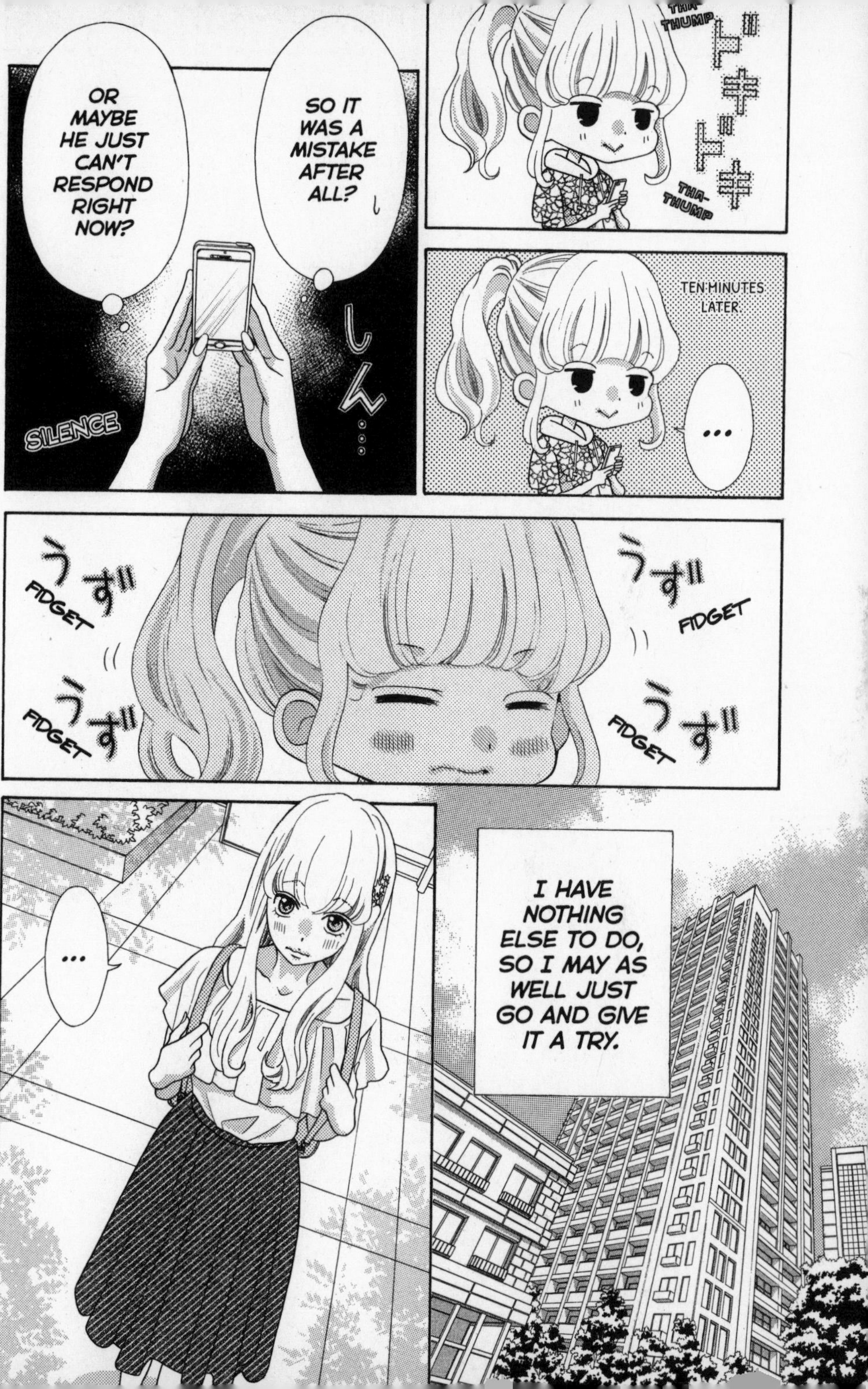
THA-THUMP
ドキドキ
THA-THUMP
TEN MINUTES LATER.
...
SO IT WAS A MISTAKE AFTER ALL?
OR MAYBE HE JUST CAN'T RESPOND RIGHT NOW?
しん...
SILENCE
うず
FIDGET
うず
FIDGET
うず
FIDGET
うず
FIDGET
I HAVE NOTHING ELSE TO DO, SO I MAY AS WELL JUST GO AND GIVE IT A TRY.
...

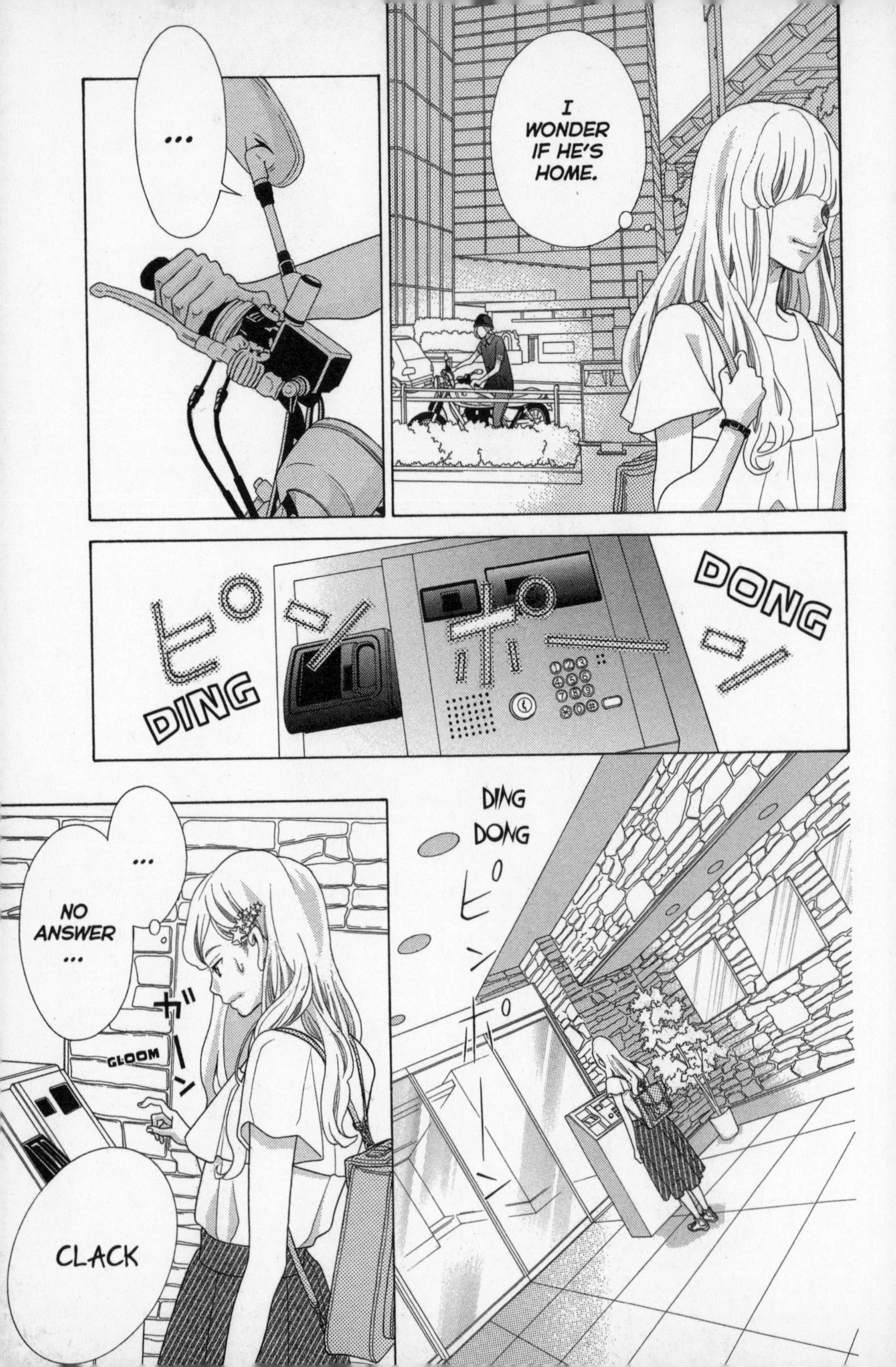
I WONDER IF HE'S HOME.
...
DONG
ピンポーン
DING
DING DONG
ピンポーン
... NO ANSWER ...
ガーン
GLOOM
CLACK

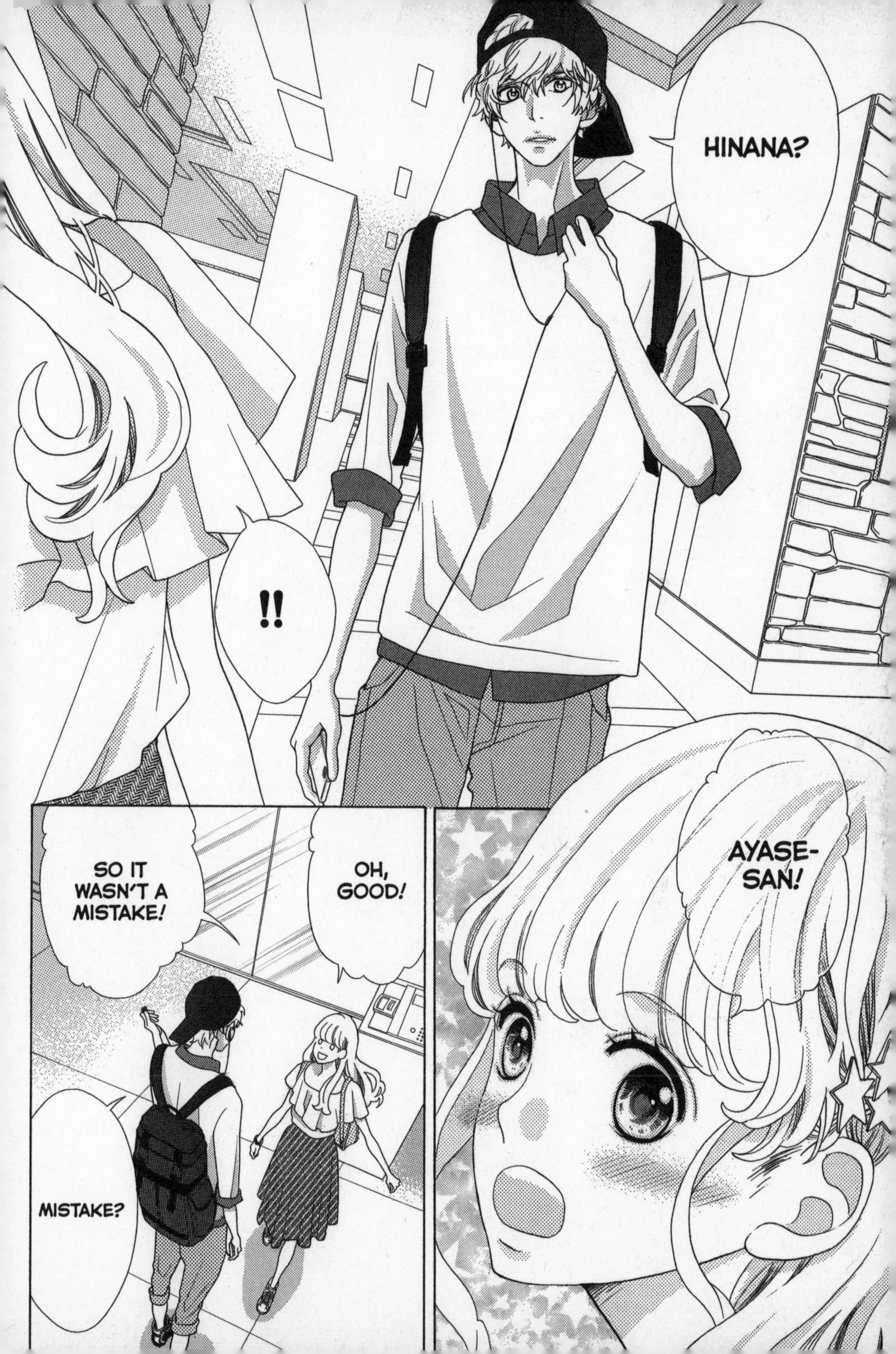
HINANA?
!!
AYASE-SAN!
OH, GOOD!
SO IT WASN'T A MISTAKE!
MISTAKE?

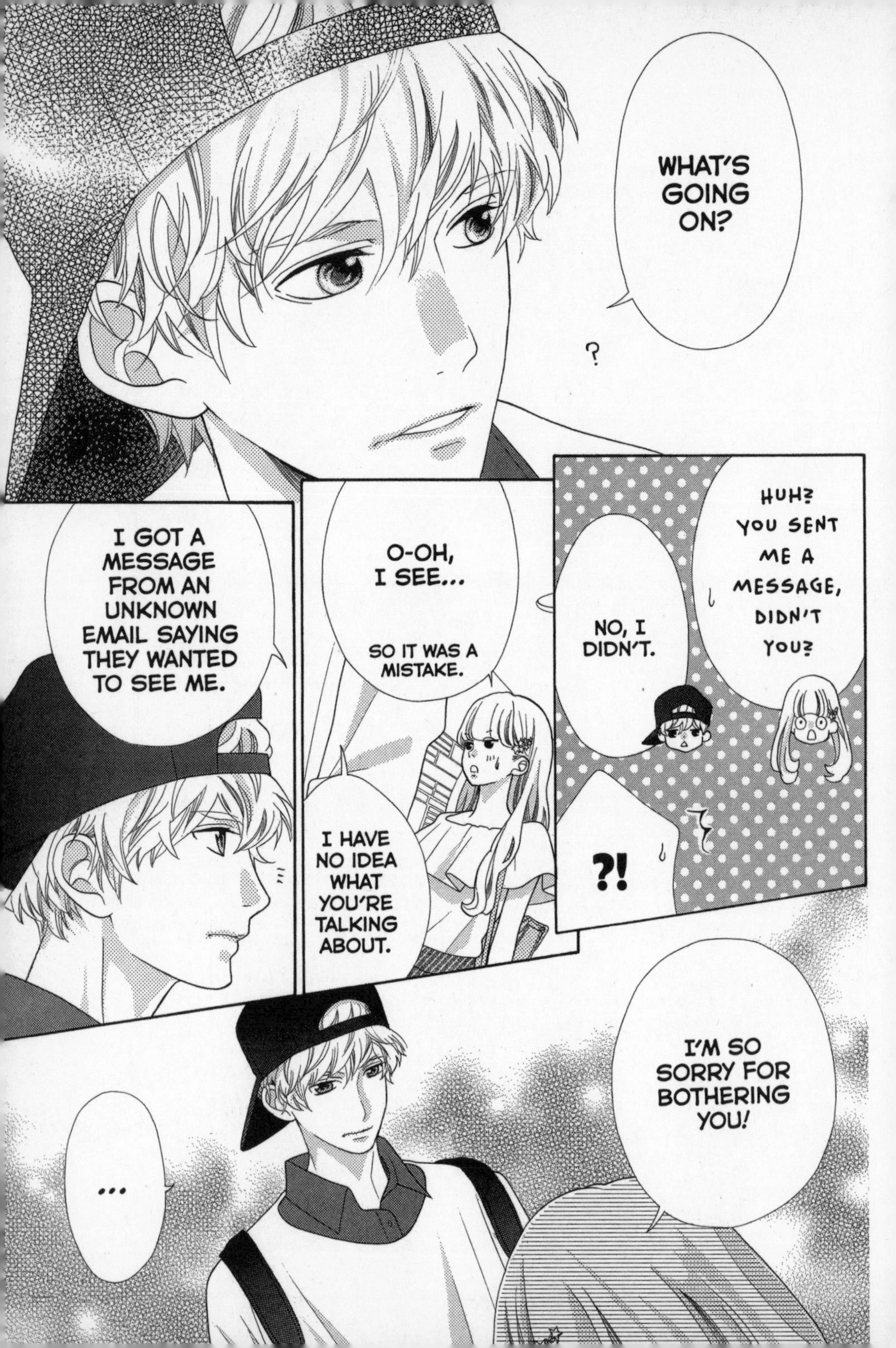
WHAT'S GOING ON?
?
HUH? YOU SENT ME A MESSAGE, DIDN'T YOU?
NO, I DIDN'T.
?!
O-OH, I SEE...
SO IT WAS A MISTAKE.
I HAVE NO IDEA WHAT YOU'RE TALKING ABOUT.
I GOT A MESSAGE FROM AN UNKNOWN EMAIL SAYING THEY WANTED TO SEE ME.
I'M SO SORRY FOR BOTHERING YOU!
...

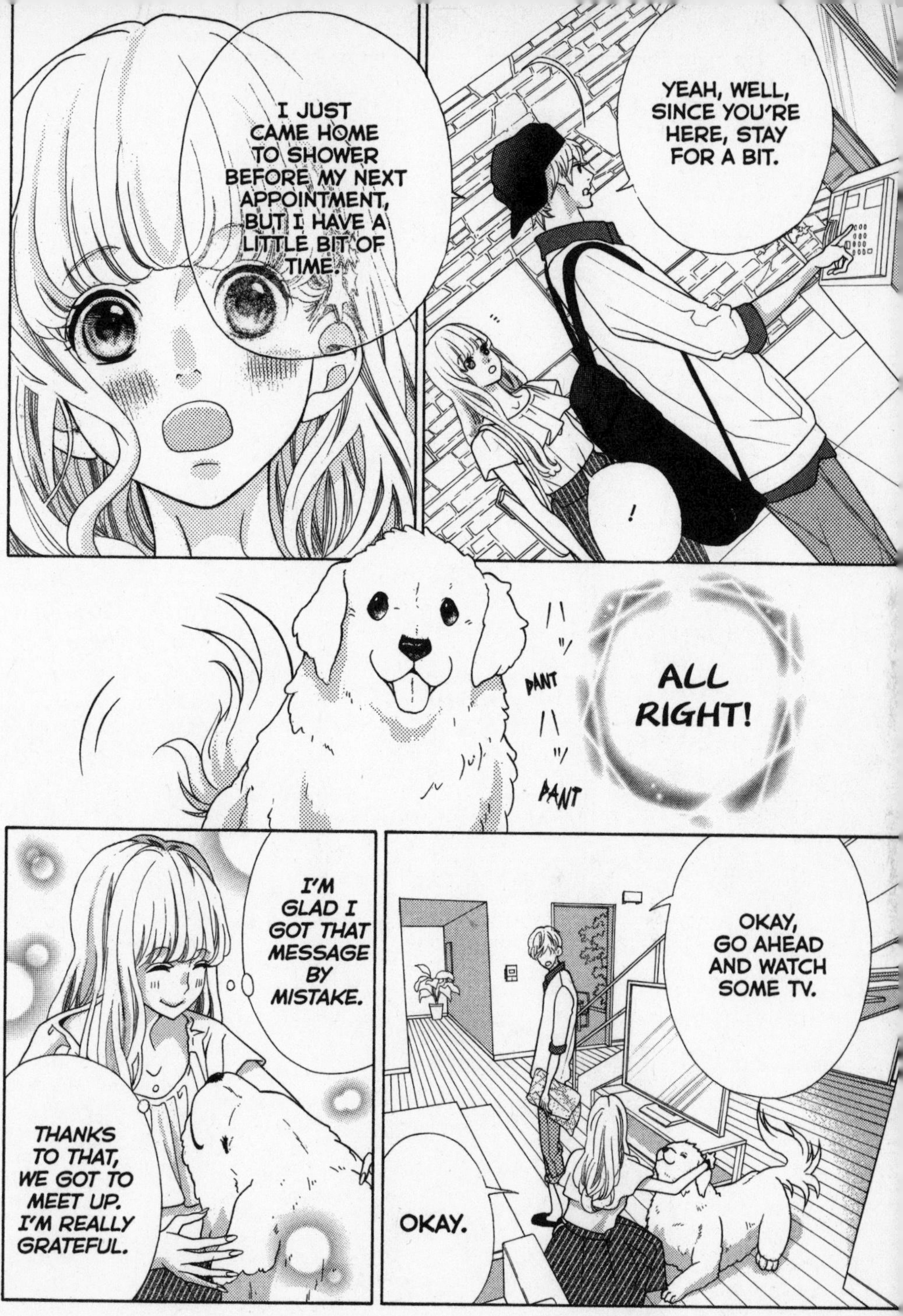
YEAH, WELL, SINCE YOU'RE HERE, STAY FOR A BIT.
!
I JUST CAME HOME TO SHOWER BEFORE MY NEXT APPOINTMENT, BUT I HAVE A LITTLE BIT OF TIME.
ALL RIGHT!
PANT
PANT
OKAY, GO AHEAD AND WATCH SOME TV.
OKAY.
I'M GLAD I GOT THAT MESSAGE BY MISTAKE.
THANKS TO THAT, WE GOT TO MEET UP. I'M REALLY GRATEFUL.

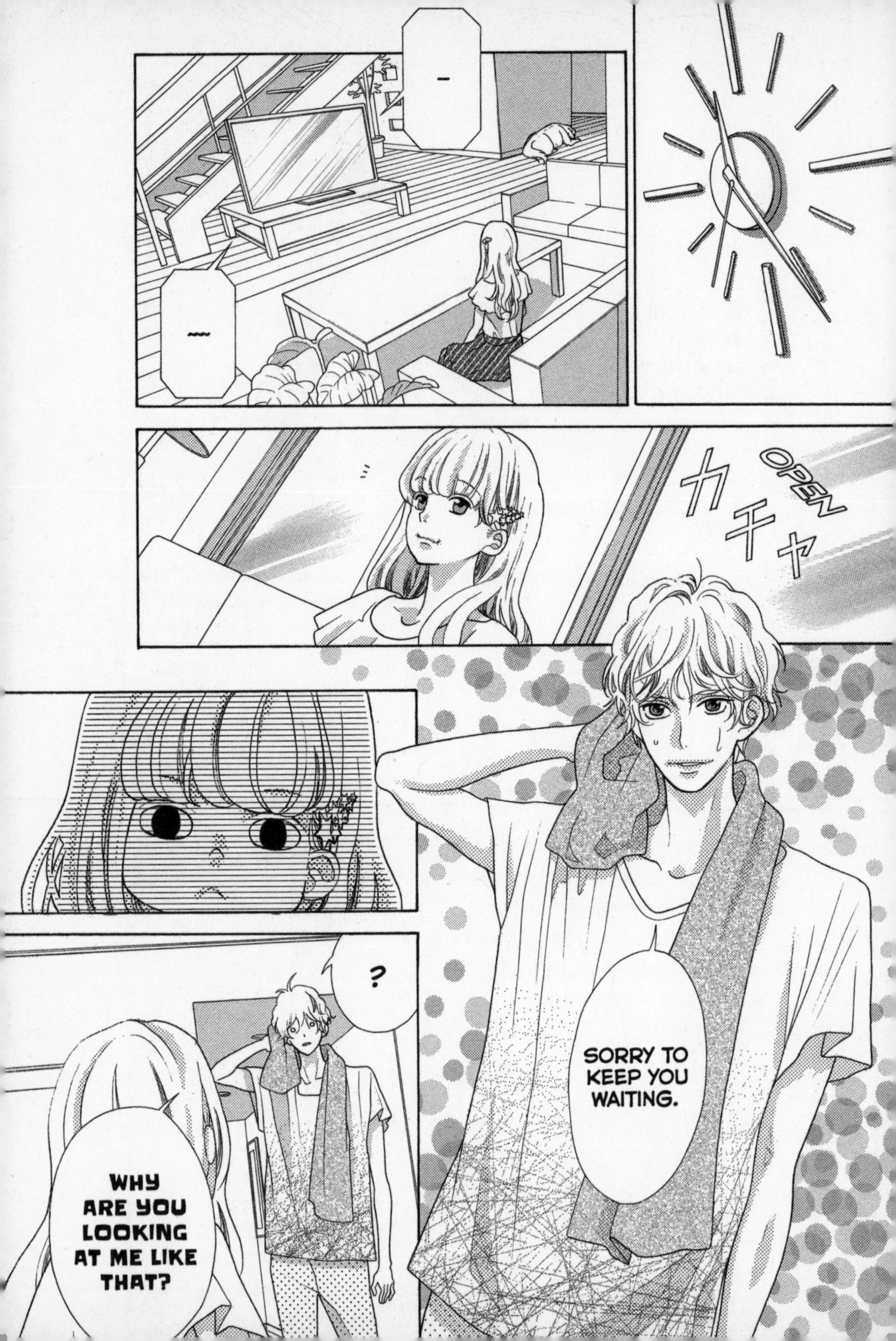
カチャ
OPEN
SORRY TO KEEP YOU WAITING.
?
WHY ARE YOU LOOKING AT ME LIKE THAT?

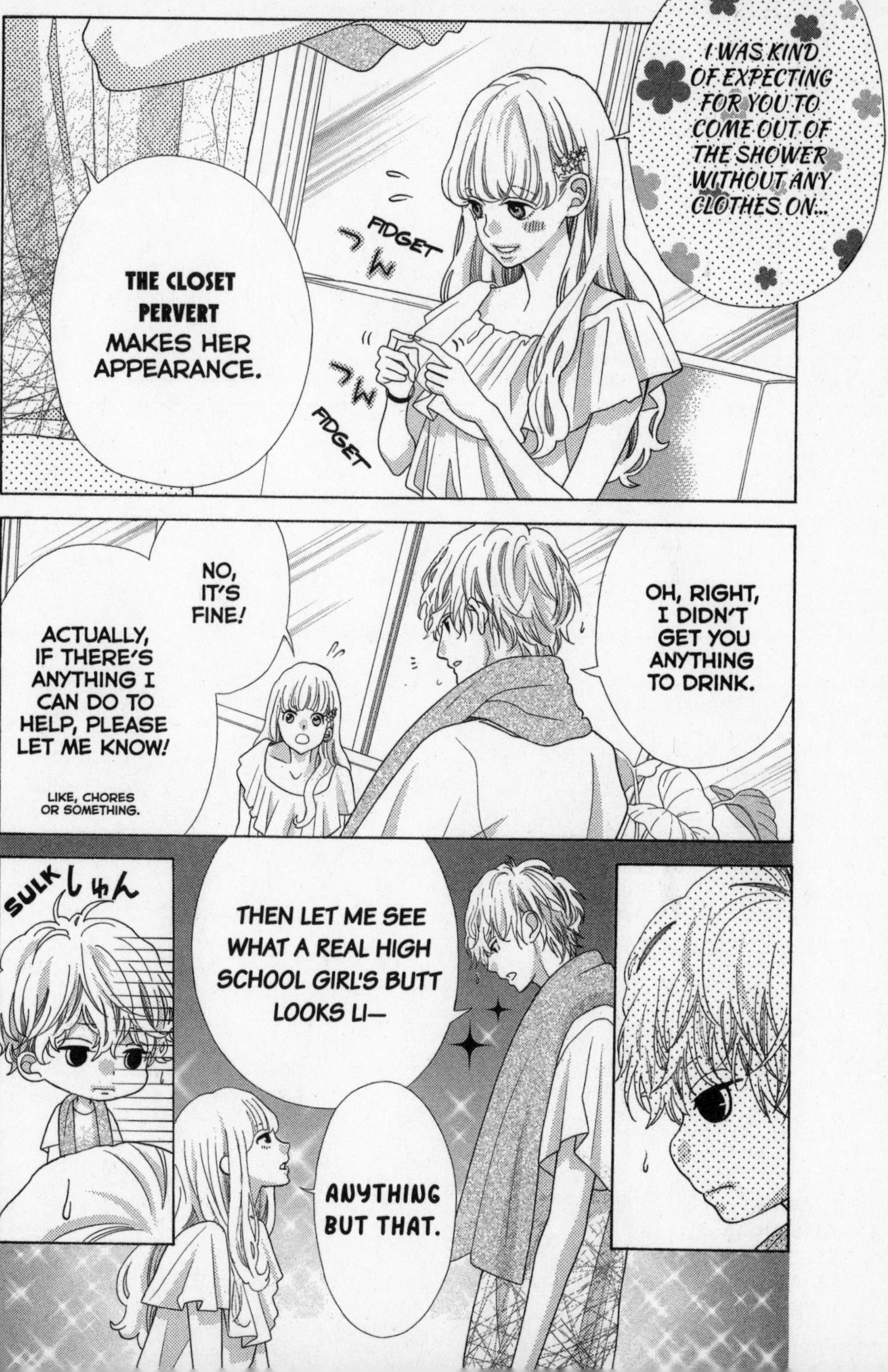
I WAS KIND OF EXPECTING FOR YOU TO COME OUT OF THE SHOWER WITHOUT ANY CLOTHES ON...
FIDGET
FIDGET
THE CLOSET PERVERT MAKES HER APPEARANCE.
OH, RIGHT, I DIDN'T GET YOU ANYTHING TO DRINK.
NO, IT'S FINE!
ACTUALLY, IF THERE'S ANYTHING I CAN DO TO HELP, PLEASE LET ME KNOW!
LIKE, CHORES OR SOMETHING.
THEN LET ME SEE WHAT A REAL HIGH SCHOOL GIRL'S BUTT LOOKS LI—
ANYTHING BUT THAT.
SULK しゅん

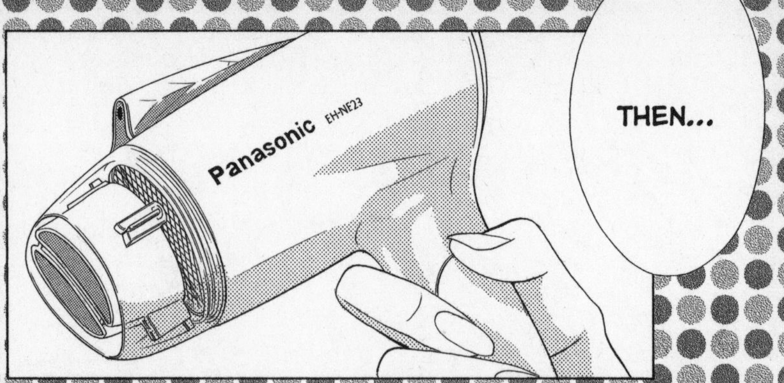
Panasonic EH-NE23
THEN...

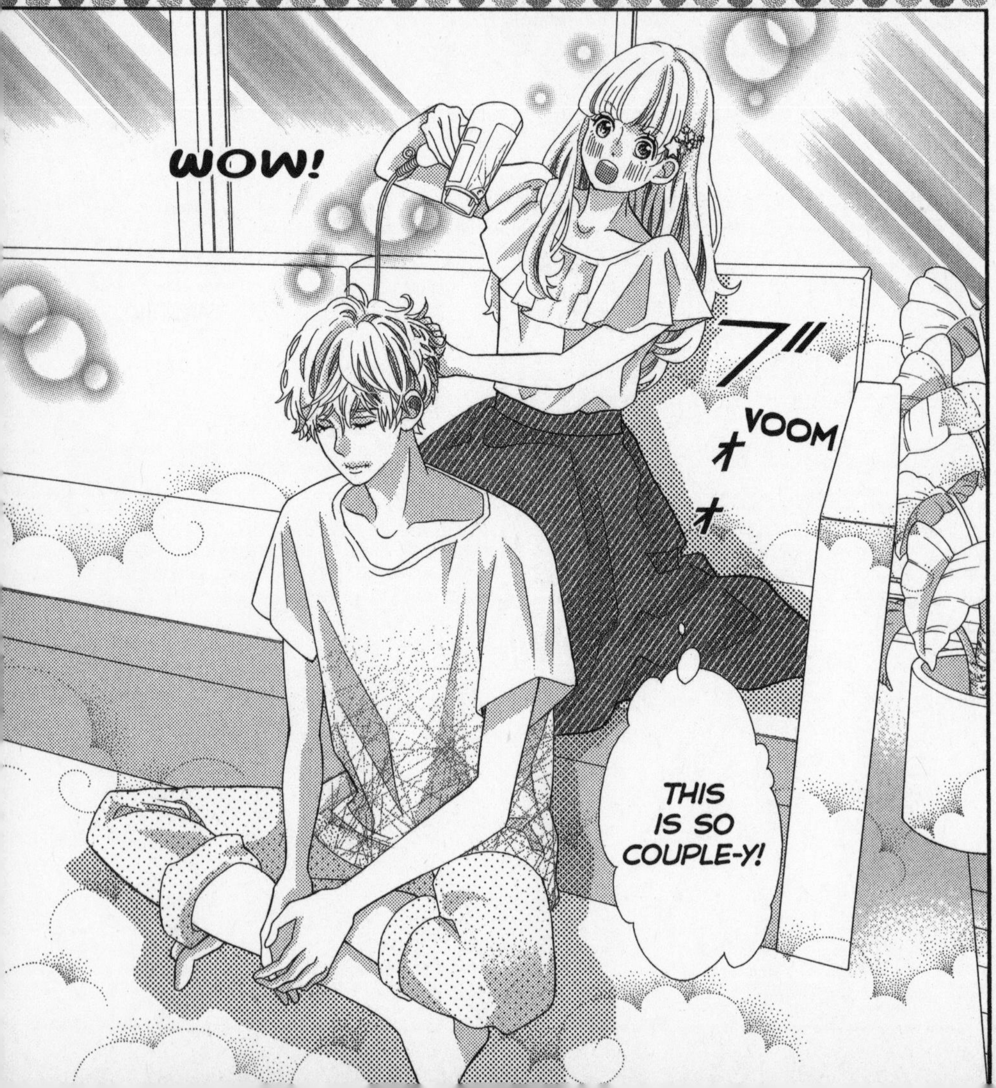
WOW!
ブオオ
VOOM
THIS IS SO COUPLE-Y!

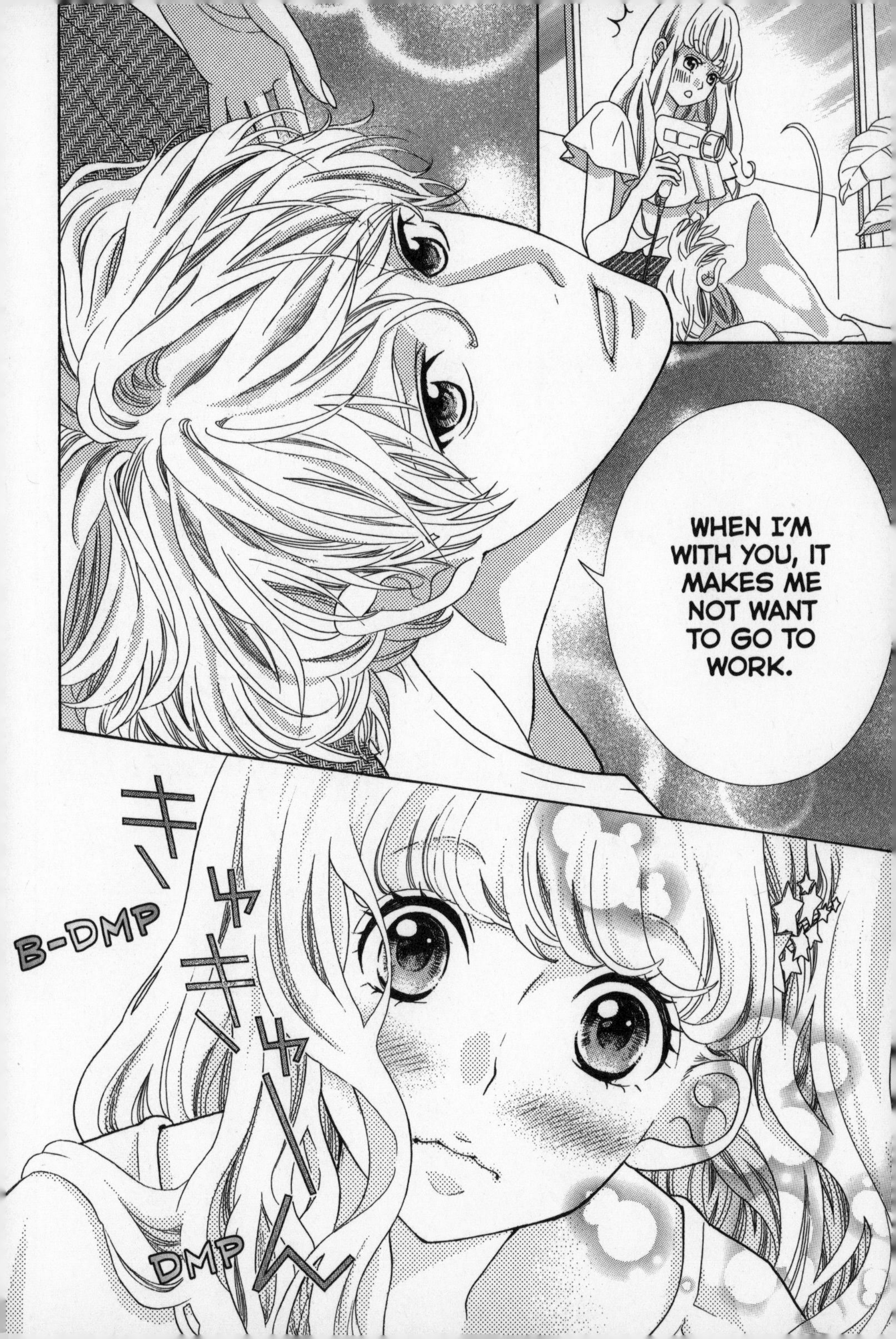
WHEN I'M WITH YOU, IT MAKES ME NOT WANT TO GO TO WORK.
B-DMP
DMP

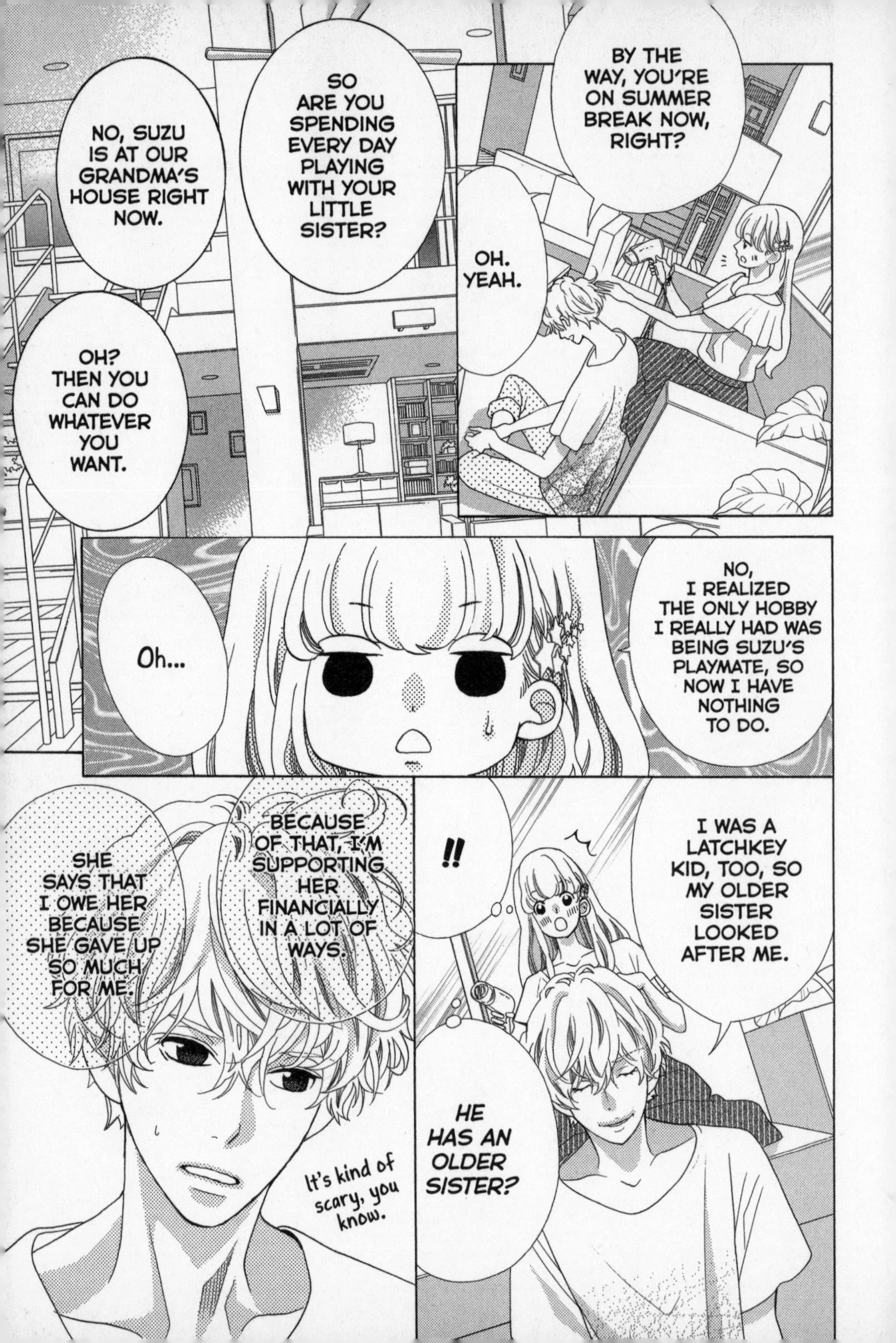
BY THE WAY, YOU'RE ON SUMMER BREAK NOW, RIGHT?
OH. YEAH.
SO ARE YOU SPENDING EVERY DAY PLAYING WITH YOUR LITTLE SISTER?
NO, SUZU IS AT OUR GRANDMA'S HOUSE RIGHT NOW.
OH? THEN YOU CAN DO WHATEVER YOU WANT.
NO, I REALIZED THE ONLY HOBBY I REALLY HAD WAS BEING SUZU'S PLAYMATE, SO NOW I HAVE NOTHING TO DO.
Oh...
I WAS A LATCHKEY KID, TOO, SO MY OLDER SISTER LOOKED AFTER ME.
!!
HE HAS AN OLDER SISTER?
SHE SAYS THAT I OWE HER BECAUSE SHE GAVE UP SO MUCH FOR ME.
BECAUSE OF THAT, I'M SUPPORTING HER FINANCIALLY IN A LOT OF WAYS.
It's kind of scary, you know.

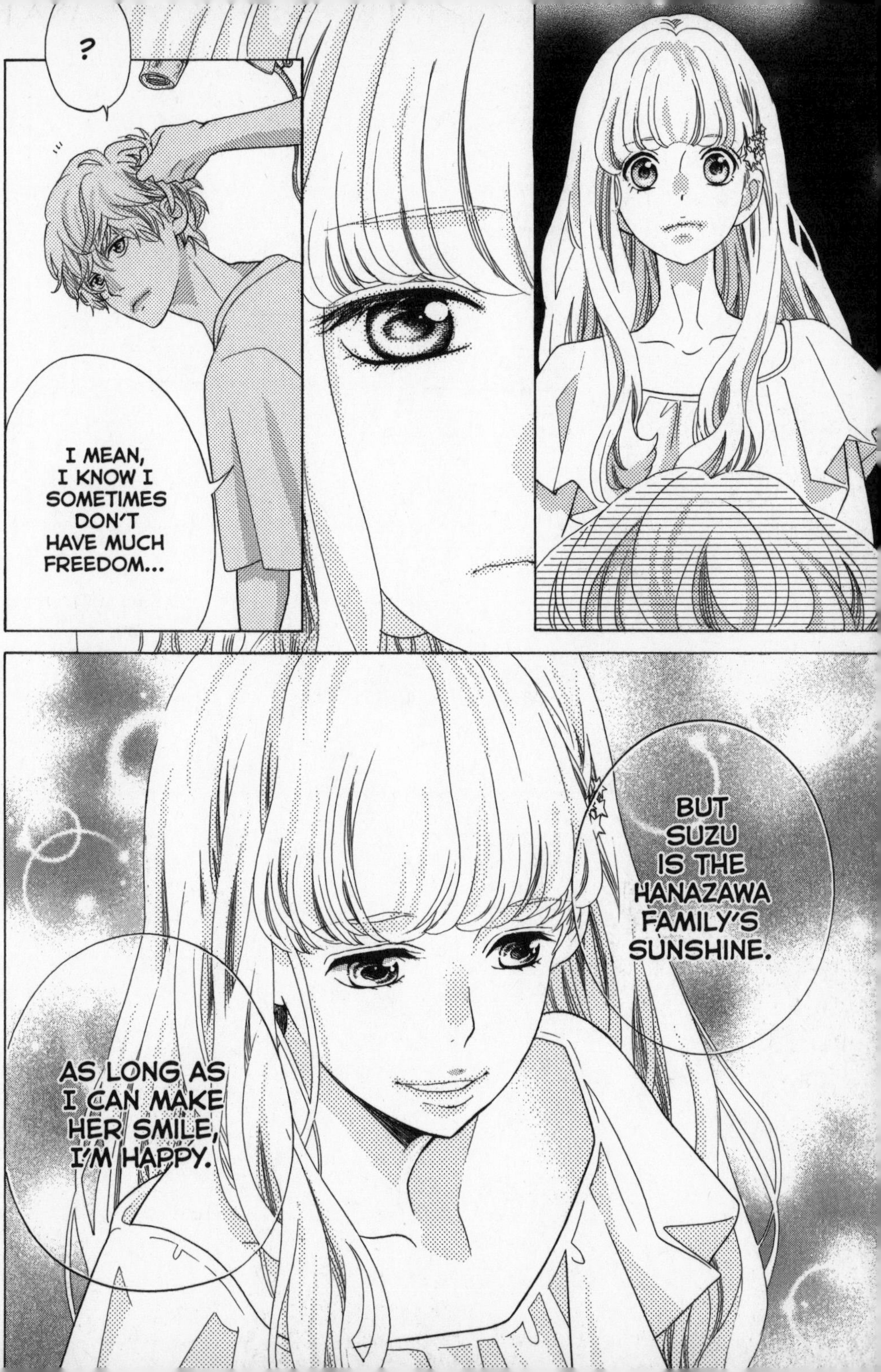
?
I MEAN, I KNOW I SOMETIMES DON'T HAVE MUCH FREEDOM...
BUT SUZU IS THE HANAZAWA FAMILY'S SUNSHINE.
AS LONG AS I CAN MAKE HER SMILE, I'M HAPPY.

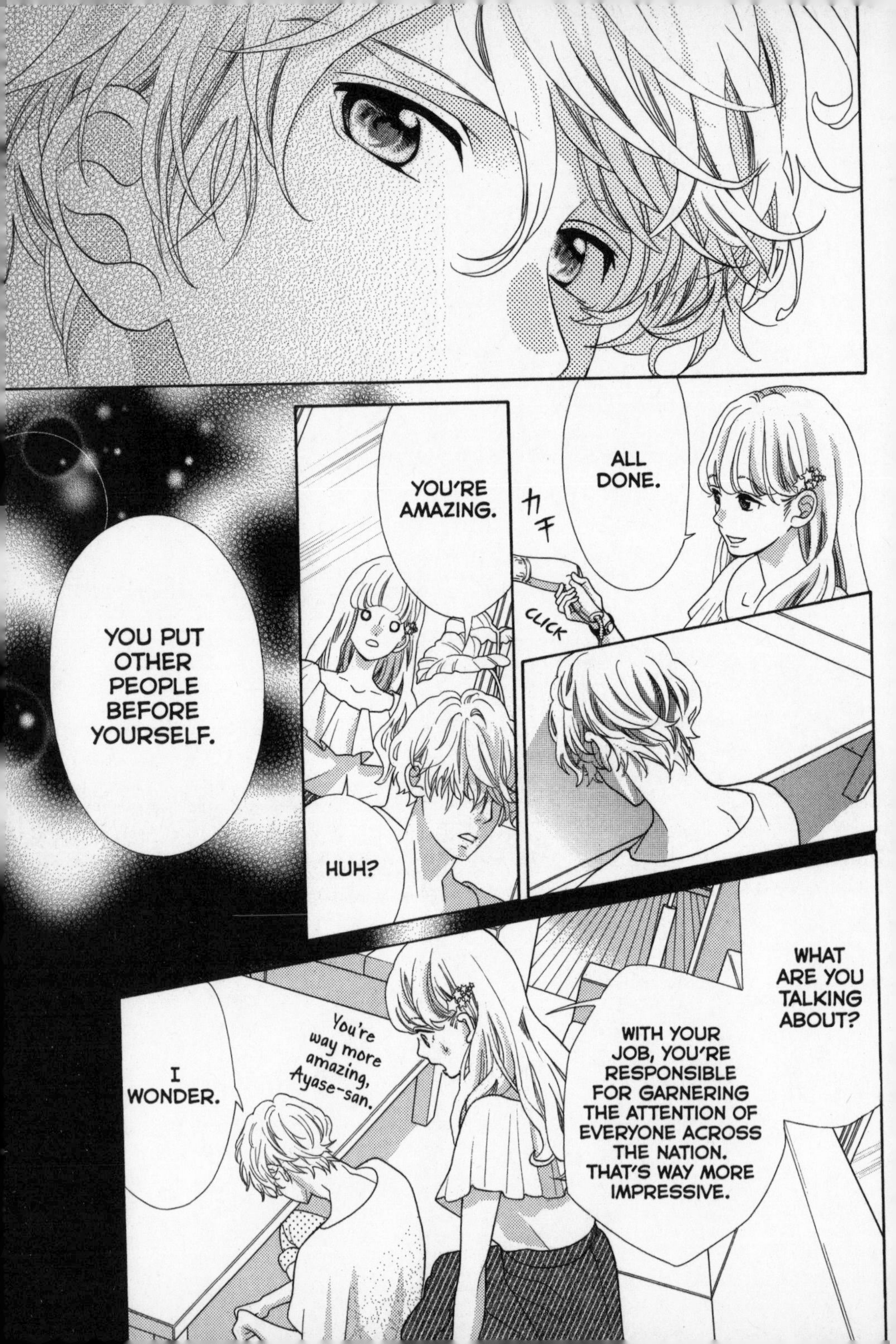
ALL DONE.
カチ
CLICK
YOU'RE AMAZING.
HUH?
YOU PUT OTHER PEOPLE BEFORE YOURSELF.
WHAT ARE YOU TALKING ABOUT?
WITH YOUR JOB, YOU'RE RESPONSIBLE FOR GARNERING THE ATTENTION OF EVERYONE ACROSS THE NATION. THAT'S WAY MORE IMPRESSIVE.
You're way more amazing, Ayase-san.
I WONDER.

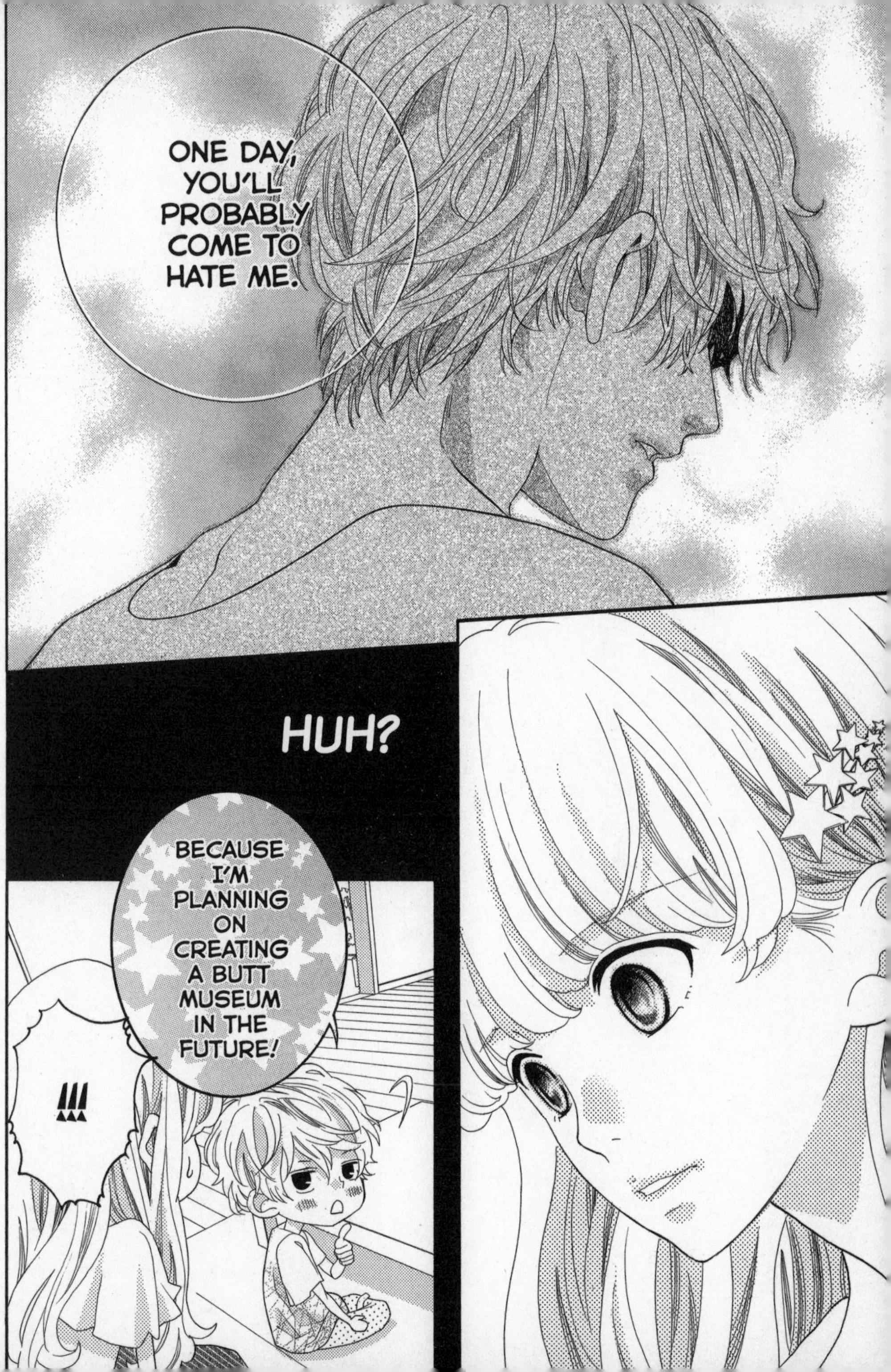
ONE DAY, YOU'LL PROBABLY COME TO HATE ME.
HUH?
BECAUSE I'M PLANNING ON CREATING A BUTT MUSEUM IN THE FUTURE!
!!!

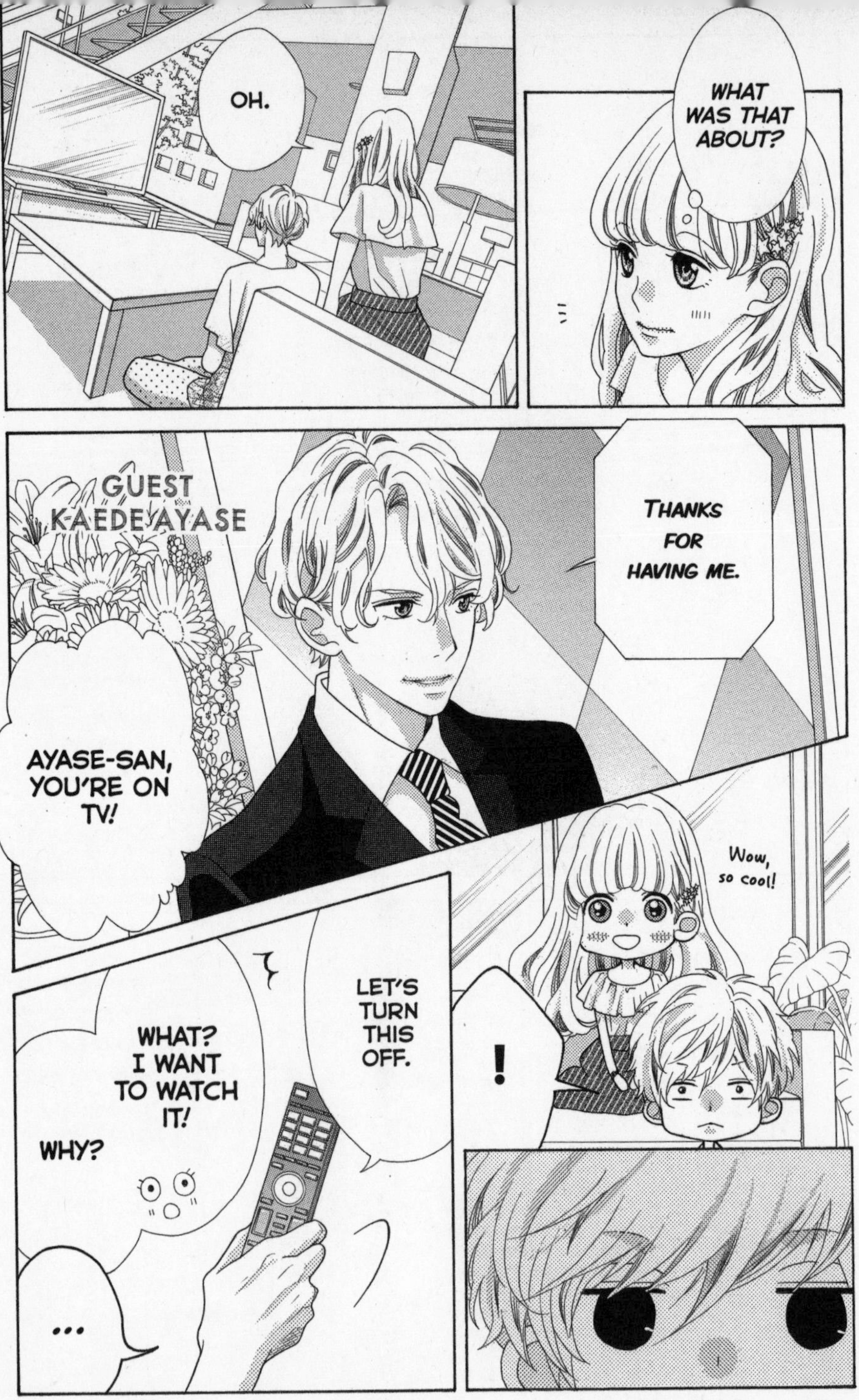
WHAT WAS THAT ABOUT?
OH.
THANKS FOR HAVING ME.
GUEST KAEDE AYASE
AYASE-SAN, YOU'RE ON TV!
Wow, so cool!
!
LET'S TURN THIS OFF.
WHAT? I WANT TO WATCH IT!
WHY?
...

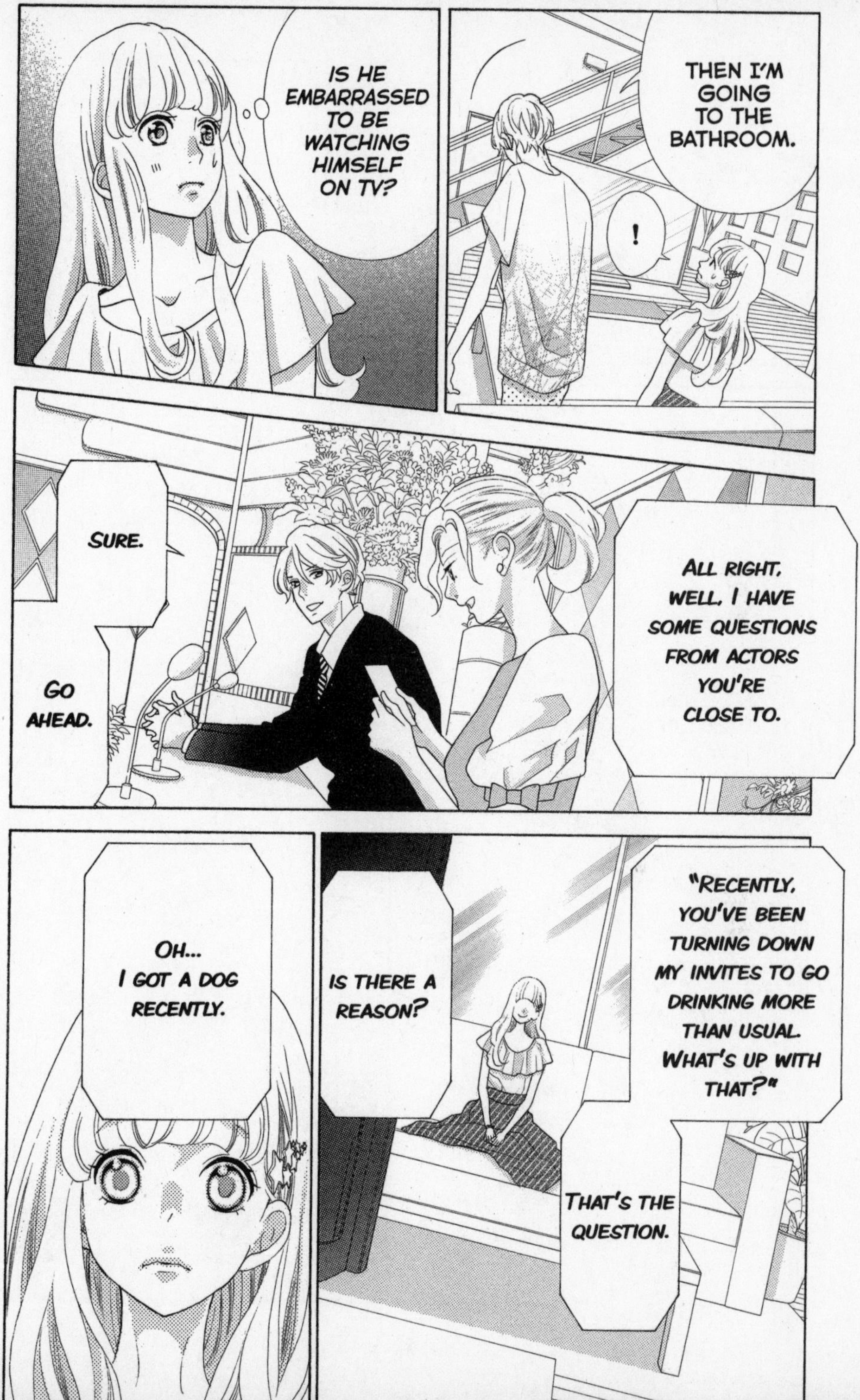
THEN I'M GOING TO THE BATHROOM.
!
IS HE EMBARRASSED TO BE WATCHING HIMSELF ON TV?
ALL RIGHT, WELL, I HAVE SOME QUESTIONS FROM ACTORS YOU'RE CLOSE TO.
SURE.
GO AHEAD.
"RECENTLY, YOU'VE BEEN TURNING DOWN MY INVITES TO GO DRINKING MORE THAN USUAL. WHAT'S UP WITH THAT?"
THAT'S THE QUESTION.
IS THERE A REASON?
OH... I GOT A DOG RECENTLY.

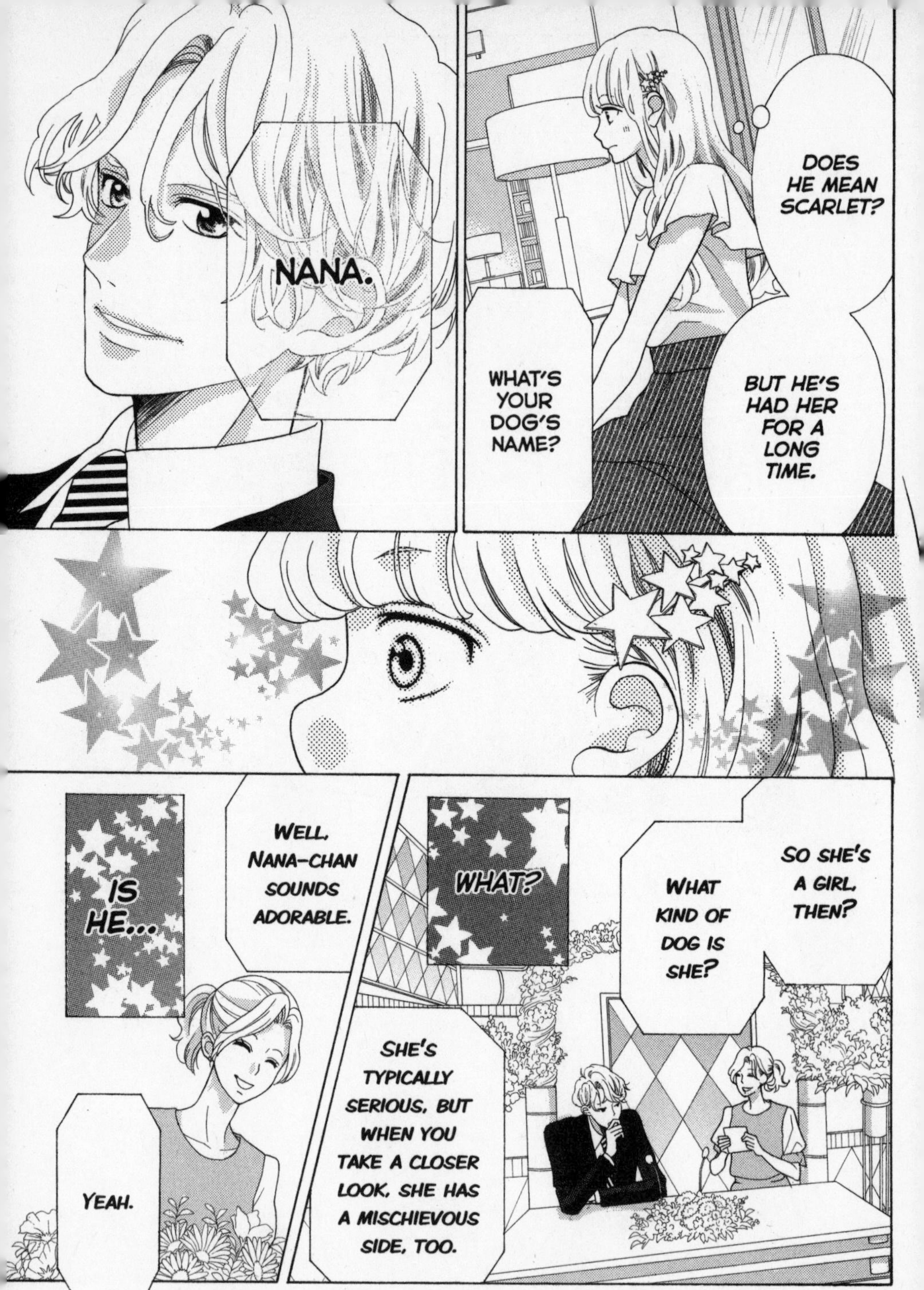
DOES HE MEAN SCARLET?
BUT HE'S HAD HER FOR A LONG TIME.
WHAT'S YOUR DOG'S NAME?
NANA.
SO SHE'S A GIRL, THEN?
WHAT KIND OF DOG IS SHE?
WHAT?
SHE'S TYPICALLY SERIOUS, BUT WHEN YOU TAKE A CLOSER LOOK, SHE HAS A MISCHIEVOUS SIDE, TOO.
WELL, NANA-CHAN SOUNDS ADORABLE.
IS HE...
YEAH.

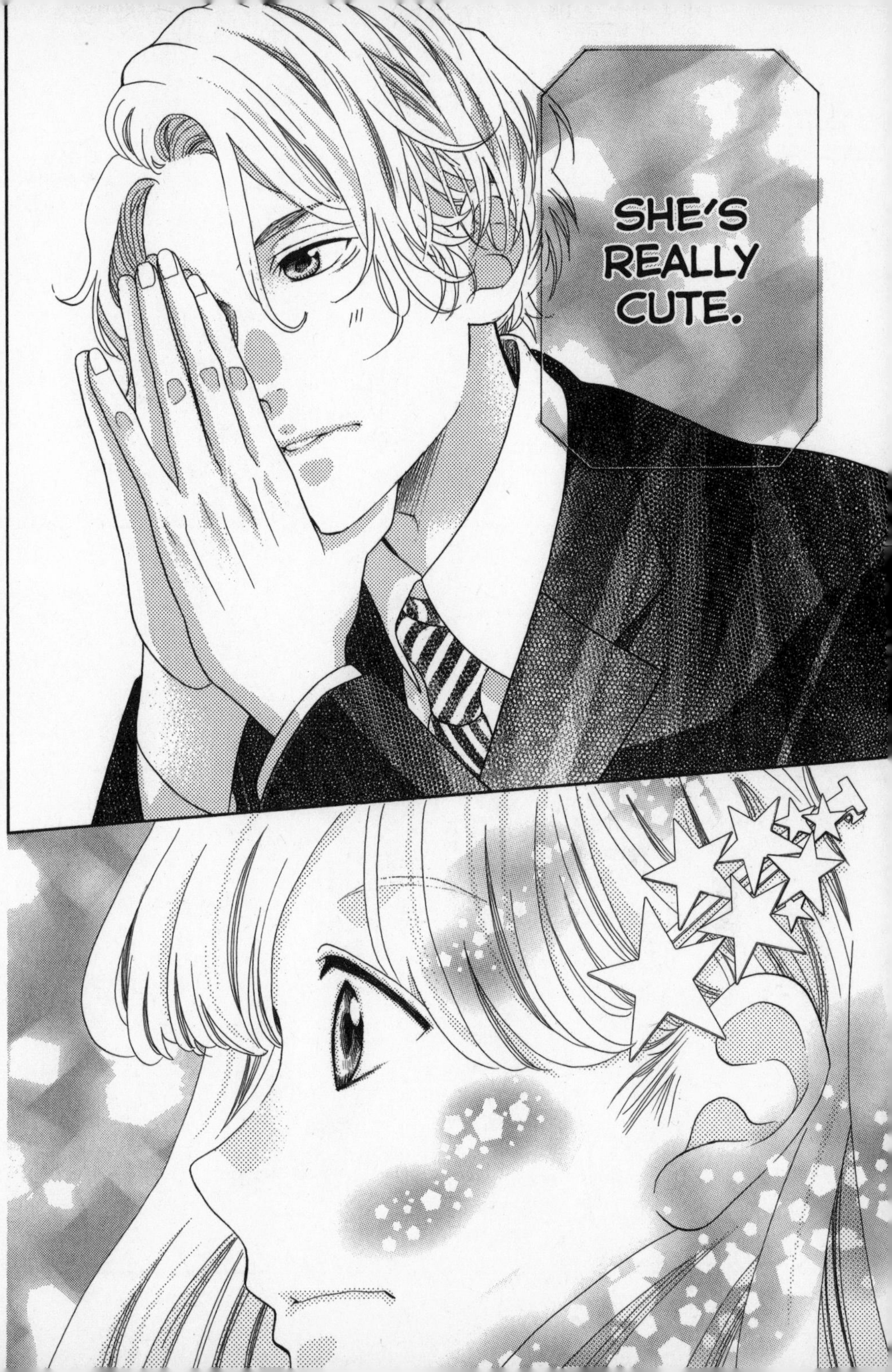
SHE'S REALLY CUTE.

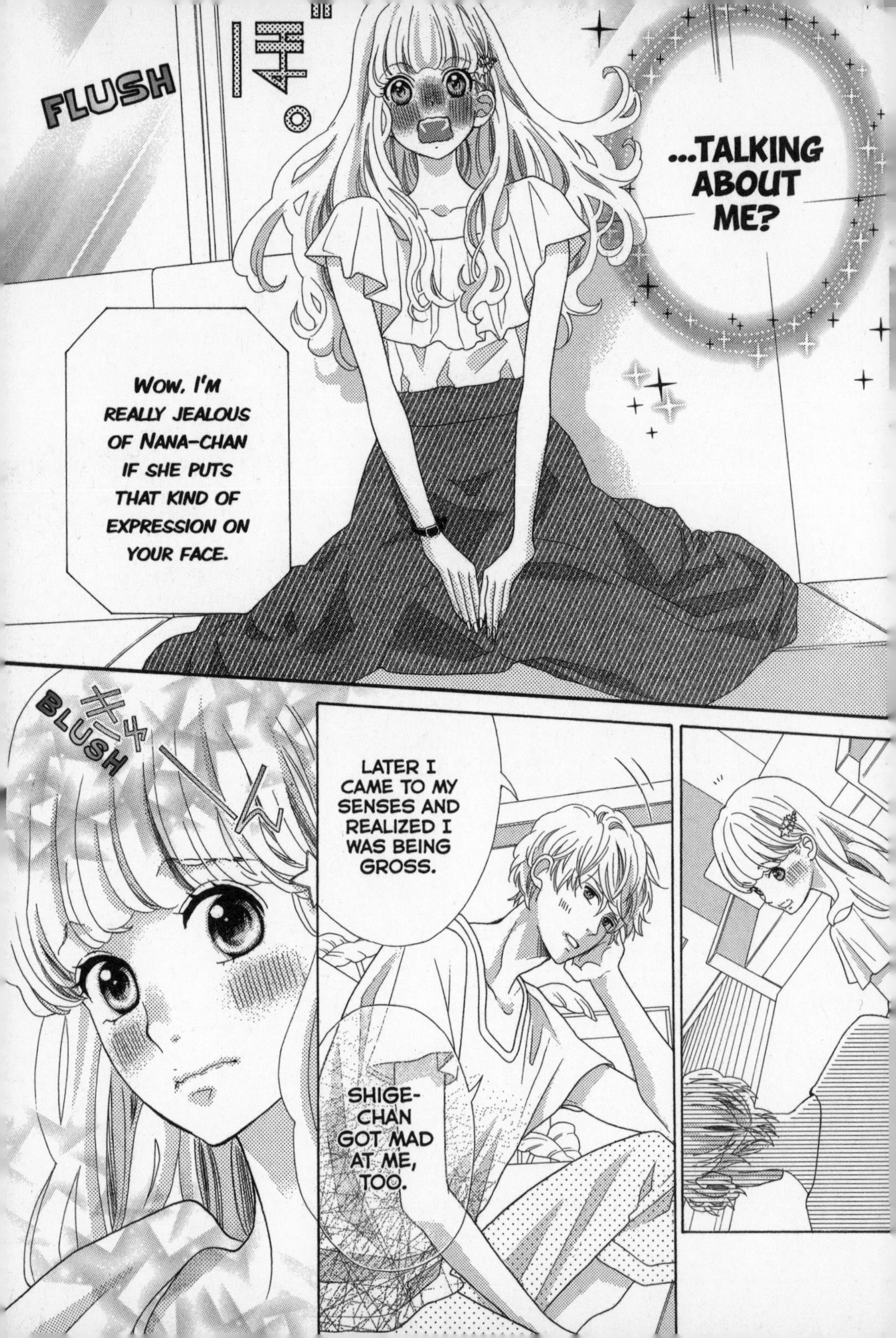
...TALKING ABOUT ME?
FLUSH
WOW, I'M REALLY JEALOUS OF NANA-CHAN IF SHE PUTS THAT KIND OF EXPRESSION ON YOUR FACE.
LATER I CAME TO MY SENSES AND REALIZED I WAS BEING GROSS.
SHIGE-CHAN GOT MAD AT ME, TOO.
BLUSH

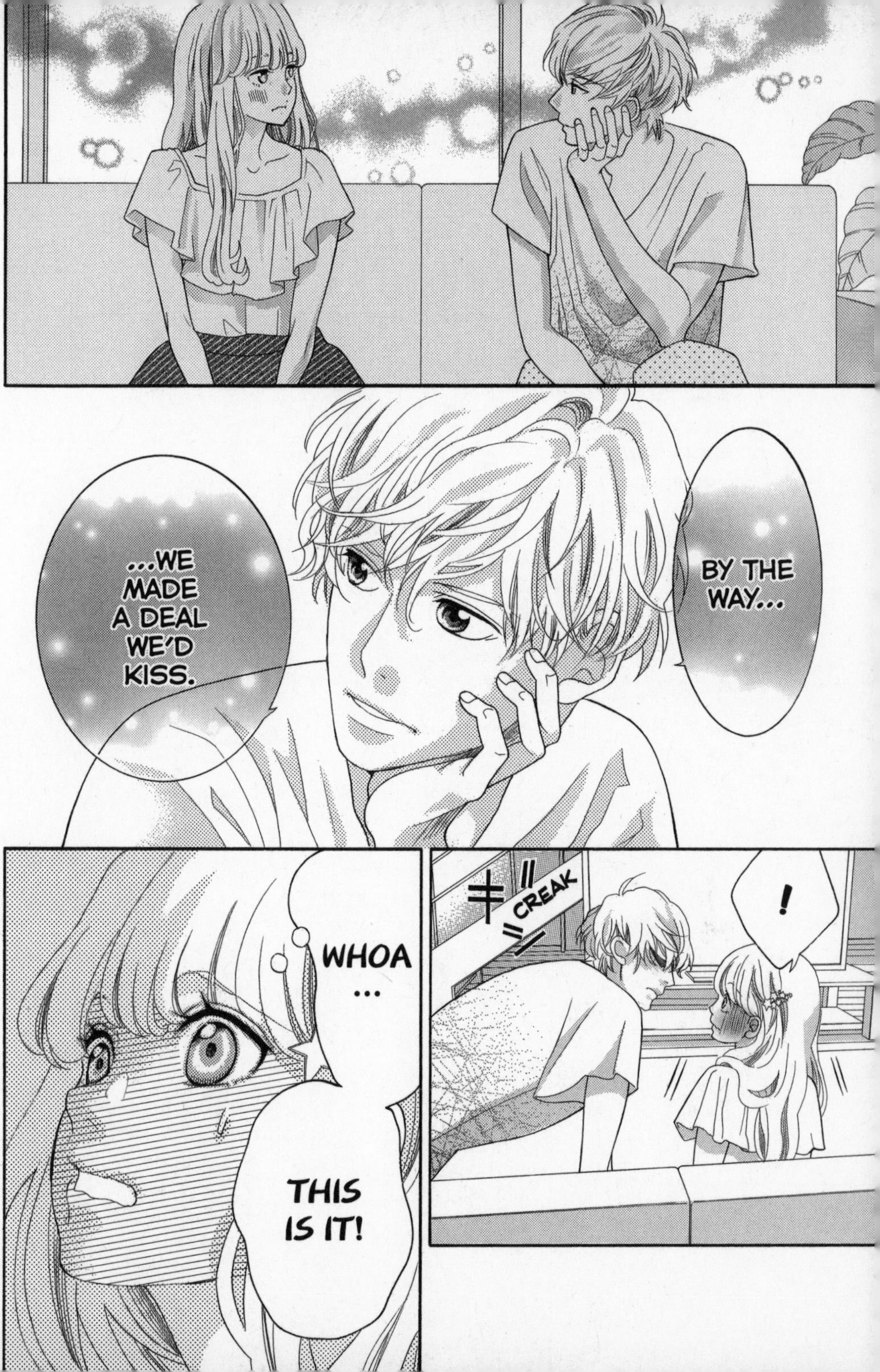
BY THE WAY...
...WE MADE A DEAL WE'D KISS.
CREAK
!
WHOA ...
THIS IS IT!

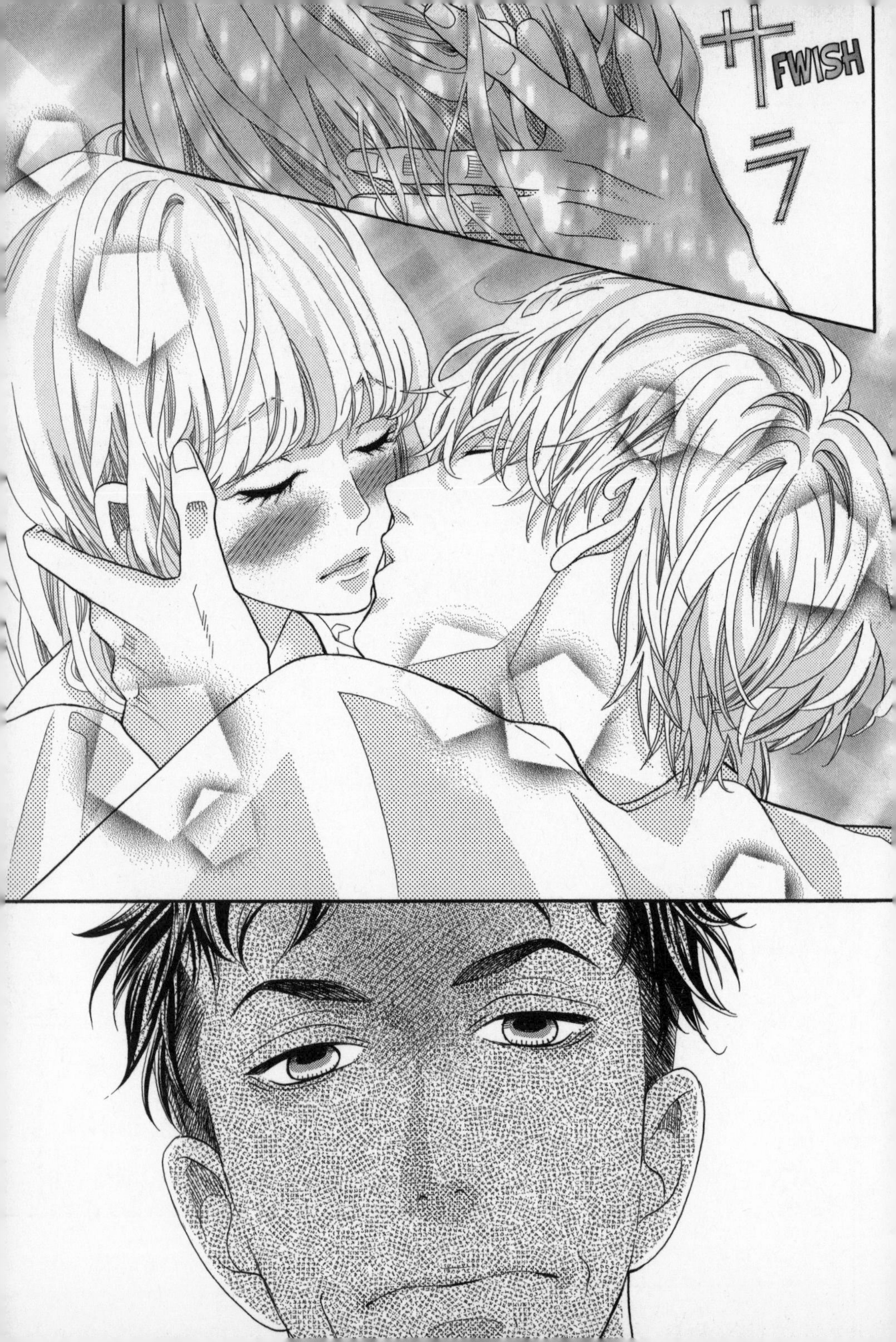
サラ
FWISH

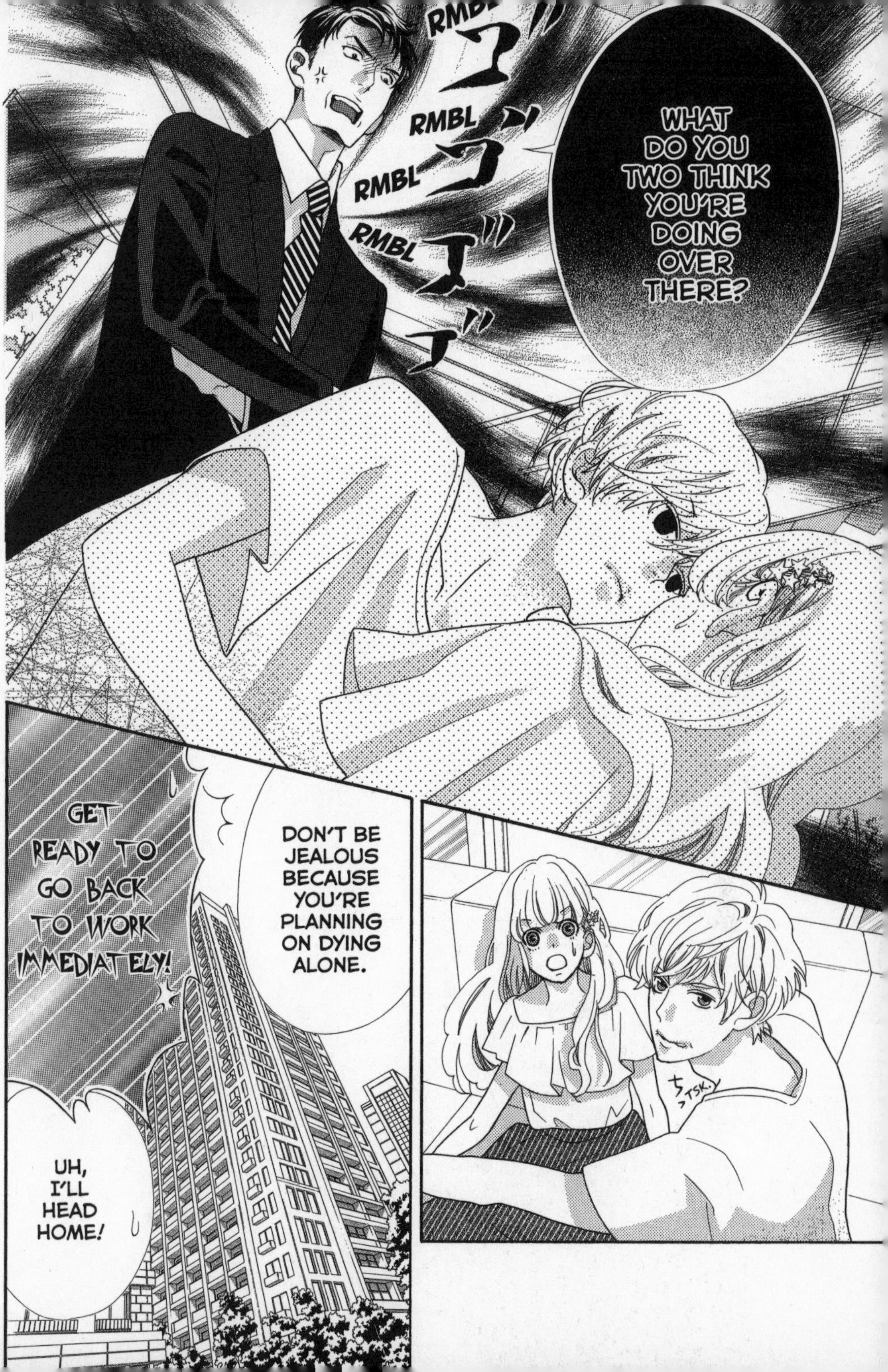
WHAT DO YOU TWO THINK YOU'RE DOING OVER THERE?
RMBL
RMBL
RMBL
RMBL
TSK
DON'T BE JEALOUS BECAUSE YOU'RE PLANNING ON DYING ALONE.
GET READY TO GO BACK TO WORK IMMEDIATELY!
UH, I'LL HEAD HOME!

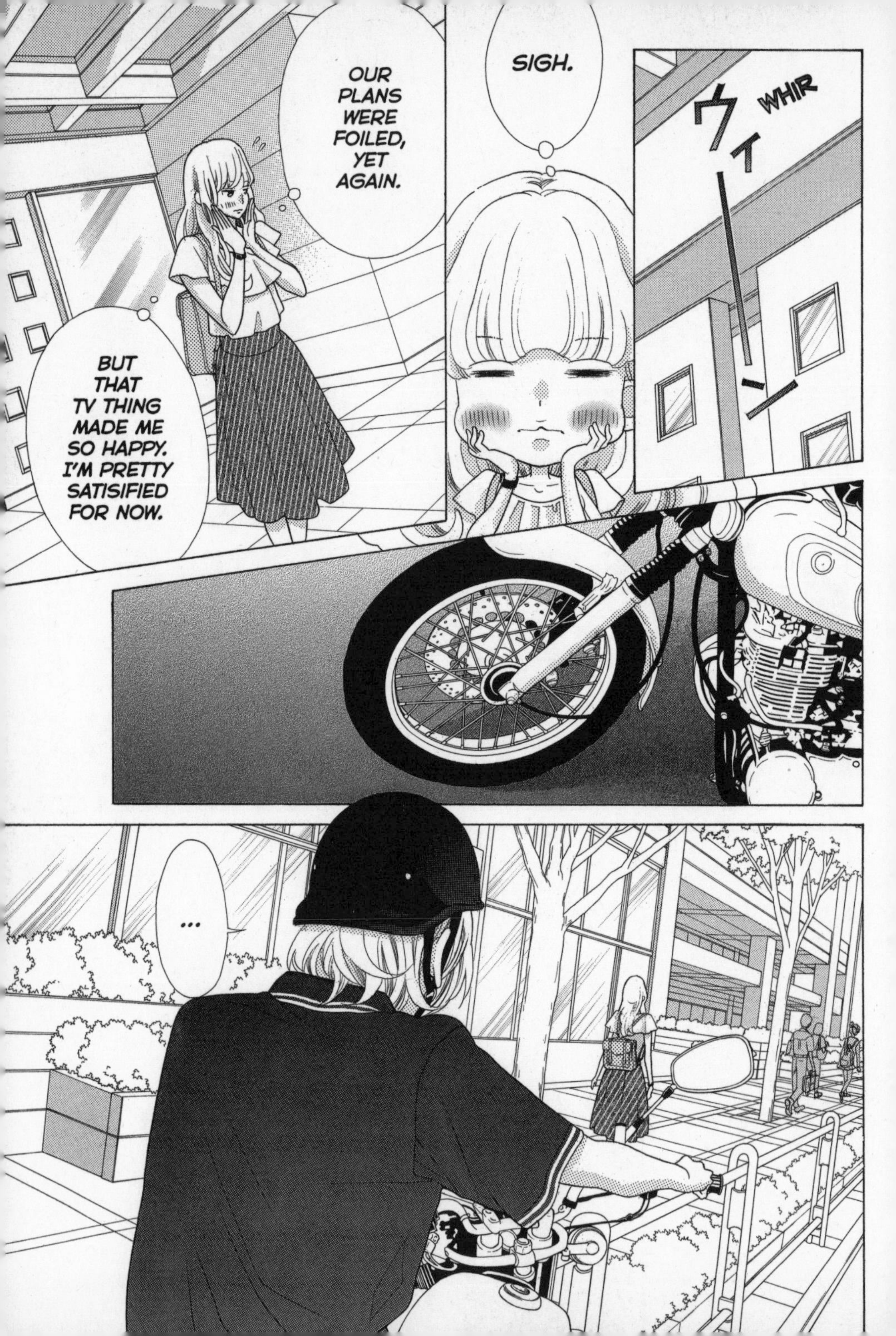
ウィーン
WHIR
SIGH.
OUR PLANS WERE FOILED, YET AGAIN.
BUT THAT TV THING MADE ME SO HAPPY. I'M PRETTY SATISIFIED FOR NOW.
...

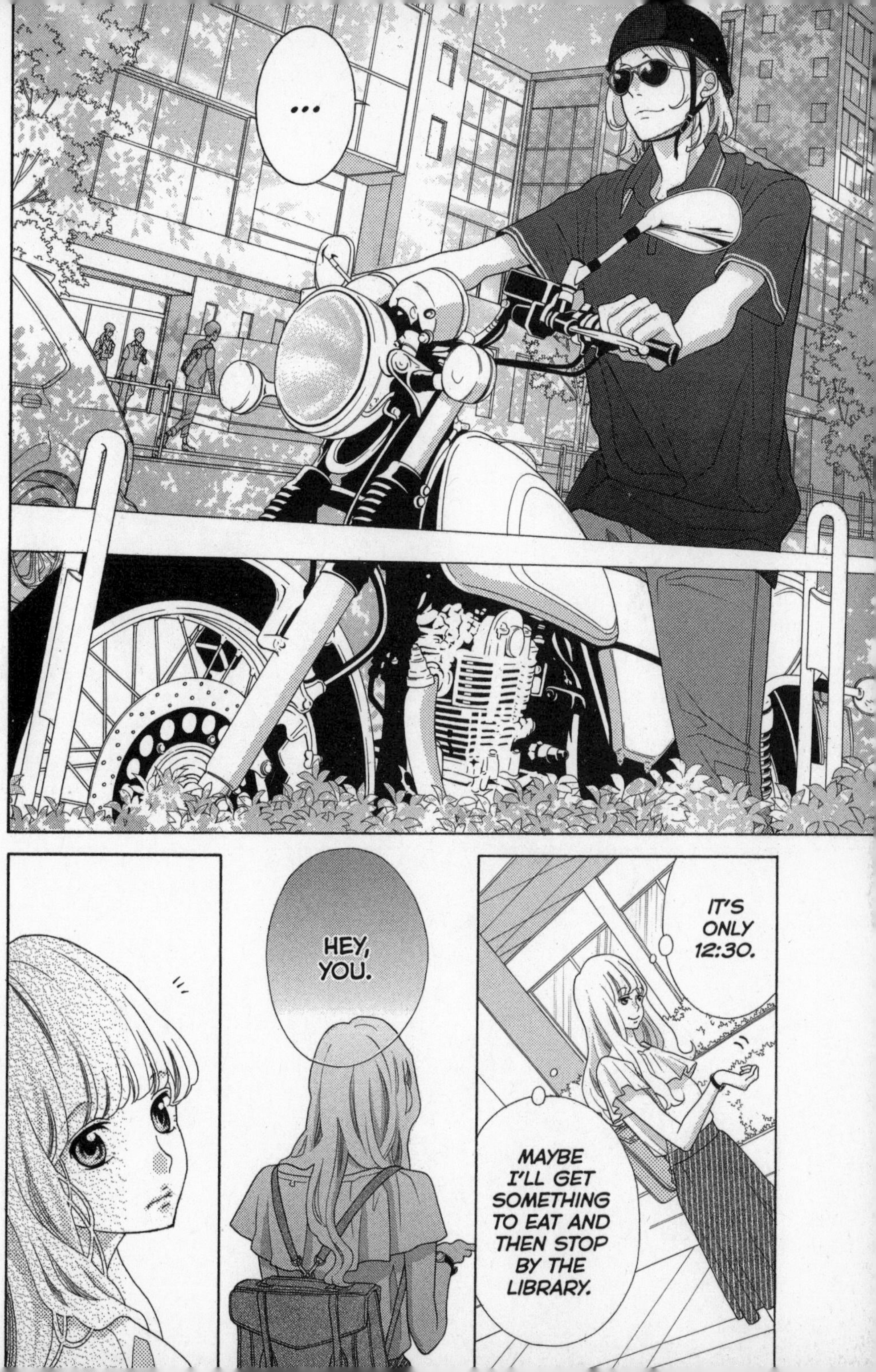
...
IT'S ONLY 12:30.
MAYBE I'LL GET SOMETHING TO EAT AND THEN STOP BY THE LIBRARY.
HEY, YOU.

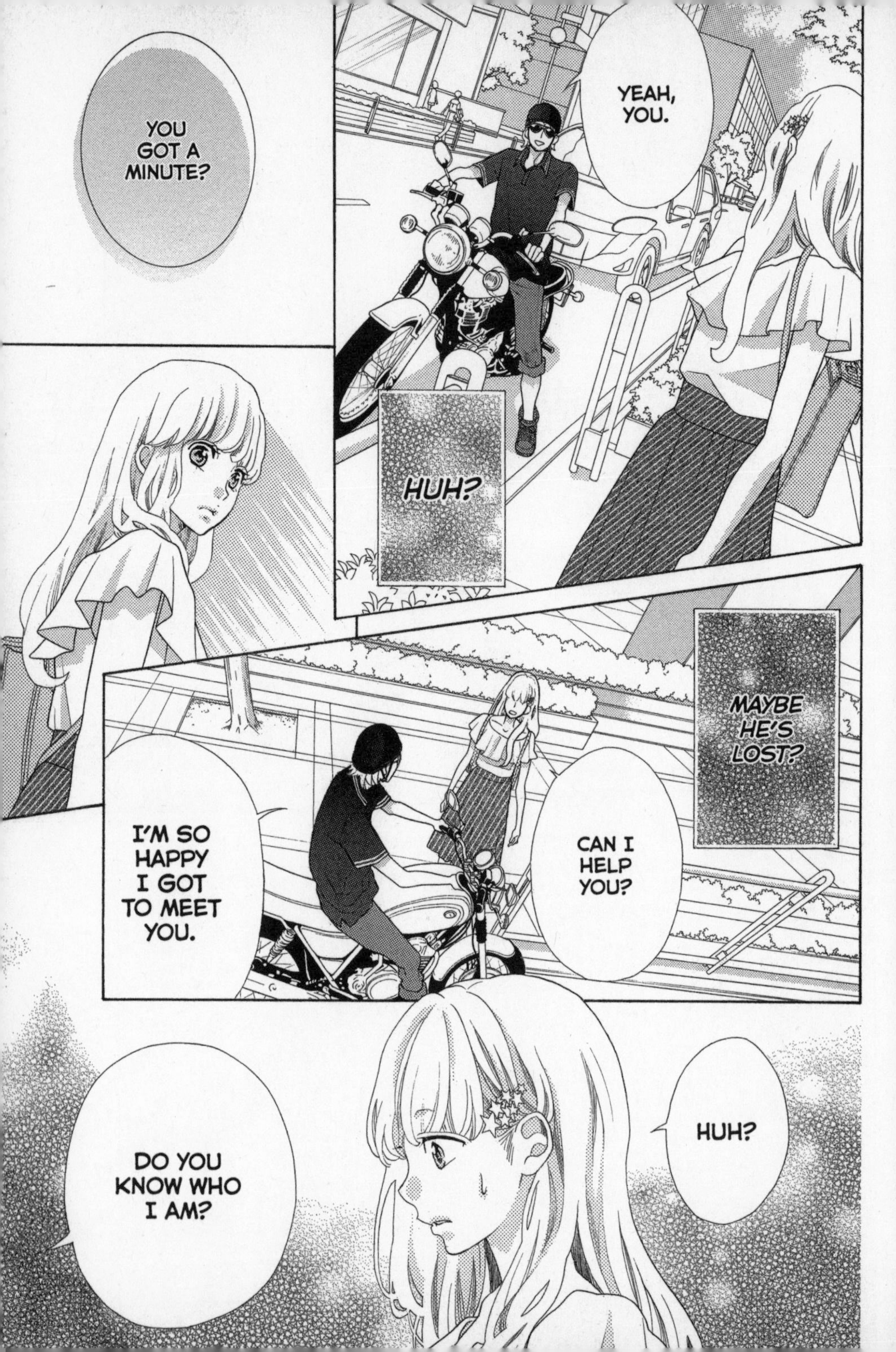
YEAH, YOU.
HUH?
YOU GOT A MINUTE?
MAYBE HE'S LOST?
CAN I HELP YOU?
I'M SO HAPPY I GOT TO MEET YOU.
HUH?
DO YOU KNOW WHO I AM?

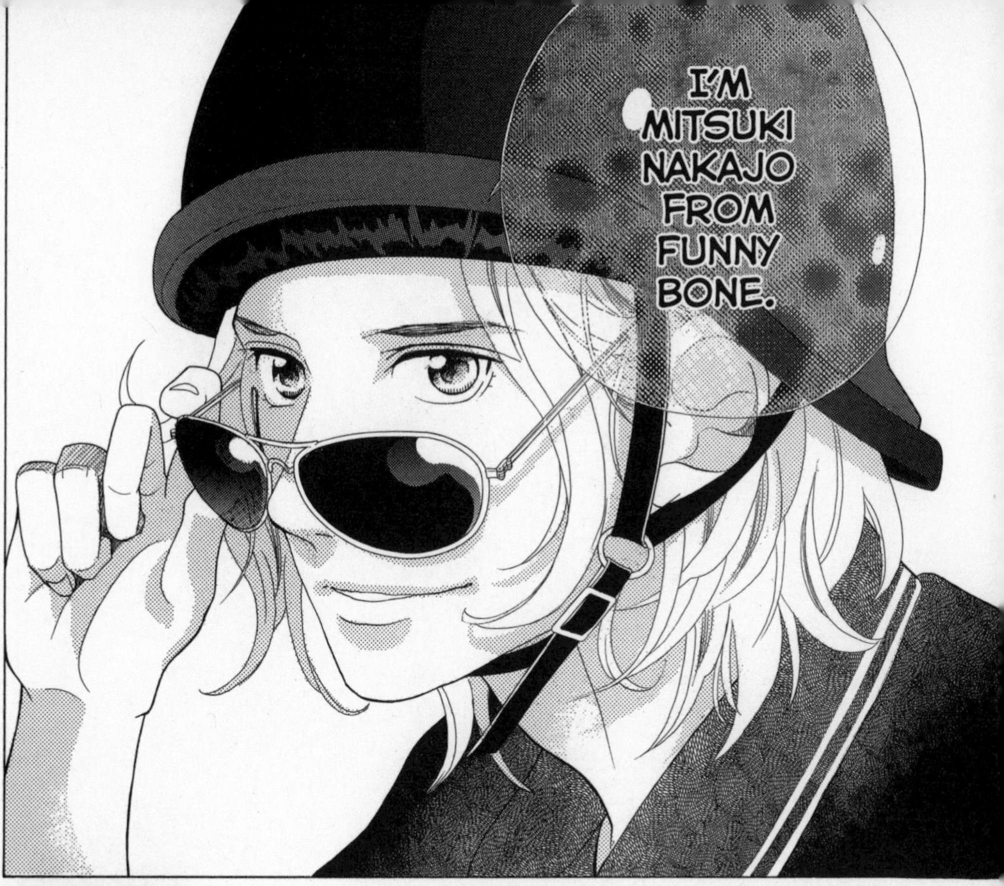
I'M MITSUKI NAKAJO FROM FUNNY BONE.
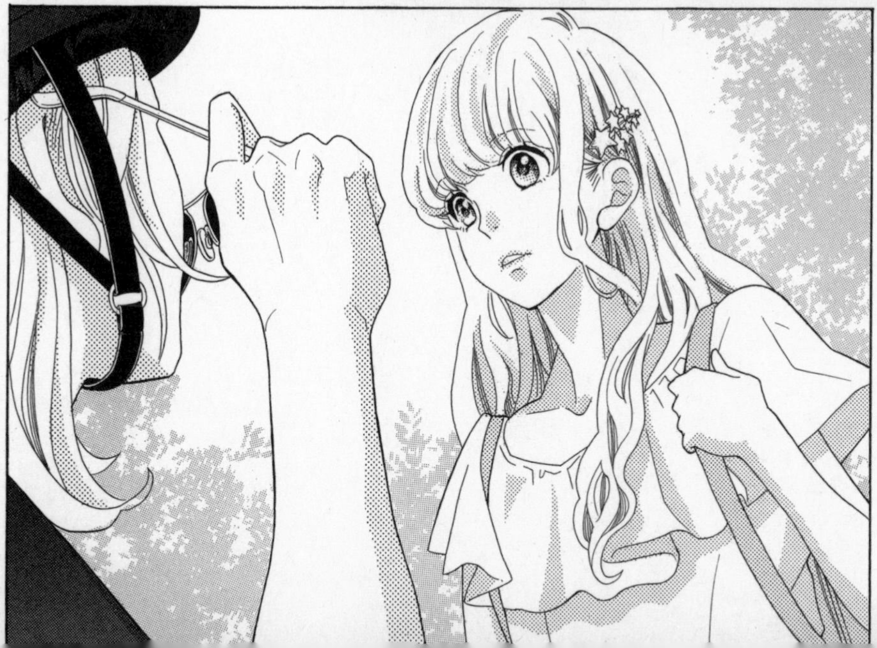

Kiss Me at the Stroke of Midnight

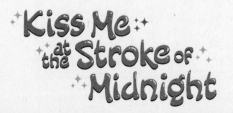

NANA THE CLOSET PERVERT GIRL

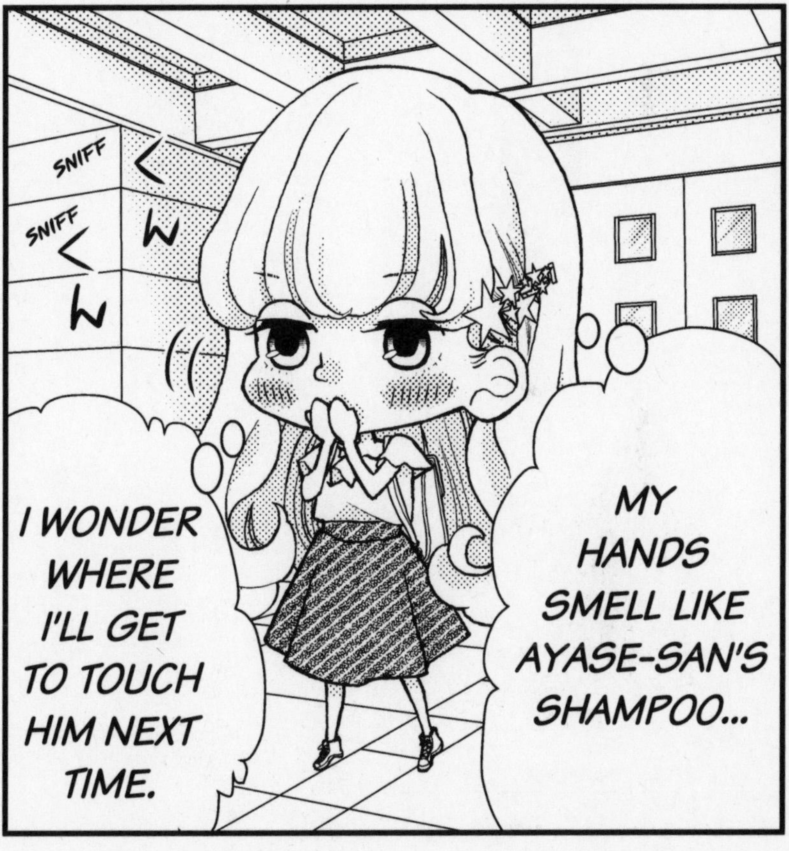
SNIFF
SNIFF
MY HANDS SMELL LIKE AYASE-SAN'S SHAMPOO...
I WONDER WHERE I'LL GET TO TOUCH HIM NEXT TIME.

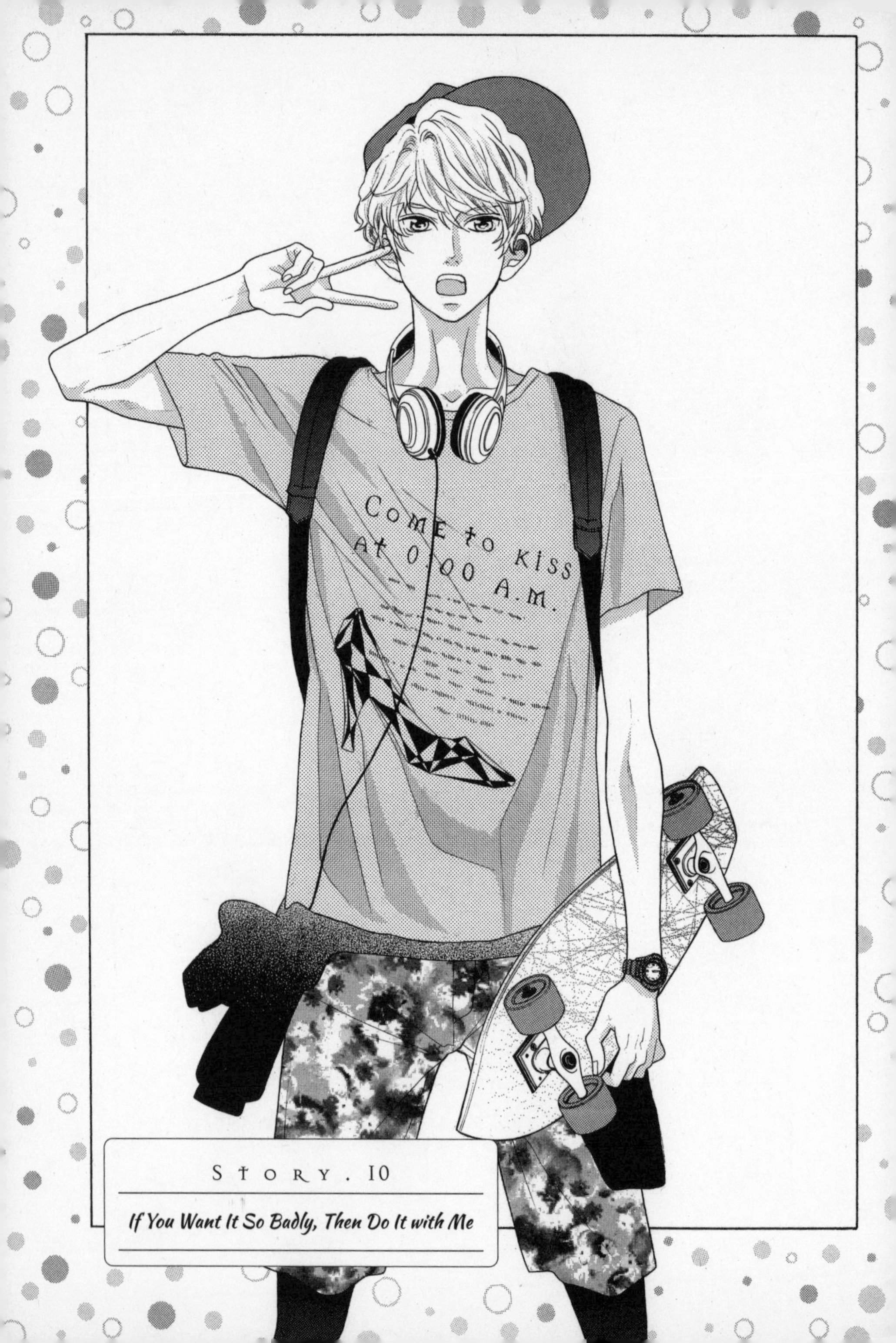
Come to Kiss
At 0:00 A.M.

Story. 10

If You Want It So Badly, Then Do It with Me

"DO YOU KNOW WHO I AM?"
"I'M MITSUKI NAKAJO FROM FUNNY BONE."

Kiss Me at the Stroke of Midnight

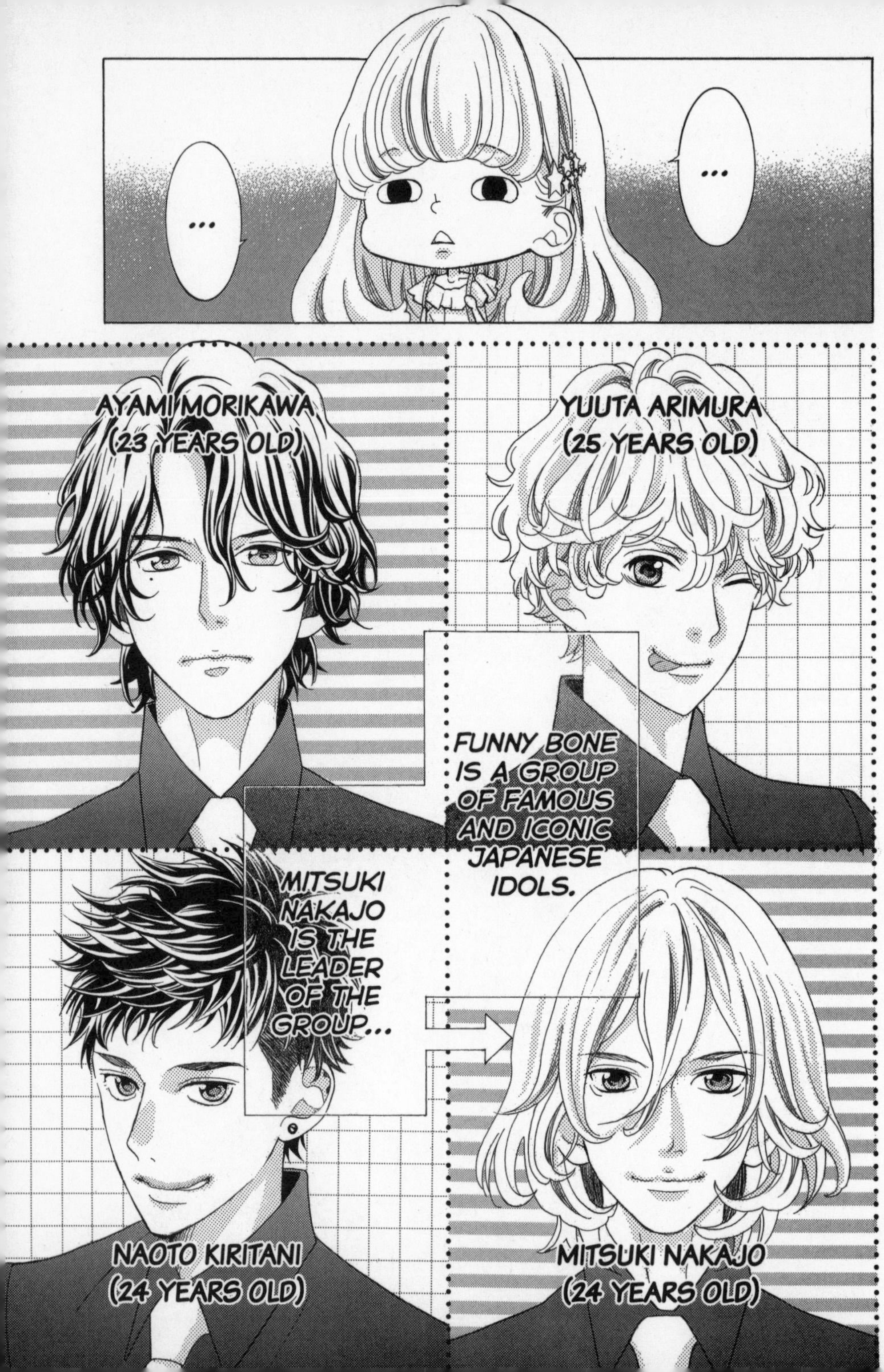
...
...
YUUTA ARIMURA (25 YEARS OLD)
AYAMI MORIKAWA (23 YEARS OLD)
FUNNY BONE IS A GROUP OF FAMOUS AND ICONIC JAPANESE IDOLS.
MITSUKI NAKAJO (24 YEARS OLD)
MITSUKI NAKAJO IS THE LEADER OF THE GROUP...
NAOTO KIRITANI (24 YEARS OLD)

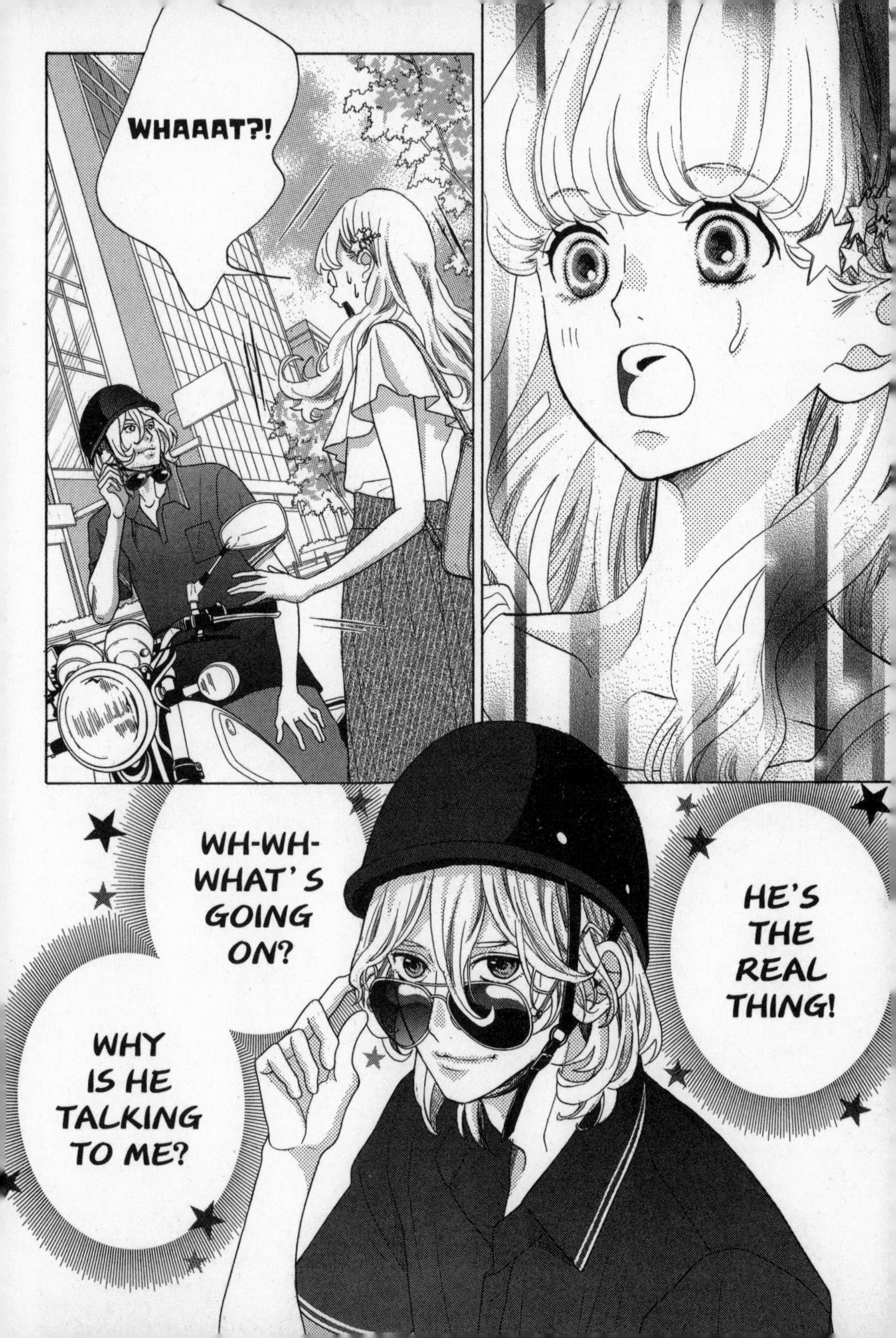
WHAAAT?!
HE'S THE REAL THING!
WH-WH-WHAT'S GOING ON?
WHY IS HE TALKING TO ME?

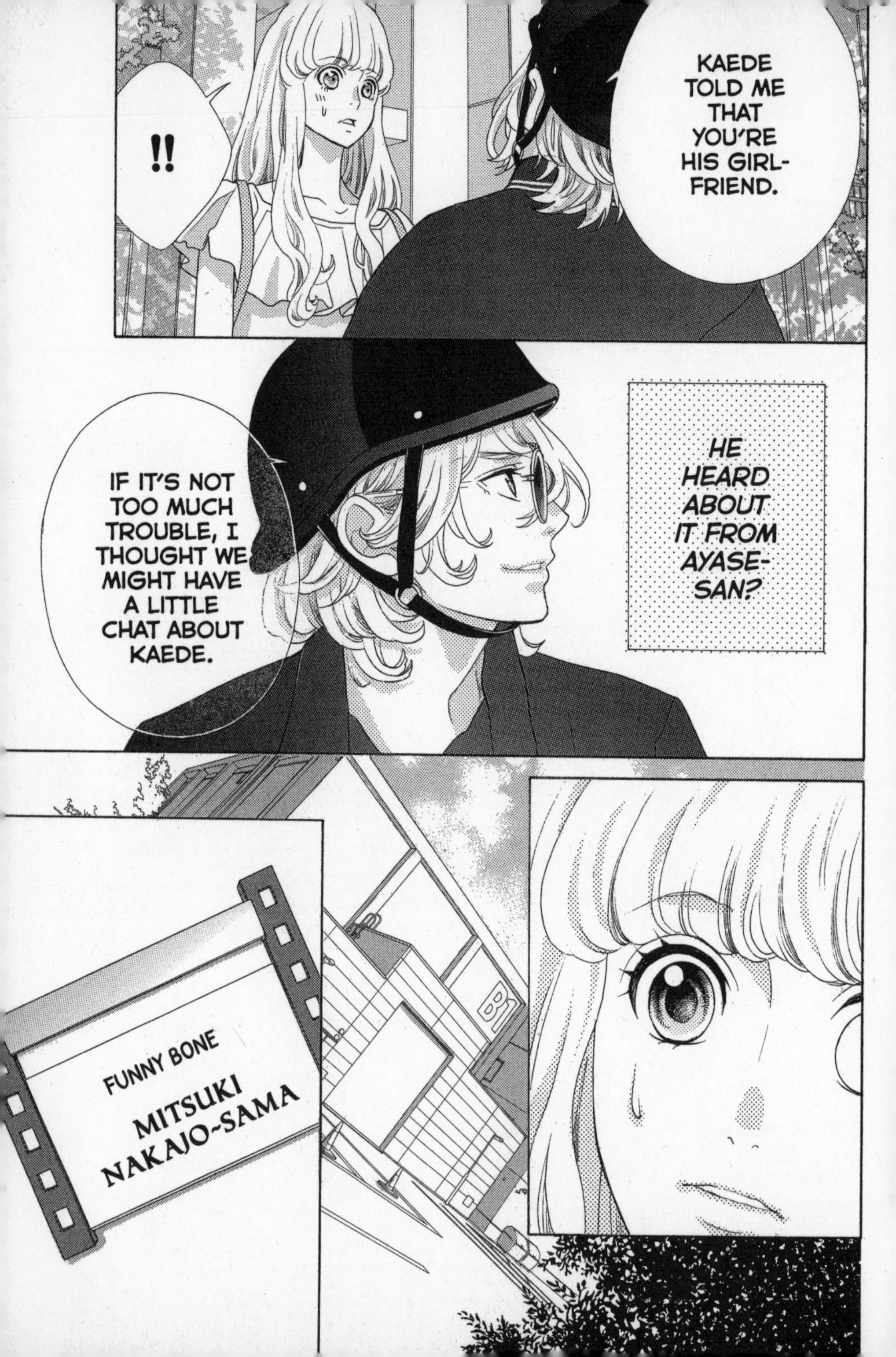
KAEDE TOLD ME THAT YOU'RE HIS GIRL-FRIEND.
!!
HE HEARD ABOUT IT FROM AYASE-SAN?
IF IT'S NOT TOO MUCH TROUBLE, I THOUGHT WE MIGHT HAVE A LITTLE CHAT ABOUT KAEDE.
B1
FUNNY BONE
MITSUKI NAKAJO-SAMA

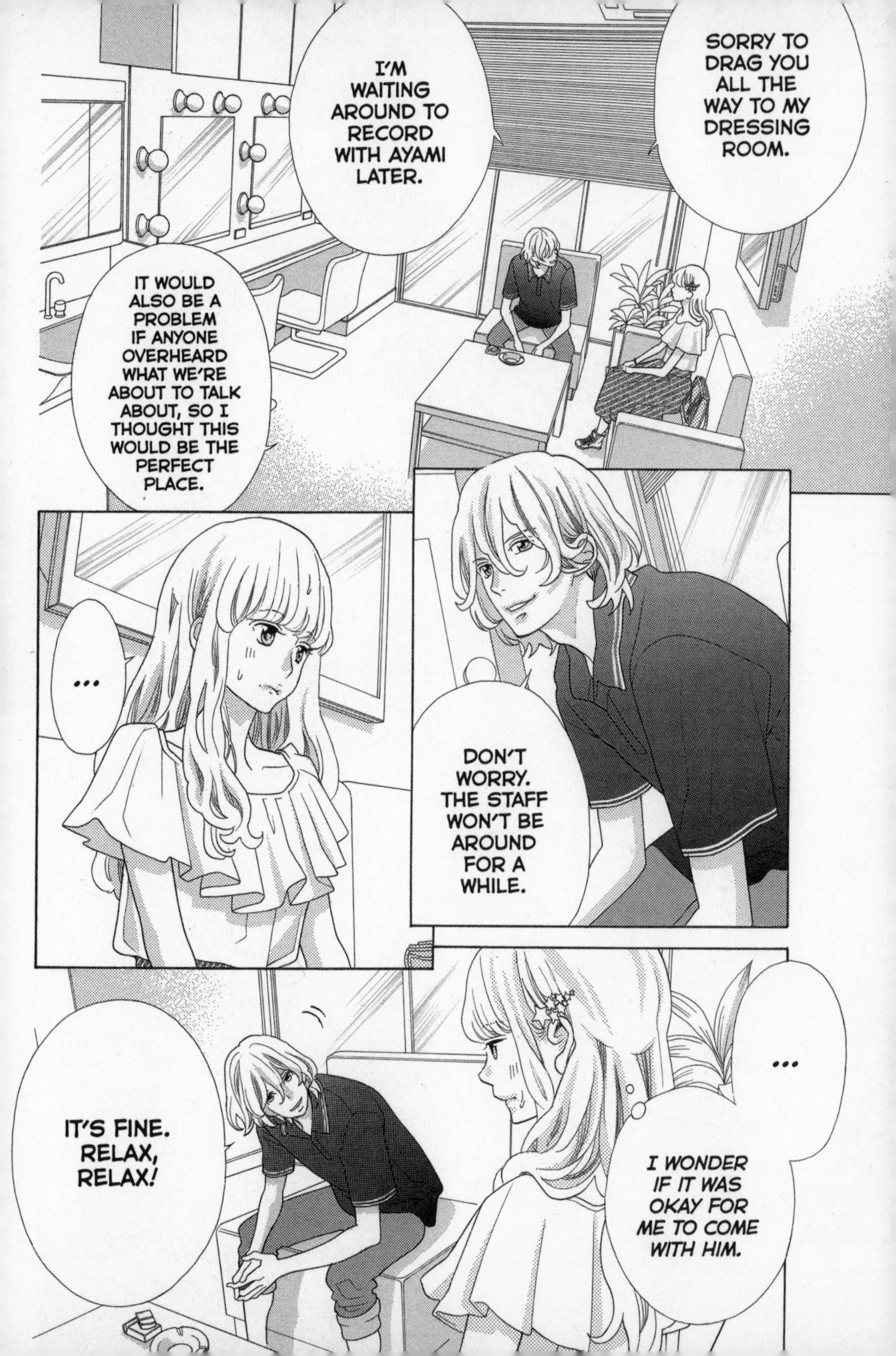
SORRY TO DRAG YOU ALL THE WAY TO MY DRESSING ROOM.
I'M WAITING AROUND TO RECORD WITH AYAMI LATER.
IT WOULD ALSO BE A PROBLEM IF ANYONE OVERHEARD WHAT WE'RE ABOUT TO TALK ABOUT, SO I THOUGHT THIS WOULD BE THE PERFECT PLACE.
DON'T WORRY. THE STAFF WON'T BE AROUND FOR A WHILE.
...
...
I WONDER IF IT WAS OKAY FOR ME TO COME WITH HIM.
IT'S FINE. RELAX, RELAX!

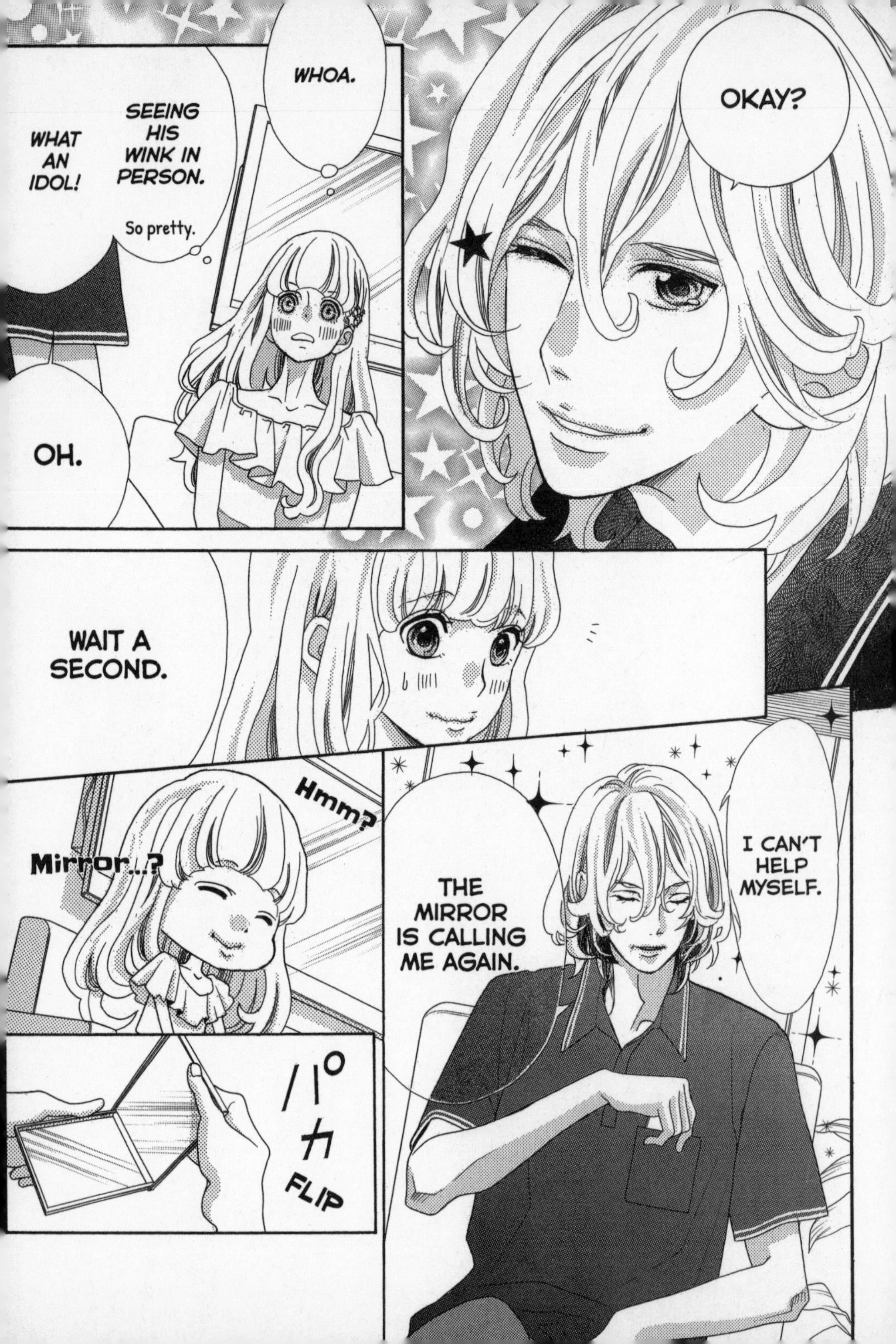
OKAY?
WHOA.
SEEING HIS WINK IN PERSON.
WHAT AN IDOL!
So pretty.
OH.
WAIT A SECOND.
I CAN'T HELP MYSELF.
THE MIRROR IS CALLING ME AGAIN.
Hmm?
Mirror..?
パカ
FLIP

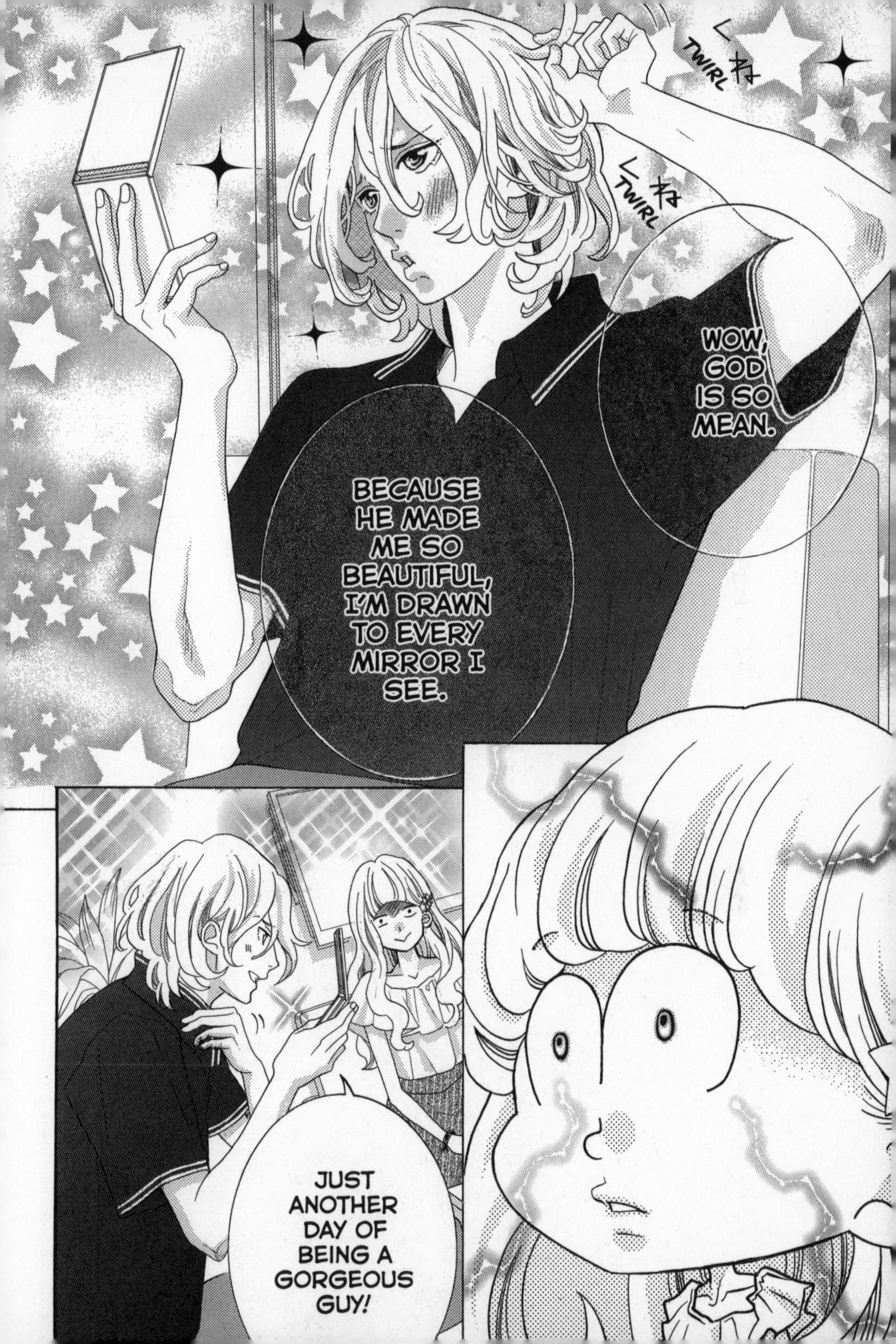
TWIRL
TWIRL
WOW, GOD IS SO MEAN.
BECAUSE HE MADE ME SO BEAUTIFUL, I'M DRAWN TO EVERY MIRROR I SEE.
JUST ANOTHER DAY OF BEING A GORGEOUS GUY!

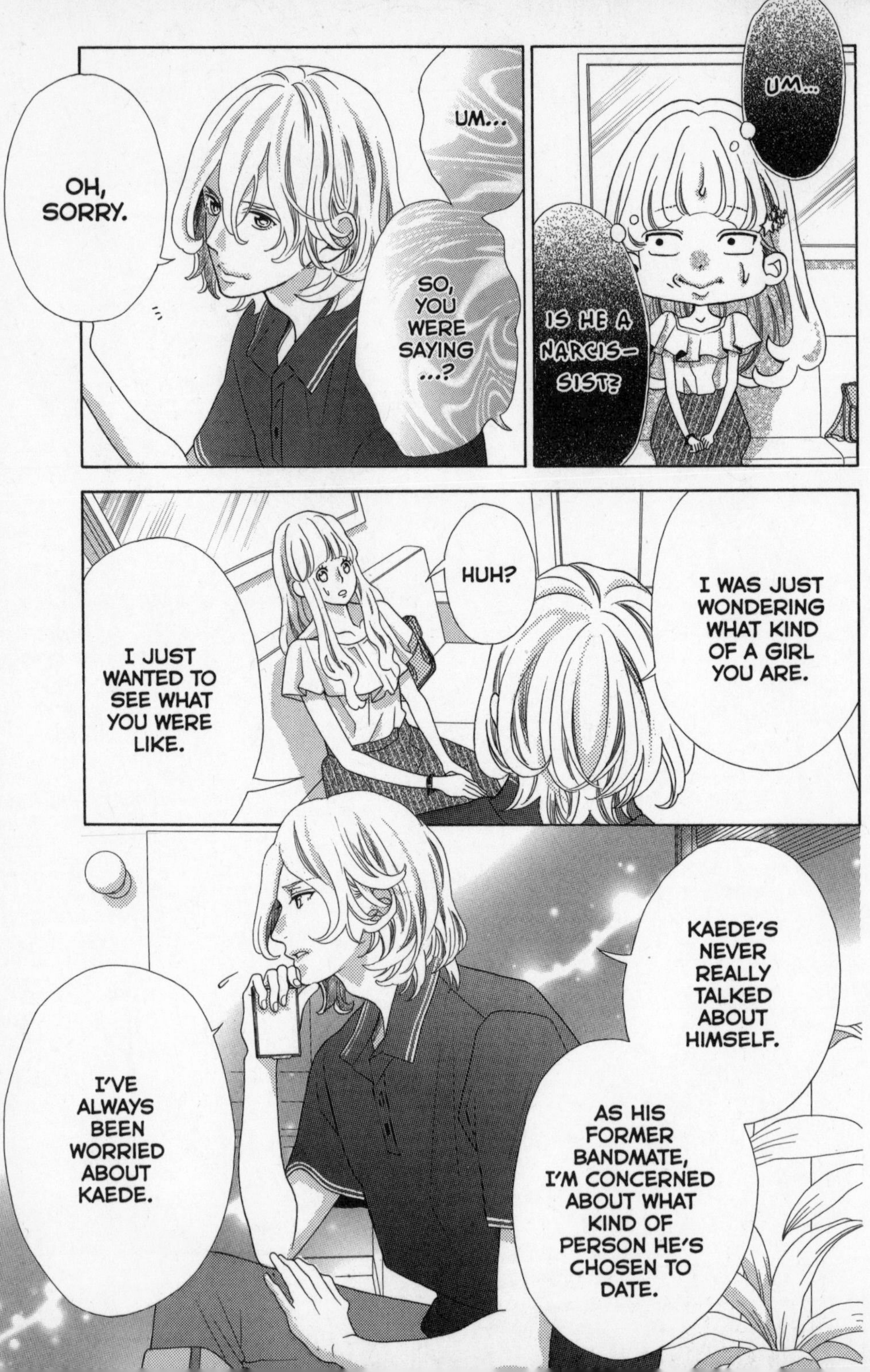
UM...
IS HE A NARCIS-SIST?
UM...
SO, YOU WERE SAYING ...?
OH, SORRY.
I WAS JUST WONDERING WHAT KIND OF A GIRL YOU ARE.
HUH?
I JUST WANTED TO SEE WHAT YOU WERE LIKE.
KAEDE'S NEVER REALLY TALKED ABOUT HIMSELF.
AS HIS FORMER BANDMATE, I'M CONCERNED ABOUT WHAT KIND OF PERSON HE'S CHOSEN TO DATE.
I'VE ALWAYS BEEN WORRIED ABOUT KAEDE.

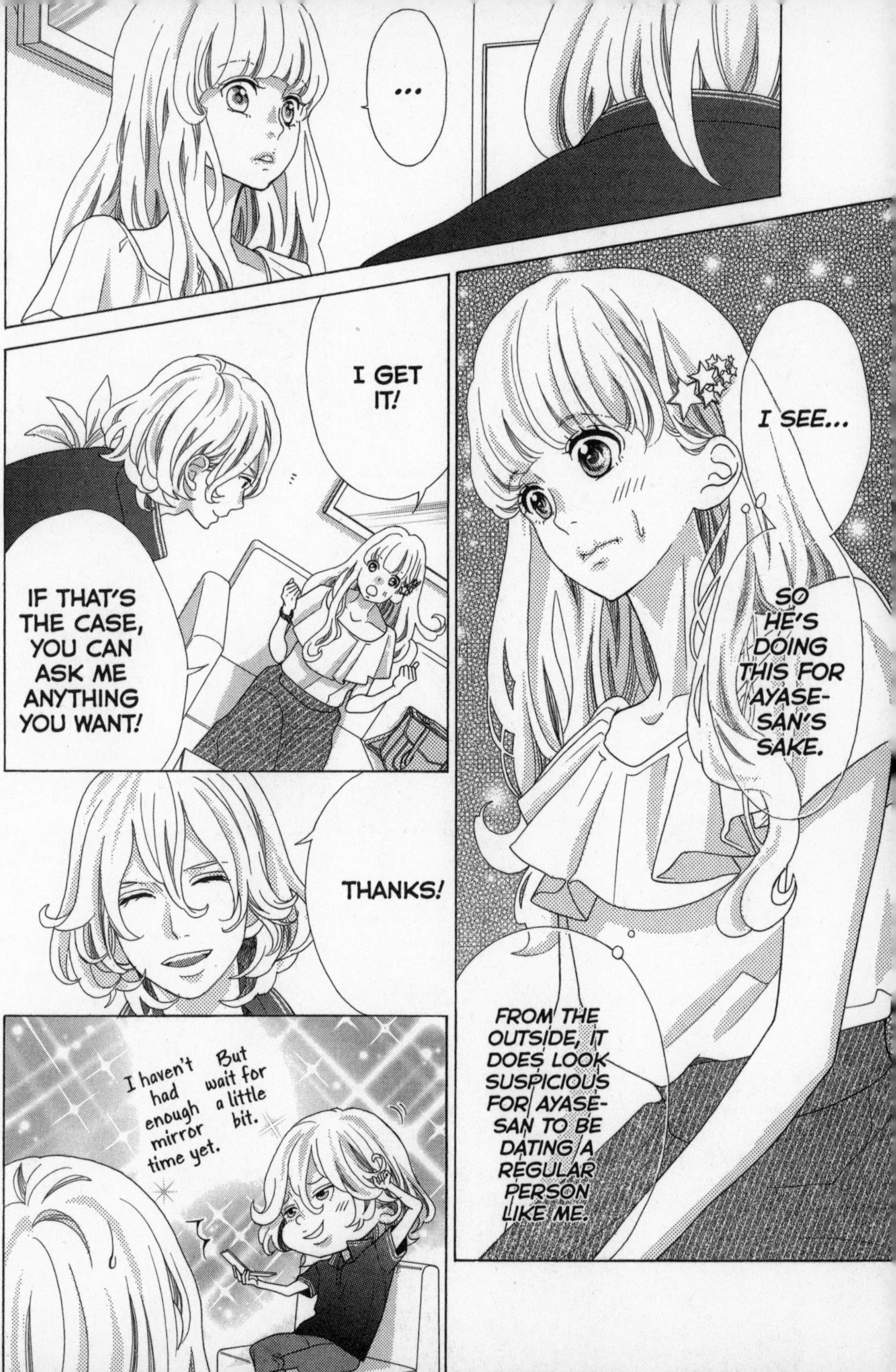
...
I SEE...
SO HE'S DOING THIS FOR AYASE-SAN'S SAKE.
FROM THE OUTSIDE, IT DOES LOOK SUSPICIOUS FOR AYASE-SAN TO BE DATING A REGULAR PERSON LIKE ME.
I GET IT!
IF THAT'S THE CASE, YOU CAN ASK ME ANYTHING YOU WANT!
THANKS!
But wait for a little bit.
I haven't had enough mirror time yet.

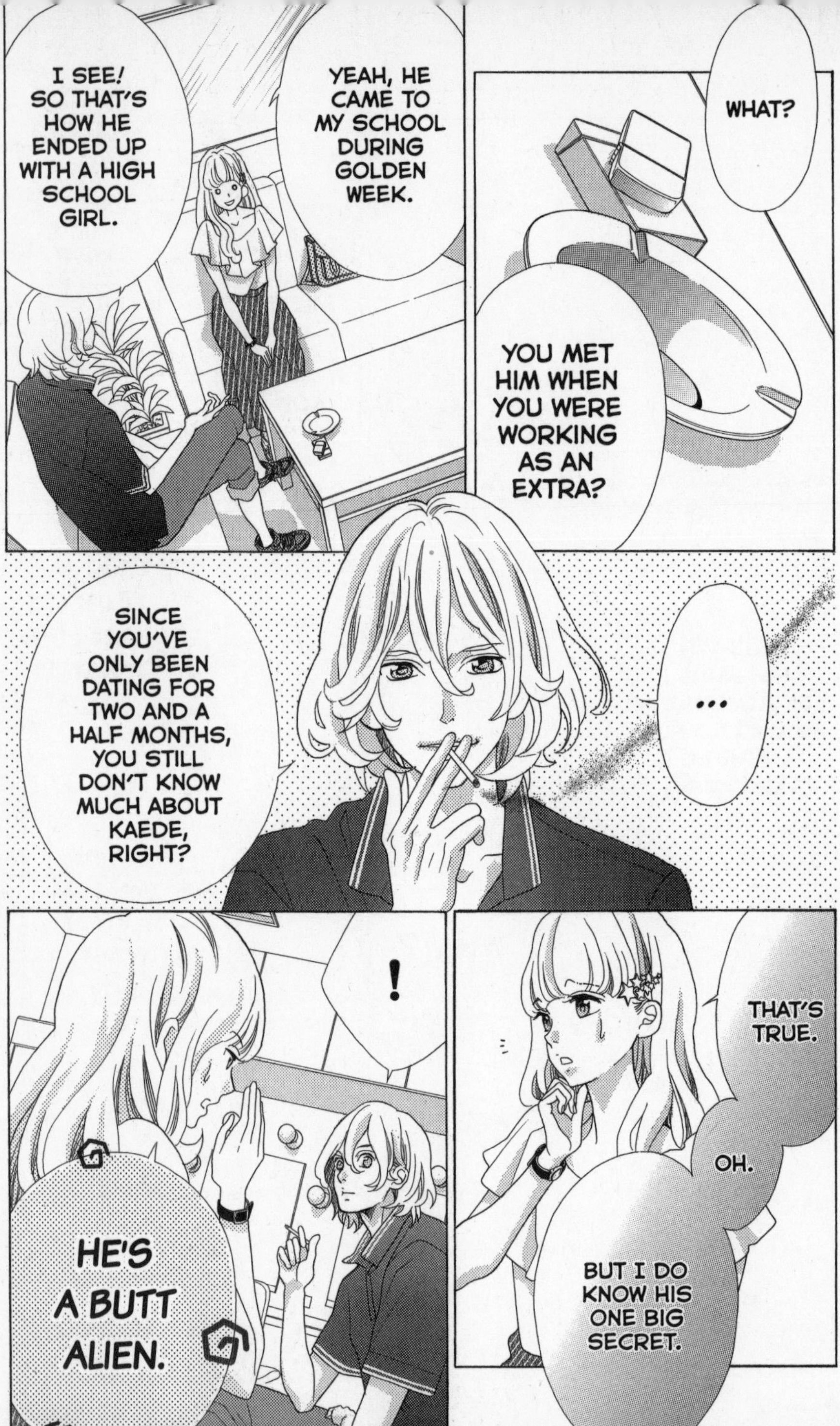
WHAT?
YOU MET HIM WHEN YOU WERE WORKING AS AN EXTRA?
YEAH, HE CAME TO MY SCHOOL DURING GOLDEN WEEK.
I SEE! SO THAT'S HOW HE ENDED UP WITH A HIGH SCHOOL GIRL.
...
SINCE YOU'VE ONLY BEEN DATING FOR TWO AND A HALF MONTHS, YOU STILL DON'T KNOW MUCH ABOUT KAEDE, RIGHT?
THAT'S TRUE.
OH.
BUT I DO KNOW HIS ONE BIG SECRET.
!
HE'S A BUTT ALIEN.

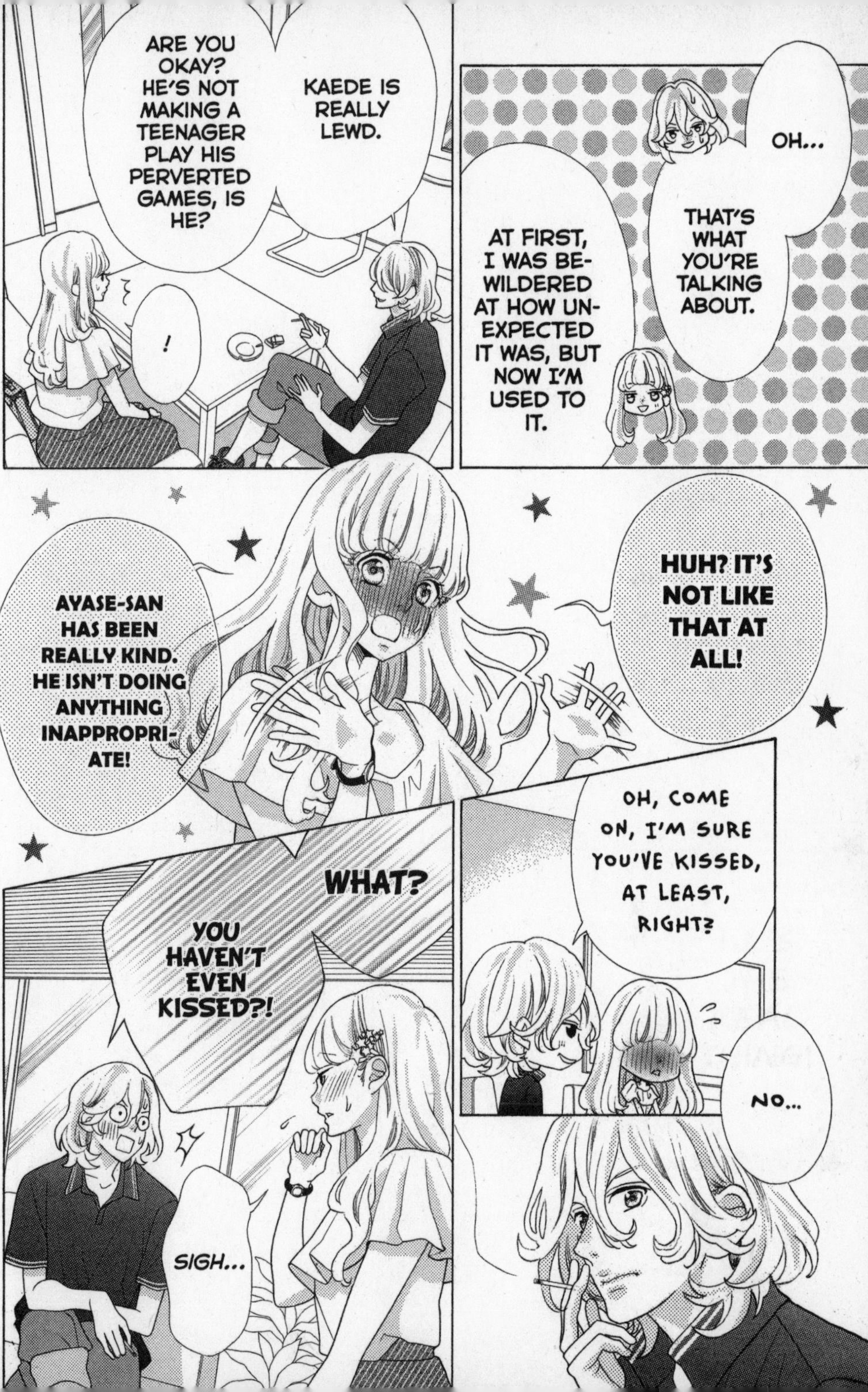
OH...
THAT'S WHAT YOU'RE TALKING ABOUT.
AT FIRST, I WAS BE-WILDERED AT HOW UN-EXPECTED IT WAS, BUT NOW I'M USED TO IT.
KAEDE IS REALLY LEWD.
ARE YOU OKAY? HE'S NOT MAKING A TEENAGER PLAY HIS PERVERTED GAMES, IS HE?
!
HUH? IT'S NOT LIKE THAT AT ALL!
AYASE-SAN HAS BEEN REALLY KIND. HE ISN'T DOING ANYTHING INAPPROPRI-ATE!
OH, COME ON, I'M SURE YOU'VE KISSED, AT LEAST, RIGHT?
NO...
WHAT?
YOU HAVEN'T EVEN KISSED?!
SIGH...

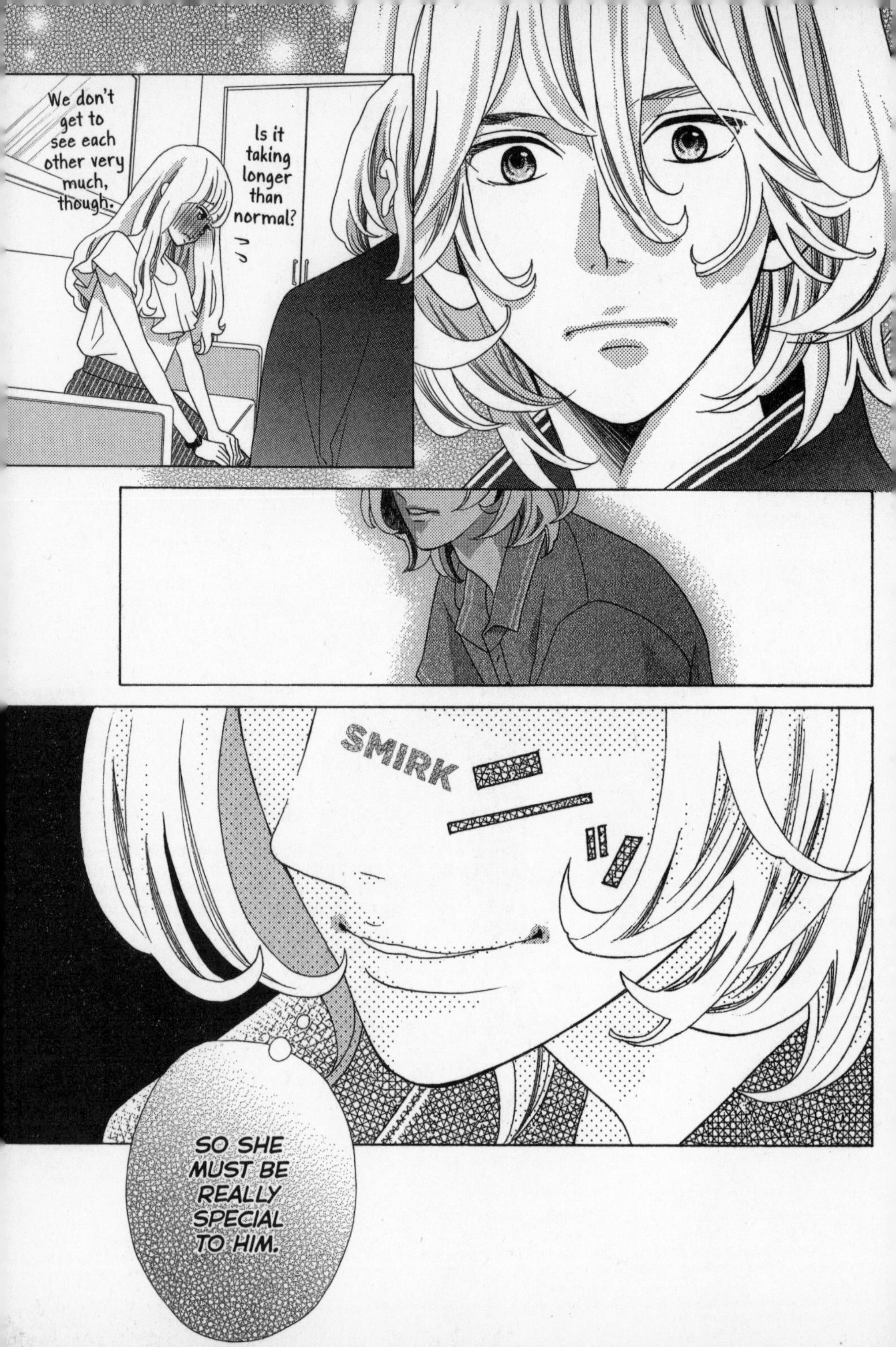
Is it taking longer than normal?
We don't get to see each other very much, though.
SMIRK
SO SHE MUST BE REALLY SPECIAL TO HIM.

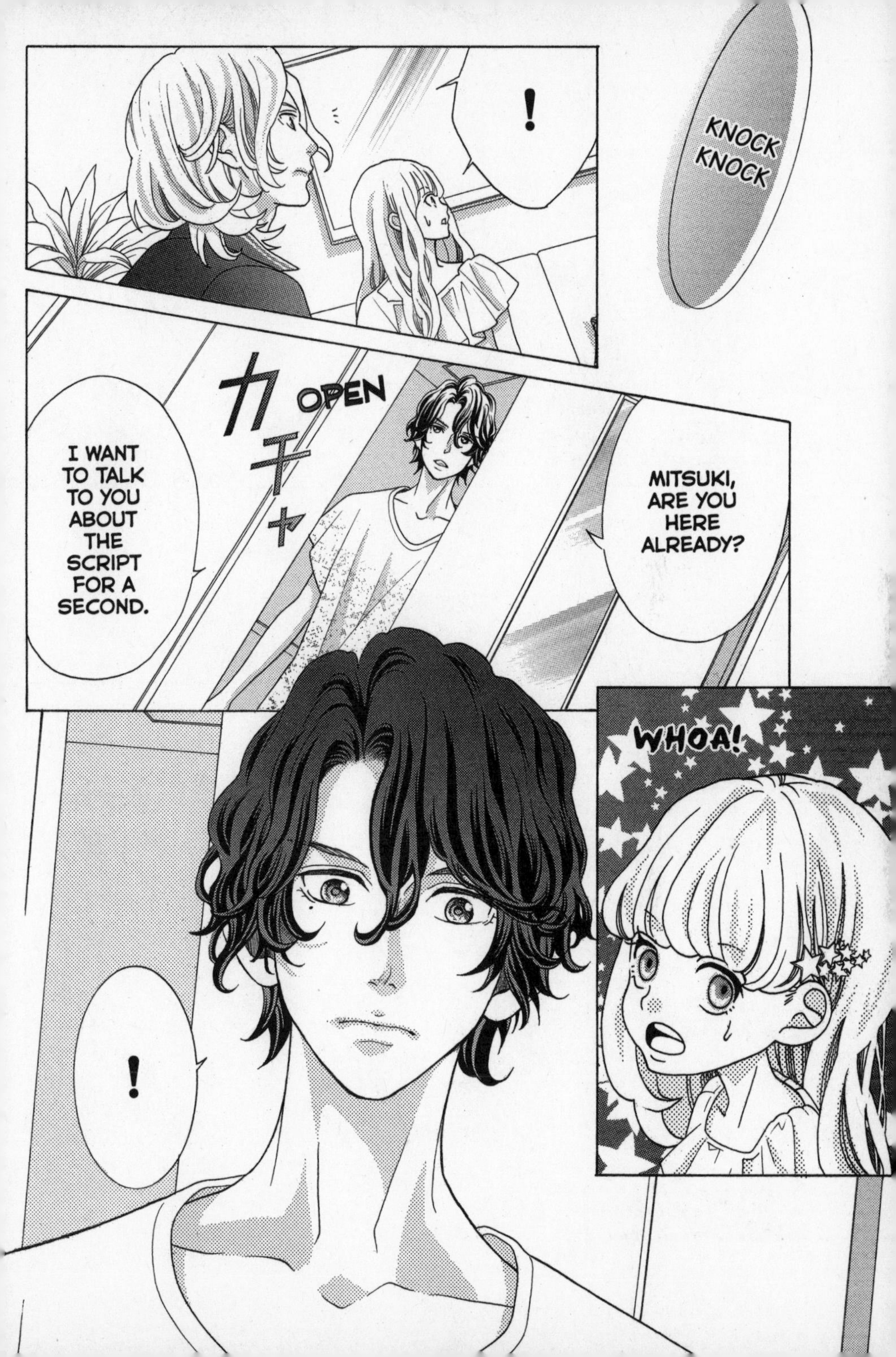
KNOCK KNOCK
!
MITSUKI, ARE YOU HERE ALREADY?
カチャ
OPEN
I WANT TO TALK TO YOU ABOUT THE SCRIPT FOR A SECOND.
WHOA!
!

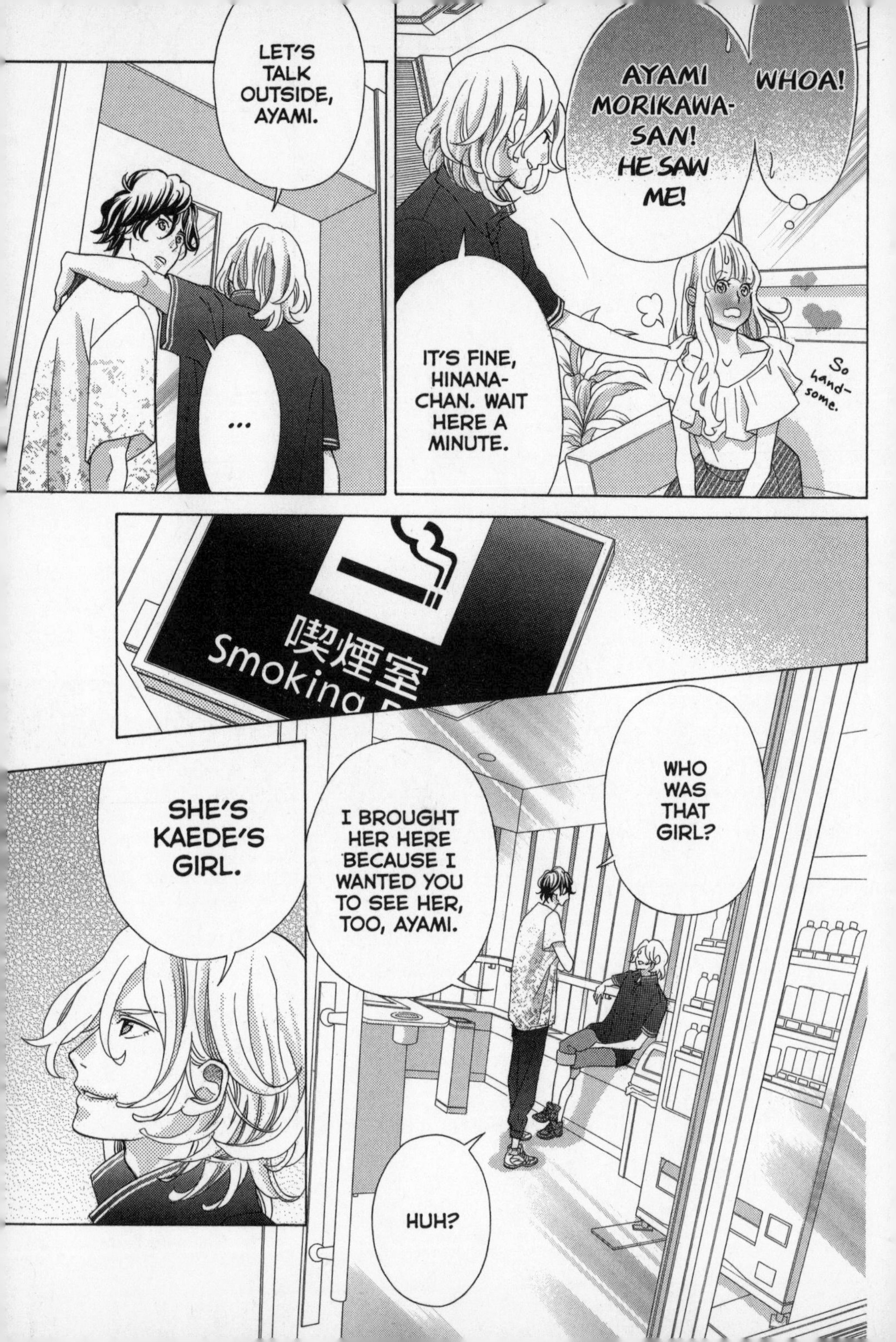
WHOA!
AYAMI MORIKAWA-SAN! HE SAW ME!
So handsome.
IT'S FINE, HINANA-CHAN. WAIT HERE A MINUTE.
LET'S TALK OUTSIDE, AYAMI.
...
喫煙室
Smoking
WHO WAS THAT GIRL?
I BROUGHT HER HERE BECAUSE I WANTED YOU TO SEE HER, TOO, AYAMI.
HUH?
SHE'S KAEDE'S GIRL.

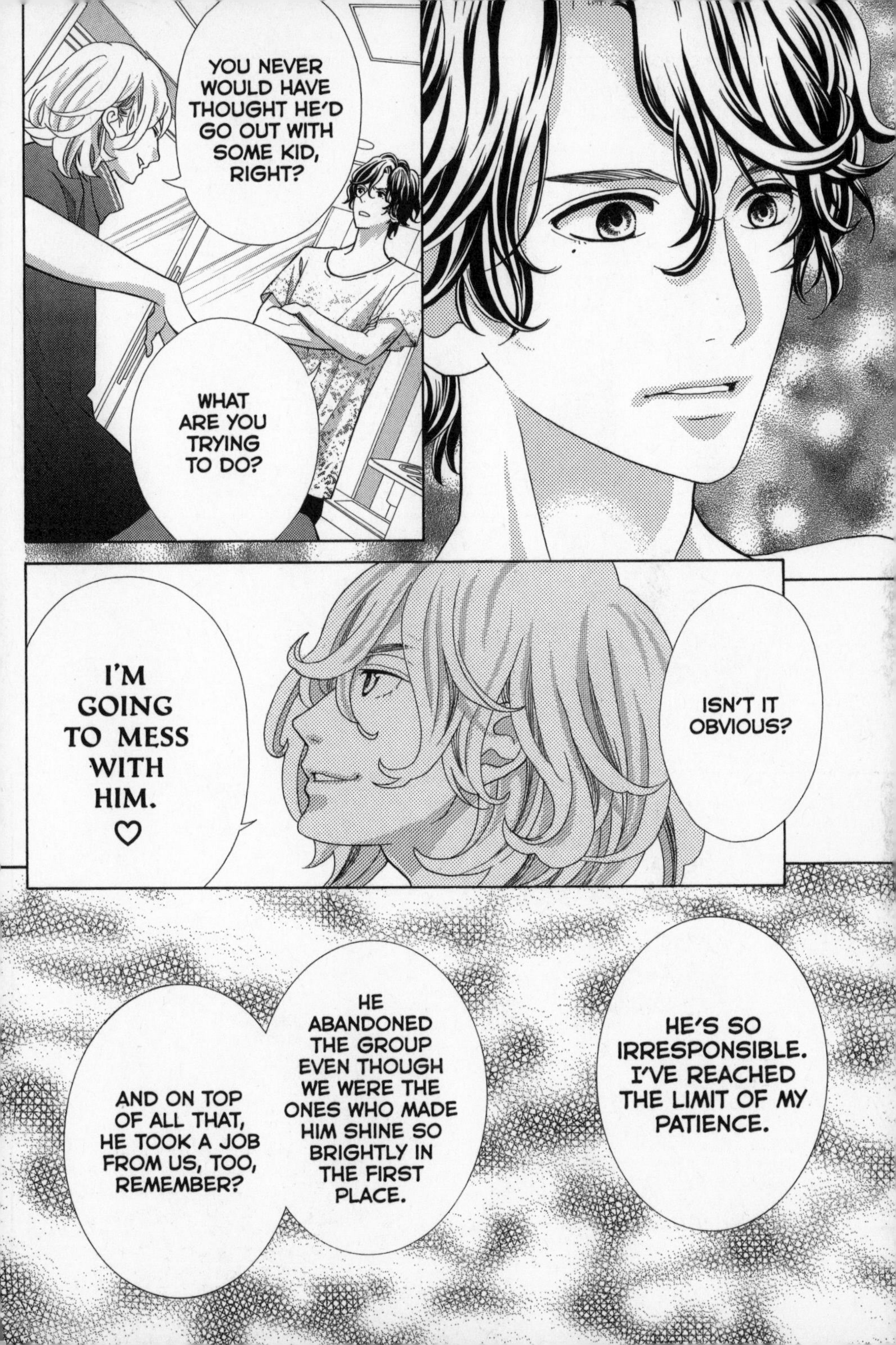
YOU NEVER WOULD HAVE THOUGHT HE'D GO OUT WITH SOME KID, RIGHT?
WHAT ARE YOU TRYING TO DO?
ISN'T IT OBVIOUS?
I'M GOING TO MESS WITH HIM. ♡
HE'S SO IRRESPONSIBLE. I'VE REACHED THE LIMIT OF MY PATIENCE.
HE ABANDONED THE GROUP EVEN THOUGH WE WERE THE ONES WHO MADE HIM SHINE SO BRIGHTLY IN THE FIRST PLACE.
AND ON TOP OF ALL THAT, HE TOOK A JOB FROM US, TOO, REMEMBER?

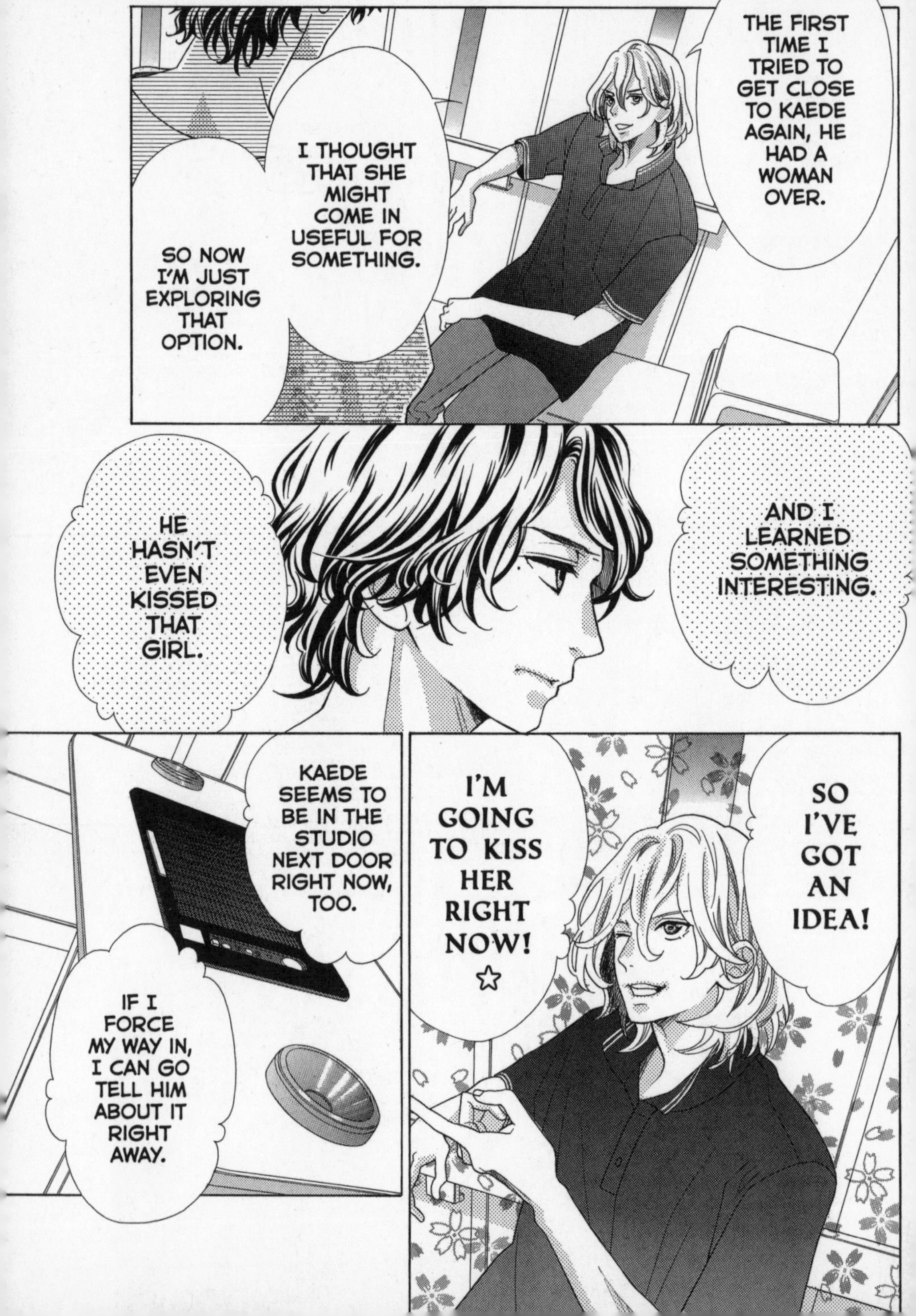
THE FIRST TIME I TRIED TO GET CLOSE TO KAEDE AGAIN, HE HAD A WOMAN OVER.
I THOUGHT THAT SHE MIGHT COME IN USEFUL FOR SOMETHING.
SO NOW I'M JUST EXPLORING THAT OPTION.
AND I LEARNED SOMETHING INTERESTING.
HE HASN'T EVEN KISSED THAT GIRL.
SO I'VE GOT AN IDEA!
I'M GOING TO KISS HER RIGHT NOW! ☆
KAEDE SEEMS TO BE IN THE STUDIO NEXT DOOR RIGHT NOW, TOO.
IF I FORCE MY WAY IN, I CAN GO TELL HIM ABOUT IT RIGHT AWAY.

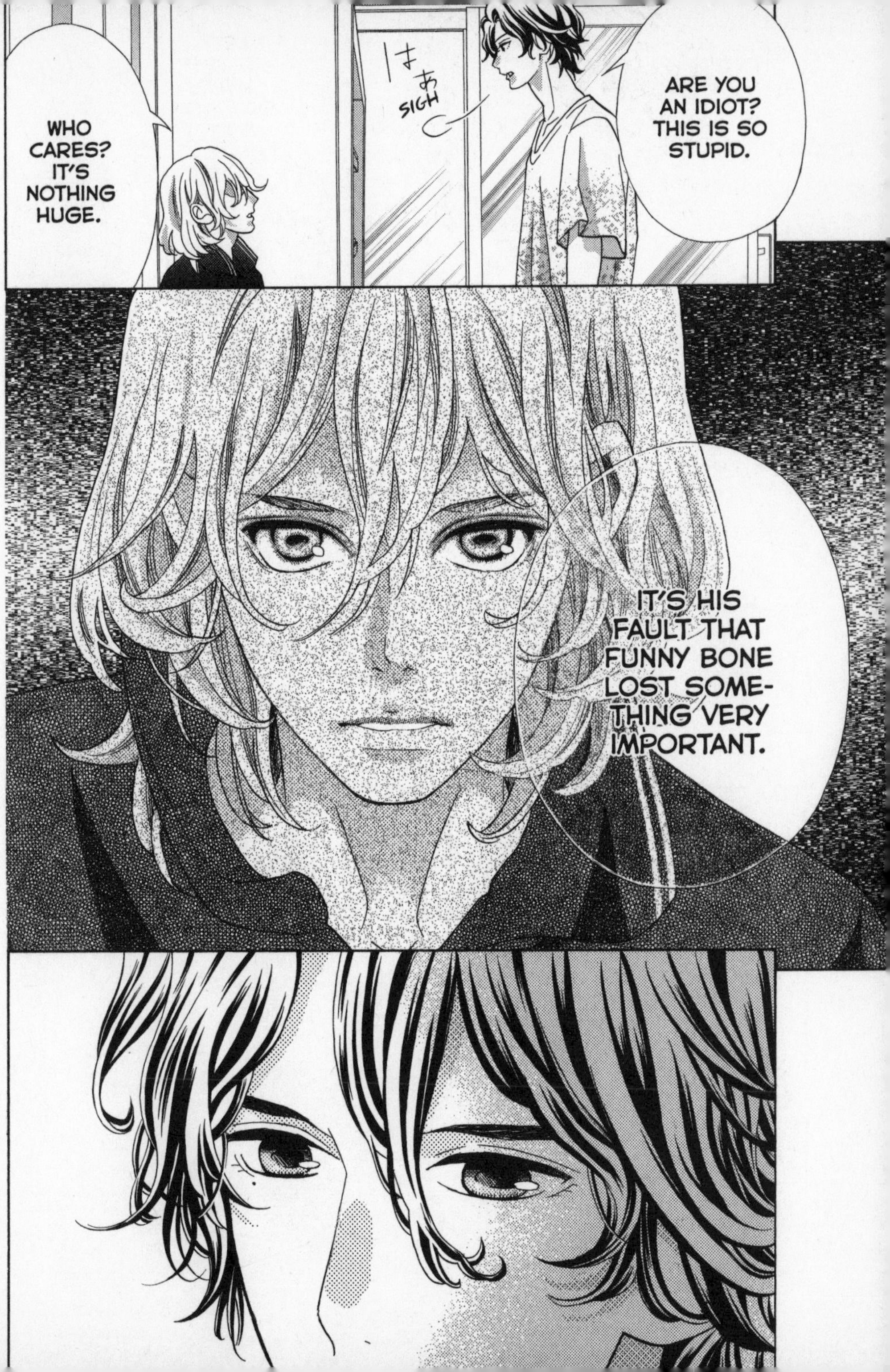
ARE YOU AN IDIOT? THIS IS SO STUPID.
はあ SIGH
WHO CARES? IT'S NOTHING HUGE.
IT'S HIS FAULT THAT FUNNY BONE LOST SOME-THING VERY IMPORTANT.

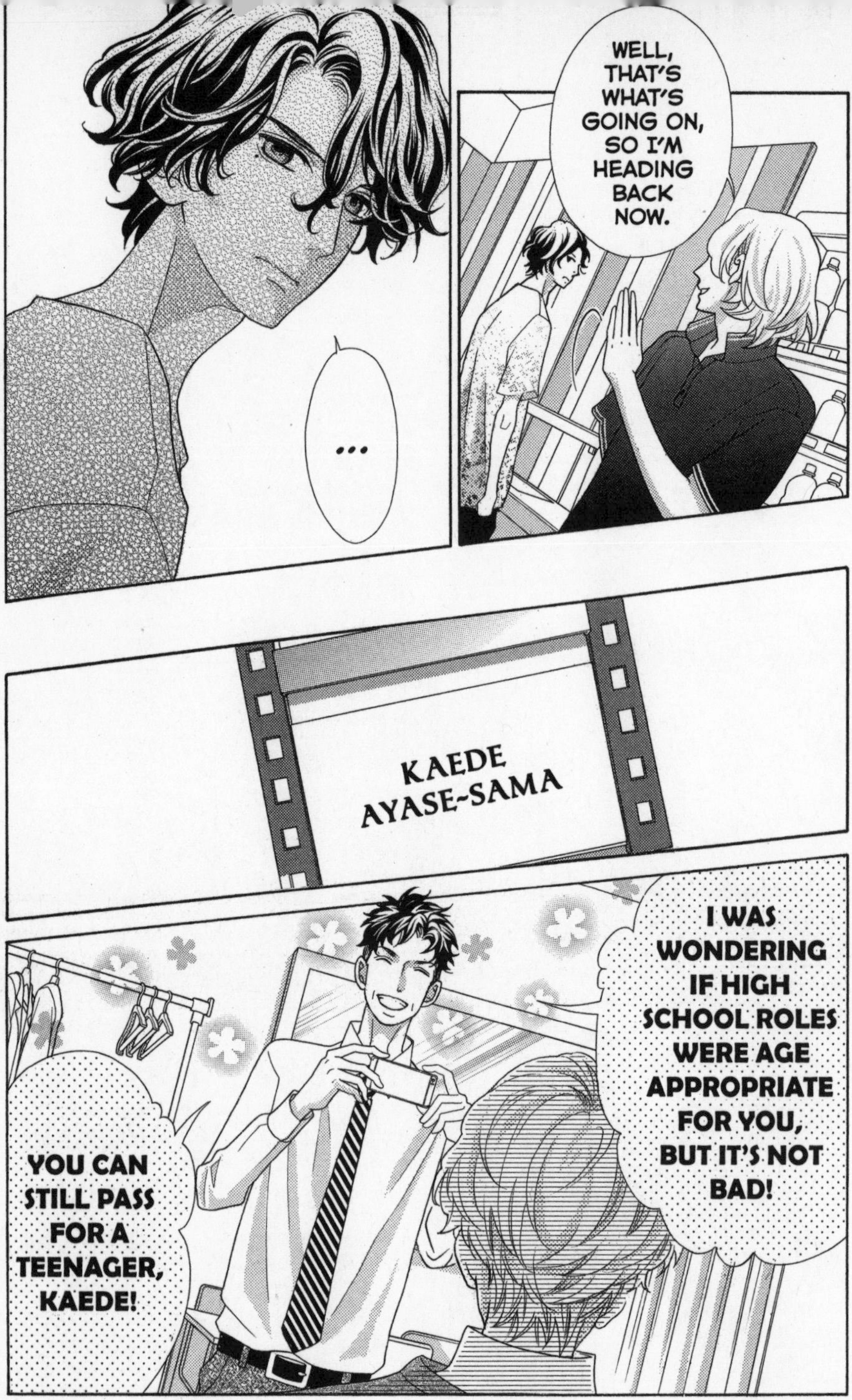
WELL, THAT'S WHAT'S GOING ON, SO I'M HEADING BACK NOW.
...
KAEDE AYASE-SAMA
I WAS WONDERING IF HIGH SCHOOL ROLES WERE AGE APPROPRIATE FOR YOU, BUT IT'S NOT BAD!
YOU CAN STILL PASS FOR A TEENAGER, KAEDE!

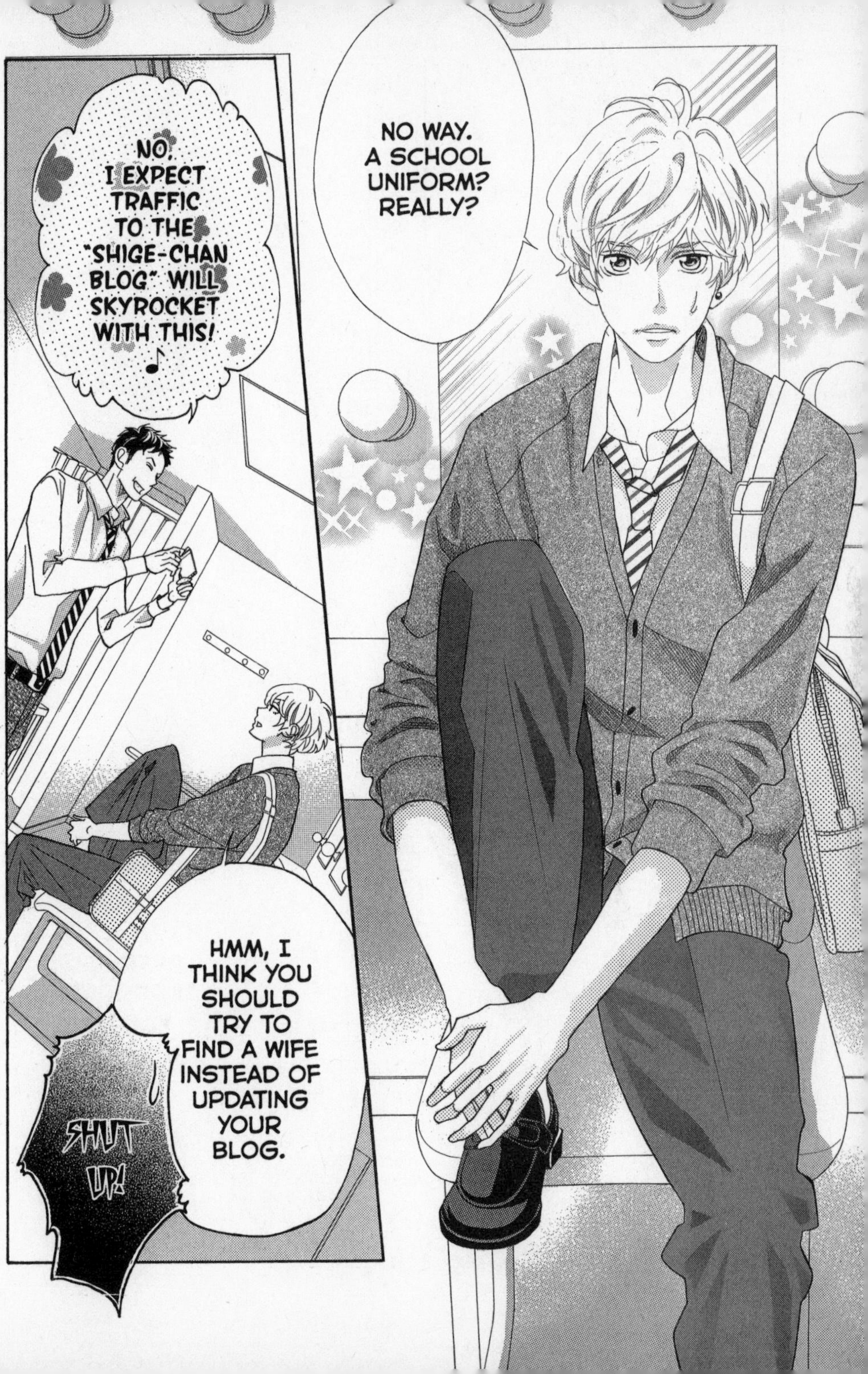
NO WAY. A SCHOOL UNIFORM? REALLY?
NO. I EXPECT TRAFFIC TO THE "SHIGE-CHAN BLOG" WILL SKYROCKET WITH THIS! ♪
HMM, I THINK YOU SHOULD TRY TO FIND A WIFE INSTEAD OF UPDATING YOUR BLOG.
SHUT UP!

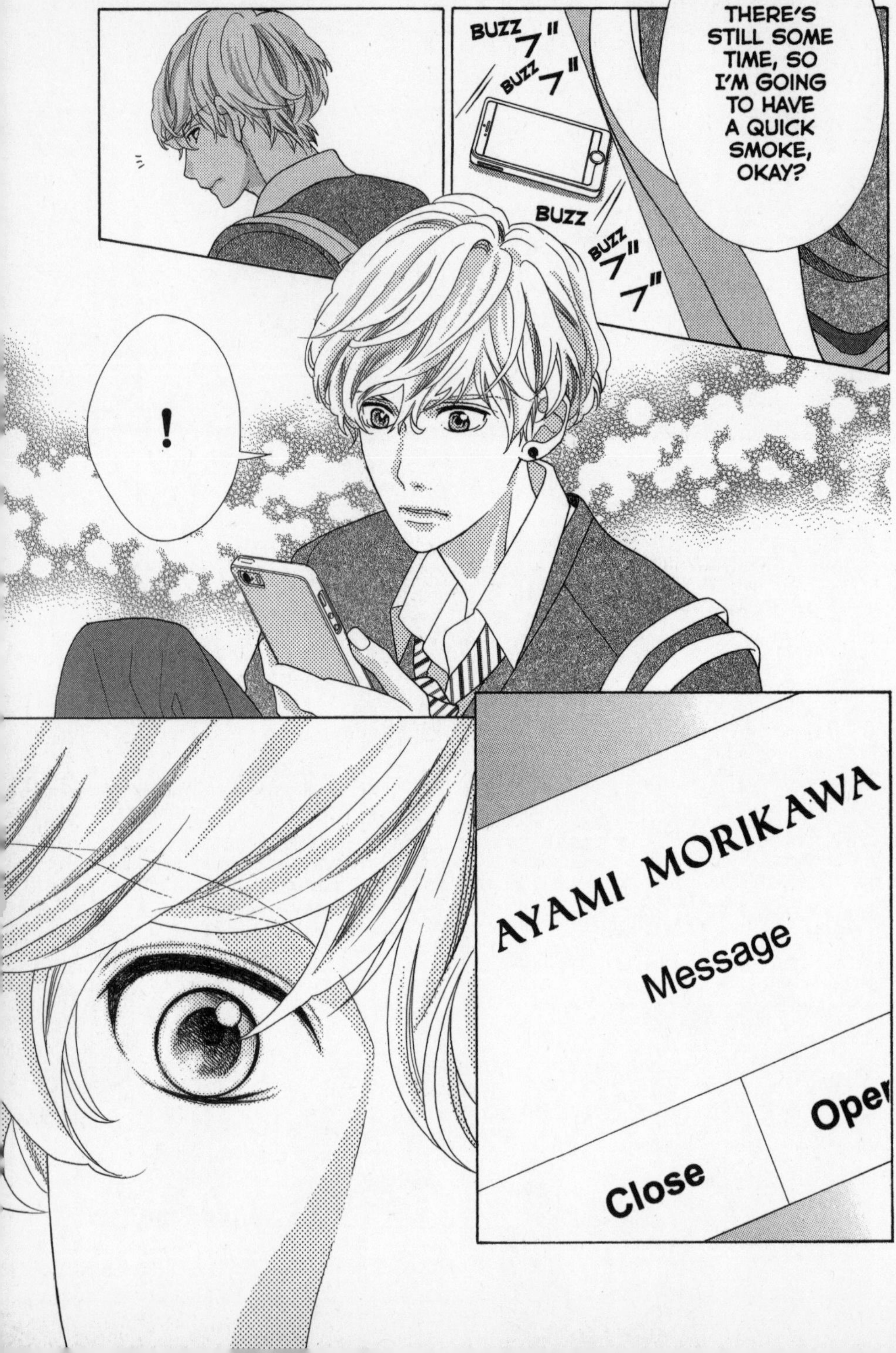

THERE'S STILL SOME TIME, SO I'M GOING TO HAVE A QUICK SMOKE, OKAY?
BUZZ
BUZZ
BUZZ
BUZZ
!
AYAMI MORIKAWA
Message
Close
Open

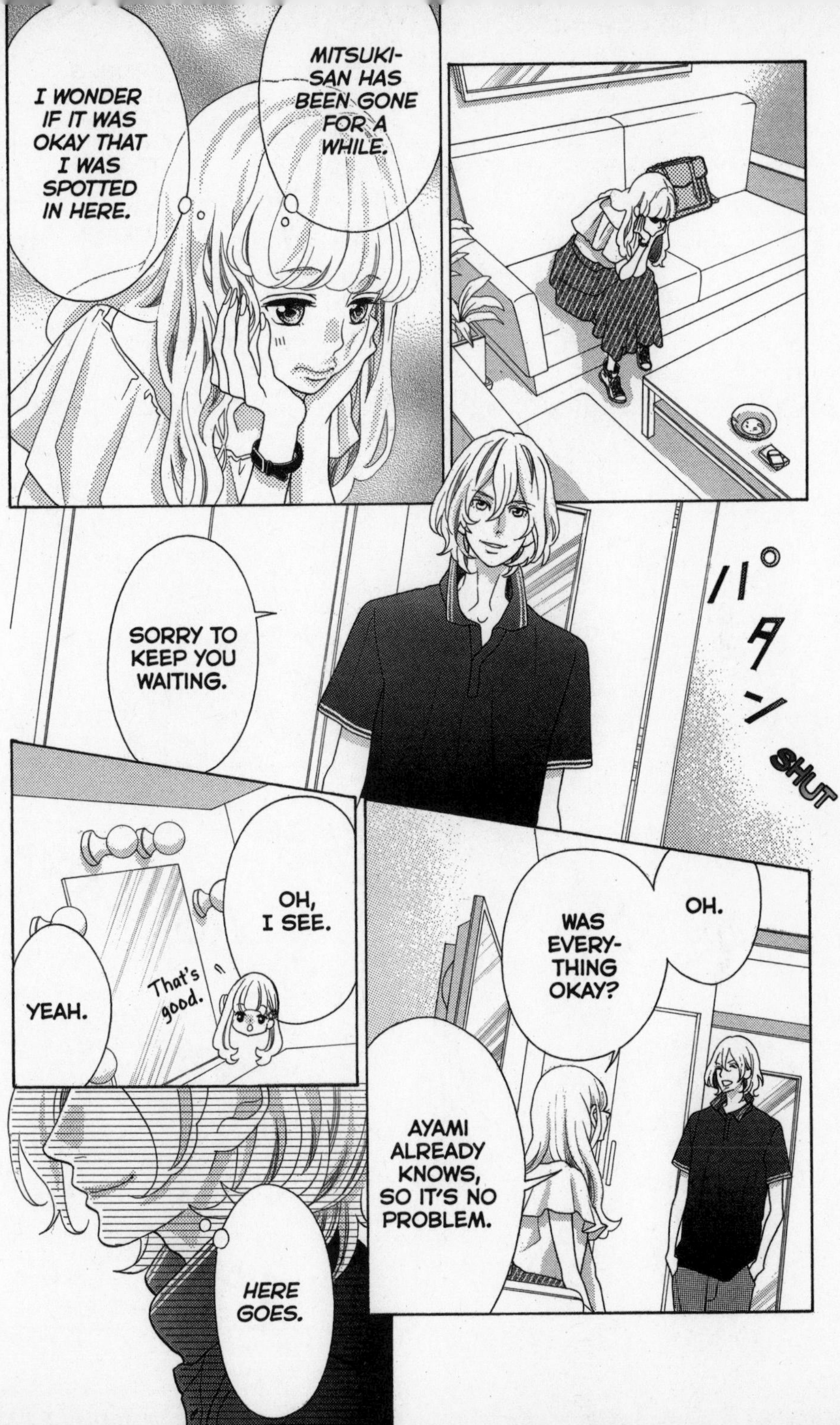
MITSUKI-SAN HAS BEEN GONE FOR A WHILE.
I WONDER IF IT WAS OKAY THAT I WAS SPOTTED IN HERE.
パタン
SHUT
SORRY TO KEEP YOU WAITING.
OH.
WAS EVERYTHING OKAY?
AYAMI ALREADY KNOWS, SO IT'S NO PROBLEM.
OH, I SEE.
That's good.
YEAH.
HERE GOES.

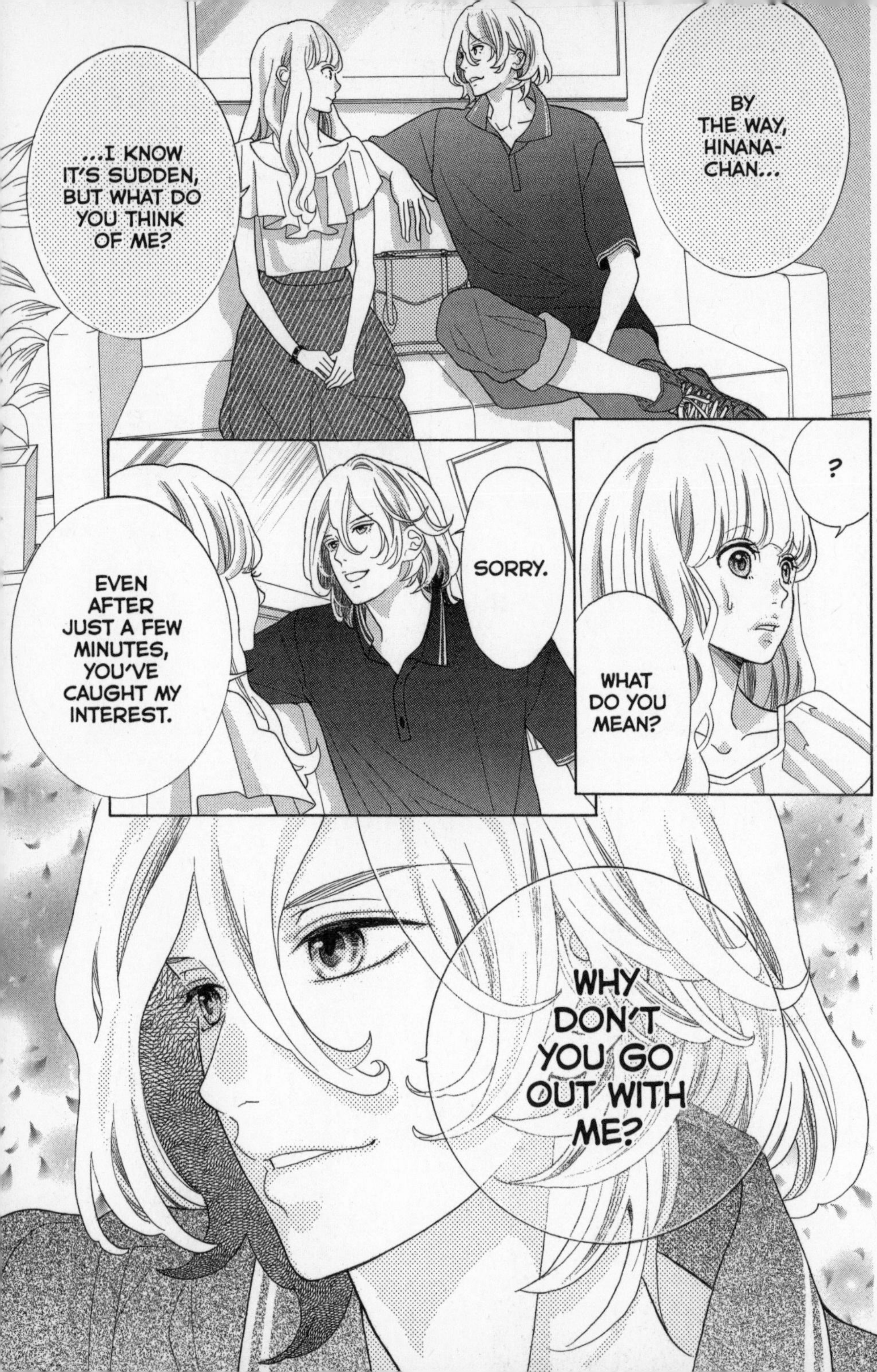
BY THE WAY, HINANA-CHAN...
...I KNOW IT'S SUDDEN, BUT WHAT DO YOU THINK OF ME?
?
WHAT DO YOU MEAN?
SORRY.
EVEN AFTER JUST A FEW MINUTES, YOU'VE CAUGHT MY INTEREST.
WHY DON'T YOU GO OUT WITH ME?

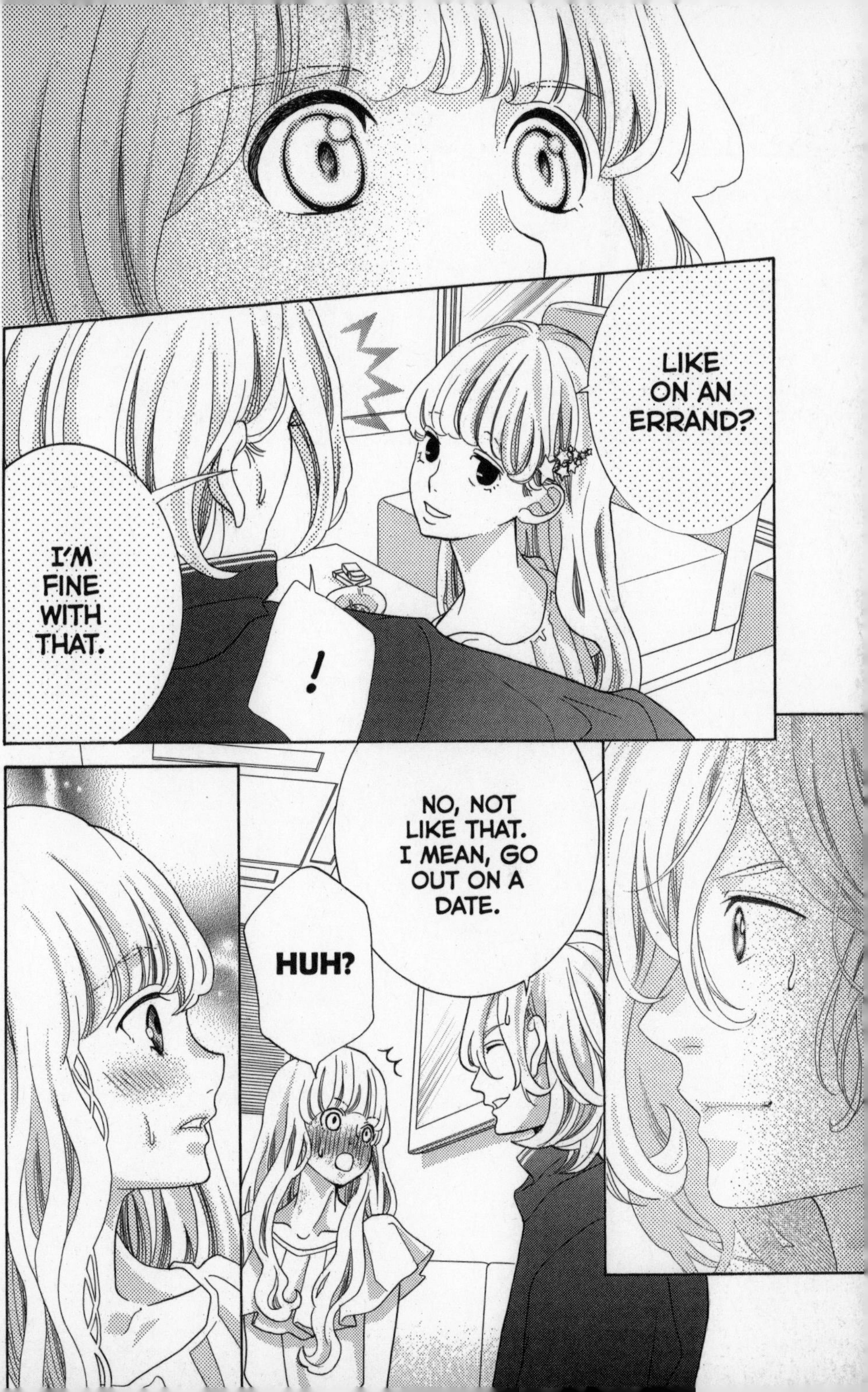
LIKE ON AN ERRAND?
I'M FINE WITH THAT.
!
NO, NOT LIKE THAT. I MEAN, GO OUT ON A DATE.
HUH?

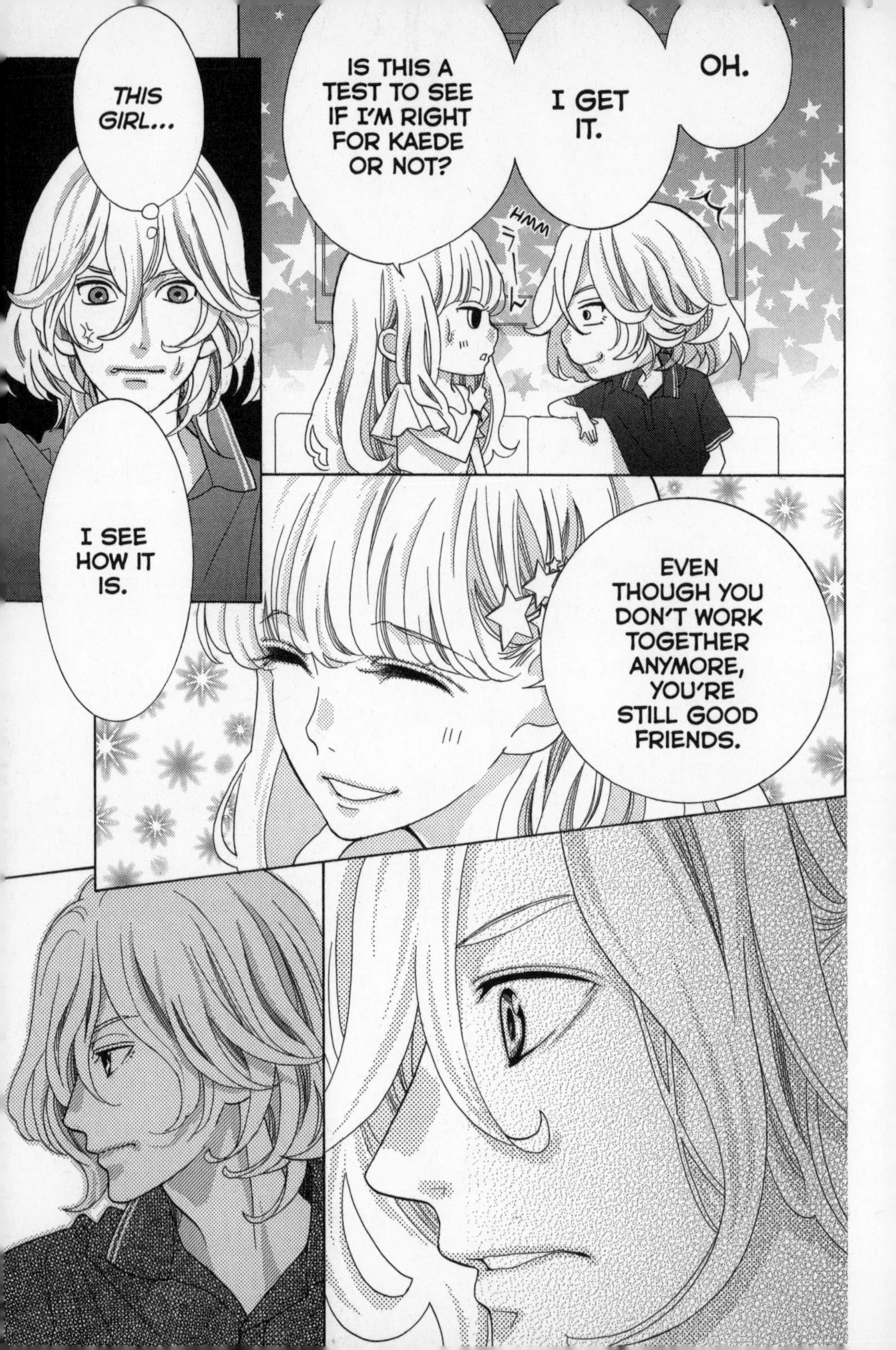
OH.
I GET IT.
IS THIS A TEST TO SEE IF I'M RIGHT FOR KAEDE OR NOT?
HMM
EVEN THOUGH YOU DON'T WORK TOGETHER ANYMORE, YOU'RE STILL GOOD FRIENDS.
THIS GIRL...
I SEE HOW IT IS.

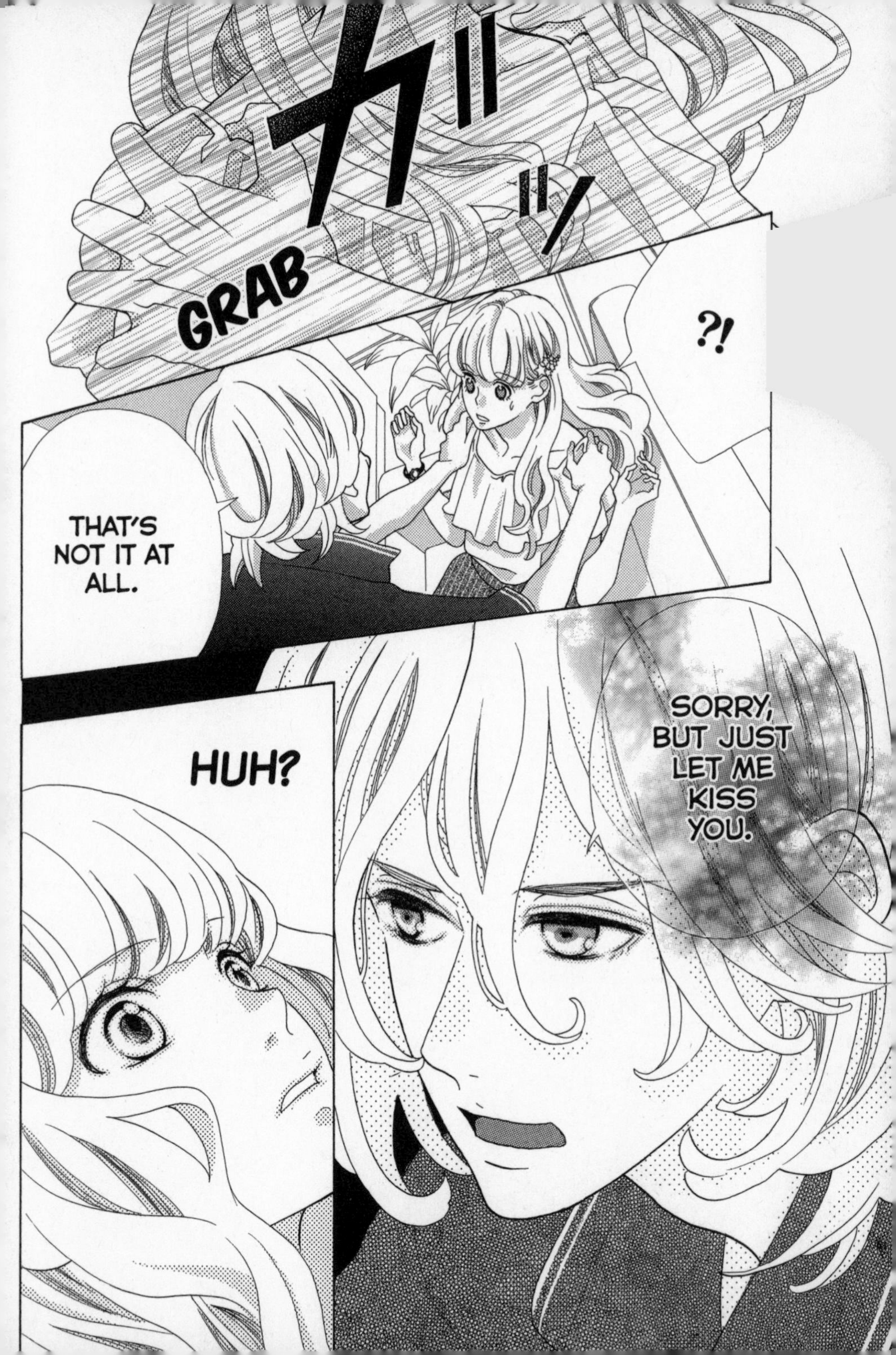
GRAB
?!
THAT'S NOT IT AT ALL.
HUH?
SORRY, BUT JUST LET ME KISS YOU.

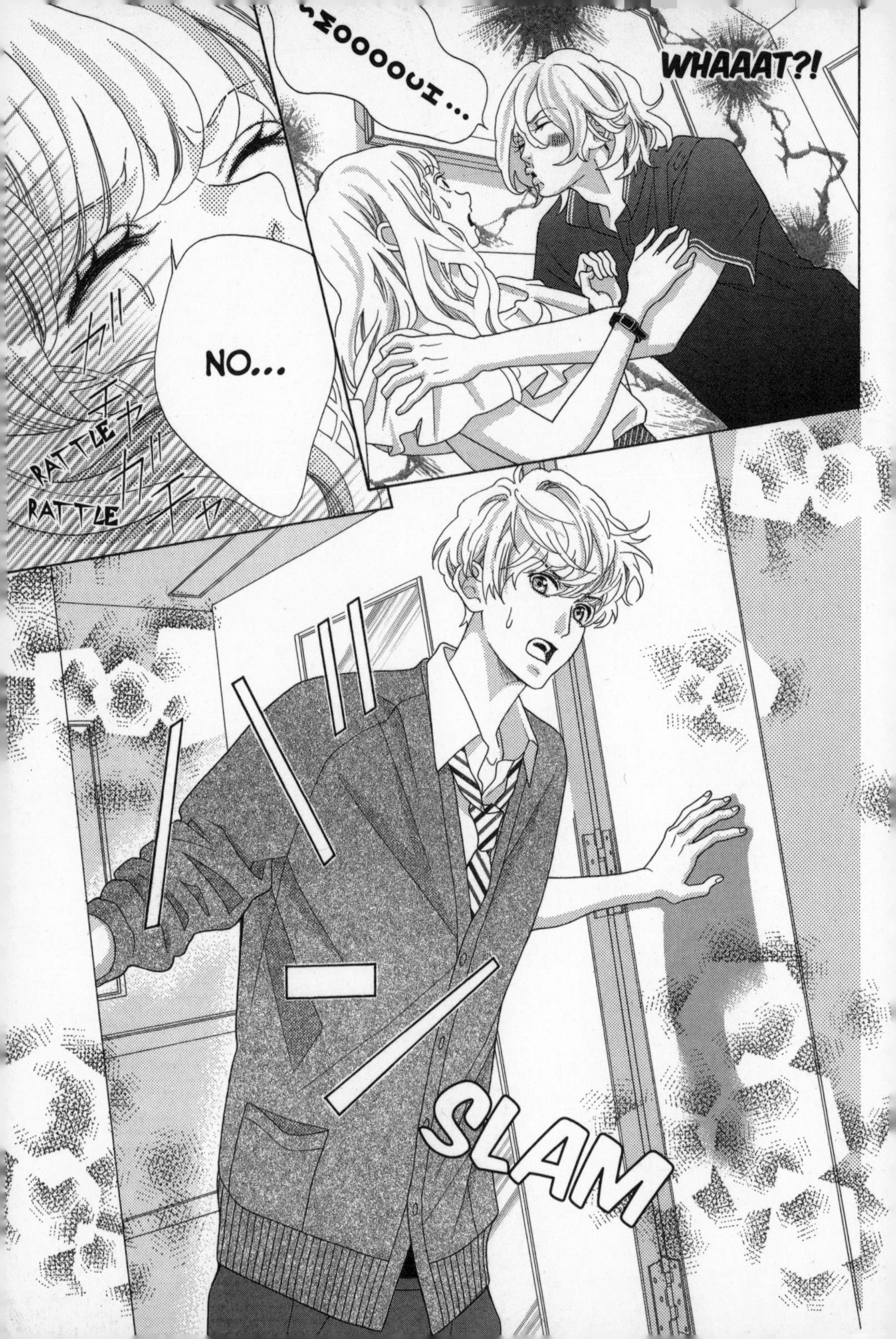
WHAAAT?!
SMOOOOCH...
NO...
RATTLE
RATTLE
SLAM

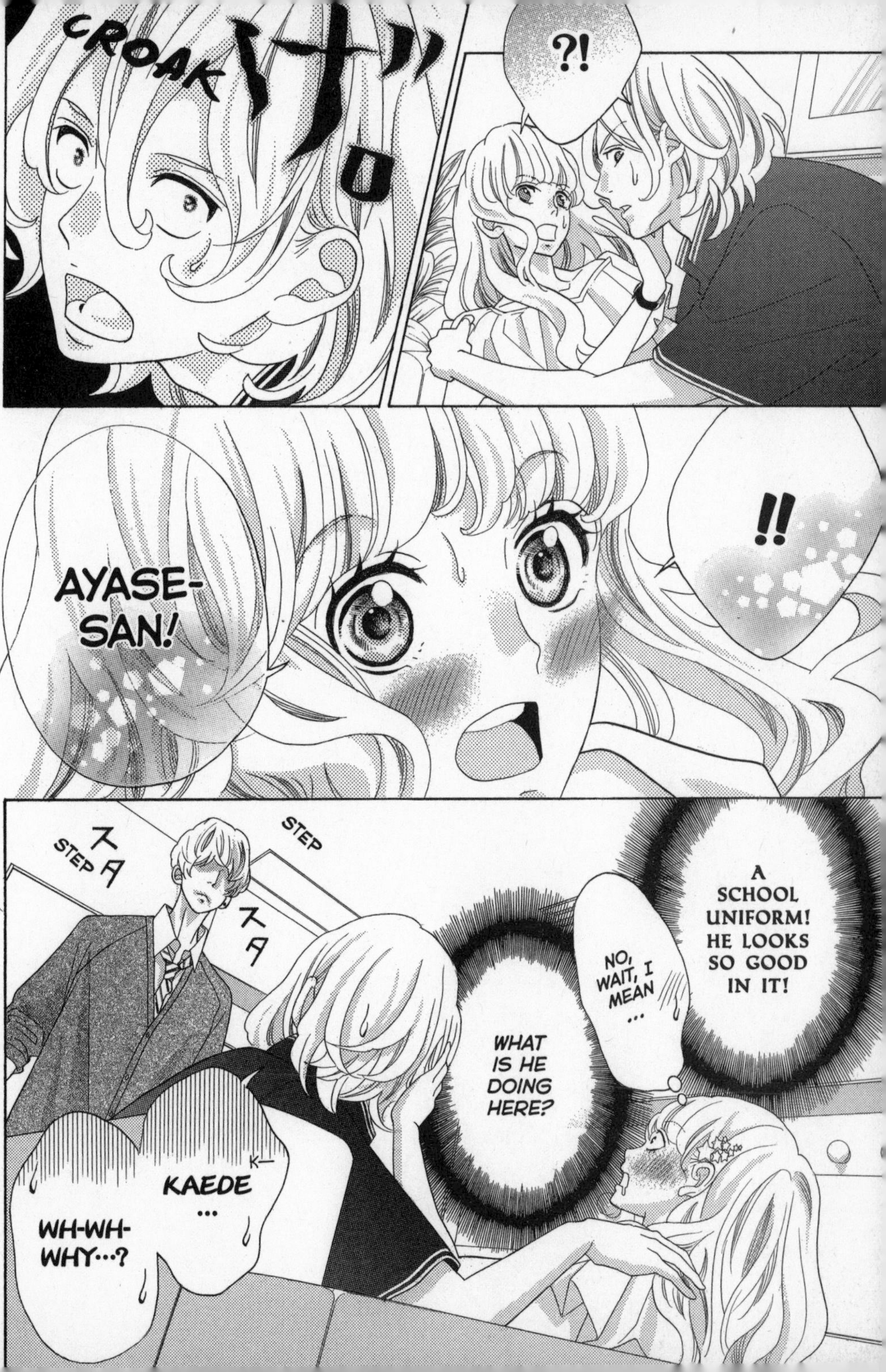
?!
CROAK
!!
AYASE-SAN!
STEP
STEP
A SCHOOL UNIFORM! HE LOOKS SO GOOD IN IT!
NO, WAIT, I MEAN ...
WHAT IS HE DOING HERE?
K—
KAEDE ...
WH-WH-WHY...?

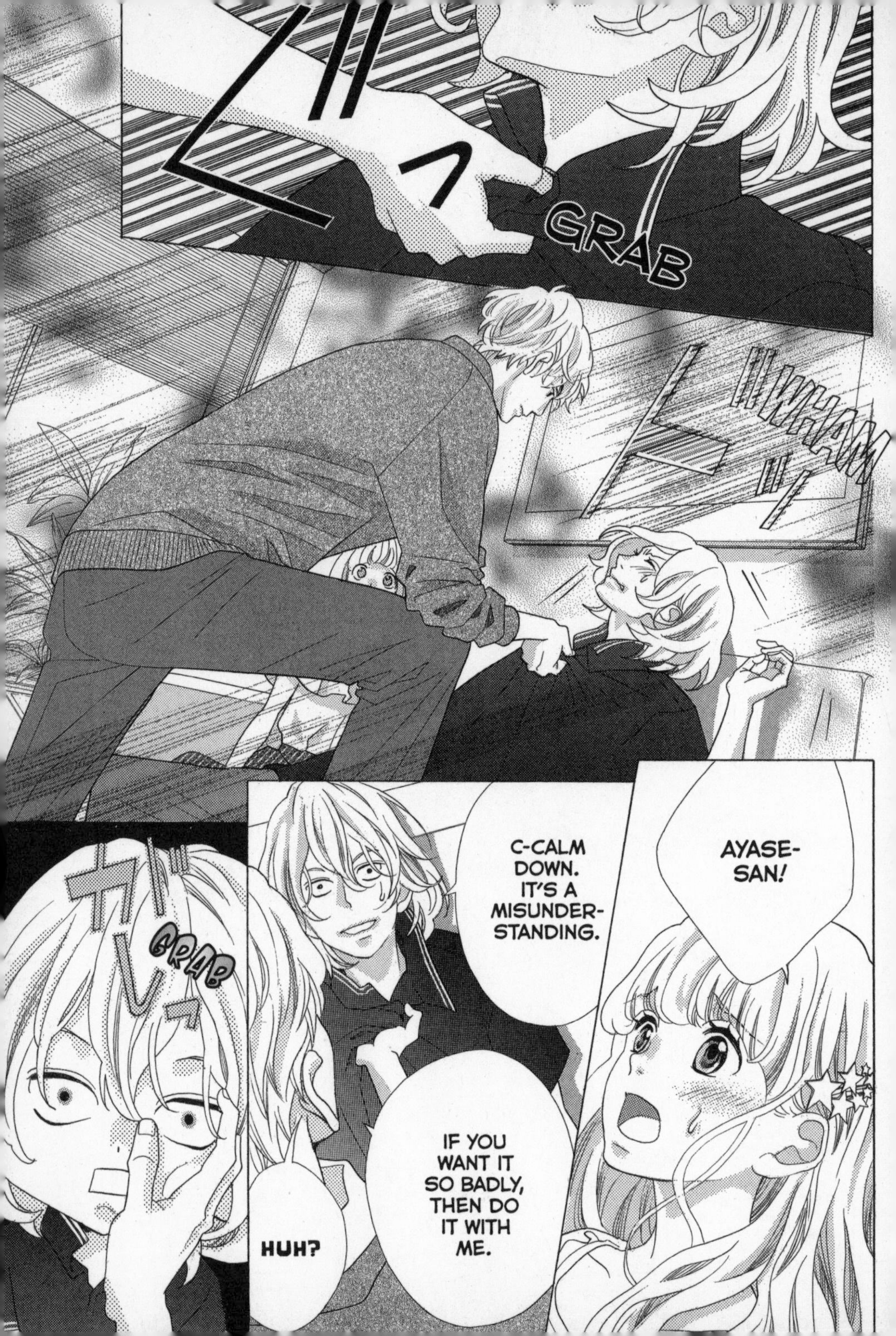
GRAB
AYASE-SAN!
C-CALM DOWN. IT'S A MISUNDERSTANDING.
IF YOU WANT IT SO BADLY, THEN DO IT WITH ME.
HUH?
GRAB

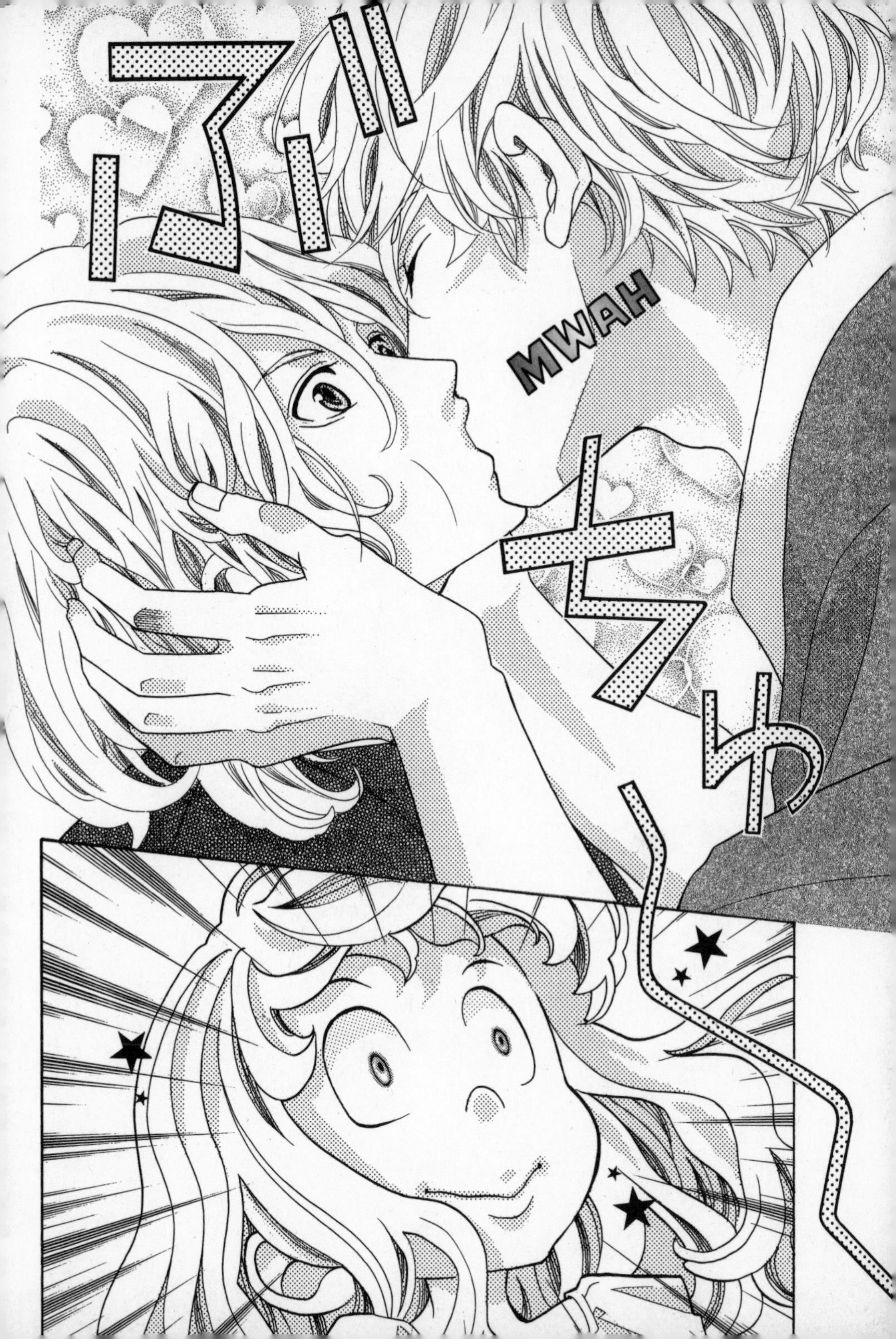
MWAH

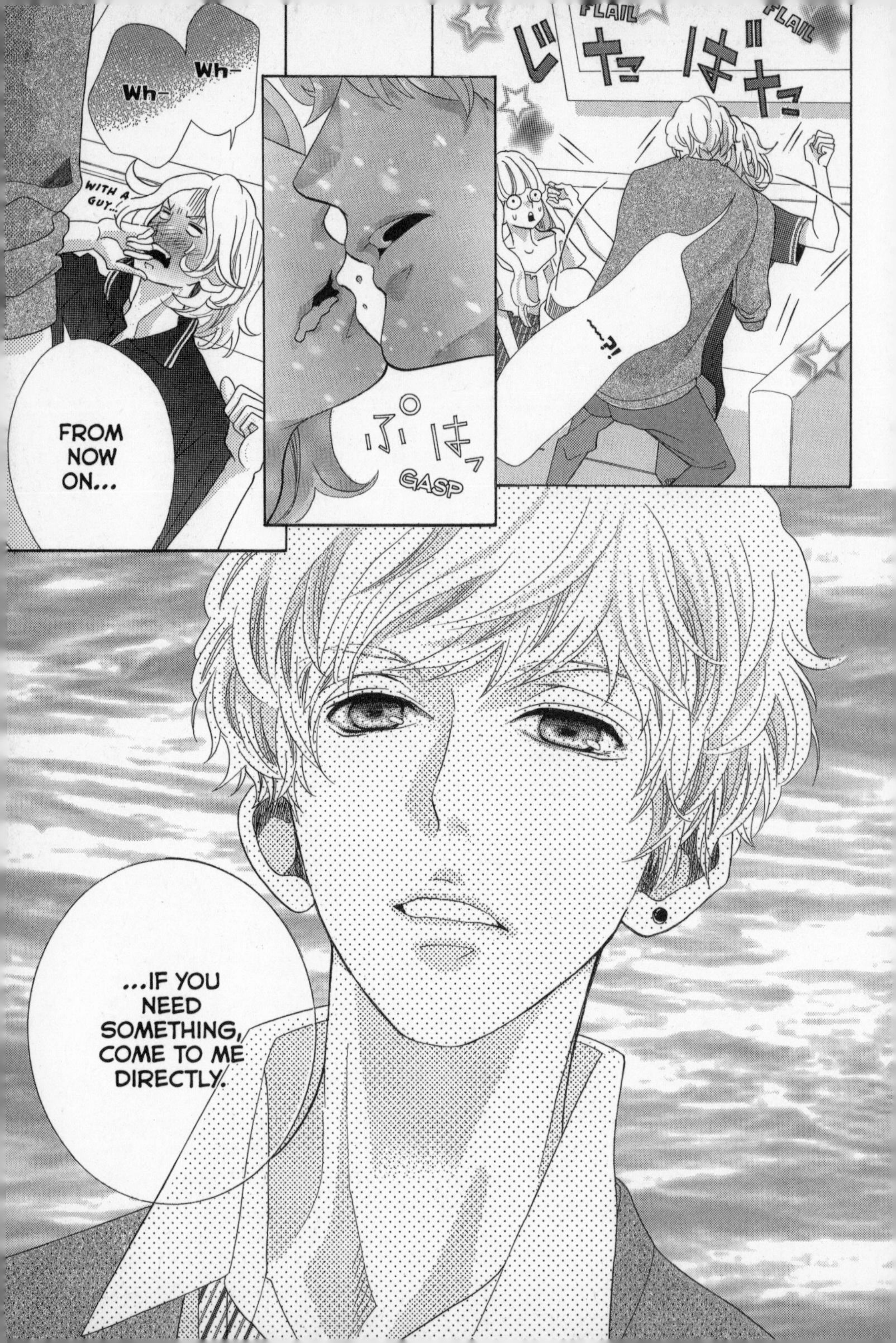
FLAIL
FLAIL
じたっ ばたっ
~~?!
ぷはっ
GASP
Wh-
Wh-
WITH A GUY...!
FROM NOW ON...
...IF YOU NEED SOMETHING, COME TO ME DIRECTLY.

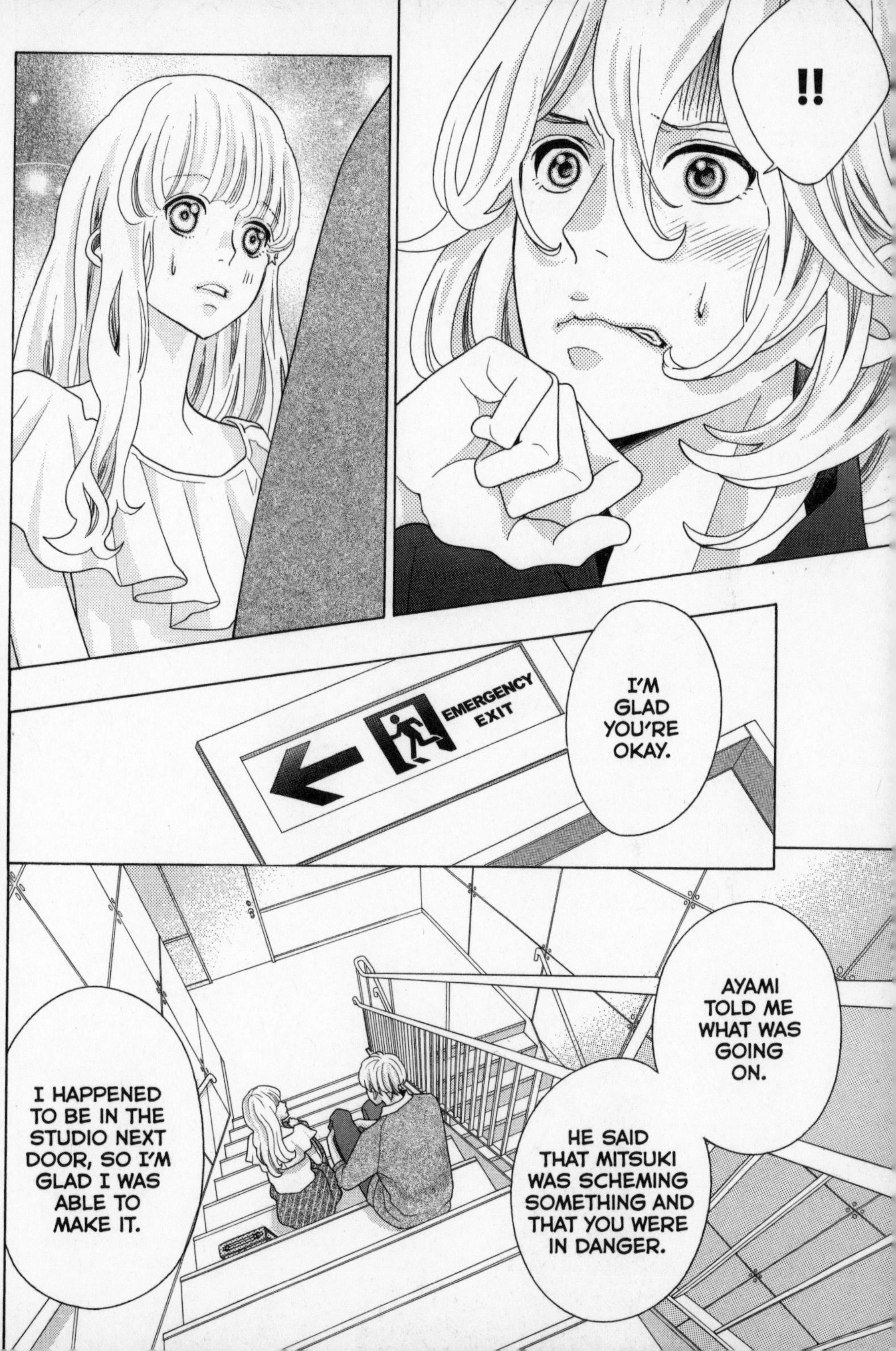
!!
EMERGENCY EXIT
I'M GLAD YOU'RE OKAY.
AYAMI TOLD ME WHAT WAS GOING ON.
HE SAID THAT MITSUKI WAS SCHEMING SOMETHING AND THAT YOU WERE IN DANGER.
I HAPPENED TO BE IN THE STUDIO NEXT DOOR, SO I'M GLAD I WAS ABLE TO MAKE IT.

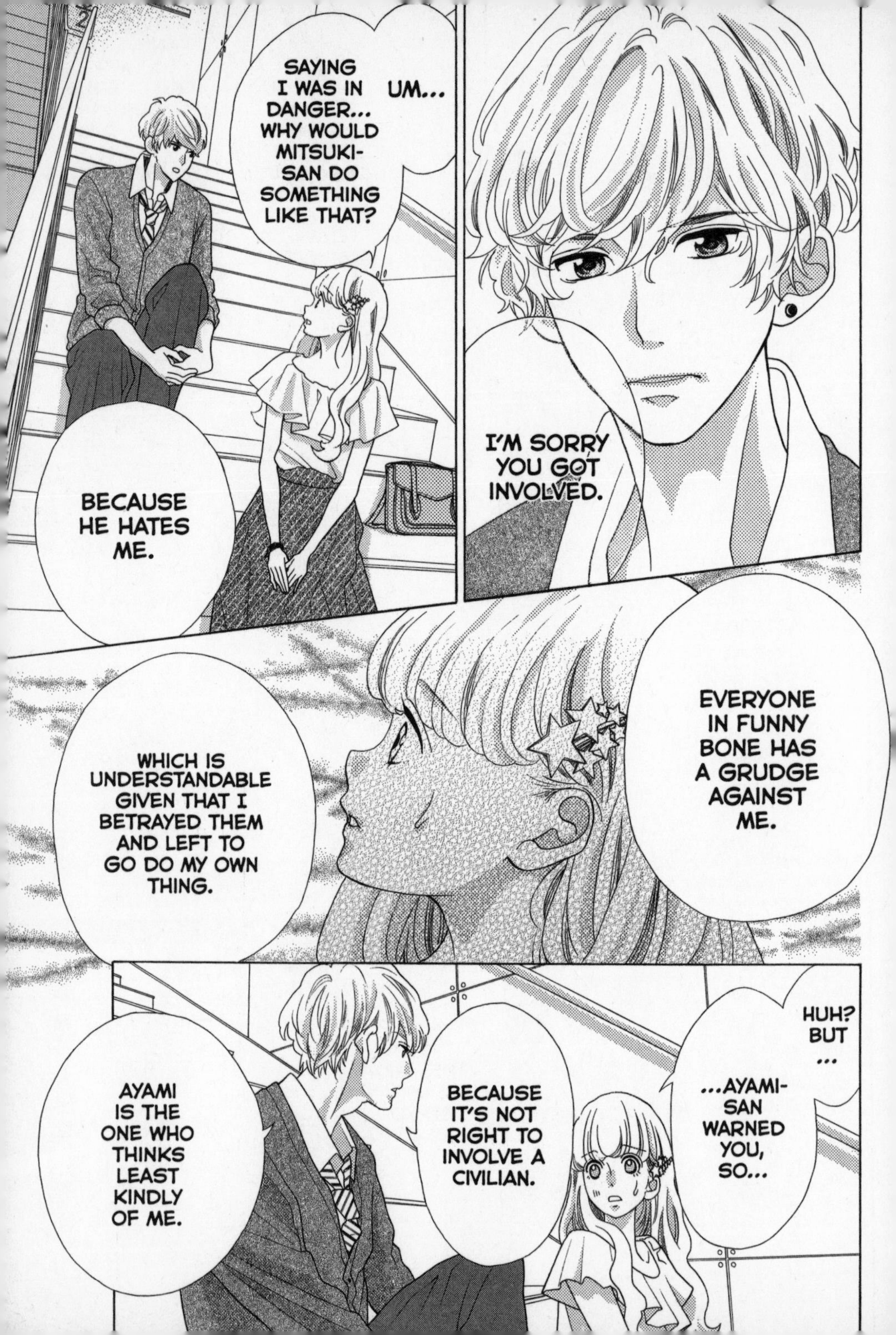
I'M SORRY YOU GOT INVOLVED.
UM...
SAYING I WAS IN DANGER... WHY WOULD MITSUKI-SAN DO SOMETHING LIKE THAT?
BECAUSE HE HATES ME.
EVERYONE IN FUNNY BONE HAS A GRUDGE AGAINST ME.
WHICH IS UNDERSTANDABLE GIVEN THAT I BETRAYED THEM AND LEFT TO GO DO MY OWN THING.
HUH? BUT ...
...AYAMI-SAN WARNED YOU, SO...
BECAUSE IT'S NOT RIGHT TO INVOLVE A CIVILIAN.
AYAMI IS THE ONE WHO THINKS LEAST KINDLY OF ME.

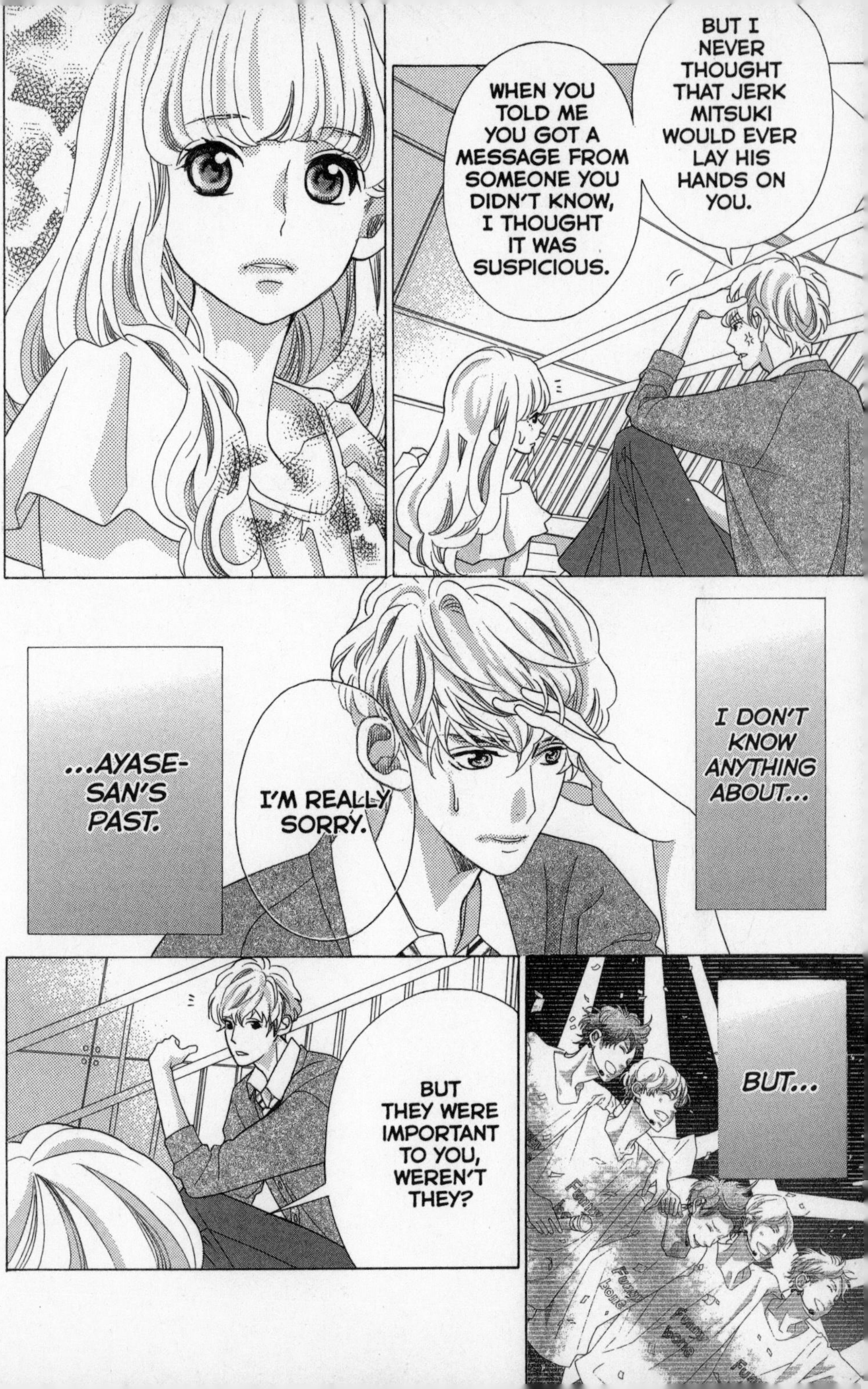
WHEN YOU TOLD ME YOU GOT A MESSAGE FROM SOMEONE YOU DIDN'T KNOW, I THOUGHT IT WAS SUSPICIOUS.
BUT I NEVER THOUGHT THAT JERK MITSUKI WOULD EVER LAY HIS HANDS ON YOU.
I DON'T KNOW ANYTHING ABOUT...
...AYASE-SAN'S PAST.
I'M REALLY SORRY.
BUT...
BUT THEY WERE IMPORTANT TO YOU, WEREN'T THEY?

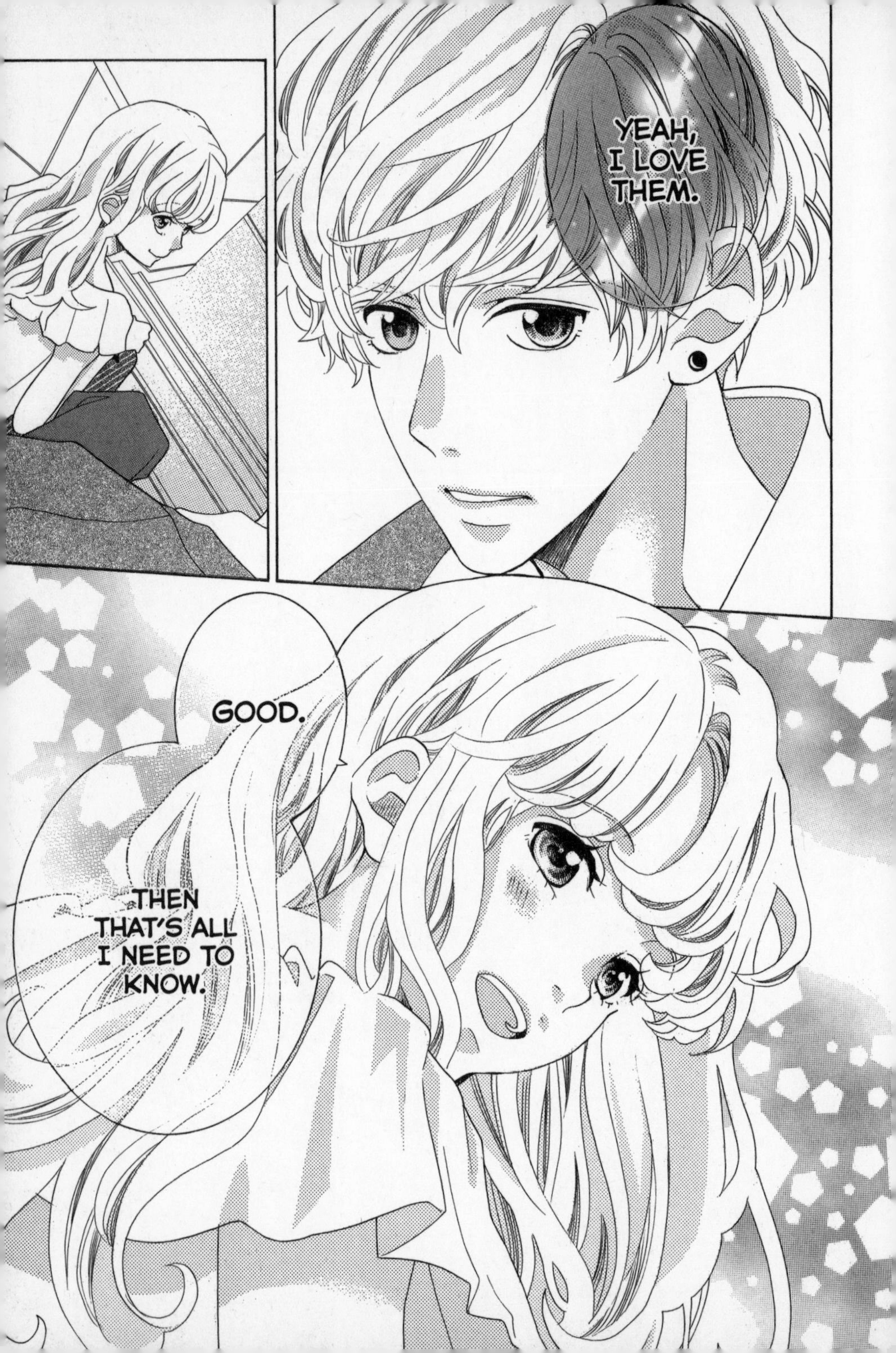
YEAH, I LOVE THEM.
GOOD.
THEN THAT'S ALL I NEED TO KNOW.

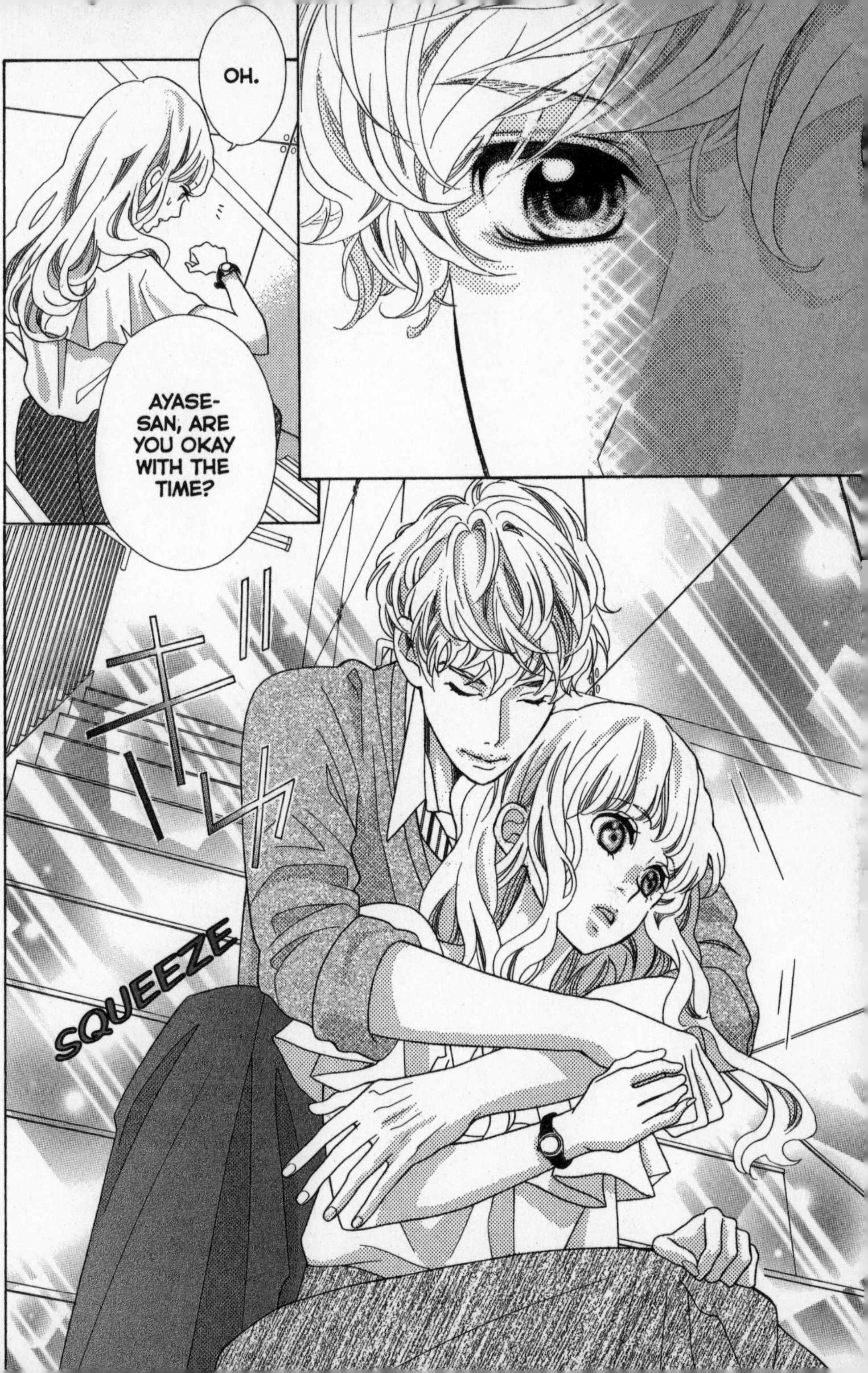
OH.
AYASE-SAN, ARE YOU OKAY WITH THE TIME?
SQUEEZE

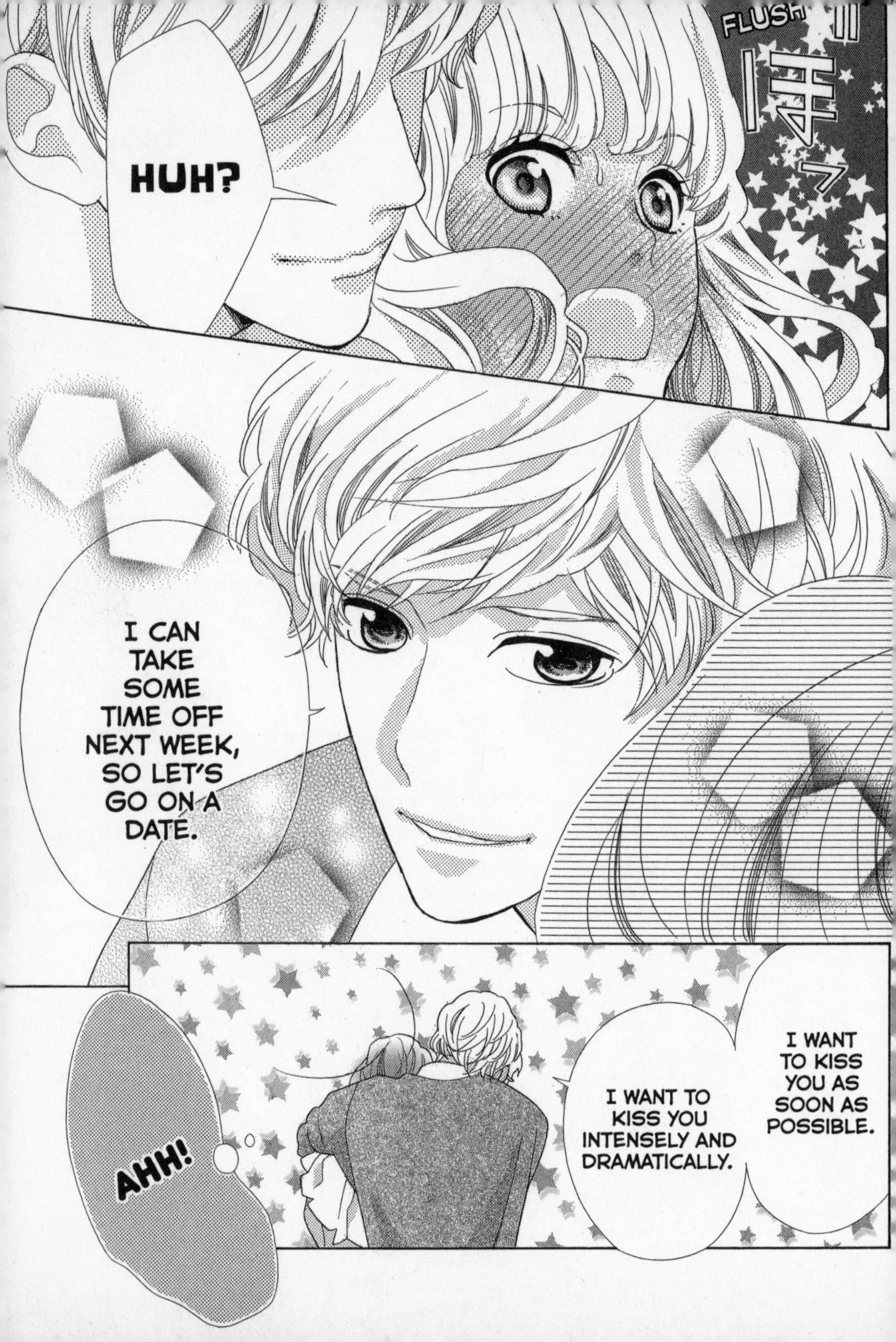
FLUSH
HUH?
I CAN TAKE SOME TIME OFF NEXT WEEK, SO LET'S GO ON A DATE.
I WANT TO KISS YOU AS SOON AS POSSIBLE.
I WANT TO KISS YOU INTENSELY AND DRAMATICALLY.
AHH!

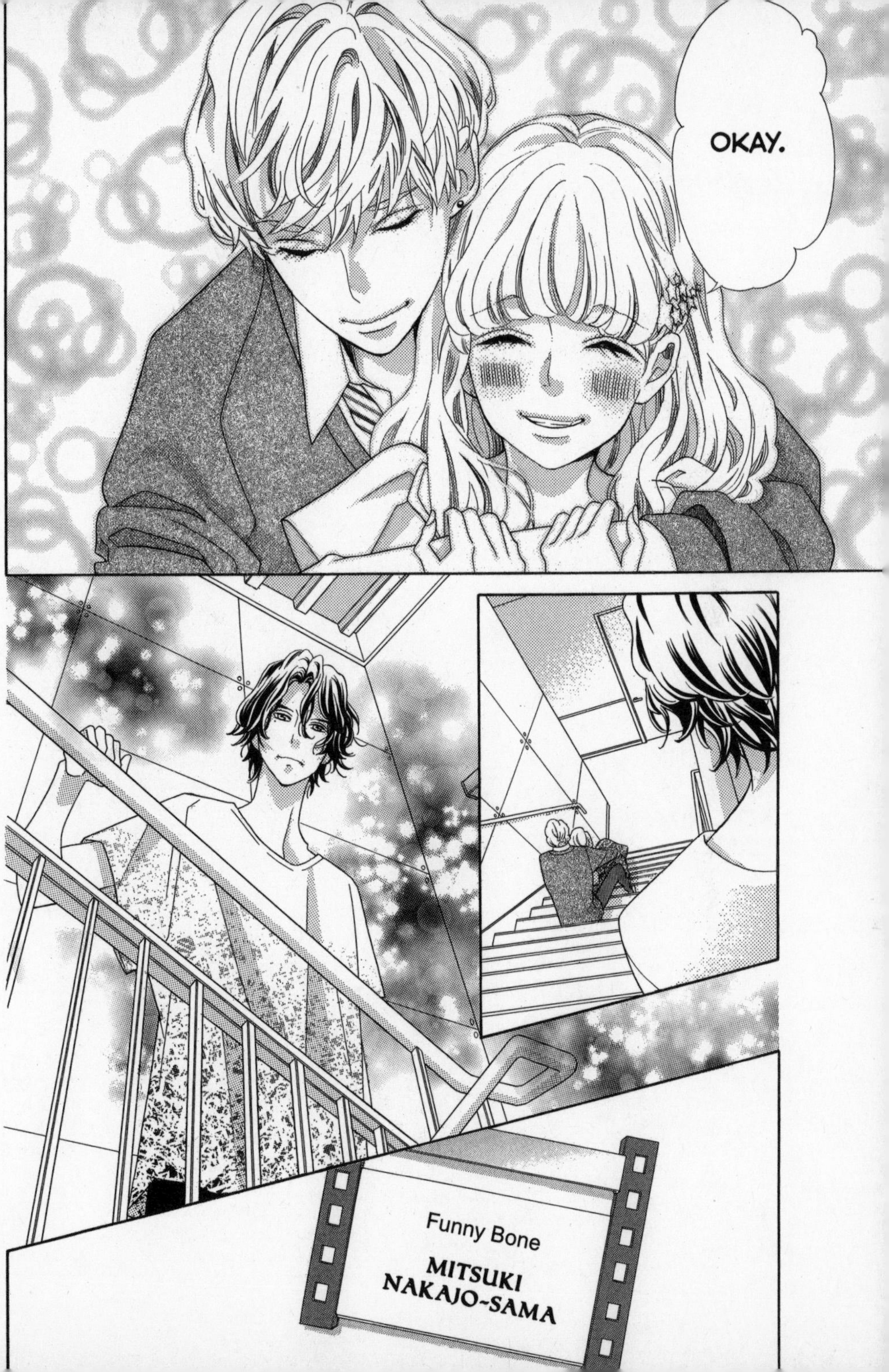
OKAY.
Funny Bone
MITSUKI NAKAJO-SAMA

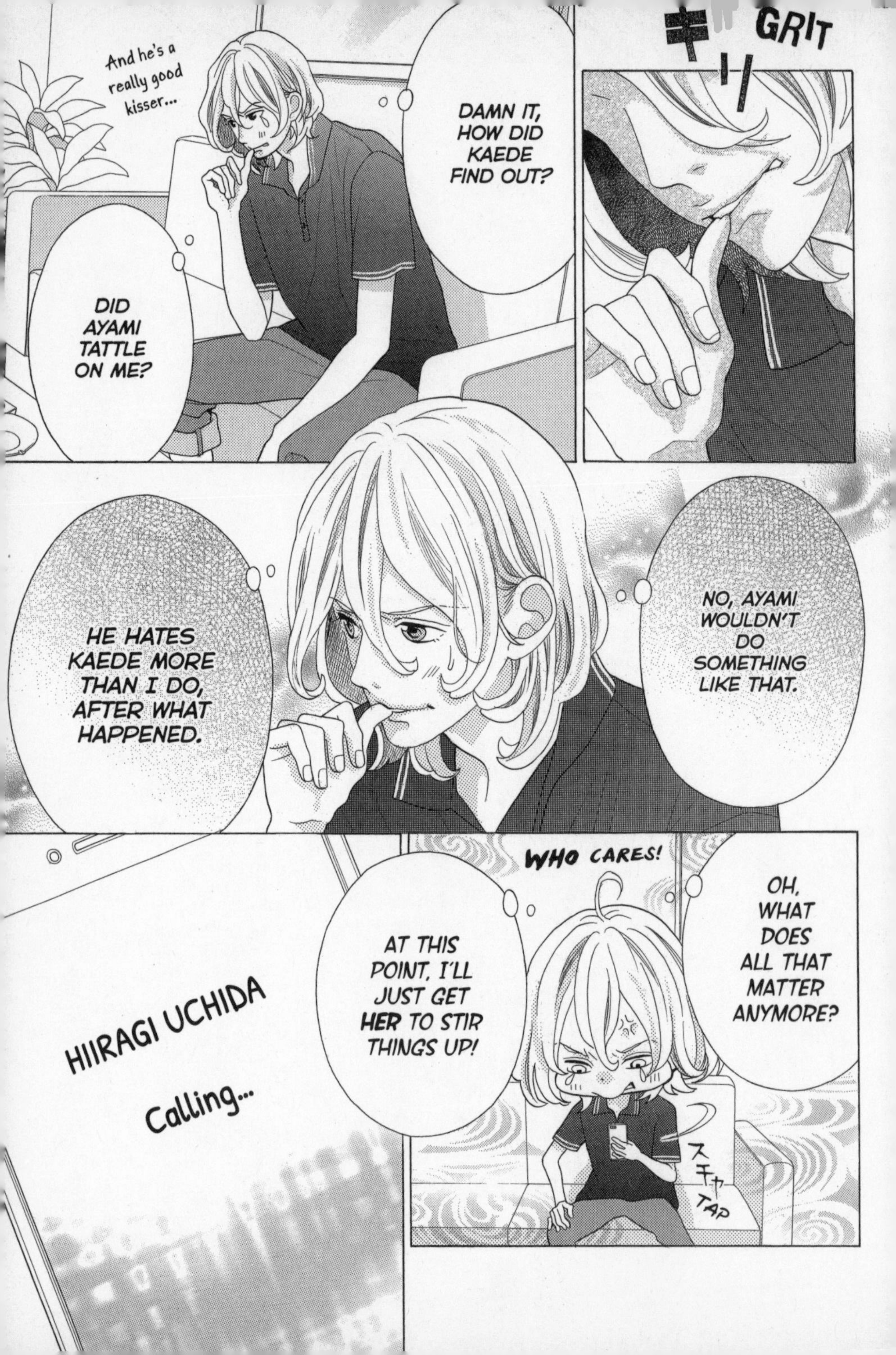
キリ
GRIT
DAMN IT, HOW DID KAEDE FIND OUT?
And he's a really good kisser...
DID AYAMI TATTLE ON ME?
NO, AYAMI WOULDN'T DO SOMETHING LIKE THAT.
HE HATES KAEDE MORE THAN I DO, AFTER WHAT HAPPENED.
OH, WHAT DOES ALL THAT MATTER ANYMORE?
WHO CARES!
AT THIS POINT, I'LL JUST GET **HER** TO STIR THINGS UP!
スチャ
TAP
HIIRAGI UCHIDA
Calling...

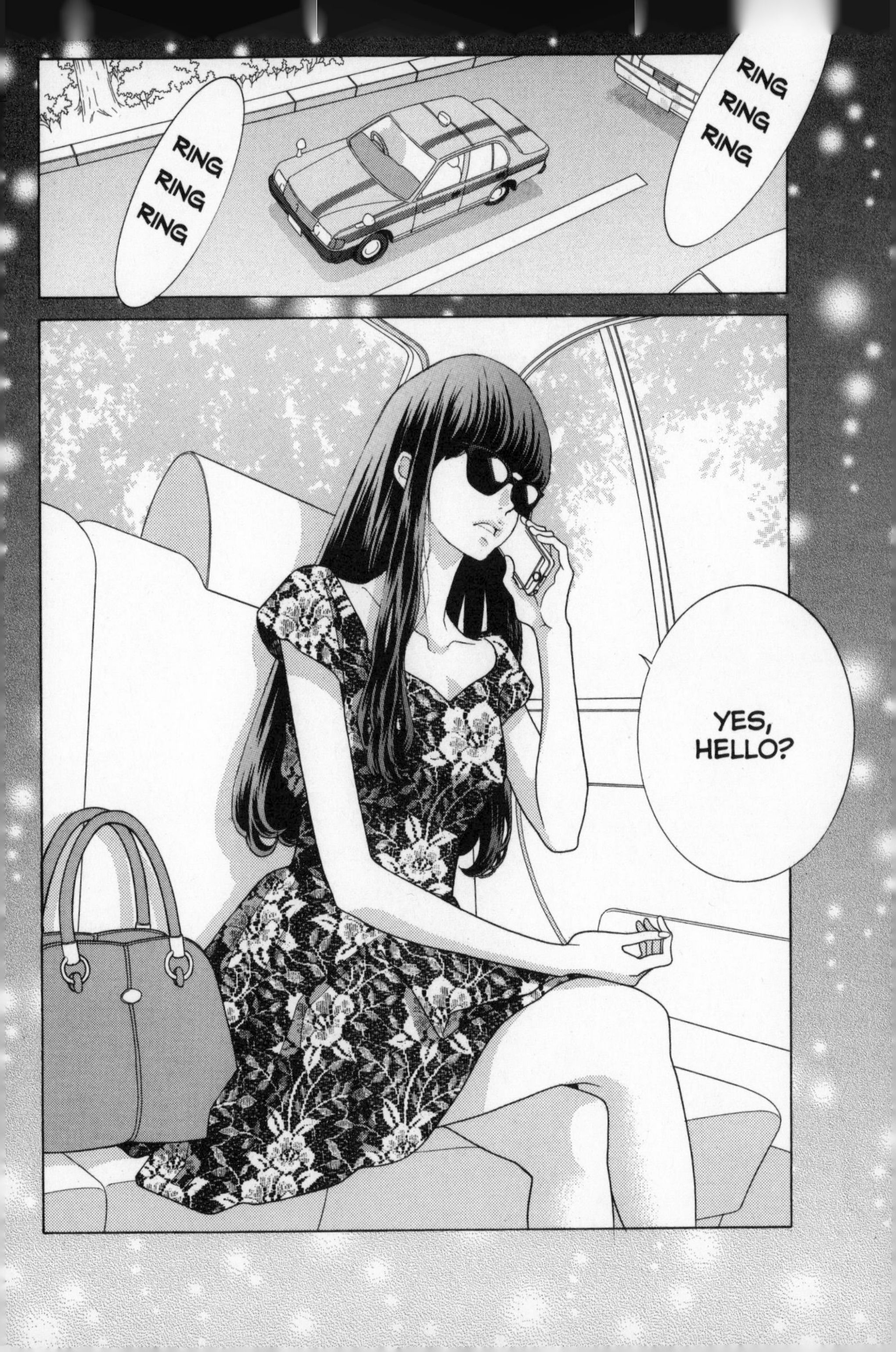
RING RING RING
RING RING RING
YES, HELLO?

TO BE CONTINUED IN
KISS ME AT THE STROKE OF MIDNIGHT
VOLUME 4

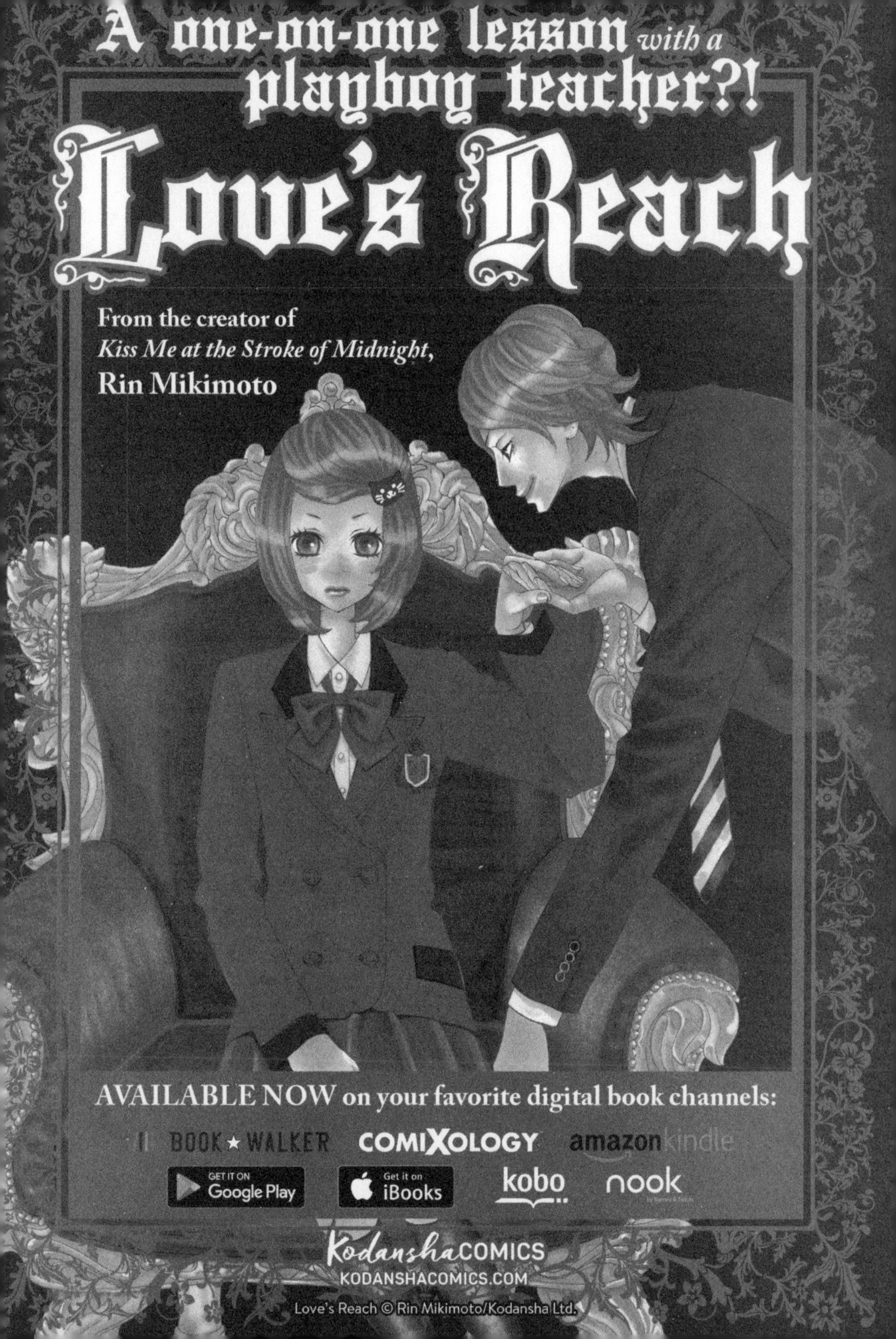
A one-on-one lesson with a playboy teacher?!
Love's Reach
From the creator of
Kiss Me at the Stroke of Midnight,
Rin Mikimoto
AVAILABLE NOW on your favorite digital book channels:
BOOK★WALKER
comiXology
amazon kindle
GET IT ON Google Play
Get it on iBooks
kobo
nook
Kodansha COMICS
KODANSHACOMICS.COM
Love's Reach © Rin Mikimoto/Kodansha Ltd.

Love's Reach

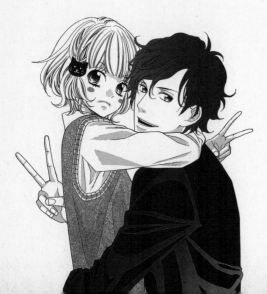

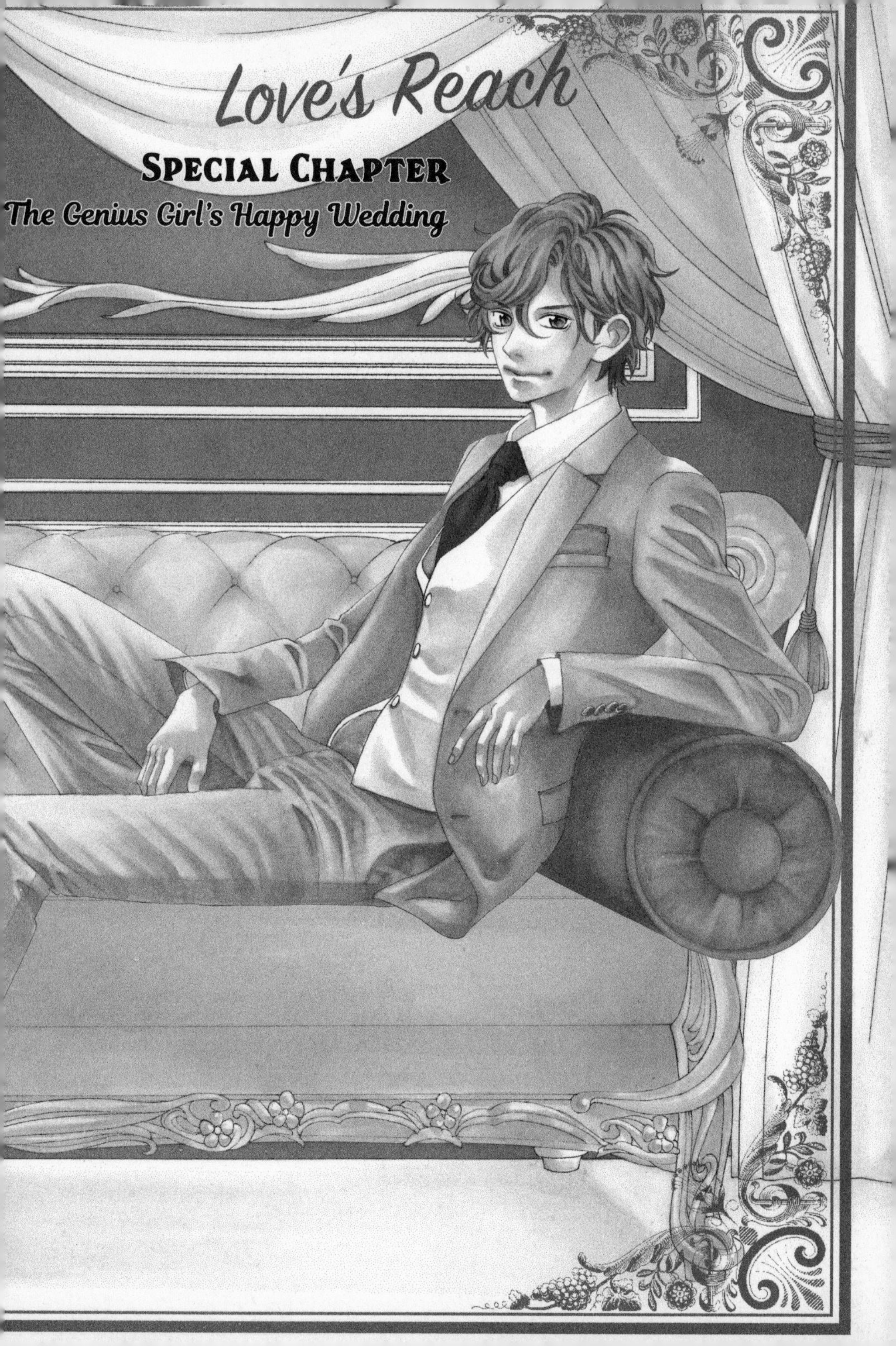
Love's Reach
Special Chapter
The Genius Girl's Happy Wedding

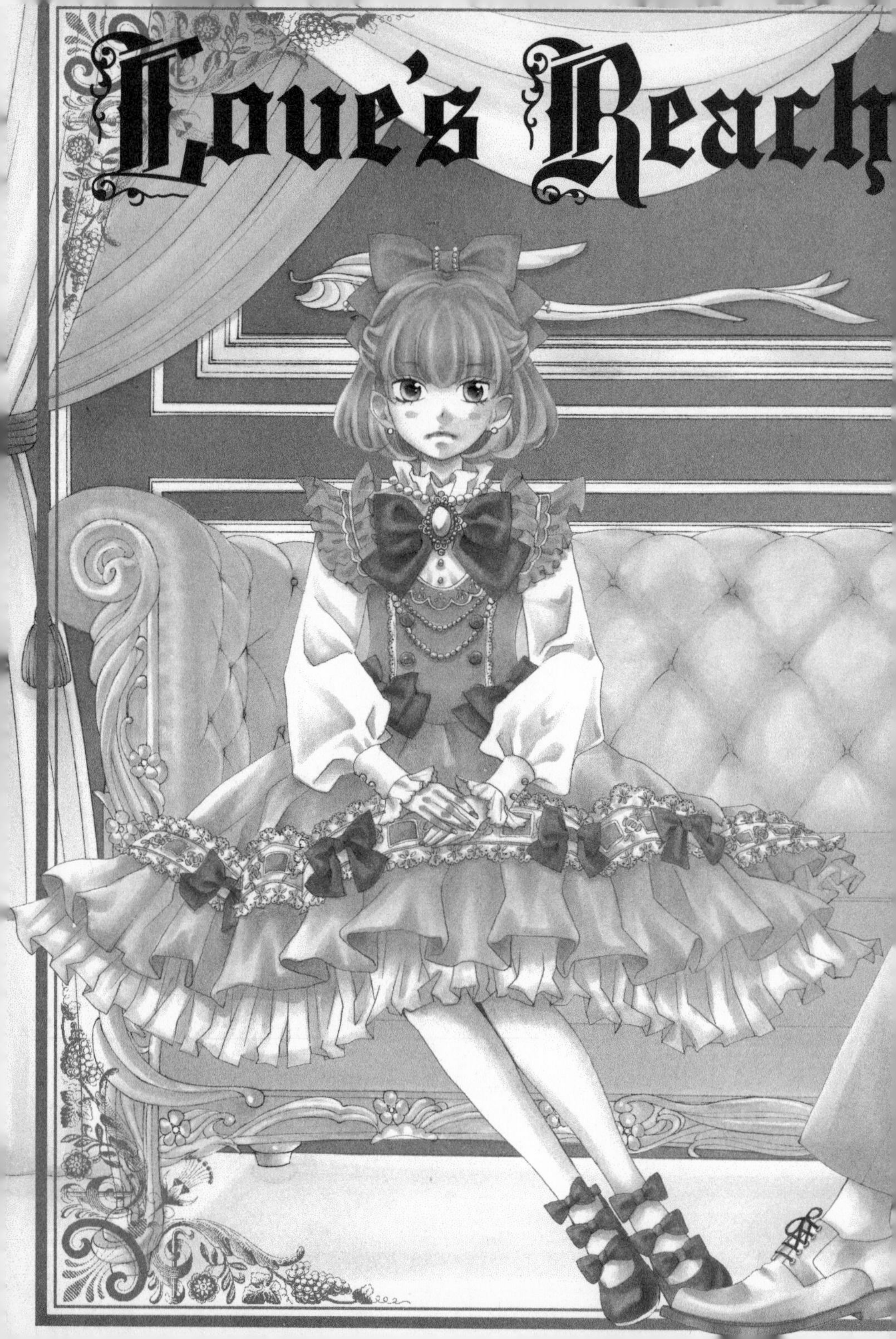
Love's Reach

Love's Reach

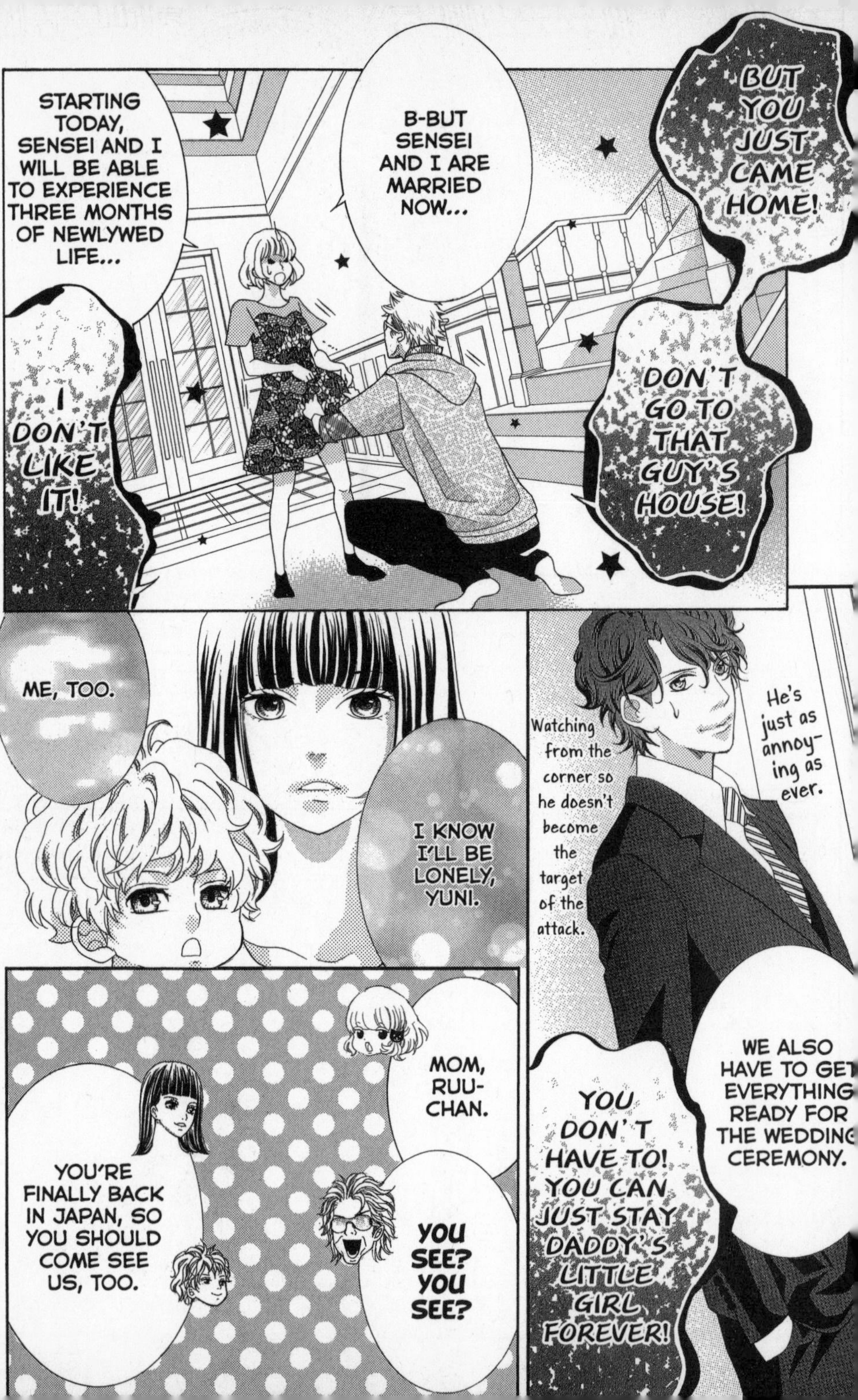
BUT YOU JUST CAME HOME!
DON'T GO TO THAT GUY'S HOUSE!
B-BUT SENSEI AND I ARE MARRIED NOW...
STARTING TODAY, SENSEI AND I WILL BE ABLE TO EXPERIENCE THREE MONTHS OF NEWLYWED LIFE...
I DON'T LIKE IT!
He's just as annoy-ing as ever.
Watching from the corner so he doesn't become the target of the attack.
WE ALSO HAVE TO GET EVERYTHING READY FOR THE WEDDING CEREMONY.
YOU DON'T HAVE TO! YOU CAN JUST STAY DADDY'S LITTLE GIRL FOREVER!
I KNOW I'LL BE LONELY, YUNI.
ME, TOO.
MOM, RUU-CHAN.
YOU SEE? YOU SEE?
YOU'RE FINALLY BACK IN JAPAN, SO YOU SHOULD COME SEE US, TOO.

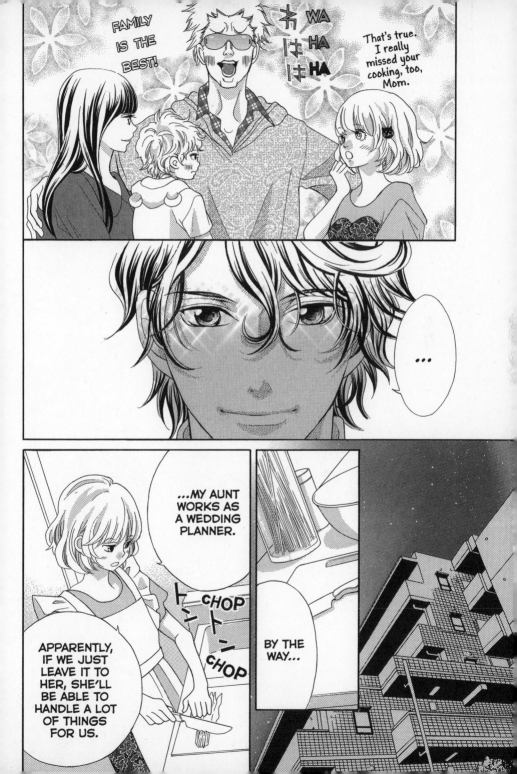

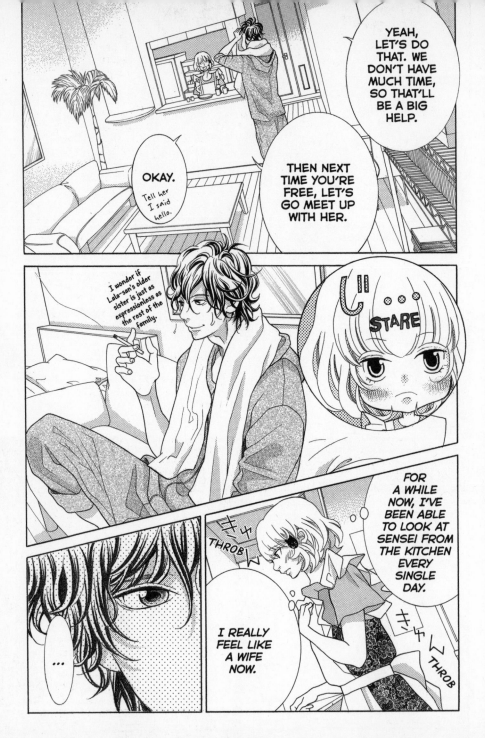

- 147 -

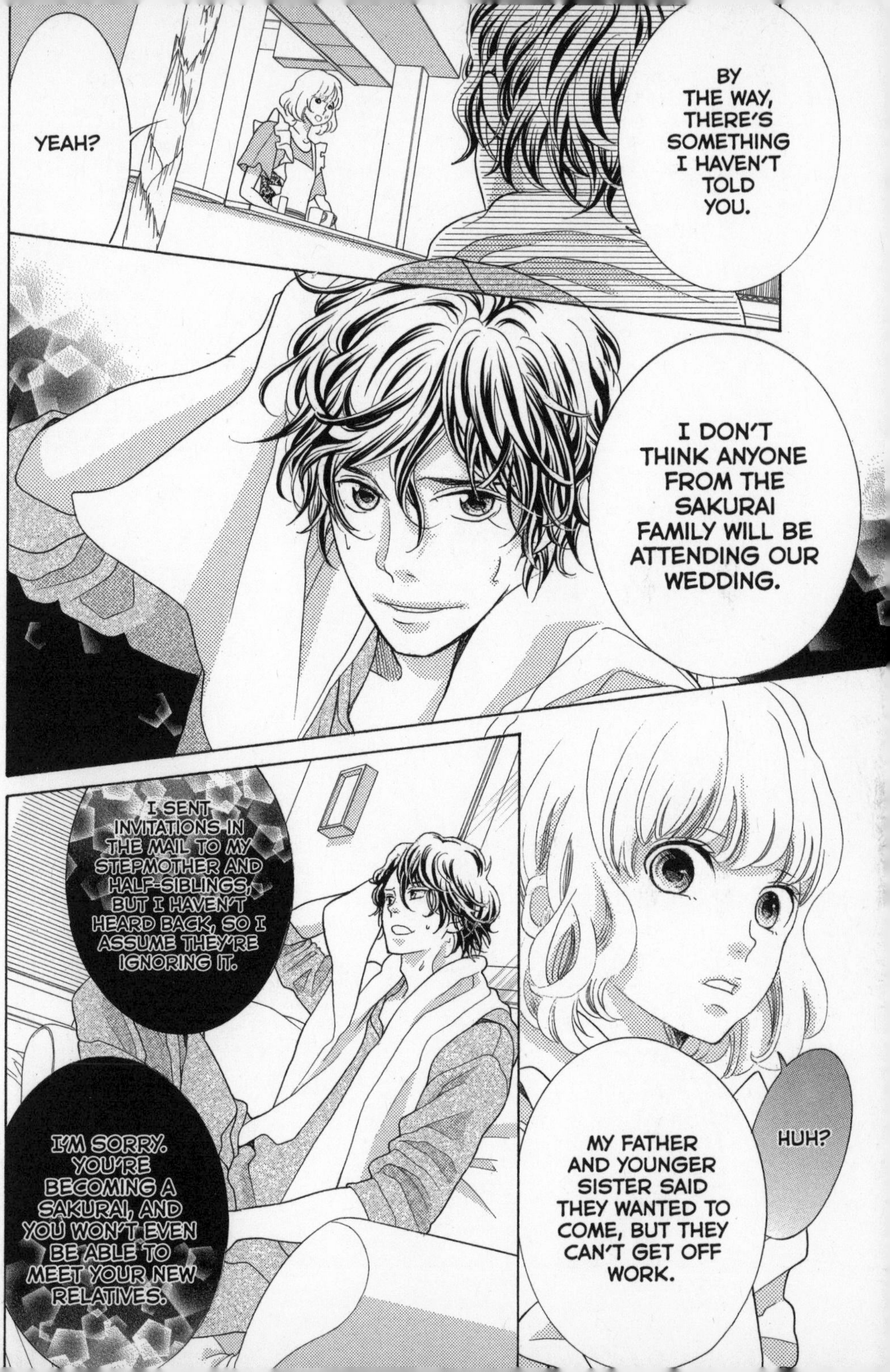
BY THE WAY, THERE'S SOMETHING I HAVEN'T TOLD YOU.
YEAH?
I DON'T THINK ANYONE FROM THE SAKURAI FAMILY WILL BE ATTENDING OUR WEDDING.
HUH?
MY FATHER AND YOUNGER SISTER SAID THEY WANTED TO COME, BUT THEY CAN'T GET OFF WORK.
I SENT INVITATIONS IN THE MAIL TO MY STEPMOTHER AND HALF-SIBLINGS, BUT I HAVEN'T HEARD BACK, SO I ASSUME THEY'RE IGNORING IT.
I'M SORRY. YOU'RE BECOMING A SAKURAI, AND YOU WON'T EVEN BE ABLE TO MEET YOUR NEW RELATIVES.

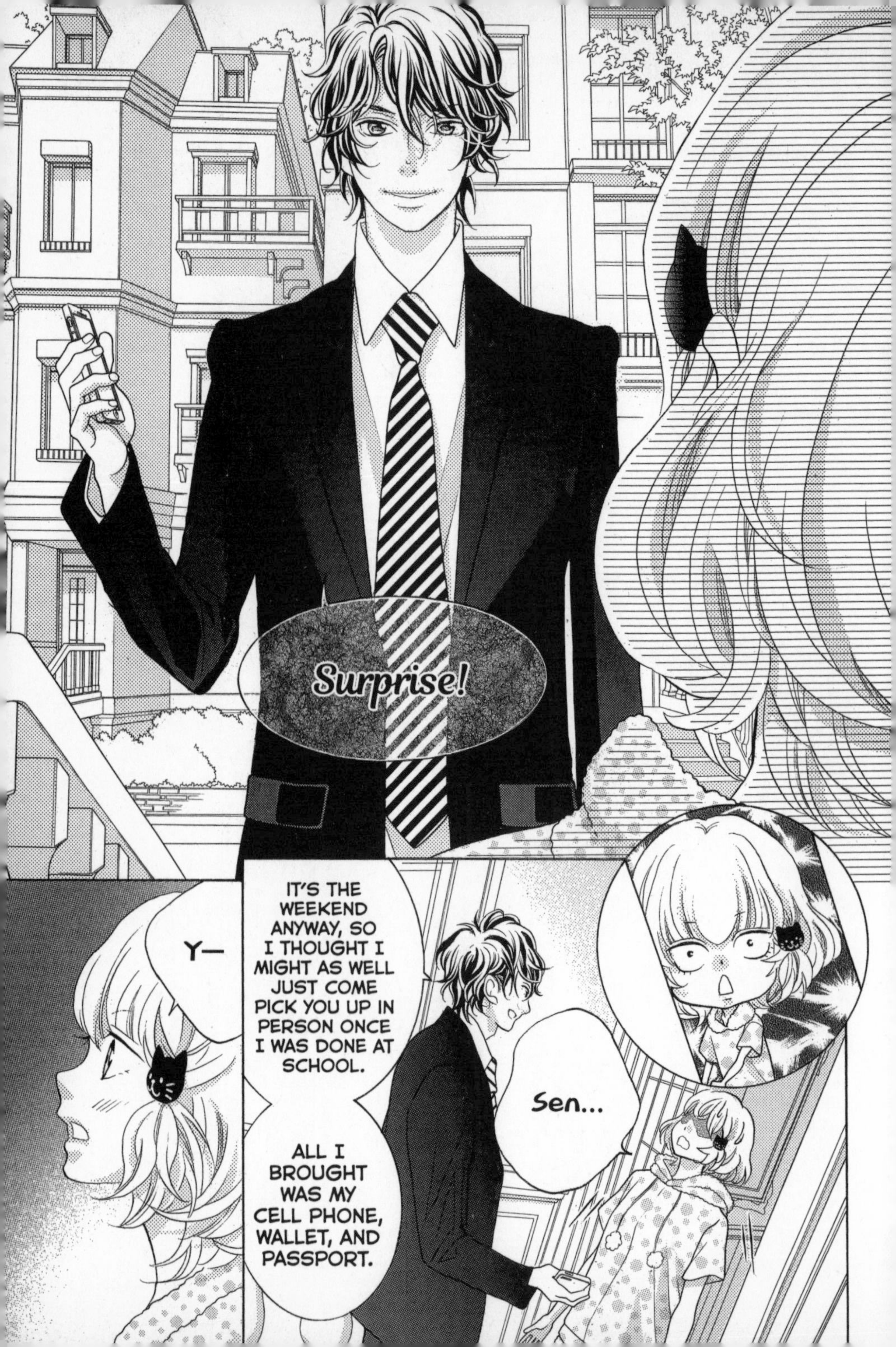
Surprise!
Sen...
IT'S THE WEEKEND ANYWAY, SO I THOUGHT I MIGHT AS WELL JUST COME PICK YOU UP IN PERSON ONCE I WAS DONE AT SCHOOL.
ALL I BROUGHT WAS MY CELL PHONE, WALLET, AND PASSPORT.
Y—

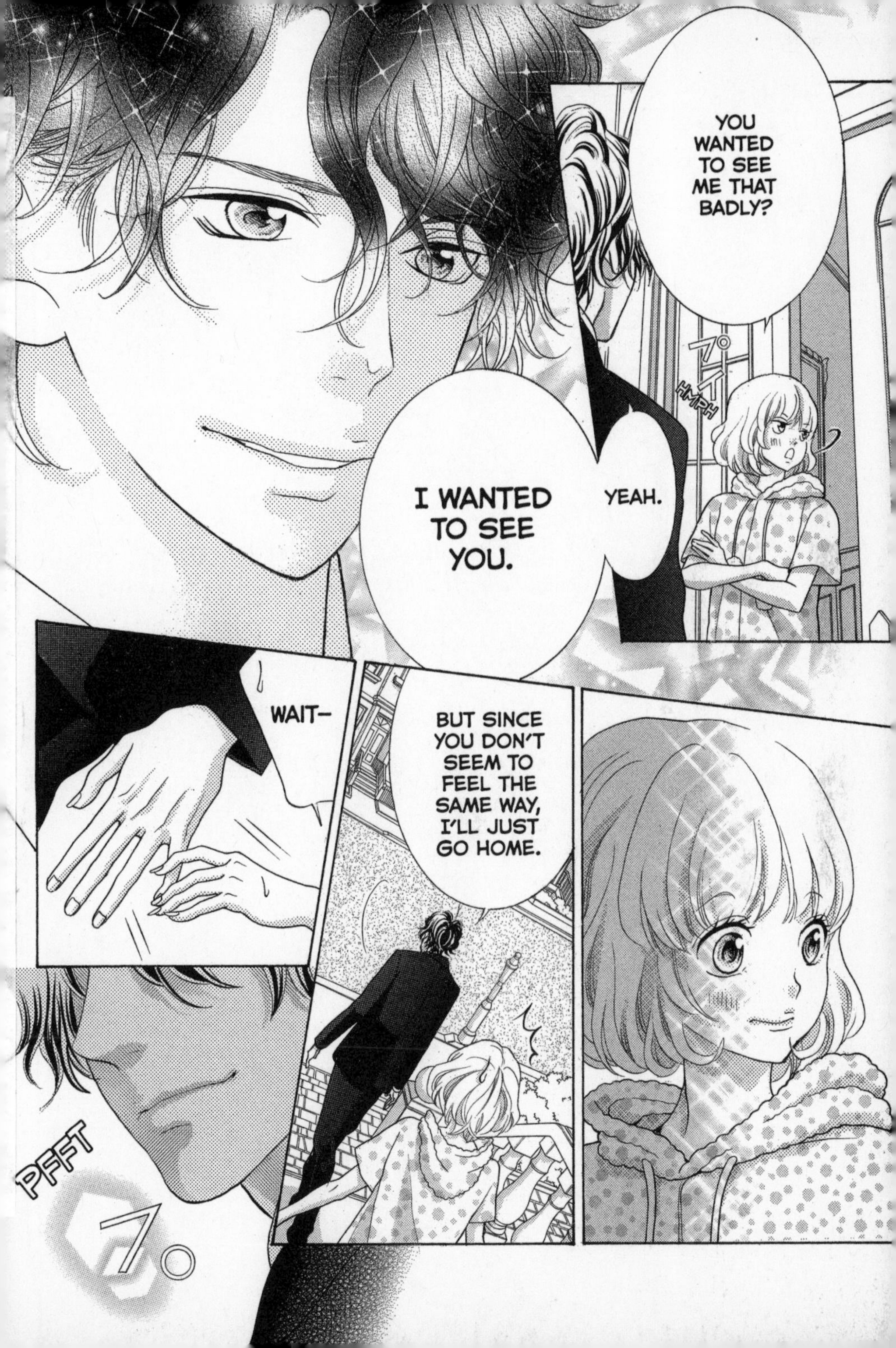
YOU WANTED TO SEE ME THAT BADLY?
HMPH
YEAH.
I WANTED TO SEE YOU.
BUT SINCE YOU DON'T SEEM TO FEEL THE SAME WAY, I'LL JUST GO HOME.
WAIT–
PFFT

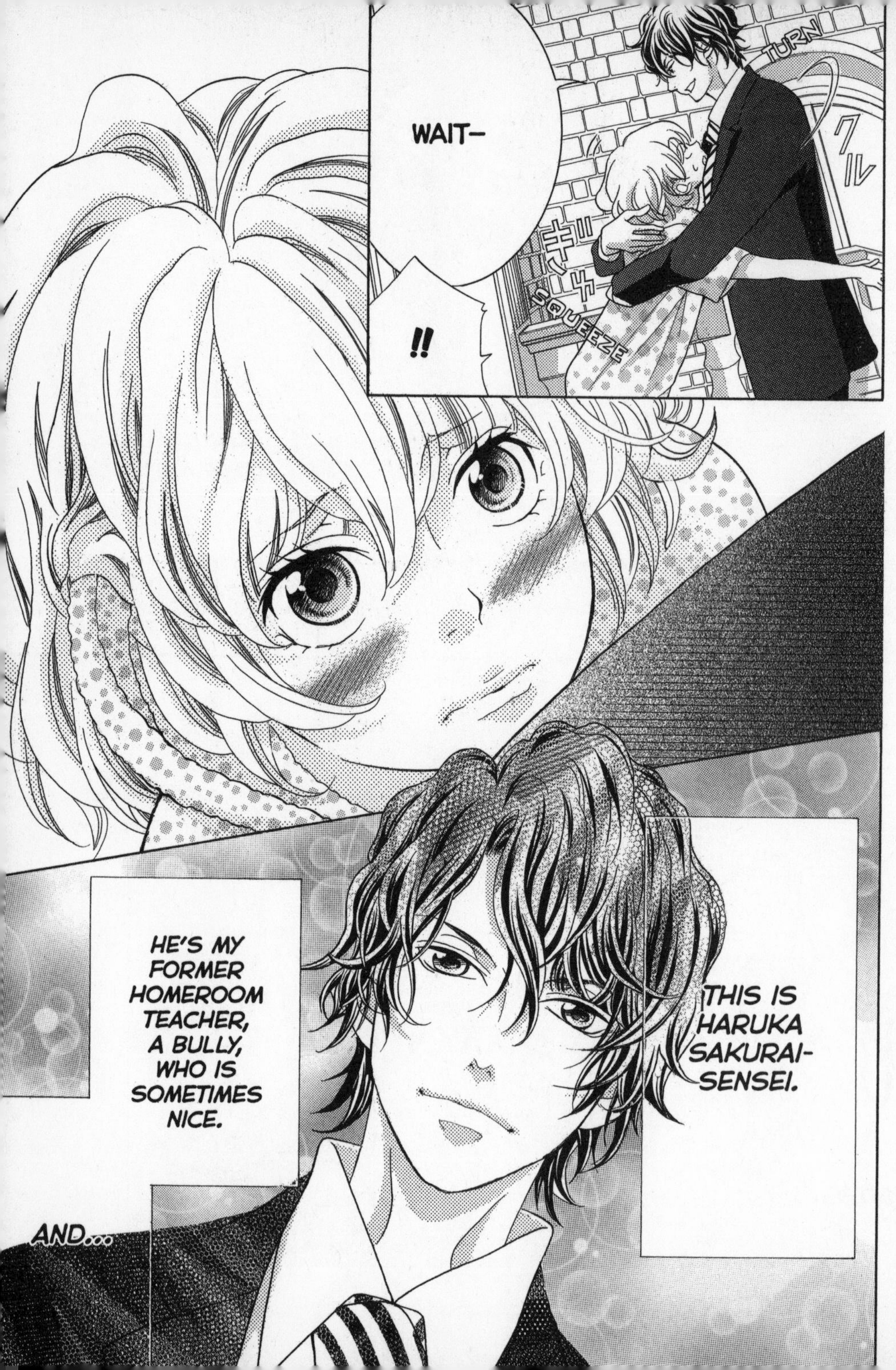
TURN
クル
WAIT-
SQUEEZE
!!
THIS IS HARUKA SAKURAI-SENSEI.
HE'S MY FORMER HOMEROOM TEACHER, A BULLY, WHO IS SOMETIMES NICE.
AND...

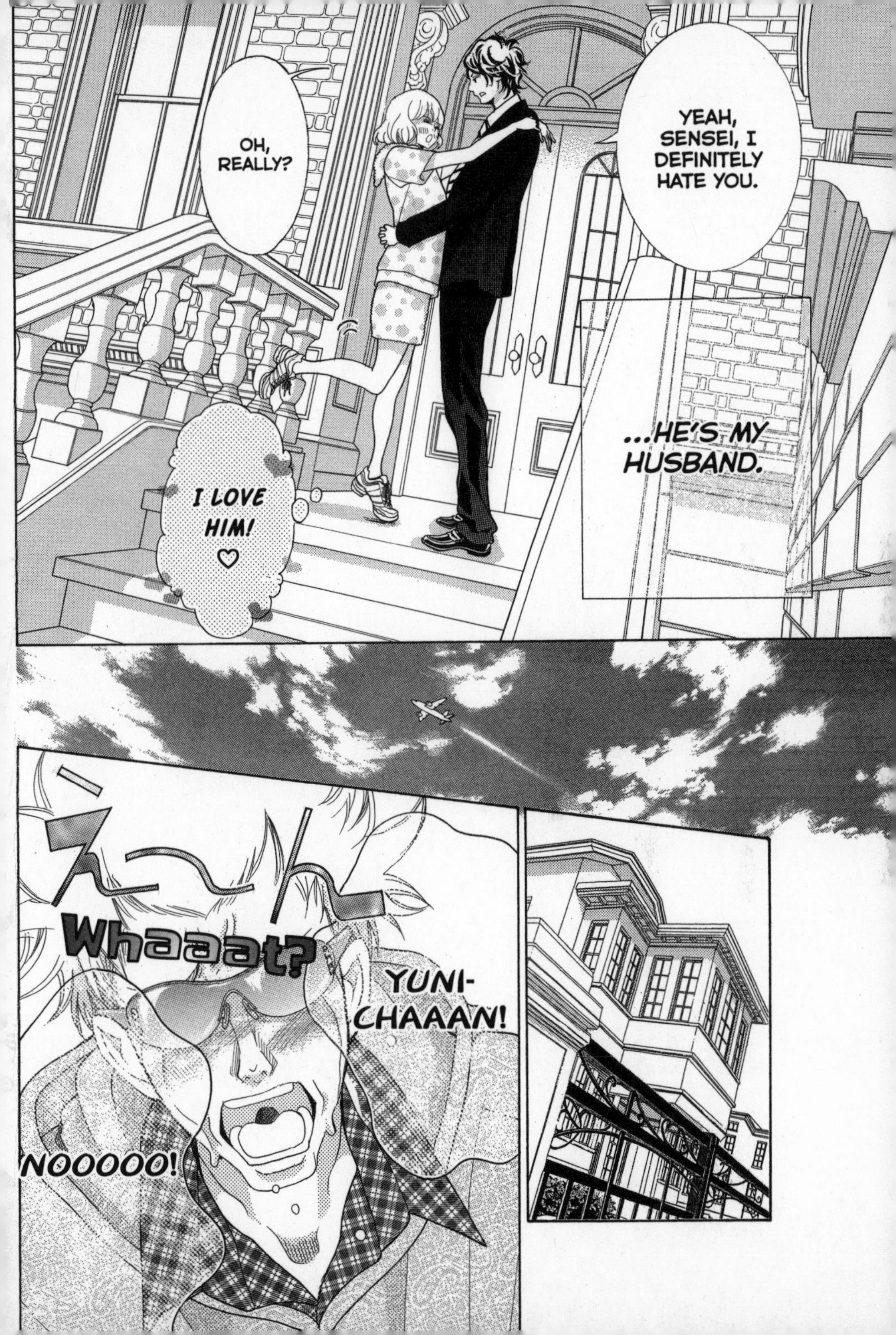
YEAH, SENSEI, I DEFINITELY HATE YOU.
OH, REALLY?
...HE'S MY HUSBAND.
I LOVE HIM! ♡
Whaaat?
YUNI-CHAAAN!
NOOOOO!

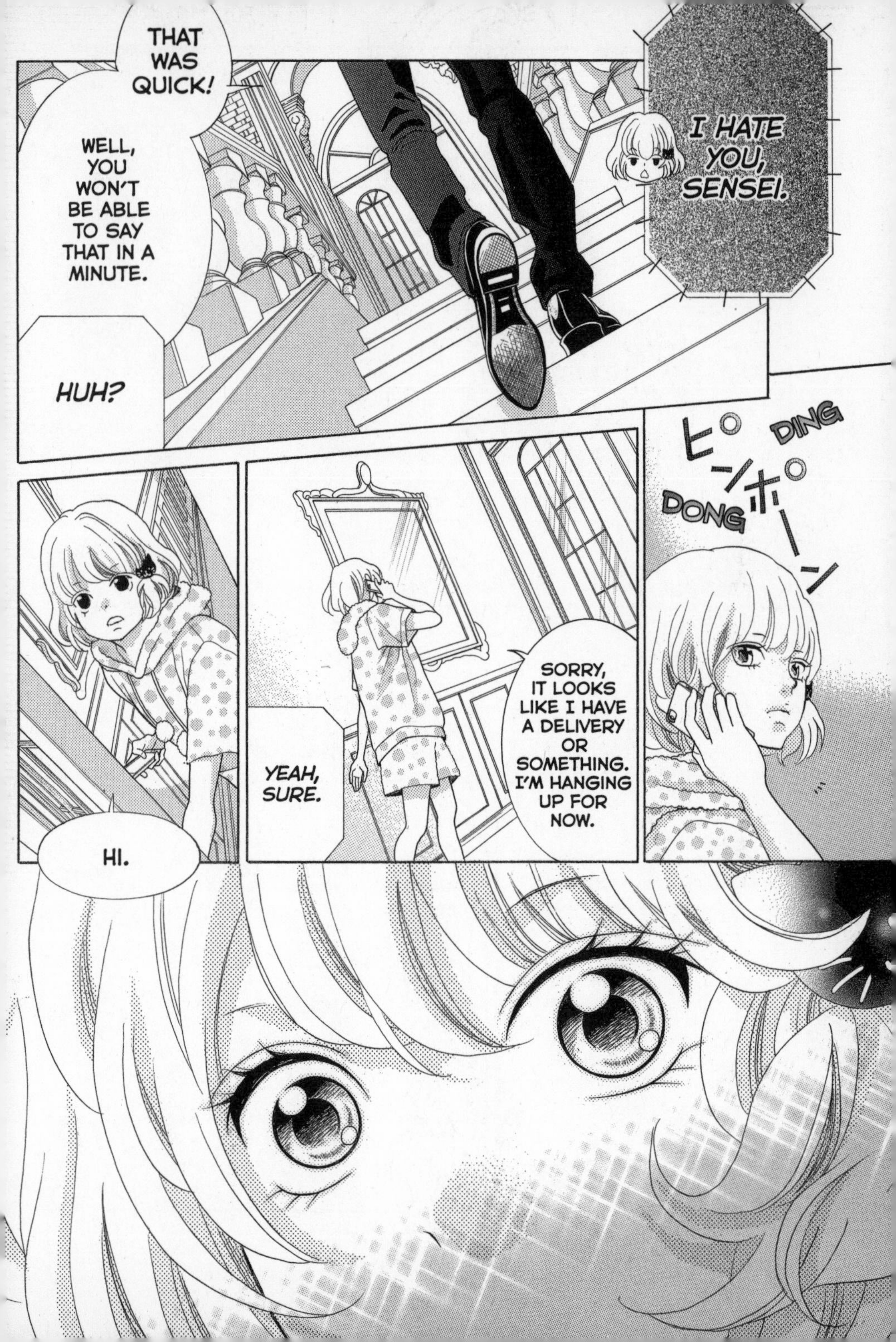
I HATE YOU, SENSEI.
THAT WAS QUICK!
WELL, YOU WON'T BE ABLE TO SAY THAT IN A MINUTE.
HUH?
ピンポーン
DING DONG
SORRY, IT LOOKS LIKE I HAVE A DELIVERY OR SOMETHING. I'M HANGING UP FOR NOW.
YEAH, SURE.
HI.

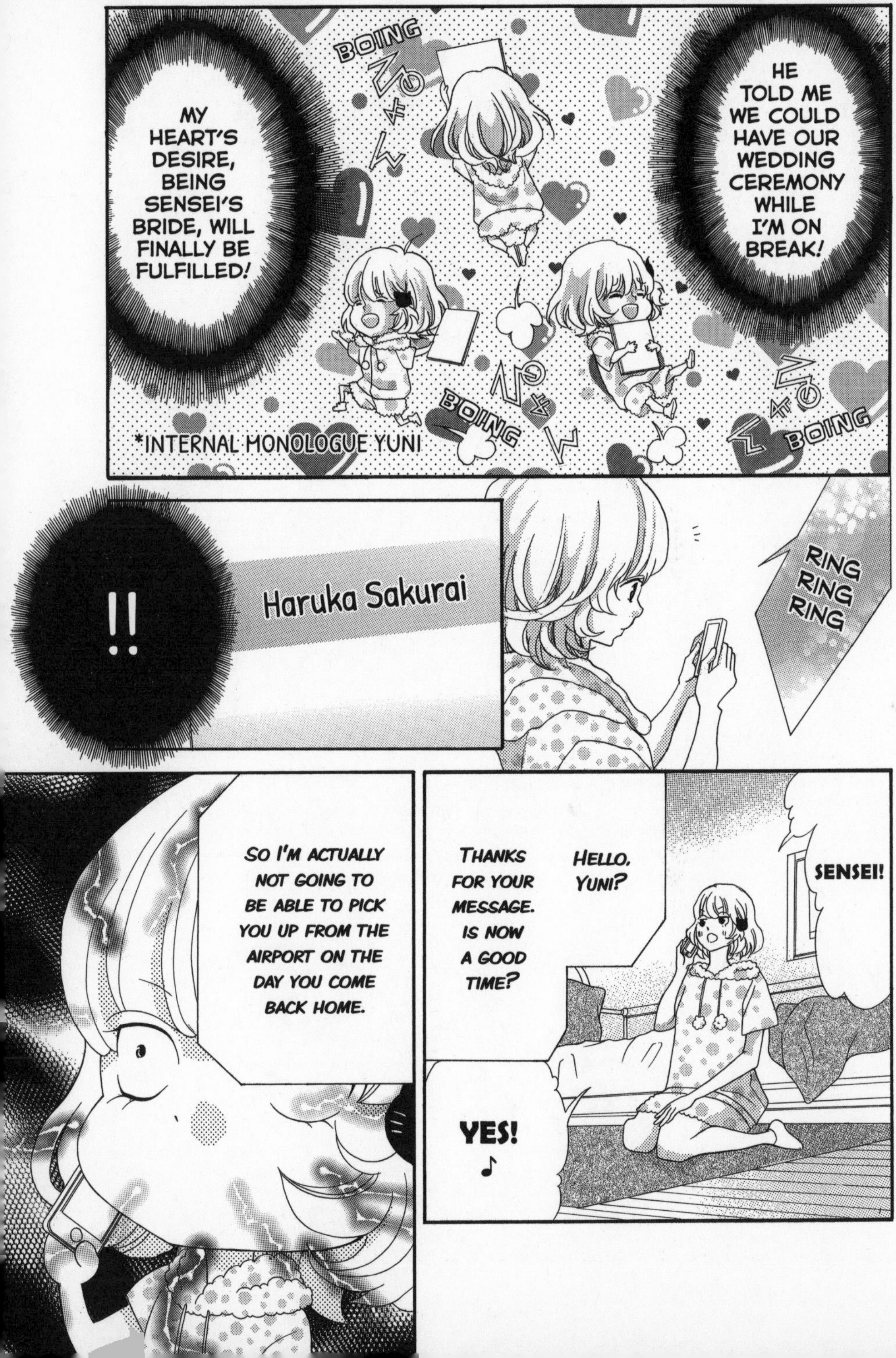
HE TOLD ME WE COULD HAVE OUR WEDDING CEREMONY WHILE I'M ON BREAK!
BOING
BOING
MY HEART'S DESIRE, BEING SENSEI'S BRIDE, WILL FINALLY BE FULFILLED!
BOING
BOING
*INTERNAL MONOLOGUE YUNI
RING RING RING
Haruka Sakurai
!!
SENSEI!
HELLO, YUNI?
THANKS FOR YOUR MESSAGE. IS NOW A GOOD TIME?
YES! ♪
SO I'M ACTUALLY NOT GOING TO BE ABLE TO PICK YOU UP FROM THE AIRPORT ON THE DAY YOU COME BACK HOME.

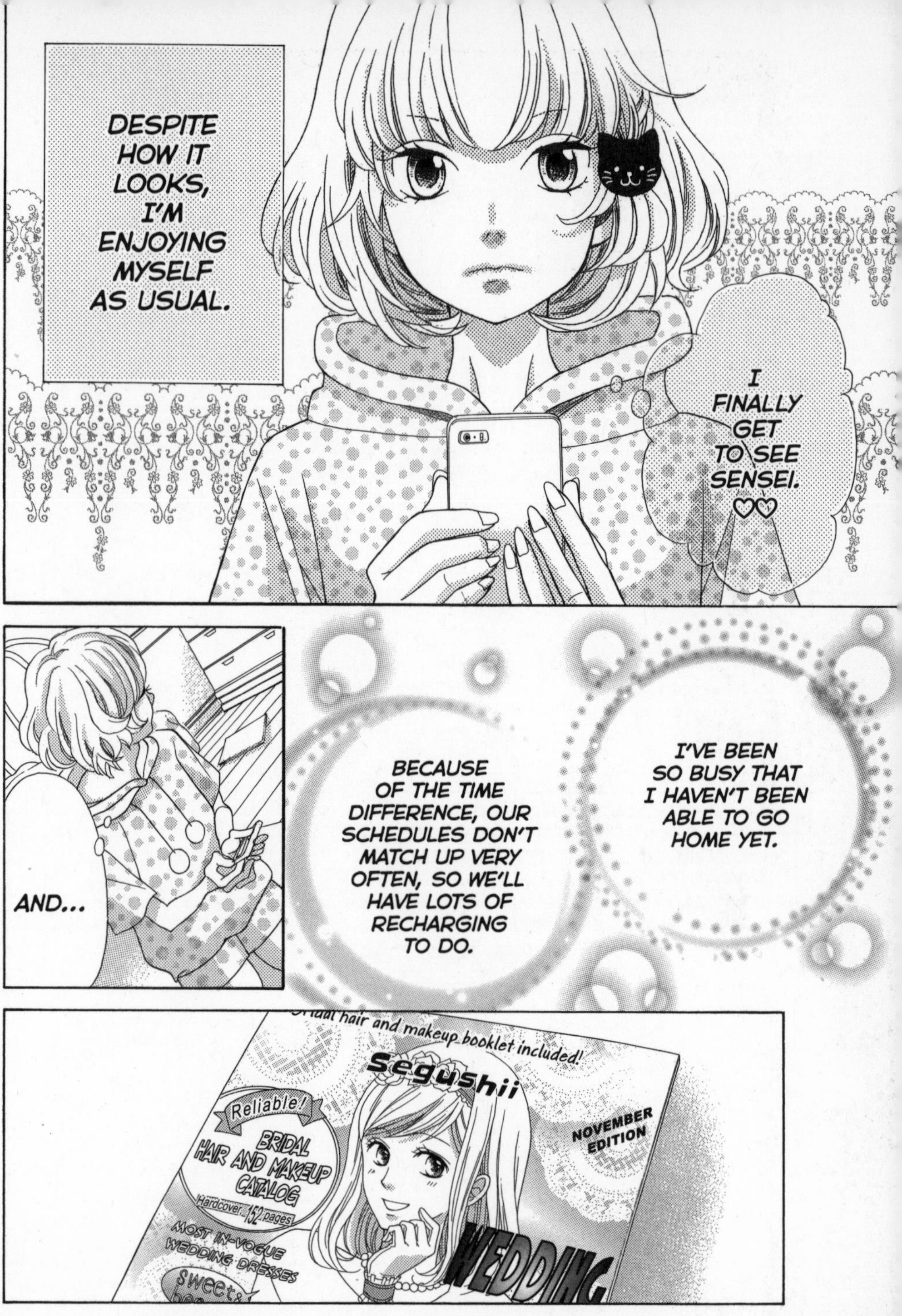

DESPITE HOW IT LOOKS, I'M ENJOYING MYSELF AS USUAL.
I FINALLY GET TO SEE SENSEI. ♡♡
I'VE BEEN SO BUSY THAT I HAVEN'T BEEN ABLE TO GO HOME YET.
BECAUSE OF THE TIME DIFFERENCE, OUR SCHEDULES DON'T MATCH UP VERY OFTEN, SO WE'LL HAVE LOTS OF RECHARGING TO DO.
AND...
hair and makeup booklet included!
Segushii
NOVEMBER EDITION
Reliable!
BRIDAL HAIR AND MAKEUP CATALOG
Hardcover: 152 pages
MOST IN-VOGUE WEDDING DRESSES
WEDDING

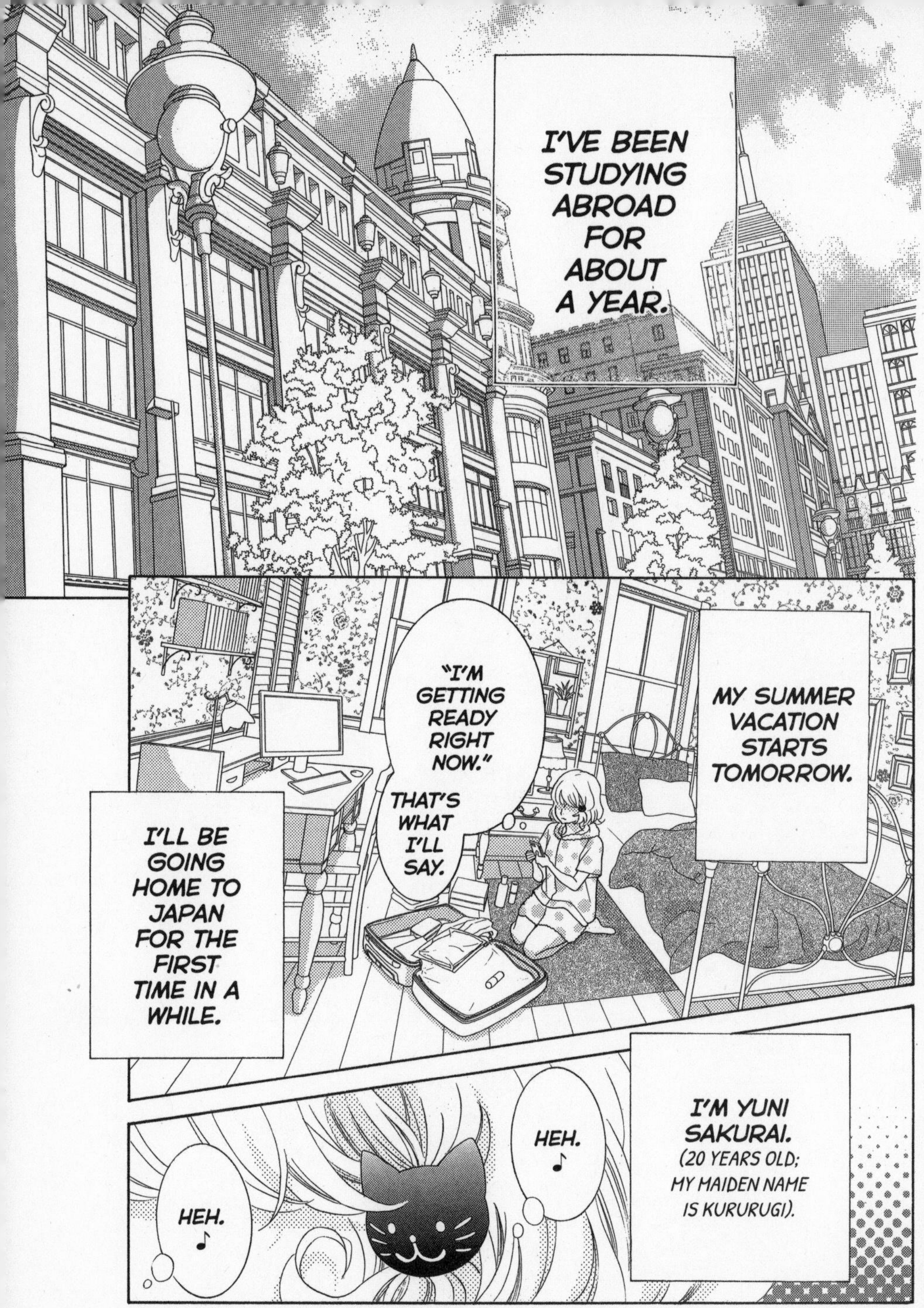
I'VE BEEN STUDYING ABROAD FOR ABOUT A YEAR.
MY SUMMER VACATION STARTS TOMORROW.
"I'M GETTING READY RIGHT NOW."
THAT'S WHAT I'LL SAY.
I'LL BE GOING HOME TO JAPAN FOR THE FIRST TIME IN A WHILE.
I'M YUNI SAKURAI. (20 YEARS OLD; MY MAIDEN NAME IS KURURUGI).
HEH. ♪
HEH. ♪

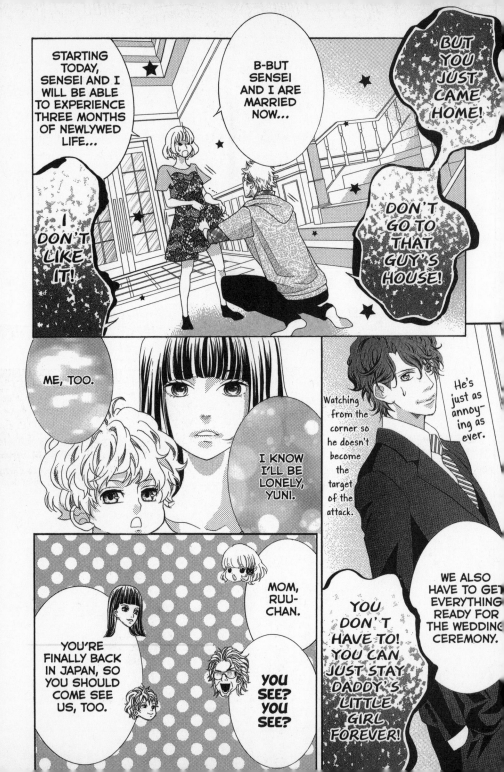

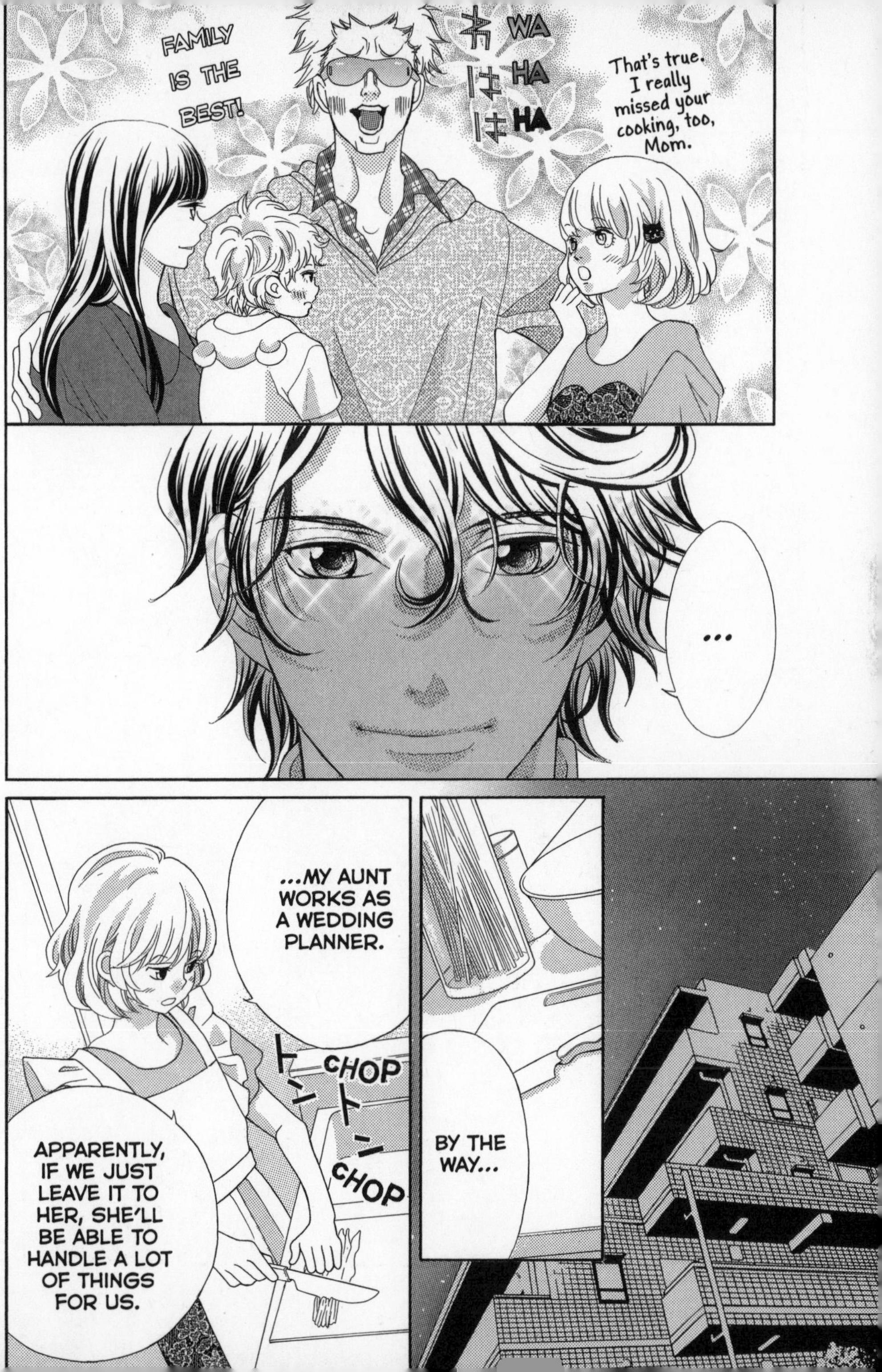
That's true. I really missed your cooking, too, Mom.
WA HA HA
FAMILY IS THE BEST!
...
BY THE WAY...
...MY AUNT WORKS AS A WEDDING PLANNER.
CHOP
CHOP
APPARENTLY, IF WE JUST LEAVE IT TO HER, SHE'LL BE ABLE TO HANDLE A LOT OF THINGS FOR US.

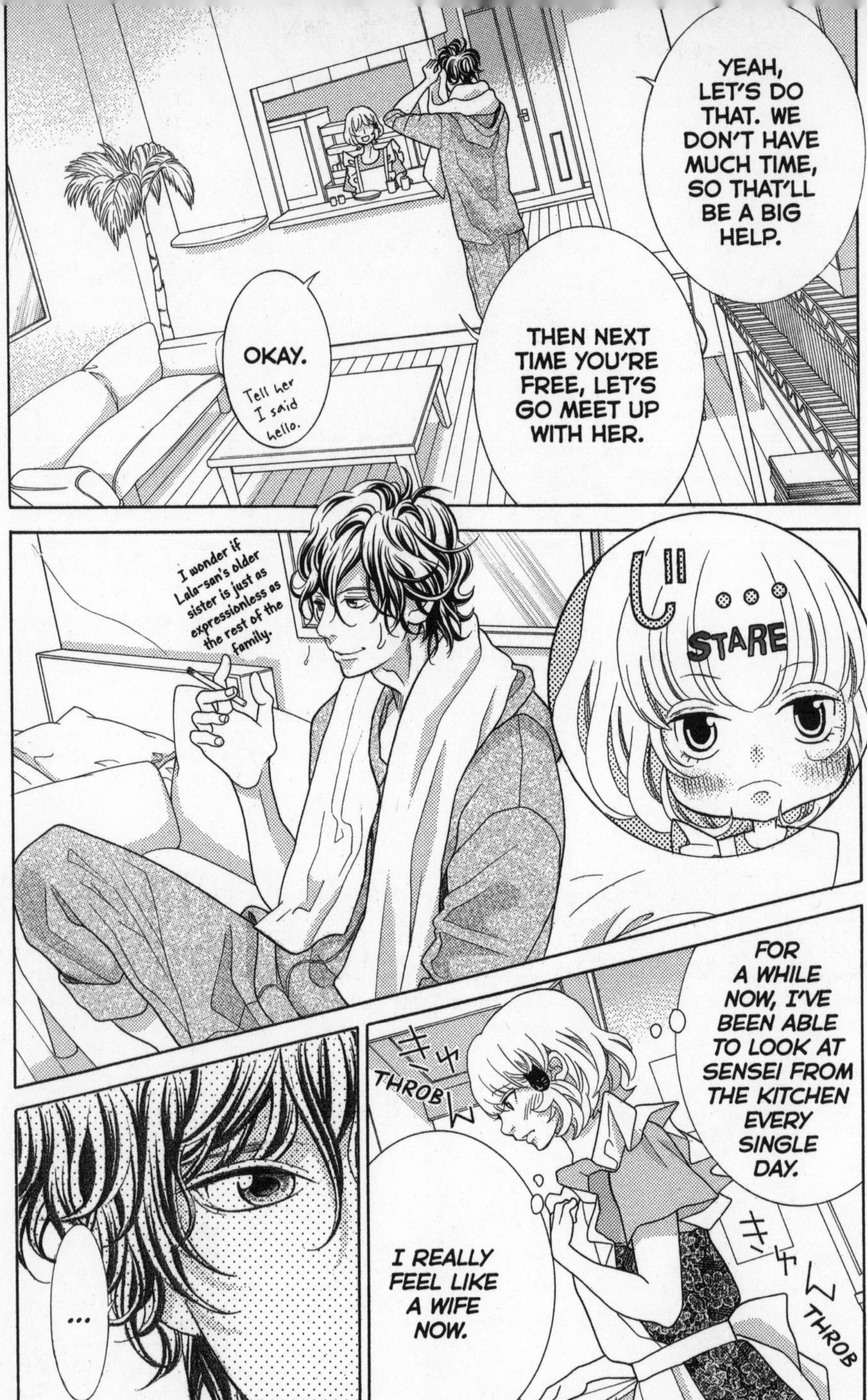
YEAH, LET'S DO THAT. WE DON'T HAVE MUCH TIME, SO THAT'LL BE A BIG HELP.
THEN NEXT TIME YOU'RE FREE, LET'S GO MEET UP WITH HER.
OKAY.
Tell her I said hello.
じー・・・
STARE
I wonder if Lala-san's older sister is just as expressionless as the rest of the family.
FOR A WHILE NOW, I'VE BEEN ABLE TO LOOK AT SENSEI FROM THE KITCHEN EVERY SINGLE DAY.
キュン
THROB
キュン
THROB
I REALLY FEEL LIKE A WIFE NOW.
...

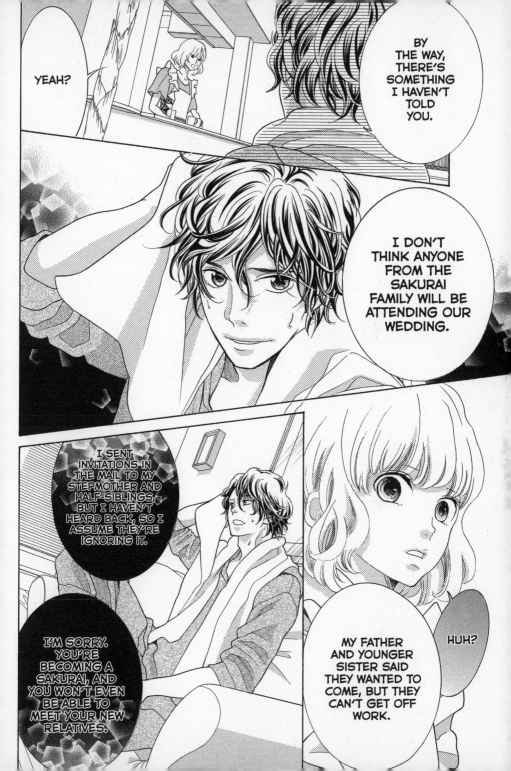

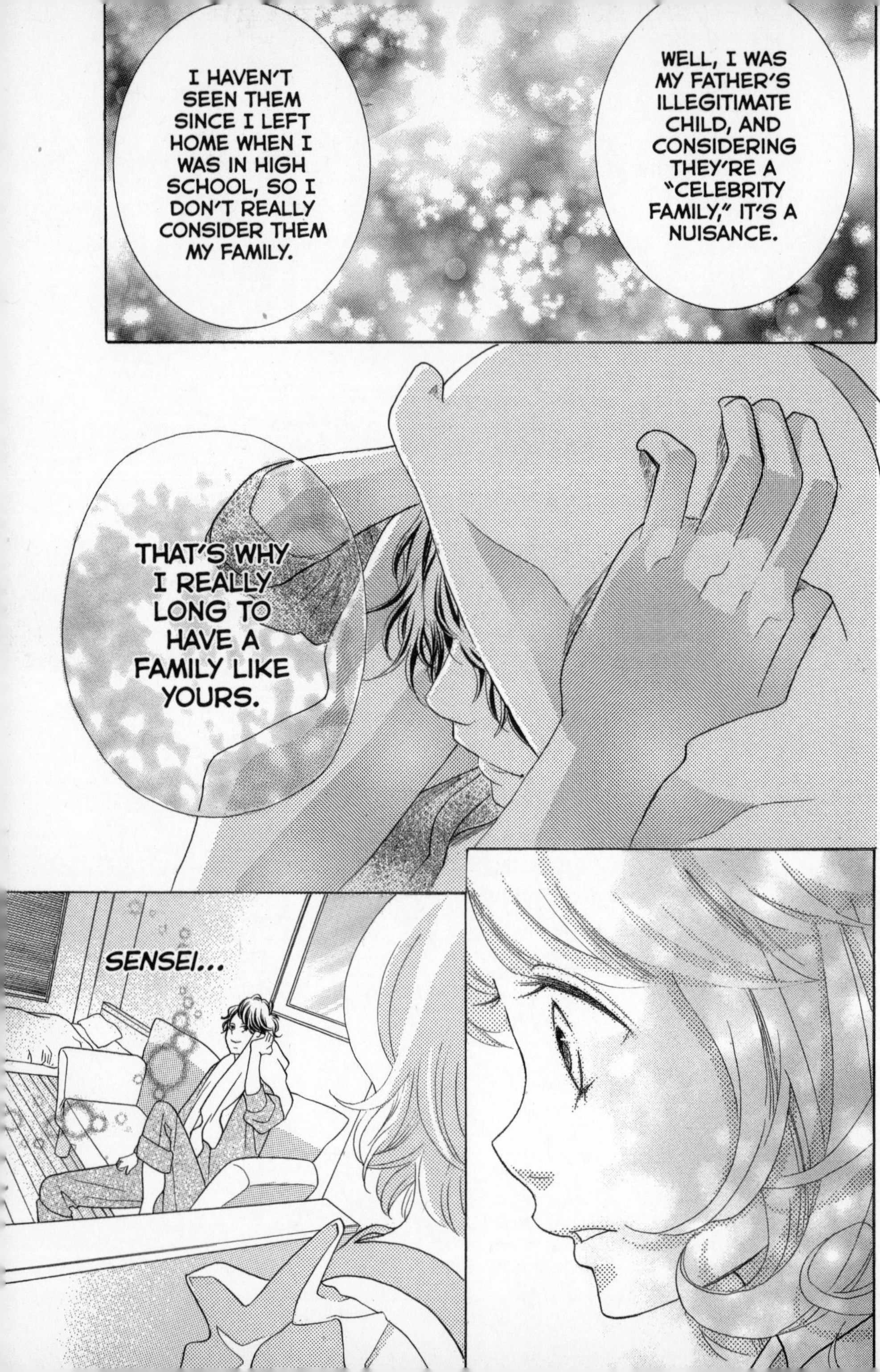
WELL, I WAS MY FATHER'S ILLEGITIMATE CHILD, AND CONSIDERING THEY'RE A "CELEBRITY FAMILY," IT'S A NUISANCE.
I HAVEN'T SEEN THEM SINCE I LEFT HOME WHEN I WAS IN HIGH SCHOOL, SO I DON'T REALLY CONSIDER THEM MY FAMILY.
THAT'S WHY I REALLY LONG TO HAVE A FAMILY LIKE YOURS.
SENSEI...

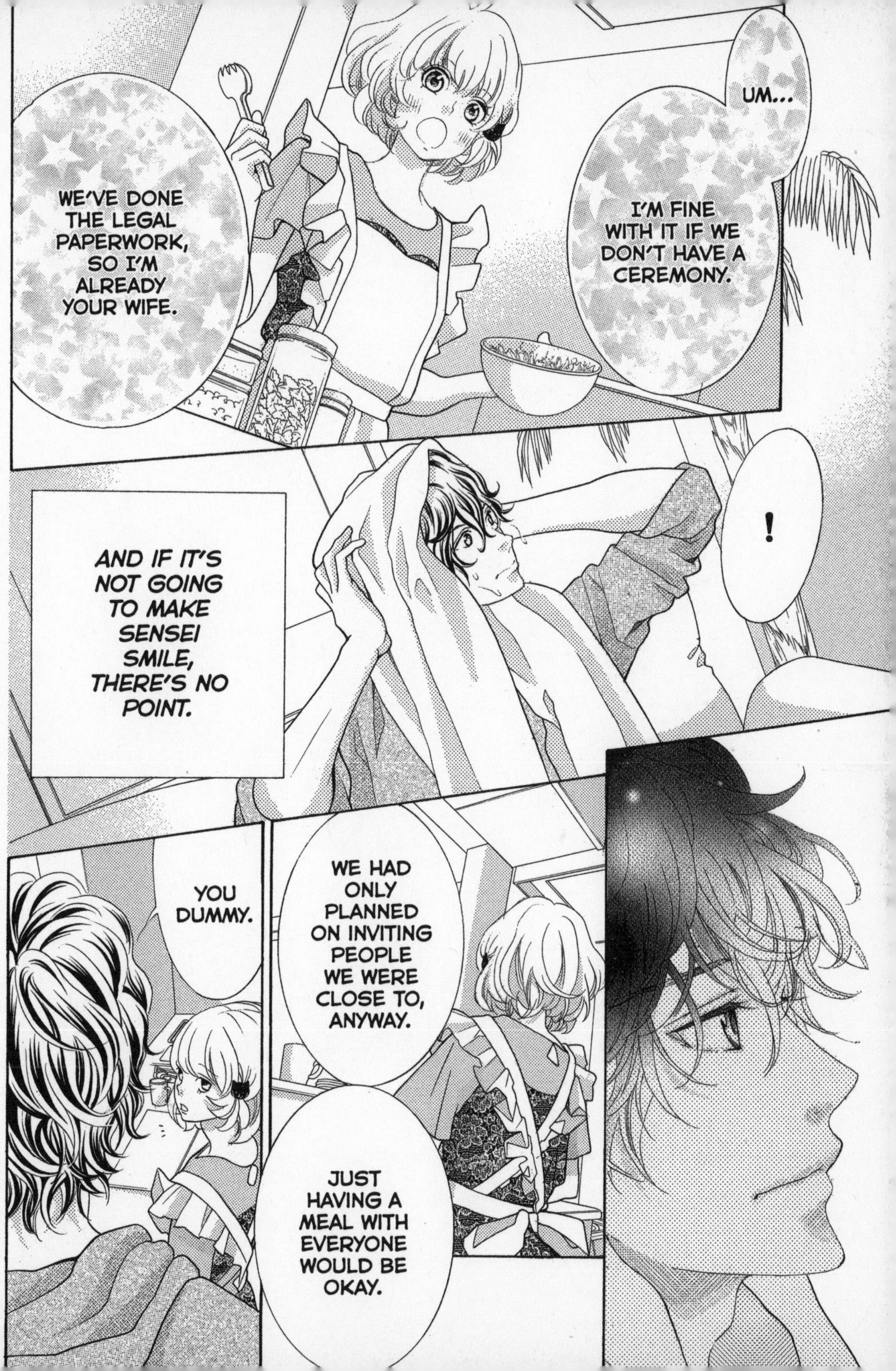
UM...
I'M FINE WITH IT IF WE DON'T HAVE A CEREMONY.
WE'VE DONE THE LEGAL PAPERWORK, SO I'M ALREADY YOUR WIFE.
!
AND IF IT'S NOT GOING TO MAKE SENSEI SMILE, THERE'S NO POINT.
WE HAD ONLY PLANNED ON INVITING PEOPLE WE WERE CLOSE TO, ANYWAY.
JUST HAVING A MEAL WITH EVERYONE WOULD BE OKAY.
YOU DUMMY.

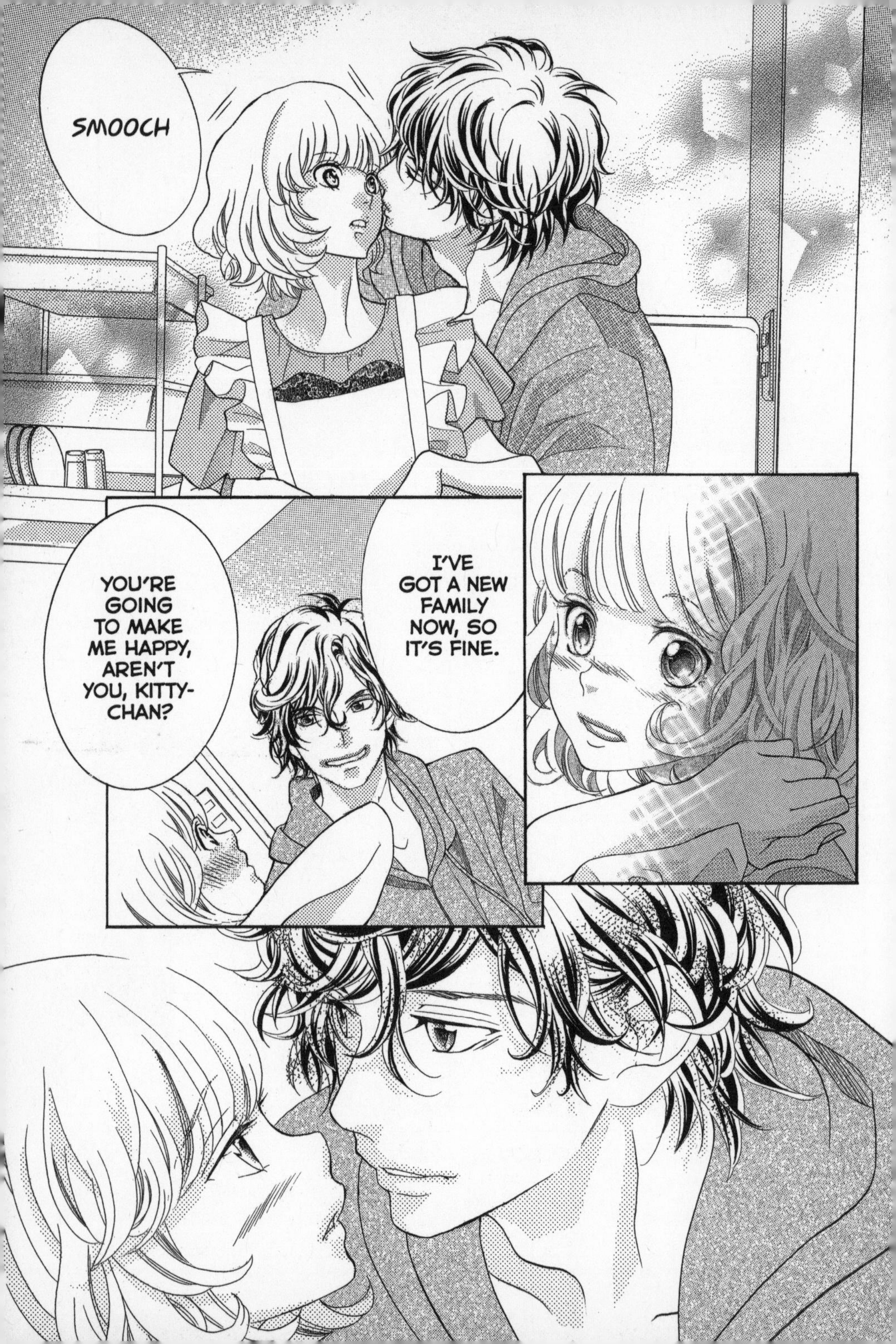
SMOOCH
I'VE GOT A NEW FAMILY NOW, SO IT'S FINE.
YOU'RE GOING TO MAKE ME HAPPY, AREN'T YOU, KITTY-CHAN?

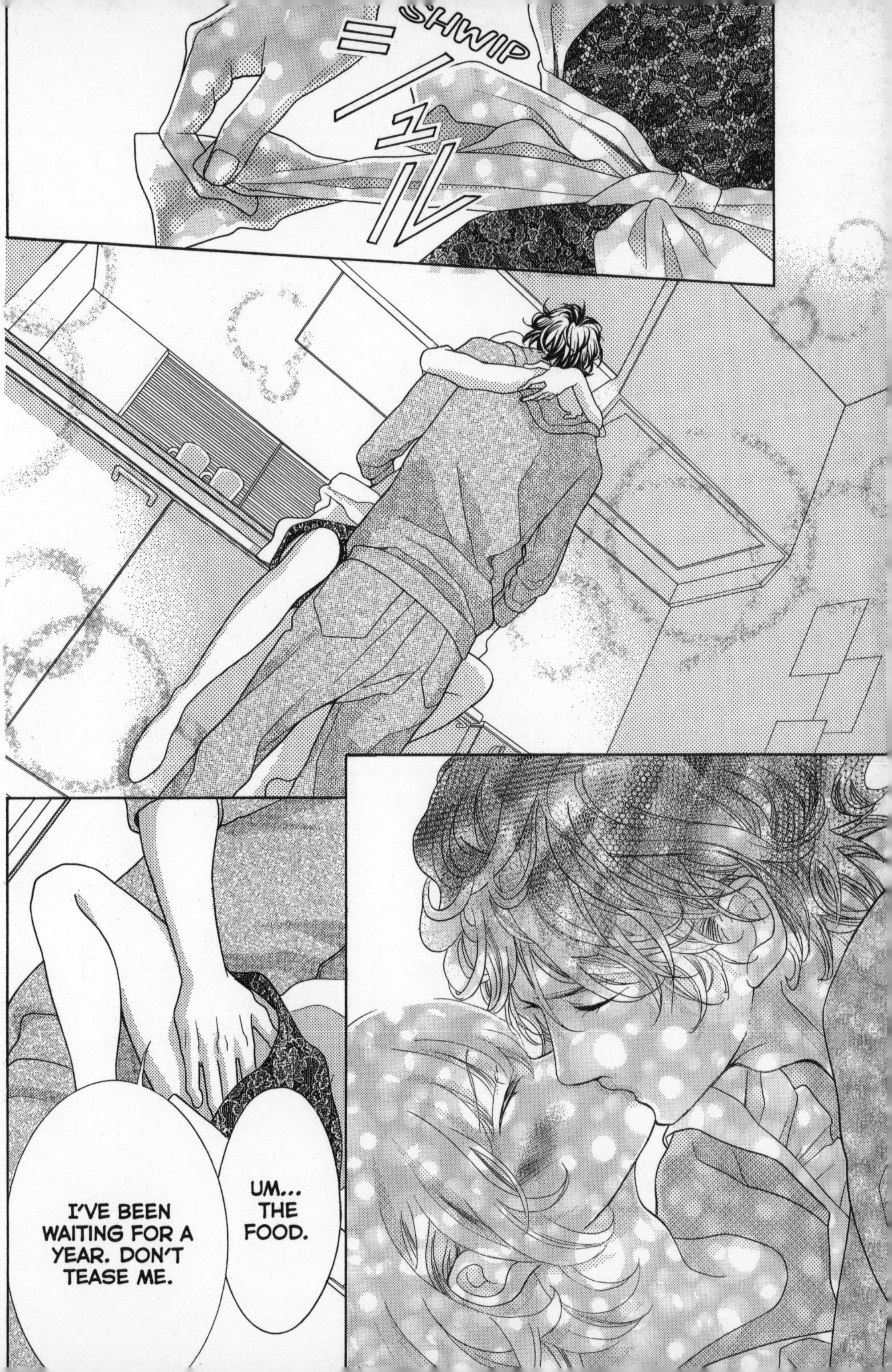
SHWIP
UM... THE FOOD.
I'VE BEEN WAITING FOR A YEAR. DON'T TEASE ME.

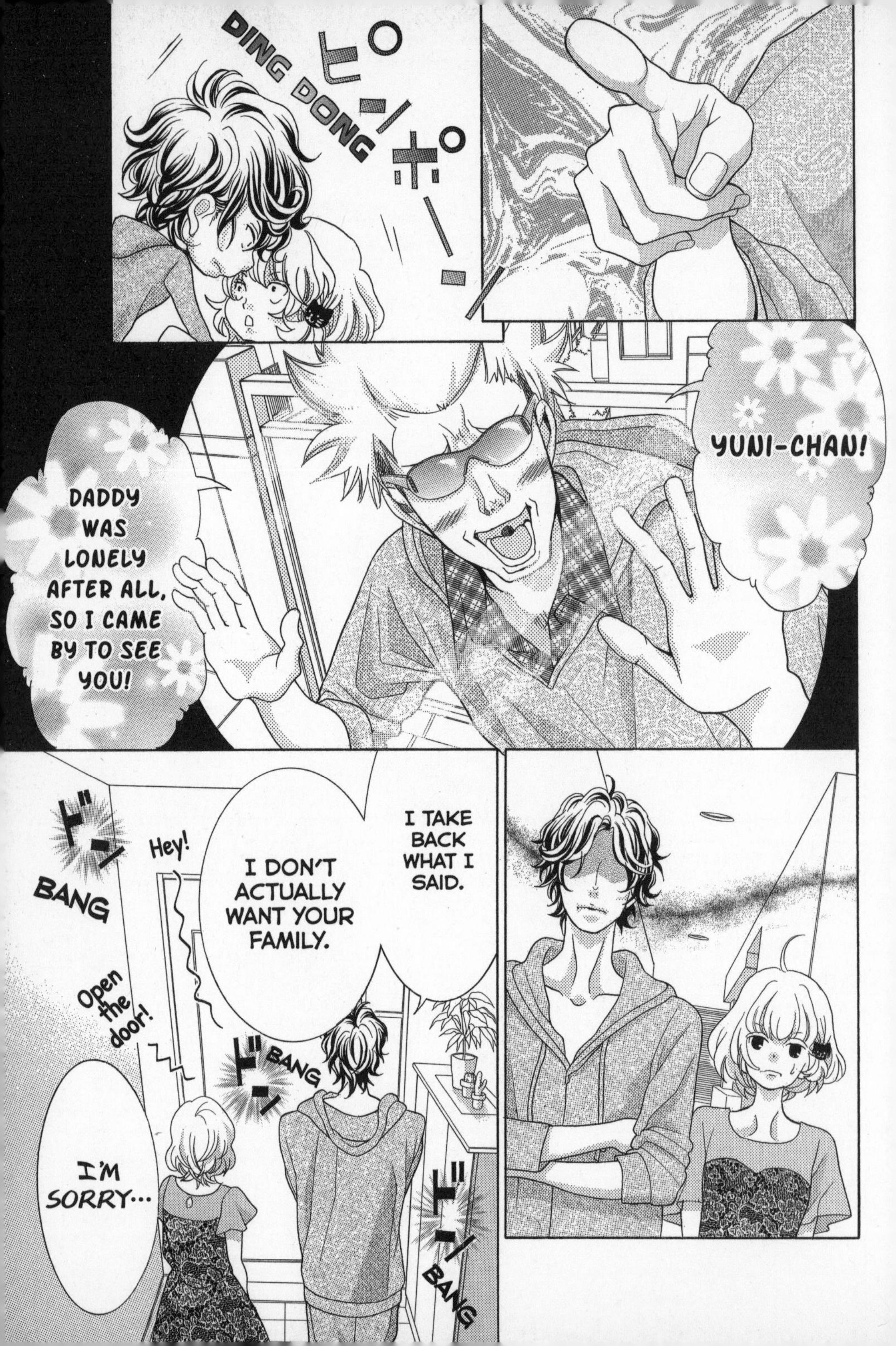
ピンポーン
DING DONG
YUNI-CHAN!
DADDY WAS LONELY AFTER ALL, SO I CAME BY TO SEE YOU!
I TAKE BACK WHAT I SAID.
I DON'T ACTUALLY WANT YOUR FAMILY.
ドーン BANG
Hey!
ドーン BANG
Open the door!
ドーン BANG
I'M SORRY...

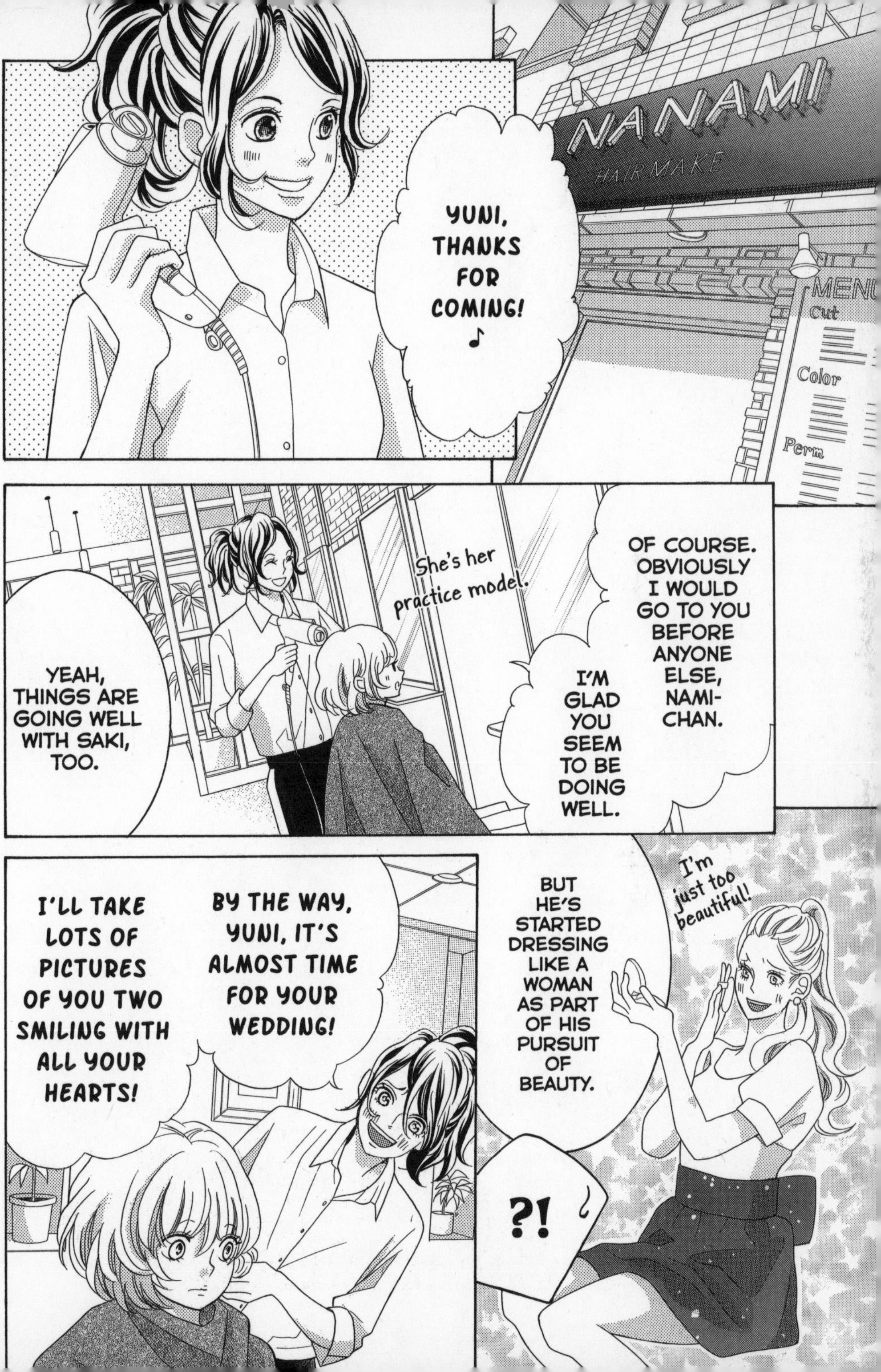
NANAMI
HAIR MAKE
MENU
Cut
Color
Perm
YUNI, THANKS FOR COMING! ♪
OF COURSE. OBVIOUSLY I WOULD GO TO YOU BEFORE ANYONE ELSE, NAMI-CHAN.
I'M GLAD YOU SEEM TO BE DOING WELL.
She's her practice model.
YEAH, THINGS ARE GOING WELL WITH SAKI, TOO.
I'm just too beautiful!
BUT HE'S STARTED DRESSING LIKE A WOMAN AS PART OF HIS PURSUIT OF BEAUTY.
?!
BY THE WAY, YUNI, IT'S ALMOST TIME FOR YOUR WEDDING!
I'LL TAKE LOTS OF PICTURES OF YOU TWO SMILING WITH ALL YOUR HEARTS!

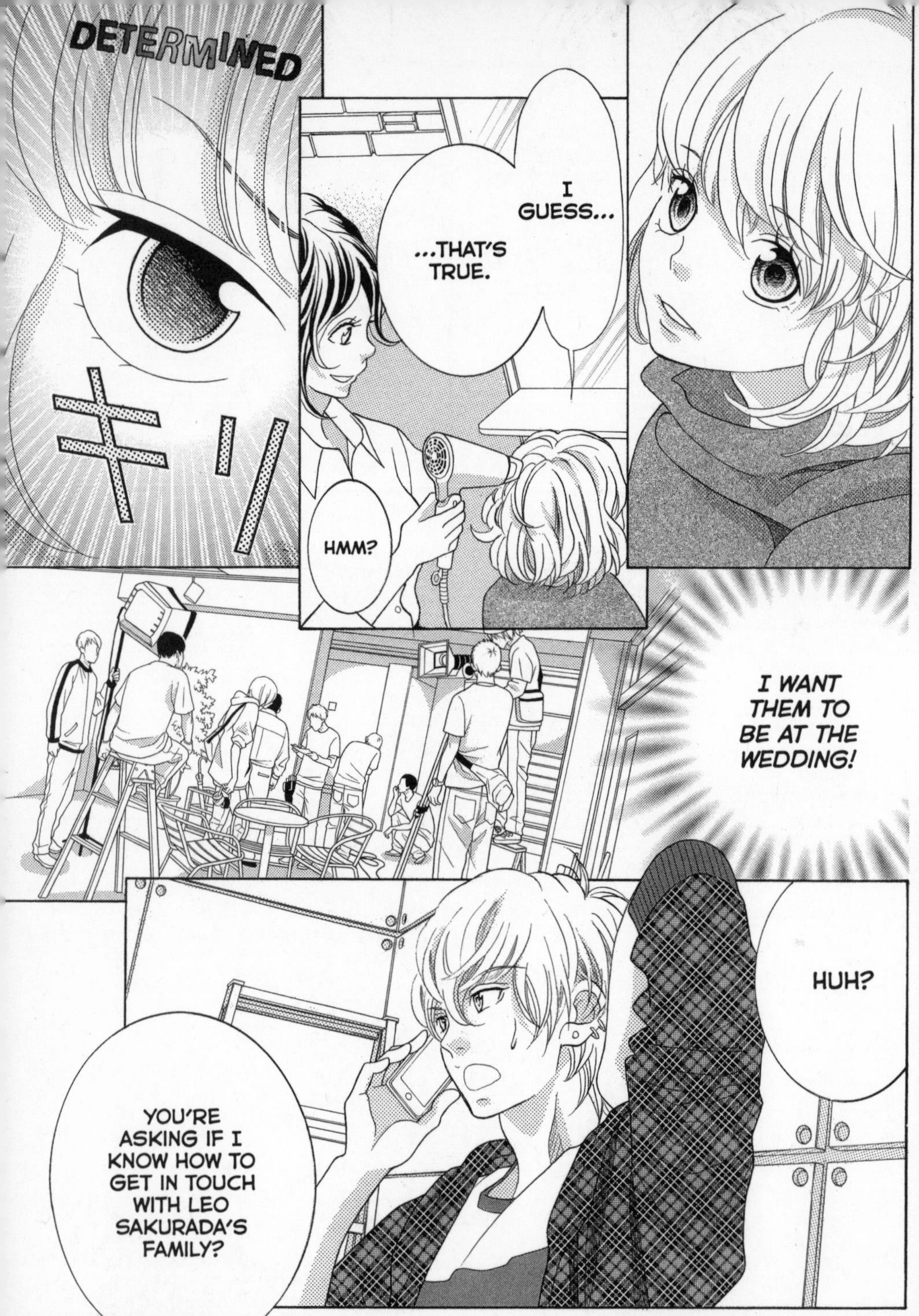
I GUESS...
...THAT'S TRUE.
HMM?
DETERMINED
キッ
I WANT THEM TO BE AT THE WEDDING!
HUH?
YOU'RE ASKING IF I KNOW HOW TO GET IN TOUCH WITH LEO SAKURADA'S FAMILY?

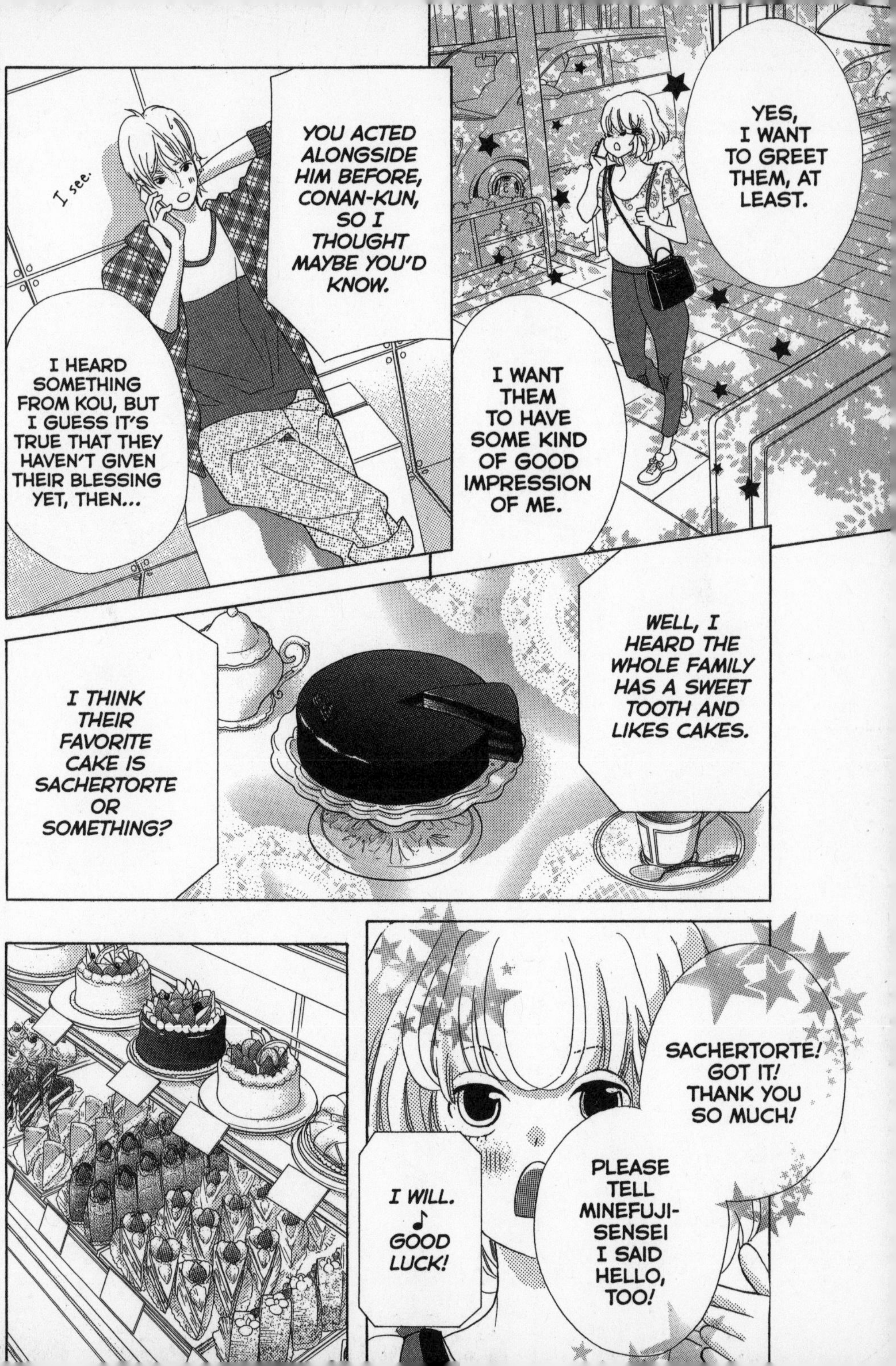
YES, I WANT TO GREET THEM, AT LEAST.
I WANT THEM TO HAVE SOME KIND OF GOOD IMPRESSION OF ME.
YOU ACTED ALONGSIDE HIM BEFORE, CONAN-KUN, SO I THOUGHT MAYBE YOU'D KNOW.
I see.
I HEARD SOMETHING FROM KOU, BUT I GUESS IT'S TRUE THAT THEY HAVEN'T GIVEN THEIR BLESSING YET, THEN...
WELL, I HEARD THE WHOLE FAMILY HAS A SWEET TOOTH AND LIKES CAKES.
I THINK THEIR FAVORITE CAKE IS SACHERTORTE OR SOMETHING?
SACHERTORTE! GOT IT! THANK YOU SO MUCH!
PLEASE TELL MINEFUJI-SENSEI I SAID HELLO, TOO!
I WILL. ♪ GOOD LUCK!

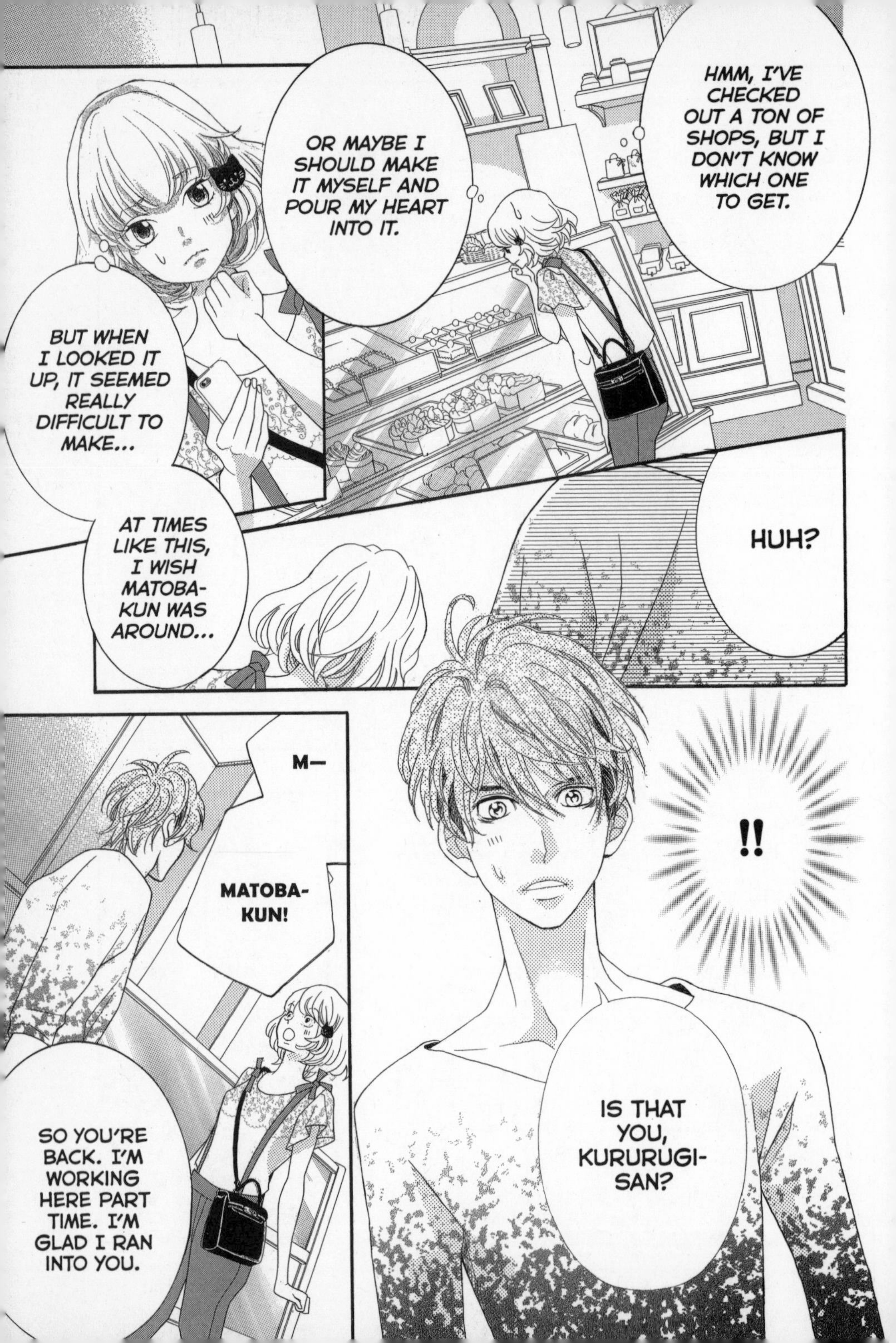
HMM, I'VE CHECKED OUT A TON OF SHOPS, BUT I DON'T KNOW WHICH ONE TO GET.
OR MAYBE I SHOULD MAKE IT MYSELF AND POUR MY HEART INTO IT.
BUT WHEN I LOOKED IT UP, IT SEEMED REALLY DIFFICULT TO MAKE...
AT TIMES LIKE THIS, I WISH MATOBA-KUN WAS AROUND...
HUH?
!!
IS THAT YOU, KURURUGI-SAN?
M—
MATOBA-KUN!
SO YOU'RE BACK. I'M WORKING HERE PART TIME. I'M GLAD I RAN INTO YOU.

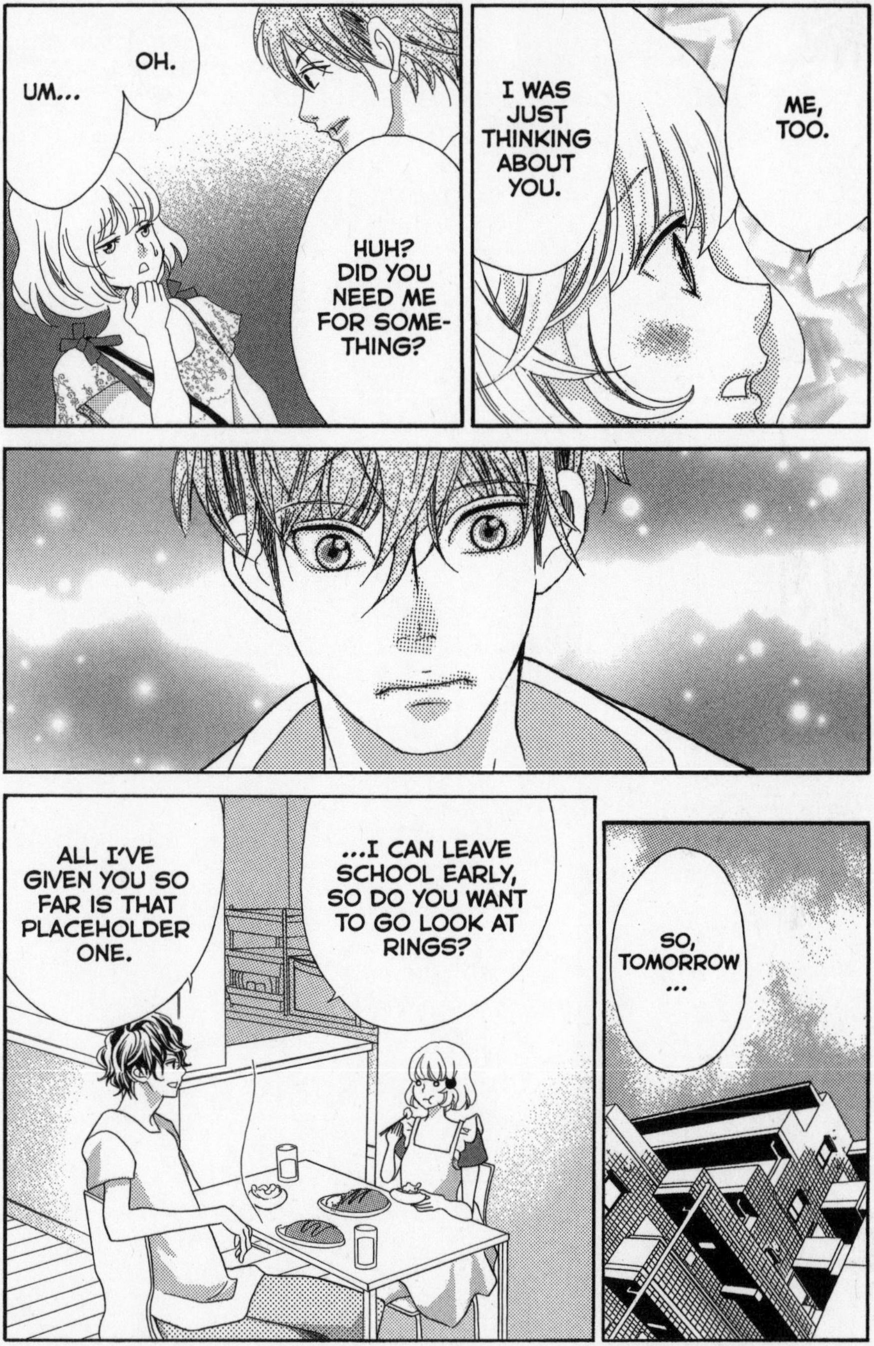
ME, TOO.
I WAS JUST THINKING ABOUT YOU.
HUH? DID YOU NEED ME FOR SOMETHING?
OH.
UM...
SO, TOMORROW...
...I CAN LEAVE SCHOOL EARLY, SO DO YOU WANT TO GO LOOK AT RINGS?
ALL I'VE GIVEN YOU SO FAR IS THAT PLACEHOLDER ONE.

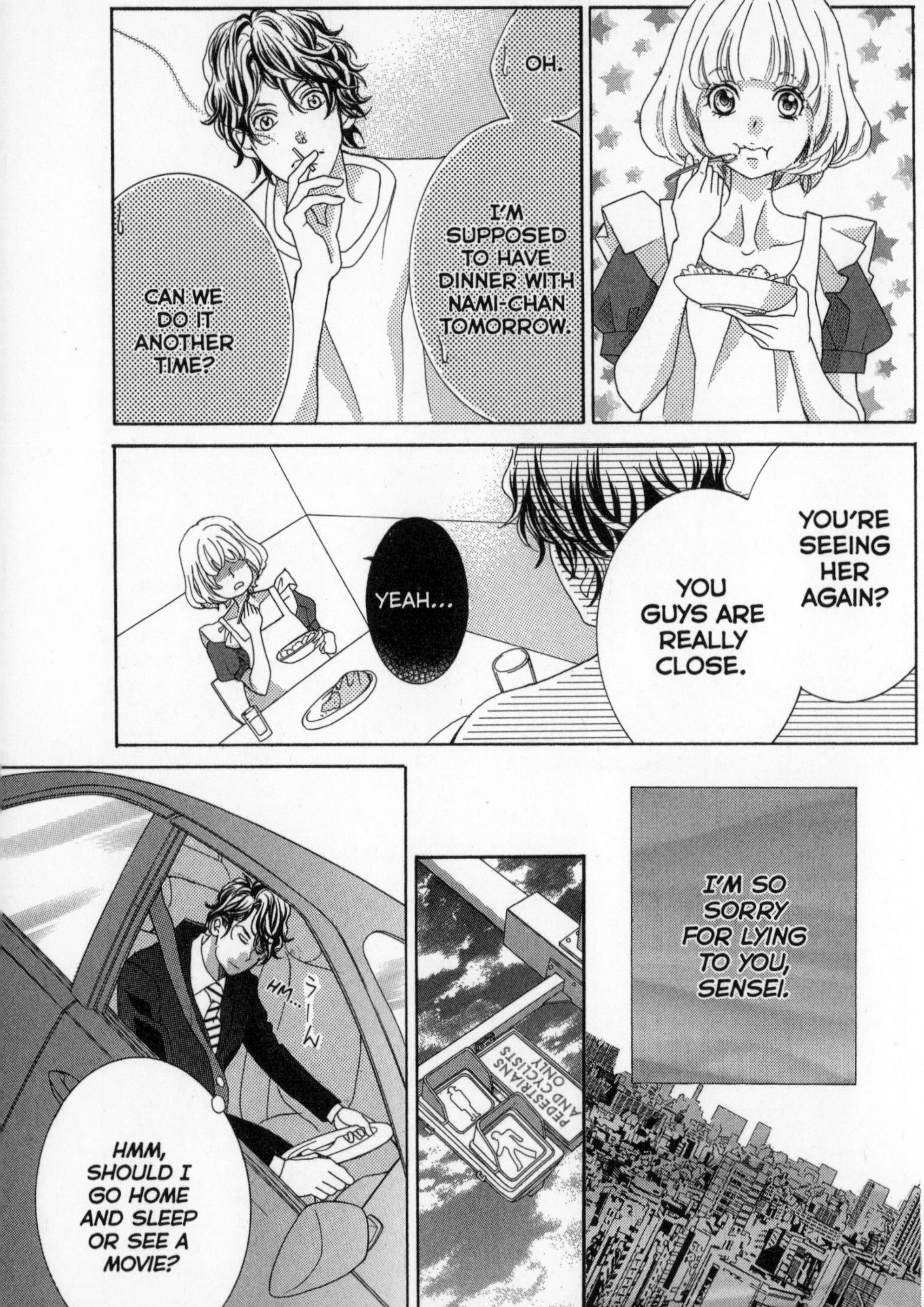
OH.
I'M SUPPOSED TO HAVE DINNER WITH NAMI-CHAN TOMORROW.
CAN WE DO IT ANOTHER TIME?
YOU'RE SEEING HER AGAIN?
YOU GUYS ARE REALLY CLOSE.
YEAH...
I'M SO SORRY FOR LYING TO YOU, SENSEI.
PEDESTRIANS AND CYCLISTS ONLY
HM...
HMM, SHOULD I GO HOME AND SLEEP OR SEE A MOVIE?

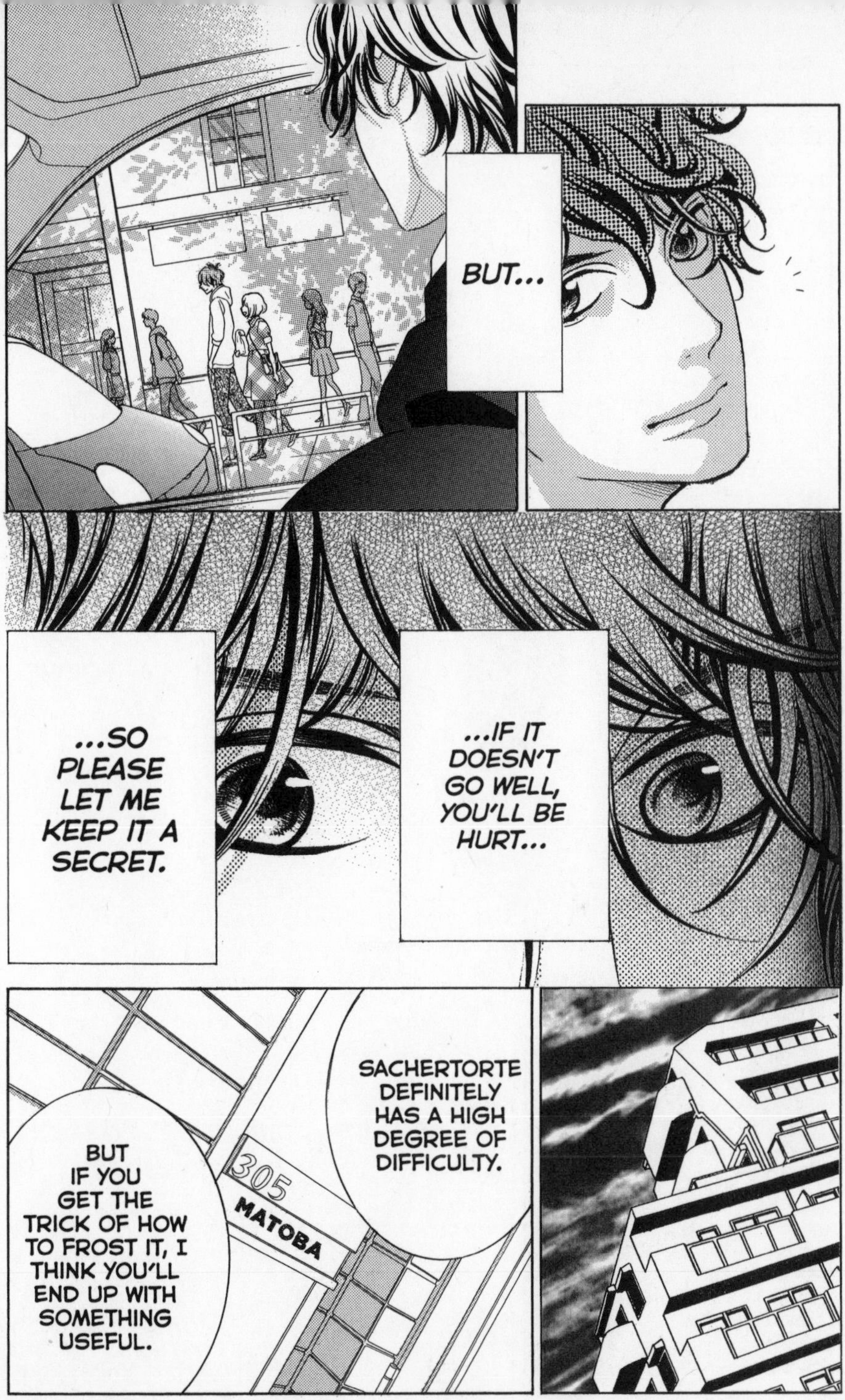
BUT...
...IF IT DOESN'T GO WELL, YOU'LL BE HURT...
...SO PLEASE LET ME KEEP IT A SECRET.
SACHERTORTE DEFINITELY HAS A HIGH DEGREE OF DIFFICULTY.
305
MATOBA
BUT IF YOU GET THE TRICK OF HOW TO FROST IT, I THINK YOU'LL END UP WITH SOMETHING USEFUL.

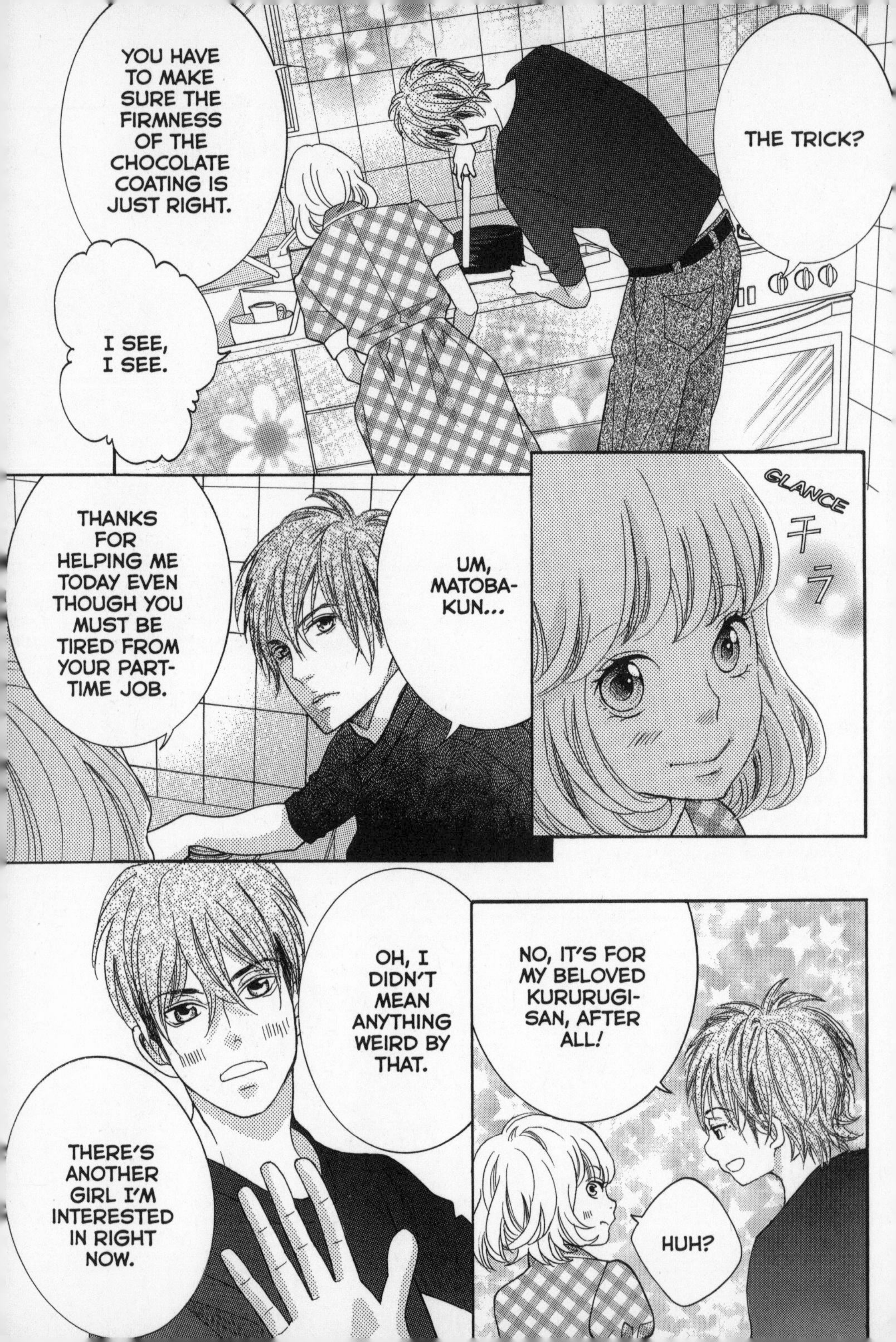
THE TRICK?
YOU HAVE TO MAKE SURE THE FIRMNESS OF THE CHOCOLATE COATING IS JUST RIGHT.
I SEE, I SEE.
GLANCE
チラ
UM, MATOBA-KUN...
THANKS FOR HELPING ME TODAY EVEN THOUGH YOU MUST BE TIRED FROM YOUR PART-TIME JOB.
NO, IT'S FOR MY BELOVED KURURUGI-SAN, AFTER ALL!
HUH?
OH, I DIDN'T MEAN ANYTHING WEIRD BY THAT.
THERE'S ANOTHER GIRL I'M INTERESTED IN RIGHT NOW.

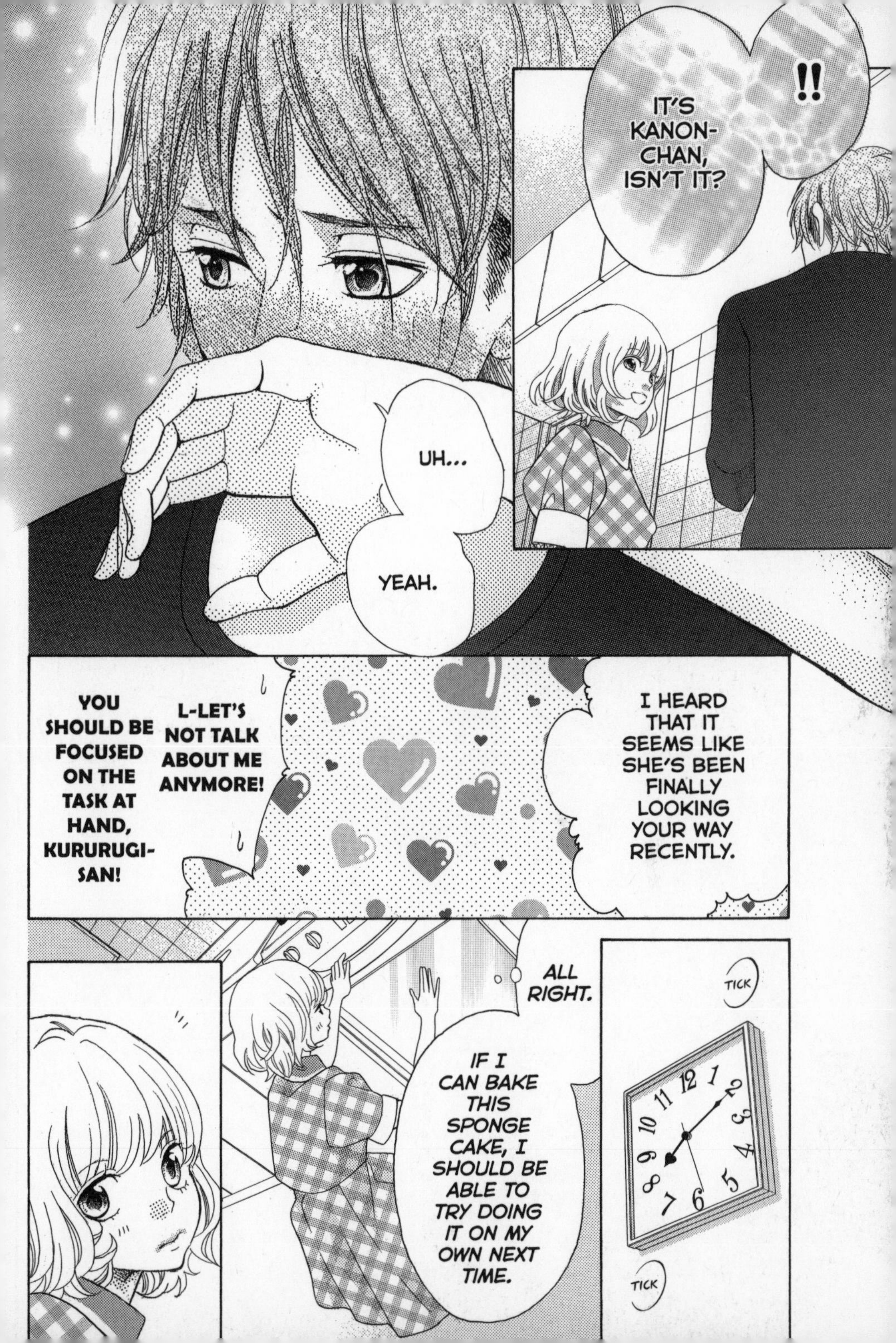
!!
IT'S KANON-CHAN, ISN'T IT?
UH...
YEAH.
I HEARD THAT IT SEEMS LIKE SHE'S BEEN FINALLY LOOKING YOUR WAY RECENTLY.
L-LET'S NOT TALK ABOUT ME ANYMORE!
YOU SHOULD BE FOCUSED ON THE TASK AT HAND, KURURUGI-SAN!
TICK
TICK
ALL RIGHT.
IF I CAN BAKE THIS SPONGE CAKE, I SHOULD BE ABLE TO TRY DOING IT ON MY OWN NEXT TIME.

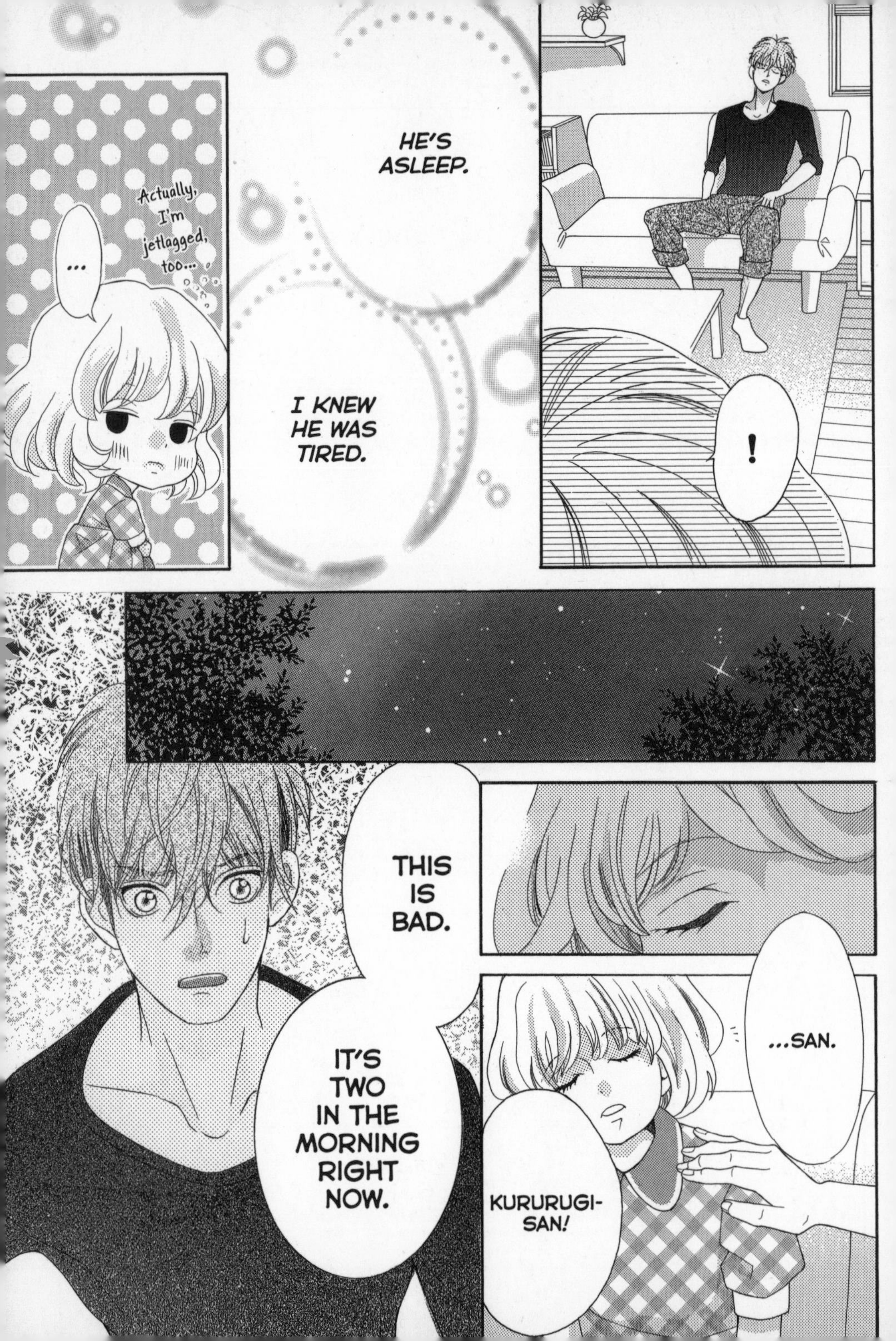
!
HE'S ASLEEP.
I KNEW HE WAS TIRED.
...
Actually, I'm jetlagged, too...
...SAN.
KURURUGI-SAN!
THIS IS BAD.
IT'S TWO IN THE MORNING RIGHT NOW.

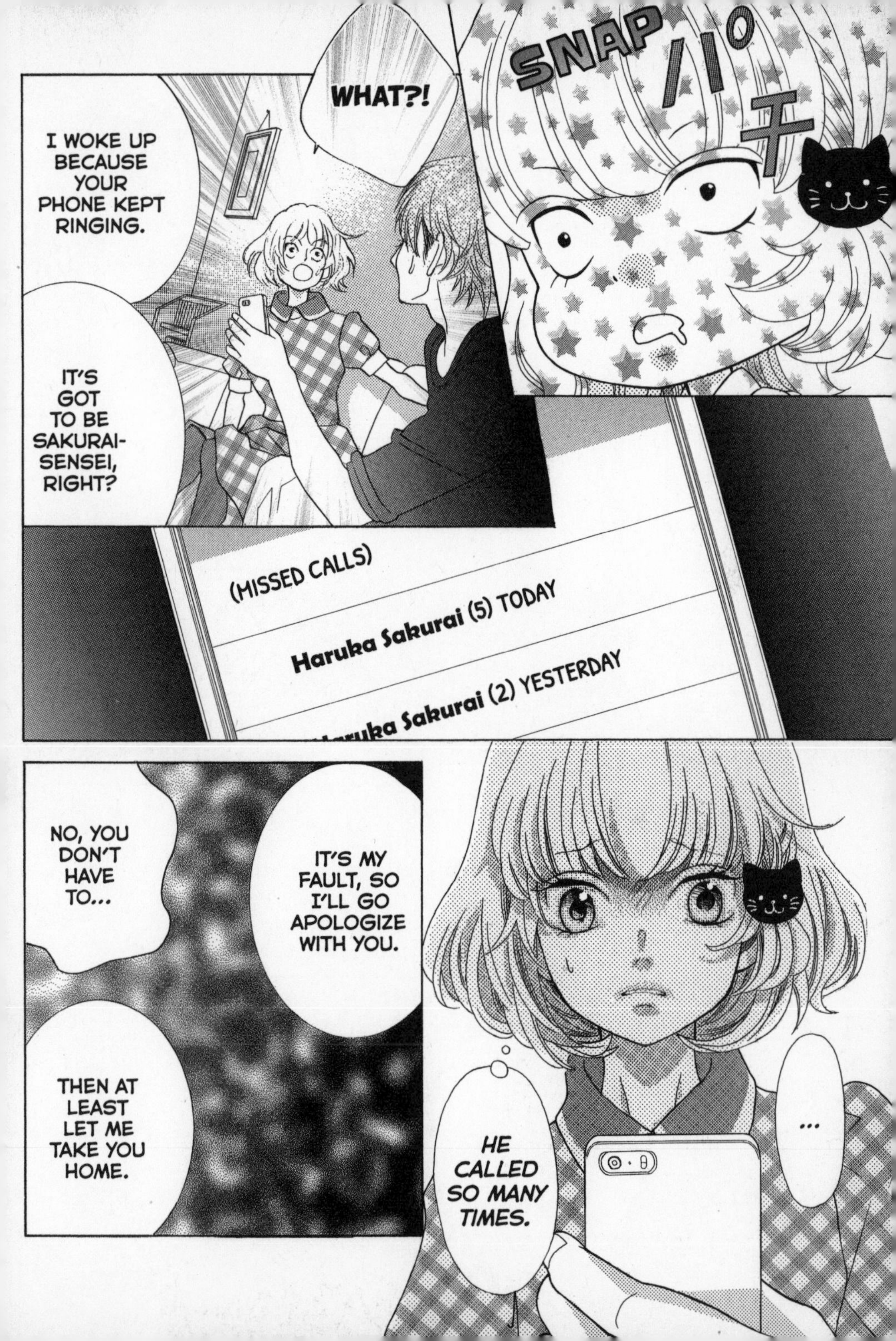
SNAP
パチ
WHAT?!
I WOKE UP BECAUSE YOUR PHONE KEPT RINGING.
IT'S GOT TO BE SAKURAI-SENSEI, RIGHT?
(MISSED CALLS)
Haruka Sakurai (5) TODAY
Haruka Sakurai (2) YESTERDAY
...
HE CALLED SO MANY TIMES.
IT'S MY FAULT, SO I'LL GO APOLOGIZE WITH YOU.
NO, YOU DON'T HAVE TO...
THEN AT LEAST LET ME TAKE YOU HOME.

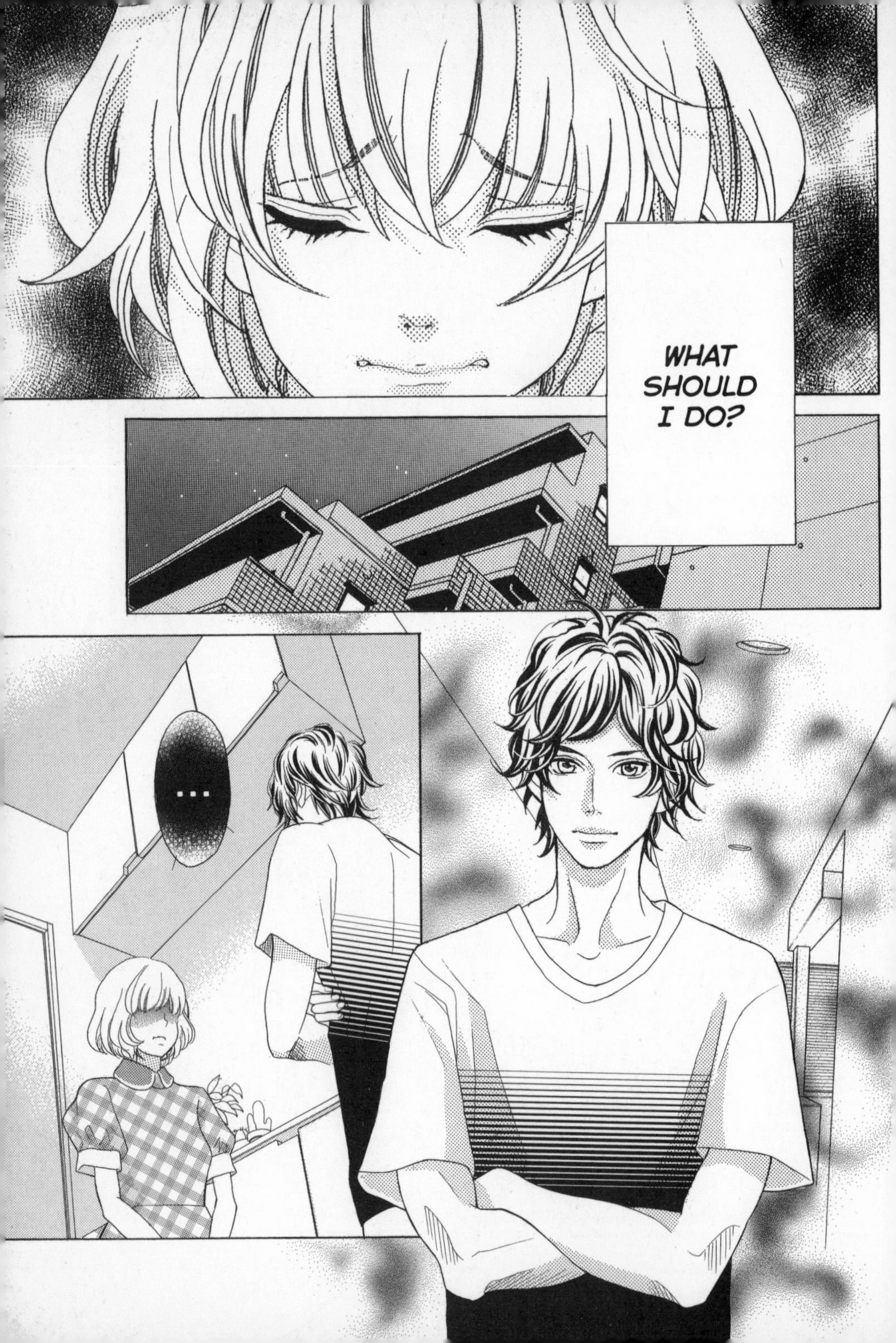
WHAT SHOULD I DO?
...

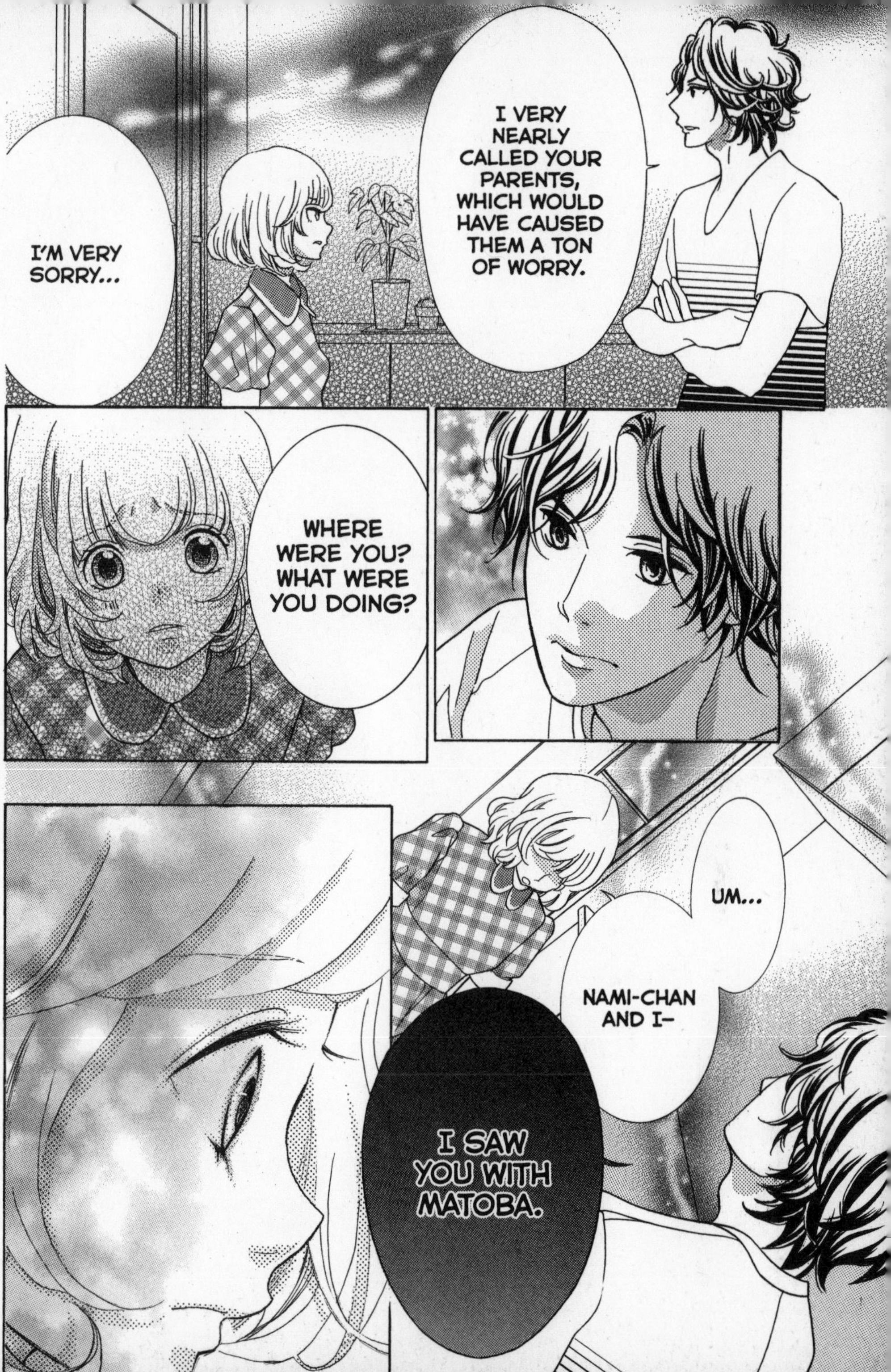
I VERY NEARLY CALLED YOUR PARENTS, WHICH WOULD HAVE CAUSED THEM A TON OF WORRY.
I'M VERY SORRY...
WHERE WERE YOU? WHAT WERE YOU DOING?
UM...
NAMI-CHAN AND I–
I SAW YOU WITH MATOBA.

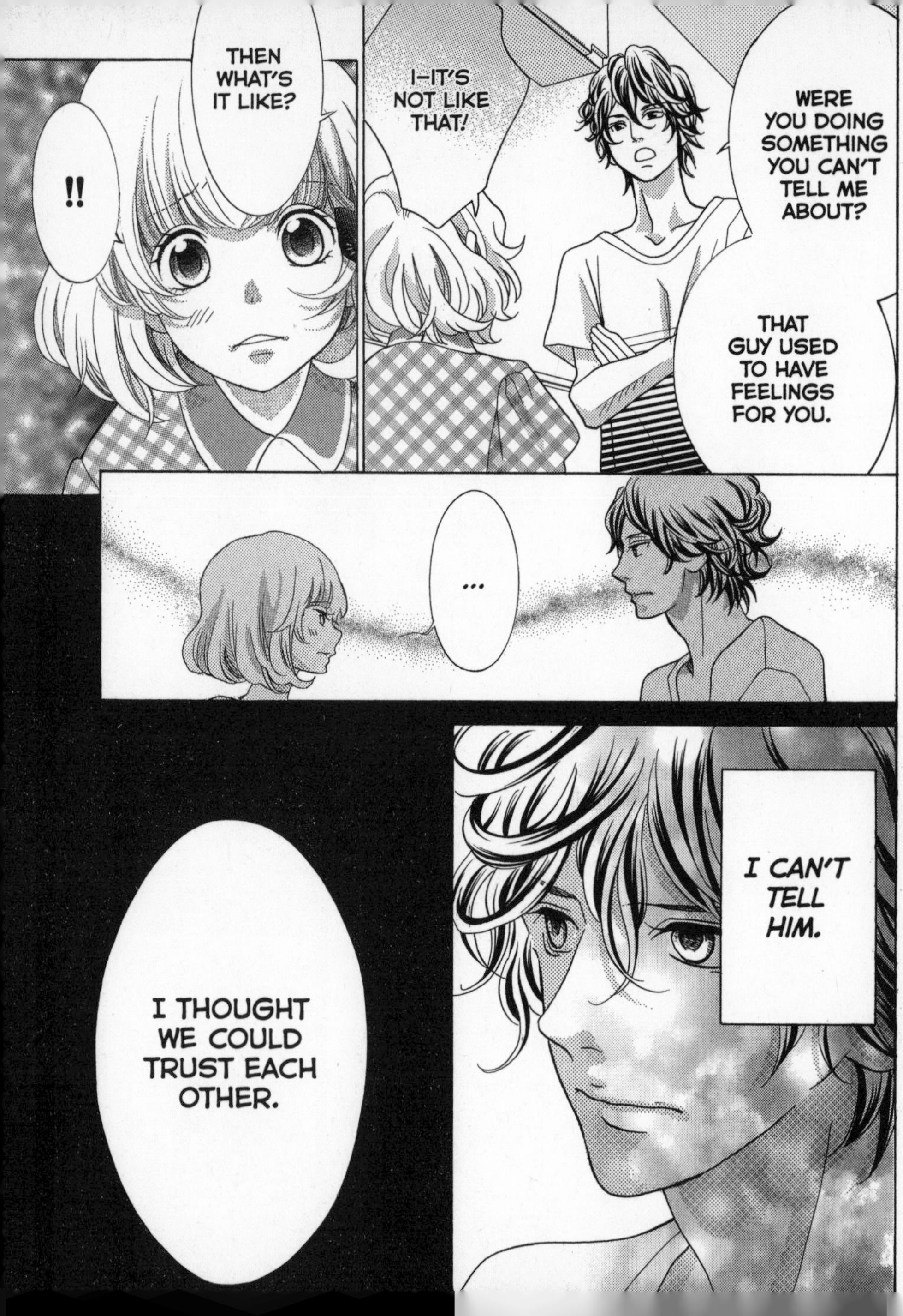
WERE YOU DOING SOMETHING YOU CAN'T TELL ME ABOUT?
I-IT'S NOT LIKE THAT!
THAT GUY USED TO HAVE FEELINGS FOR YOU.
THEN WHAT'S IT LIKE?
!!
...
I CAN'T TELL HIM.
I THOUGHT WE COULD TRUST EACH OTHER.

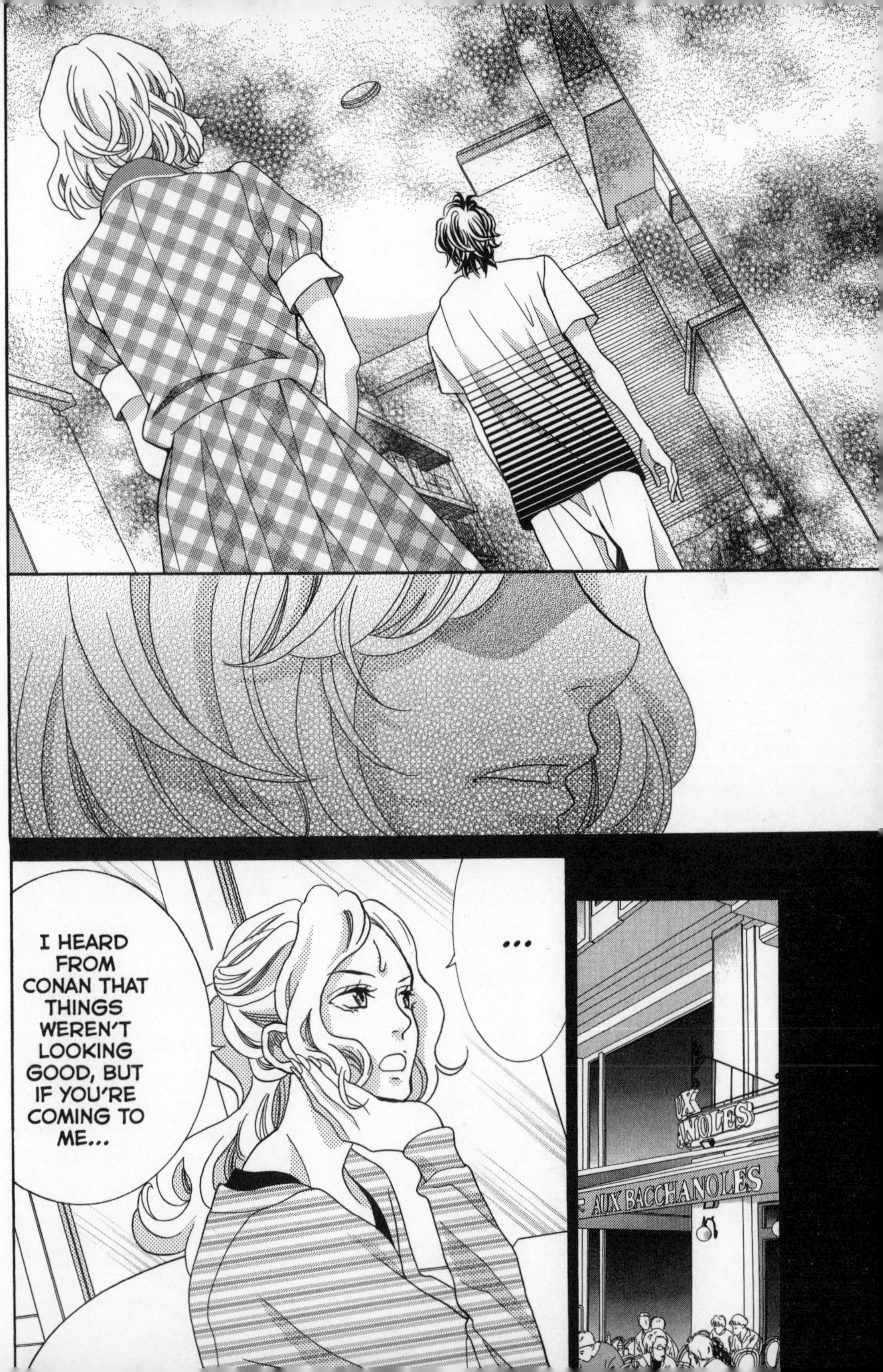
AUX BACCHANOLES
...
I HEARD FROM CONAN THAT THINGS WEREN'T LOOKING GOOD, BUT IF YOU'RE COMING TO ME...

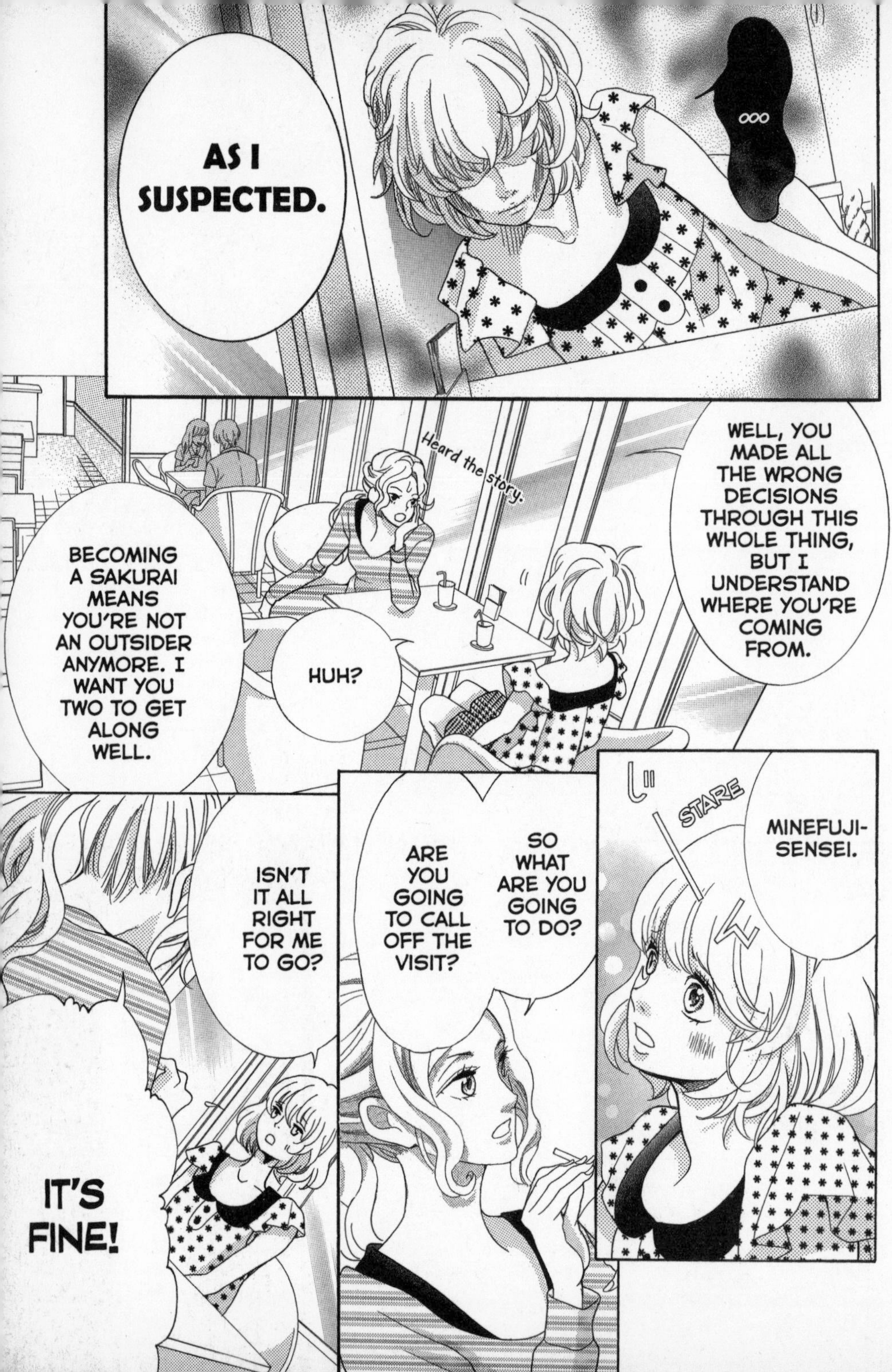
AS I SUSPECTED.
WELL, YOU MADE ALL THE WRONG DECISIONS THROUGH THIS WHOLE THING, BUT I UNDERSTAND WHERE YOU'RE COMING FROM.
Heard the story.
HUH?
BECOMING A SAKURAI MEANS YOU'RE NOT AN OUTSIDER ANYMORE. I WANT YOU TWO TO GET ALONG WELL.
STARE
MINEFUJI-SENSEI.
SO WHAT ARE YOU GOING TO DO?
ARE YOU GOING TO CALL OFF THE VISIT?
ISN'T IT ALL RIGHT FOR ME TO GO?
IT'S FINE!

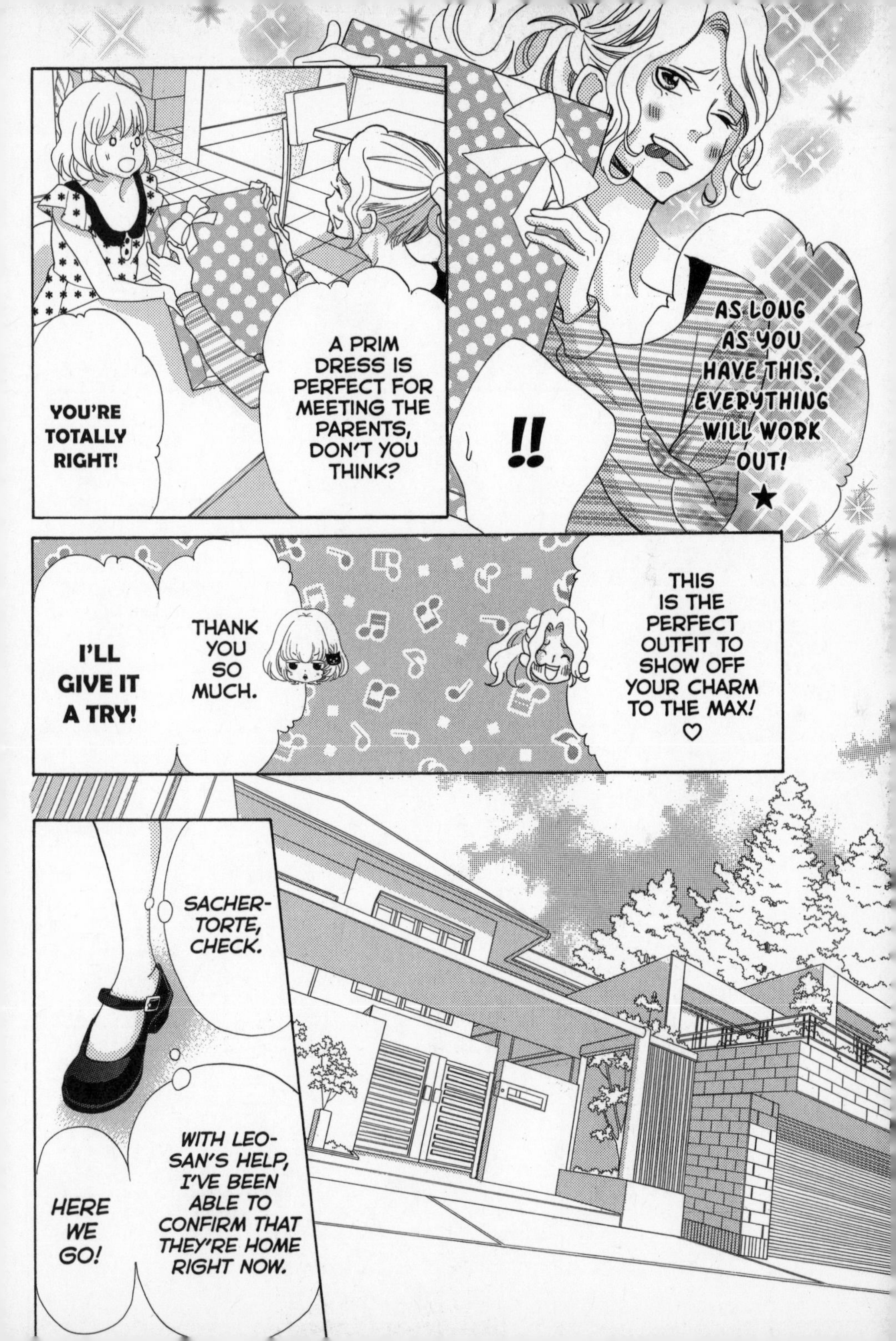
AS LONG AS YOU HAVE THIS, EVERYTHING WILL WORK OUT! ★
!!
A PRIM DRESS IS PERFECT FOR MEETING THE PARENTS, DON'T YOU THINK?
YOU'RE TOTALLY RIGHT!
THIS IS THE PERFECT OUTFIT TO SHOW OFF YOUR CHARM TO THE MAX! ♡
THANK YOU SO MUCH.
I'LL GIVE IT A TRY!
SACHER-TORTE, CHECK.
WITH LEO-SAN'S HELP, I'VE BEEN ABLE TO CONFIRM THAT THEY'RE HOME RIGHT NOW.
HERE WE GO!

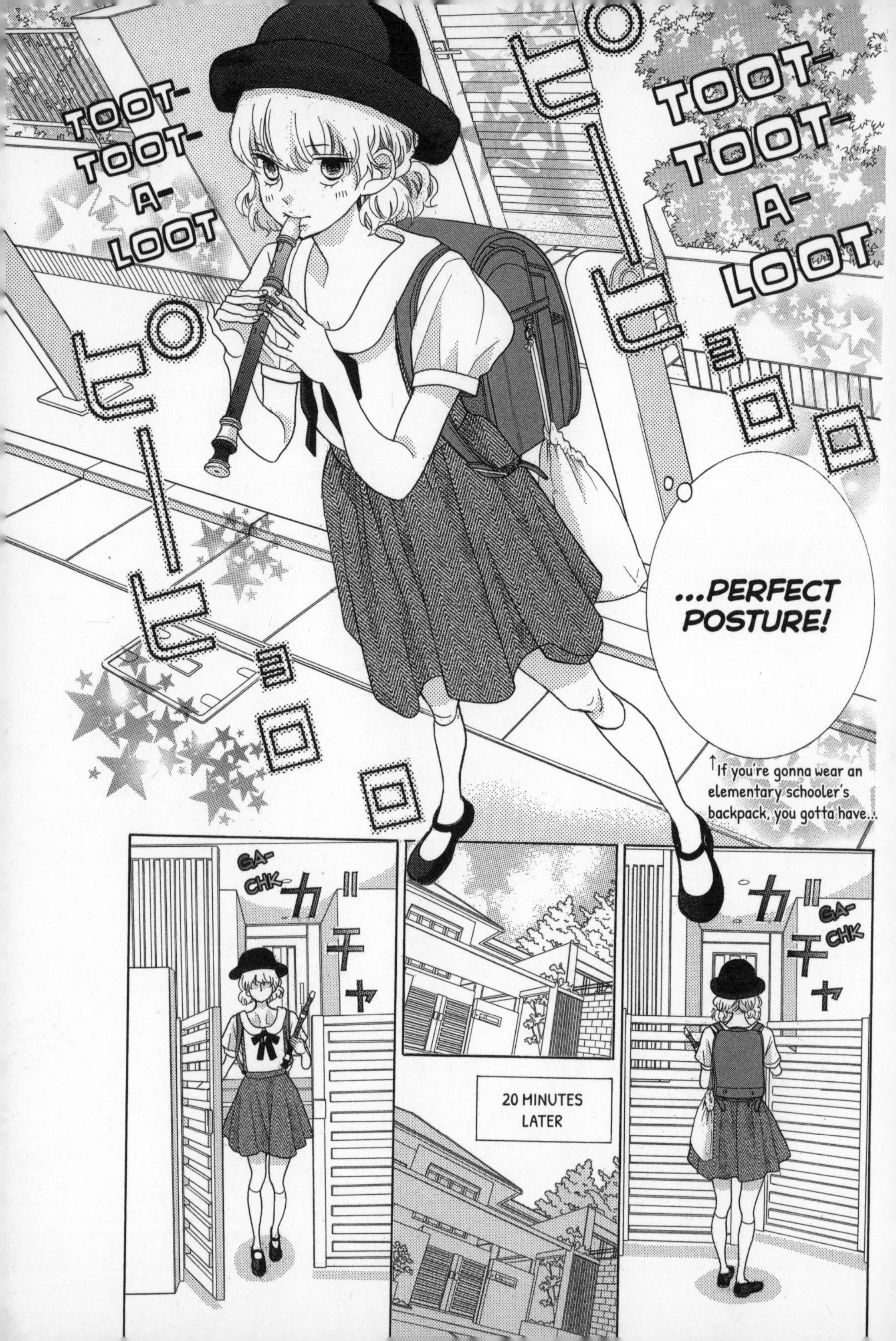
TOOT-TOOT-A-LOOT
TOOT-TOOT-A-LOOT
...PERFECT POSTURE!
↑If you're gonna wear an elementary schooler's backpack, you gotta have...
GA-CHK
20 MINUTES LATER
GA-CHK

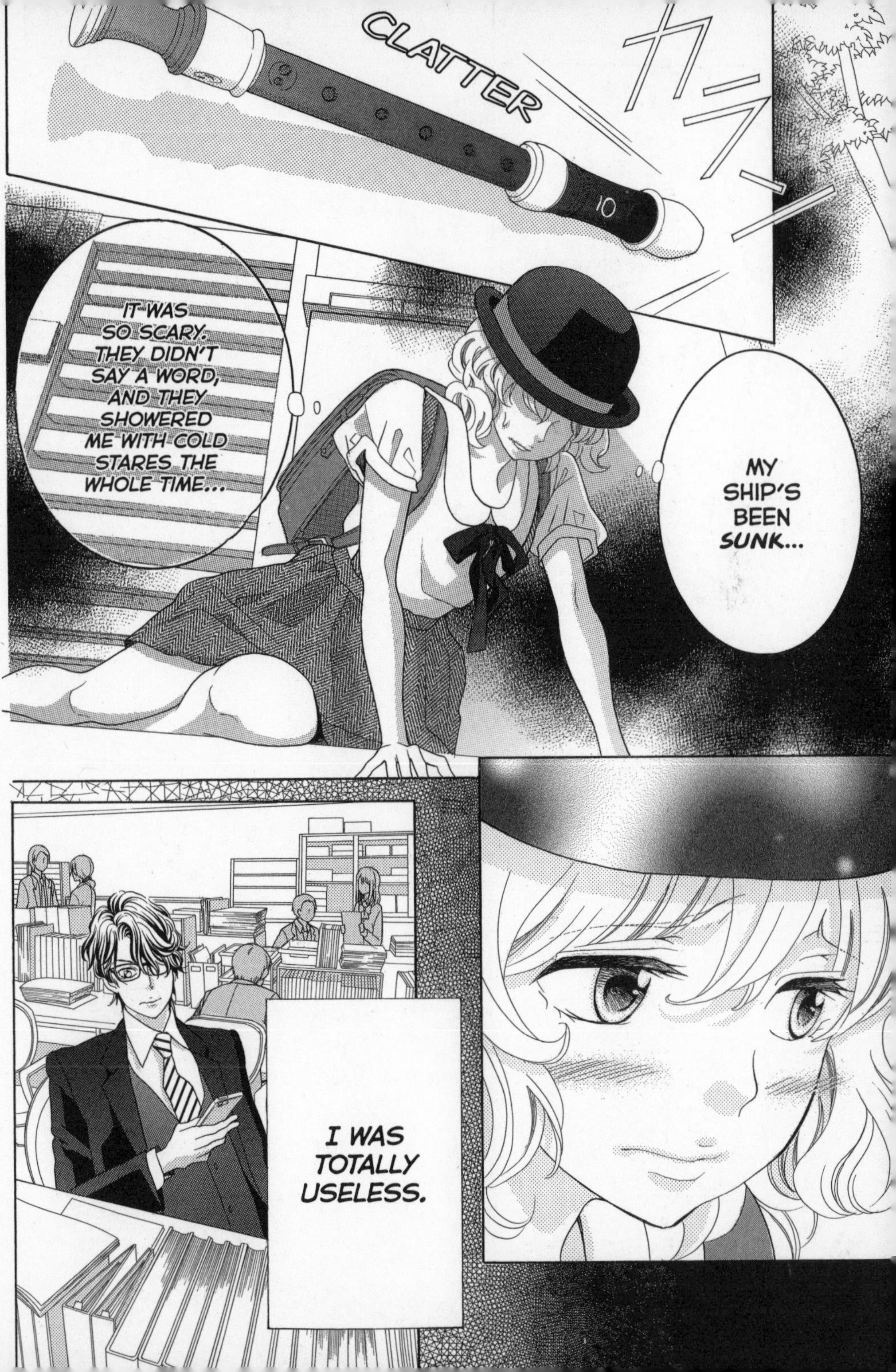
CLATTER
MY SHIP'S BEEN *SUNK*...
IT WAS SO SCARY. THEY DIDN'T SAY A WORD, AND THEY SHOWERED ME WITH COLD STARES THE WHOLE TIME...
I WAS TOTALLY USELESS.

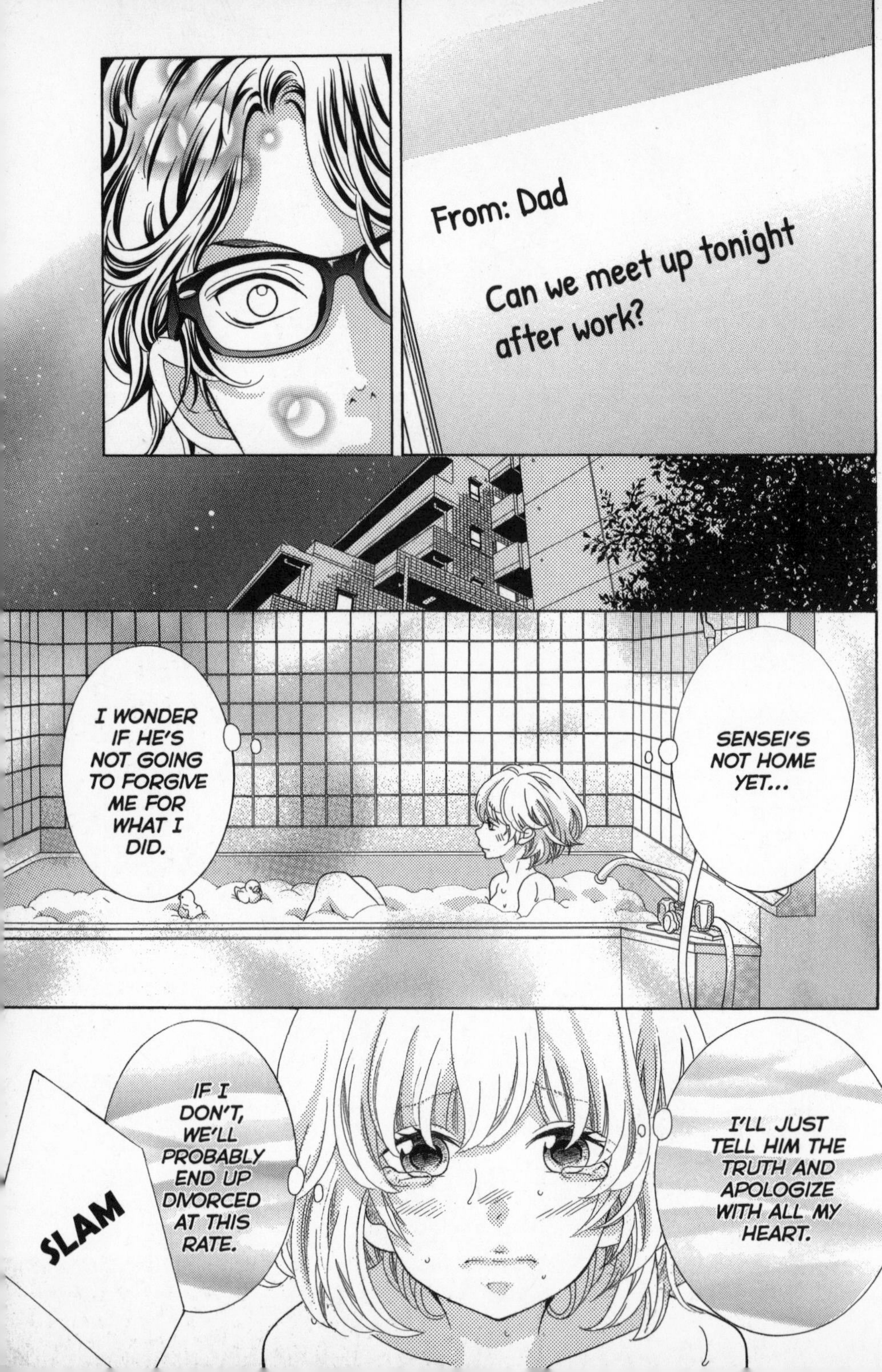
From: Dad
Can we meet up tonight after work?
SENSEI'S NOT HOME YET...
I WONDER IF HE'S NOT GOING TO FORGIVE ME FOR WHAT I DID.
I'LL JUST TELL HIM THE TRUTH AND APOLOGIZE WITH ALL MY HEART.
IF I DON'T, WE'LL PROBABLY END UP DIVORCED AT THIS RATE.
SLAM

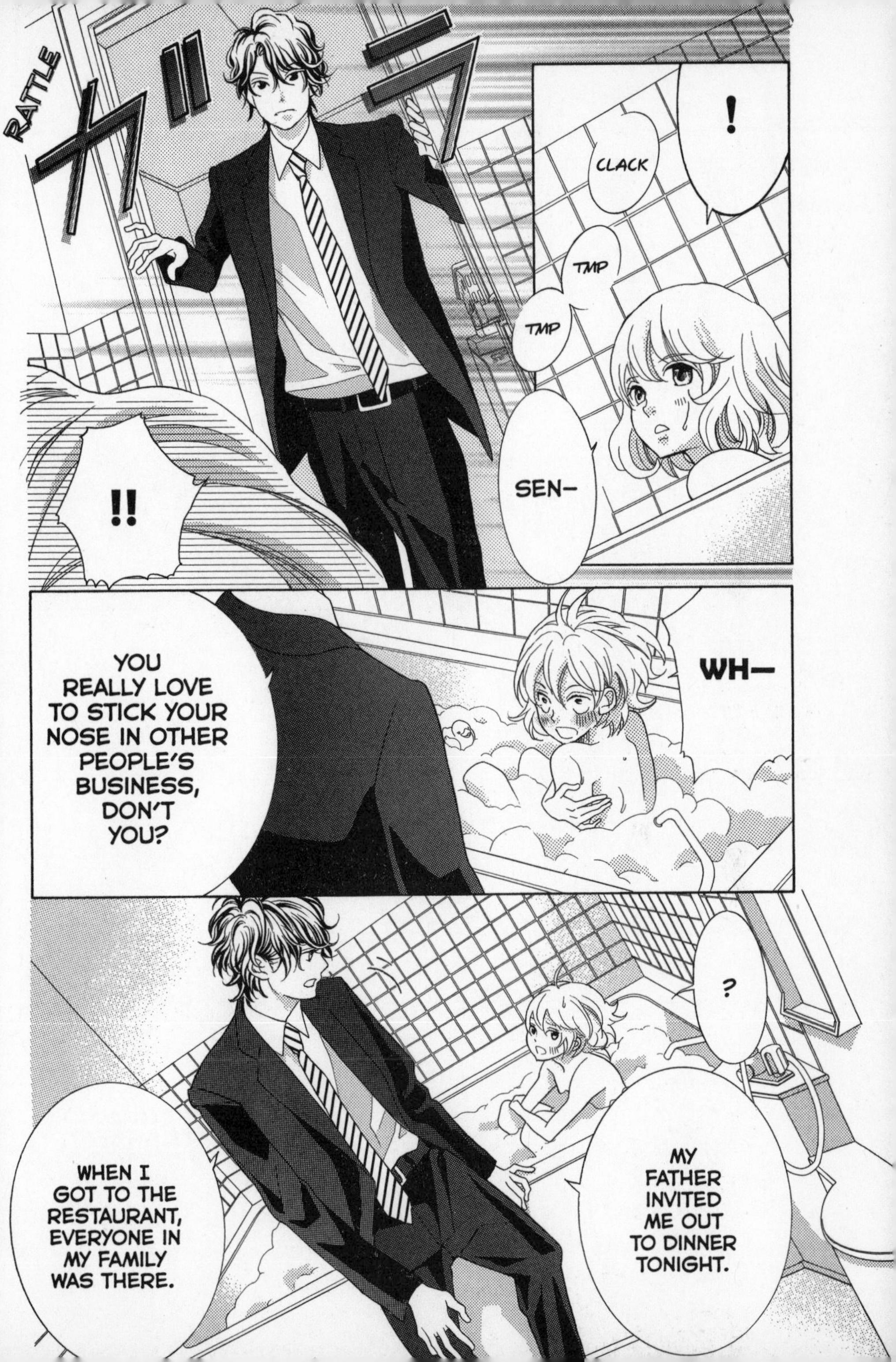
!
CLACK
TMP
TMP
SEN-
RATTLE
!!
WH—
YOU REALLY LOVE TO STICK YOUR NOSE IN OTHER PEOPLE'S BUSINESS, DON'T YOU?
?
MY FATHER INVITED ME OUT TO DINNER TONIGHT.
WHEN I GOT TO THE RESTAURANT, EVERYONE IN MY FAMILY WAS THERE.

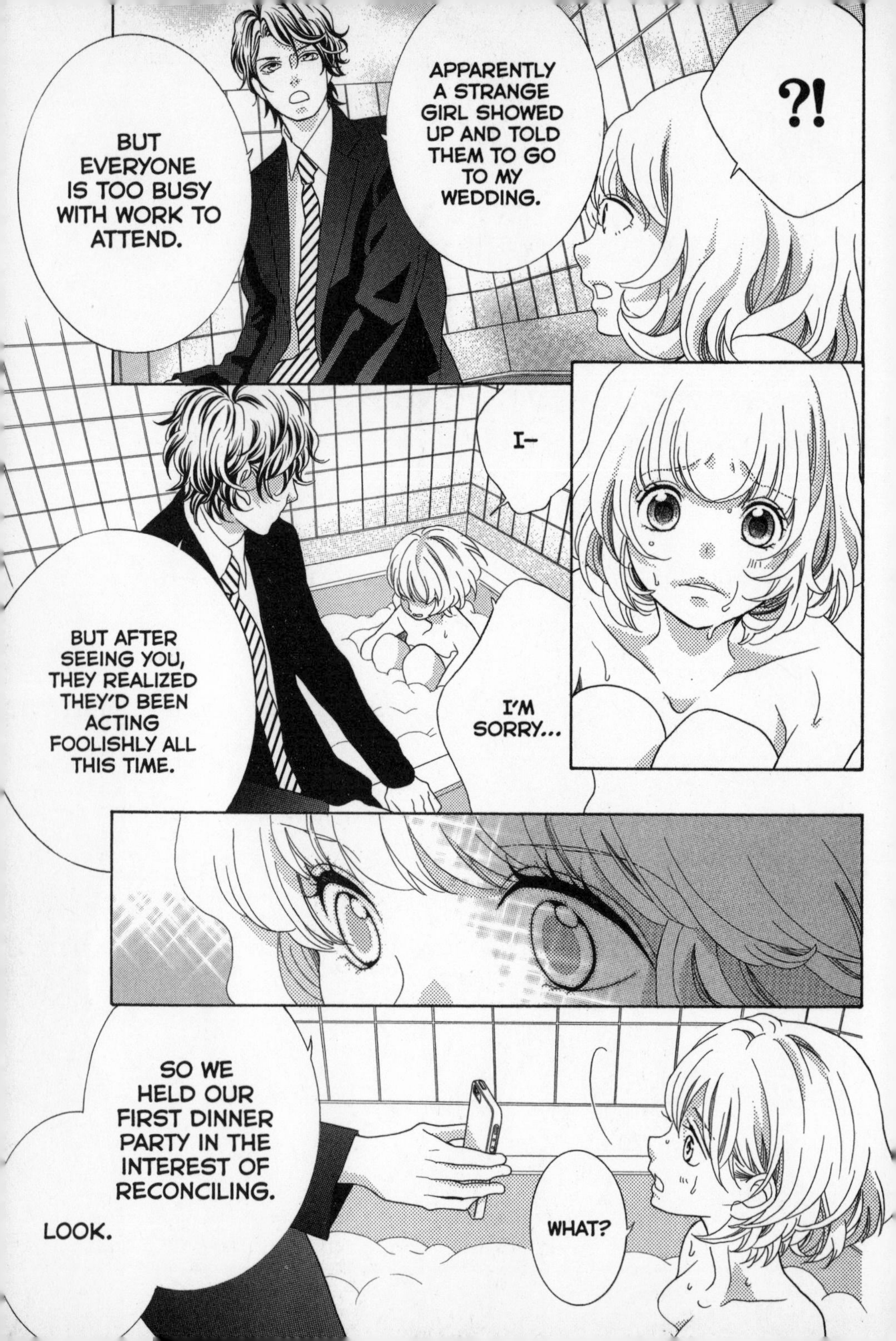
?!
APPARENTLY A STRANGE GIRL SHOWED UP AND TOLD THEM TO GO TO MY WEDDING.
BUT EVERYONE IS TOO BUSY WITH WORK TO ATTEND.
I—
I'M SORRY...
BUT AFTER SEEING YOU, THEY REALIZED THEY'D BEEN ACTING FOOLISHLY ALL THIS TIME.
WHAT?
SO WE HELD OUR FIRST DINNER PARTY IN THE INTEREST OF RECONCILING.
LOOK.

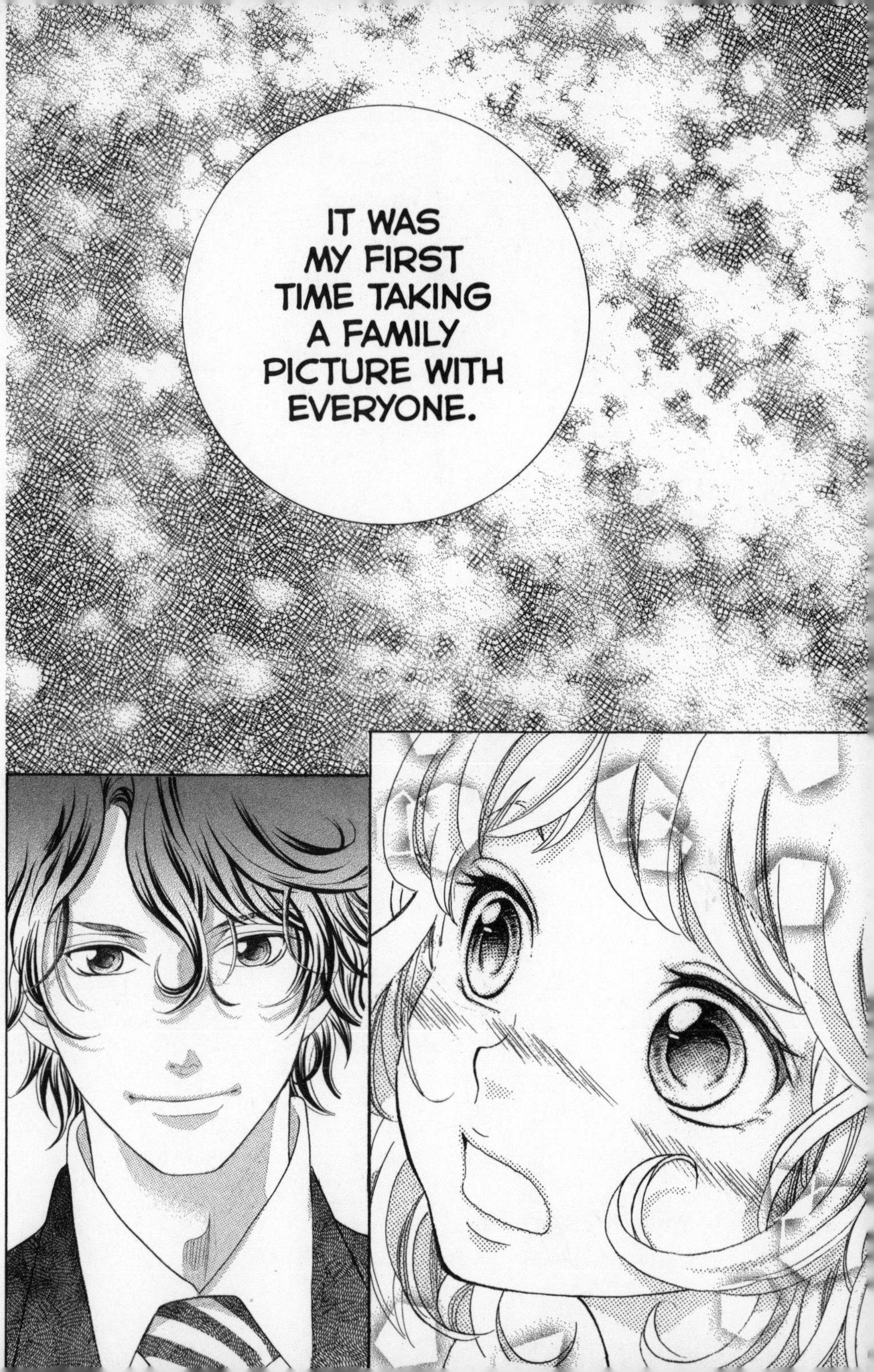
IT WAS MY FIRST TIME TAKING A FAMILY PICTURE WITH EVERYONE.

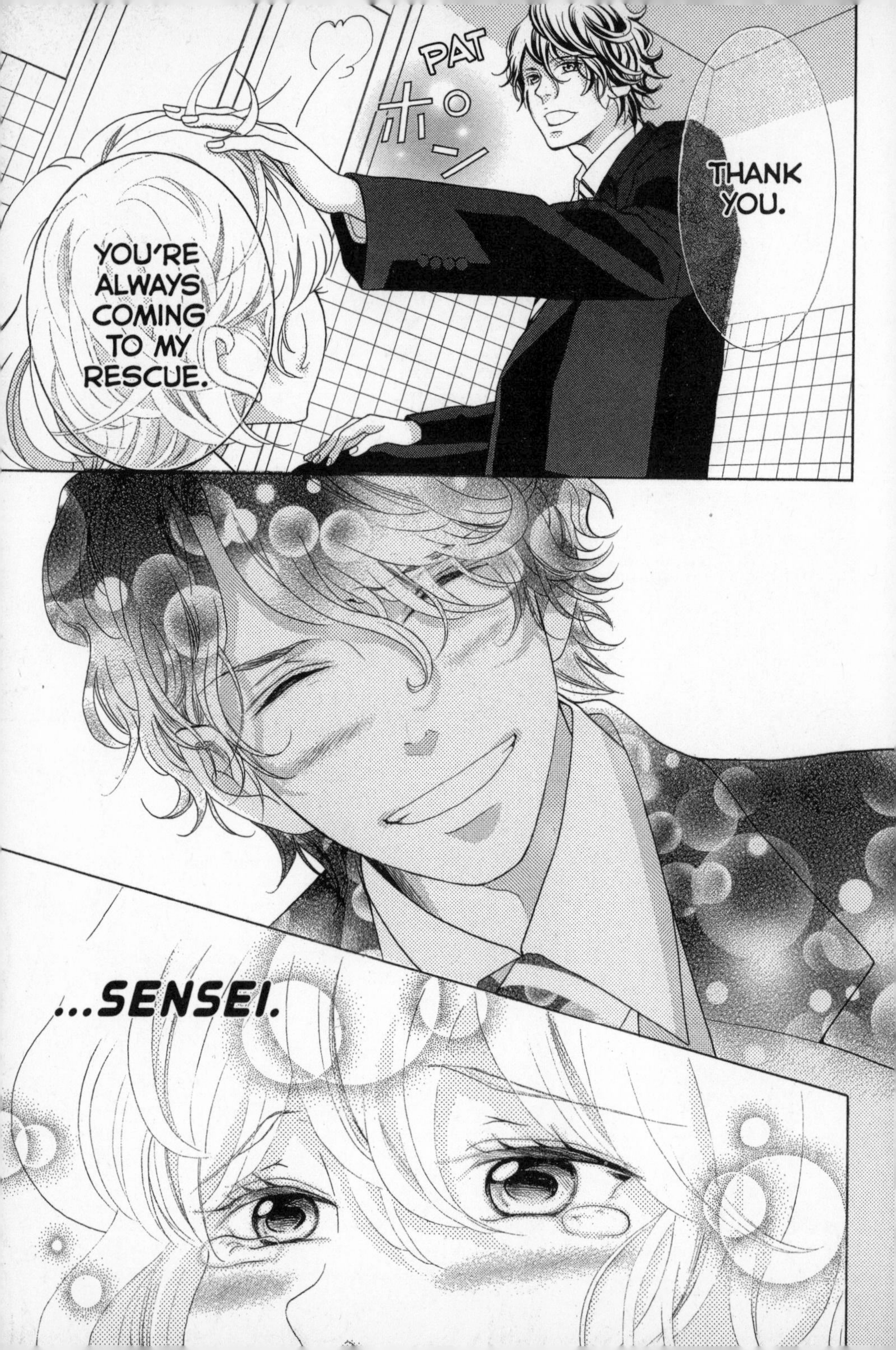
THANK YOU.
PAT
ポーン
YOU'RE ALWAYS COMING TO MY RESCUE.
...SENSEI.

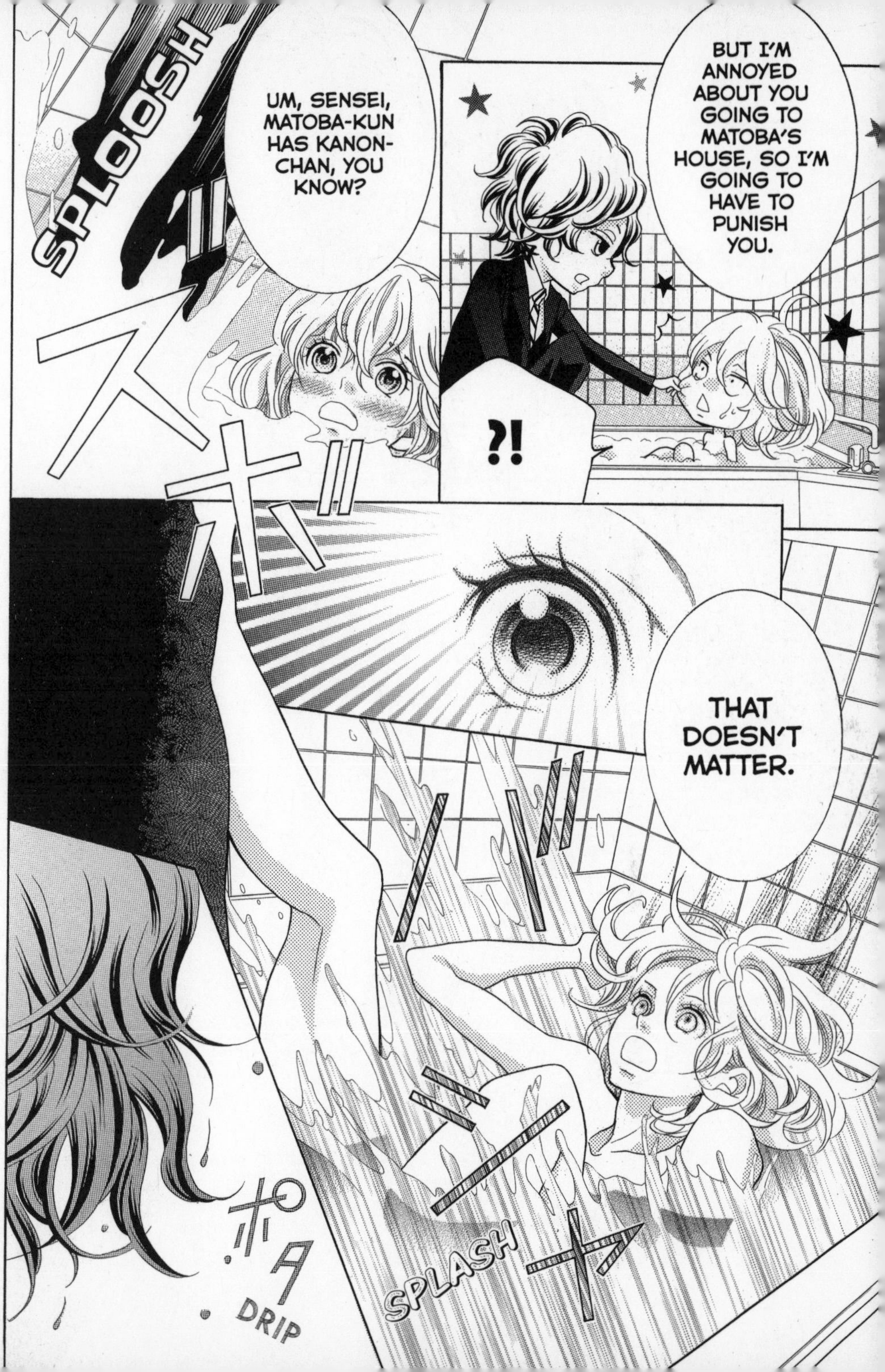
BUT I'M ANNOYED ABOUT YOU GOING TO MATOBA'S HOUSE, SO I'M GOING TO HAVE TO PUNISH YOU.
?!
UM, SENSEI, MATOBA-KUN HAS KANON-CHAN, YOU KNOW?
SPLOOSH
THAT DOESN'T MATTER.
SPLASH
DRIP

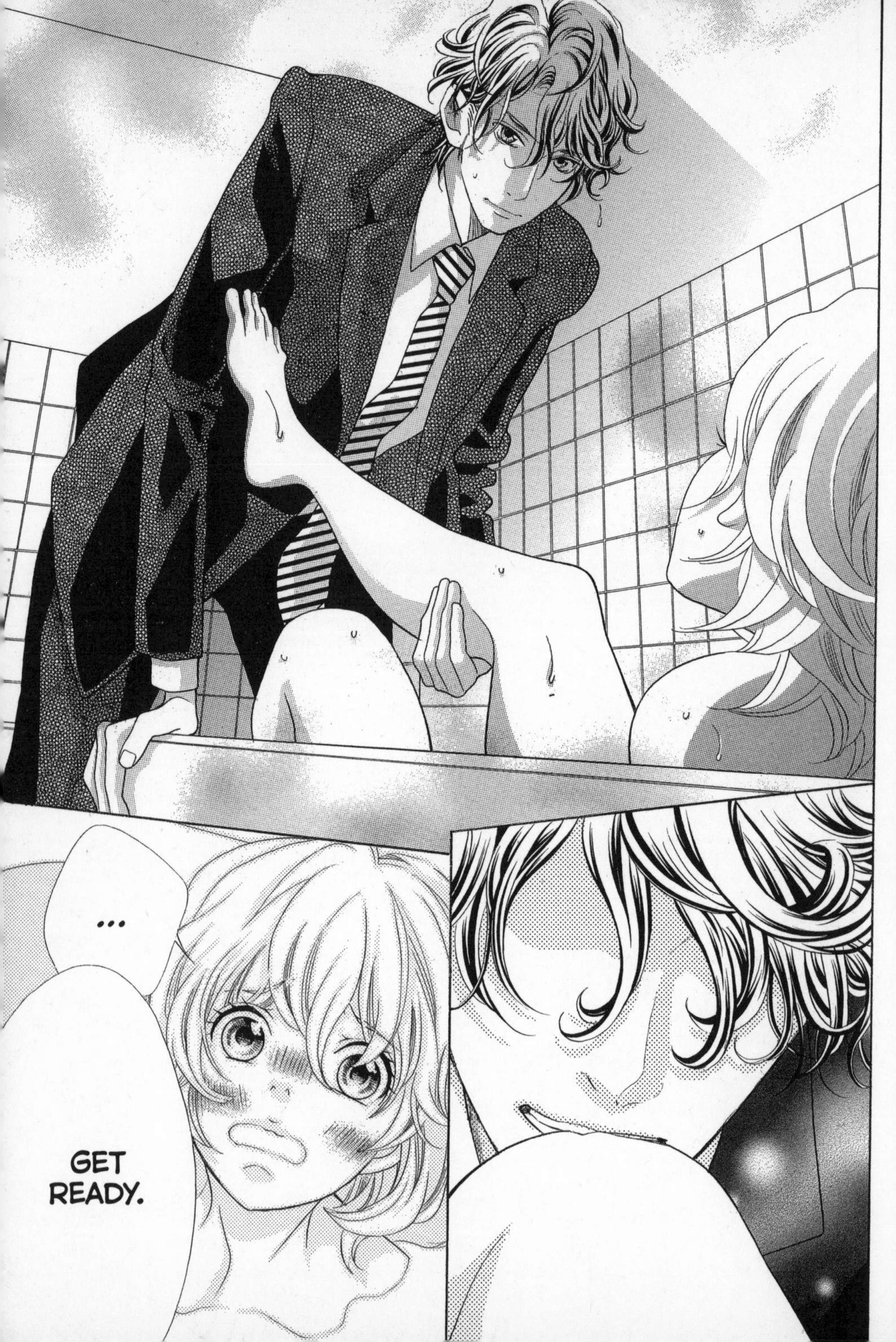
...
GET READY.

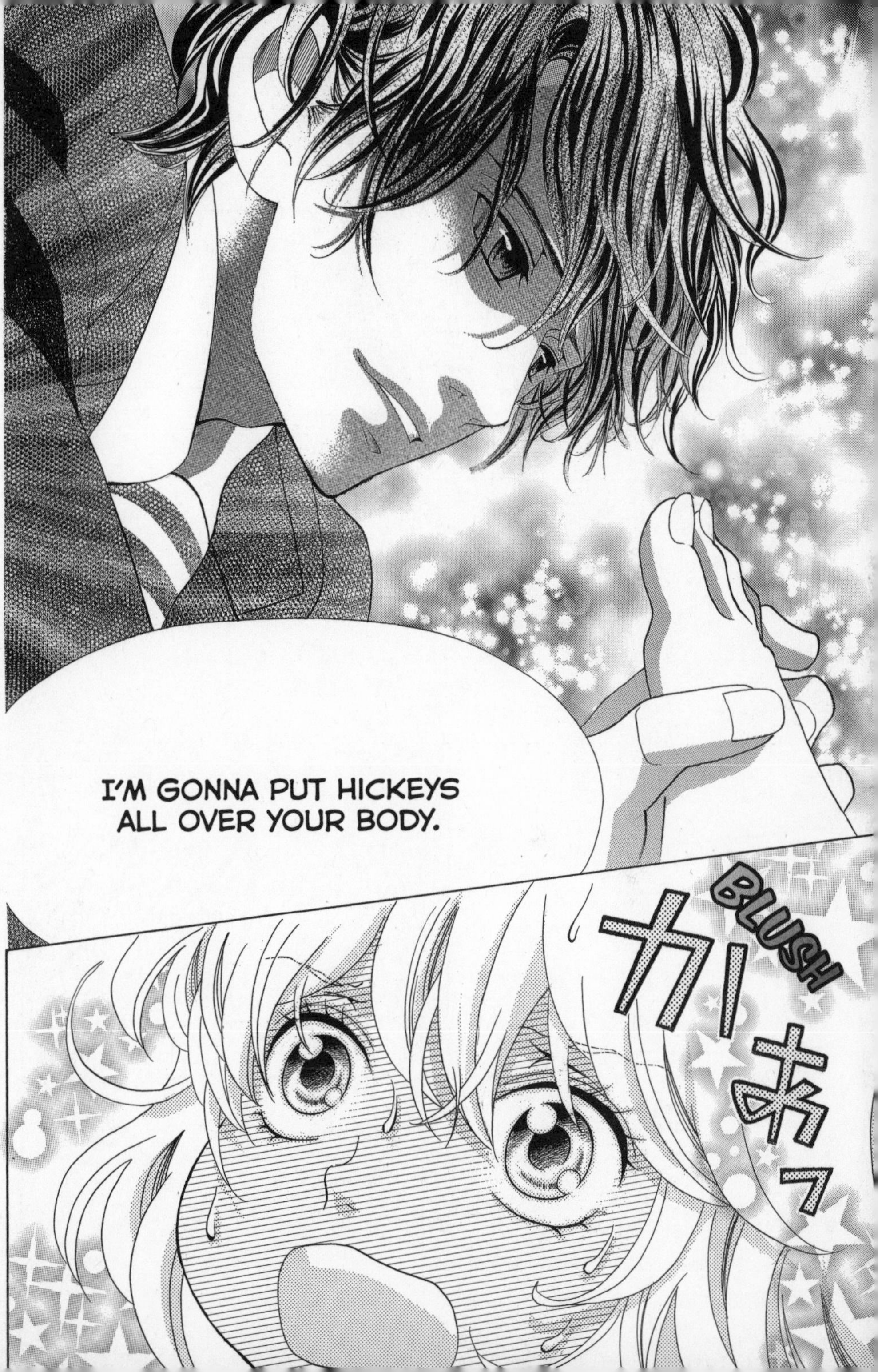
I'M GONNA PUT HICKEYS ALL OVER YOUR BODY.
BLUSH
カーあっ

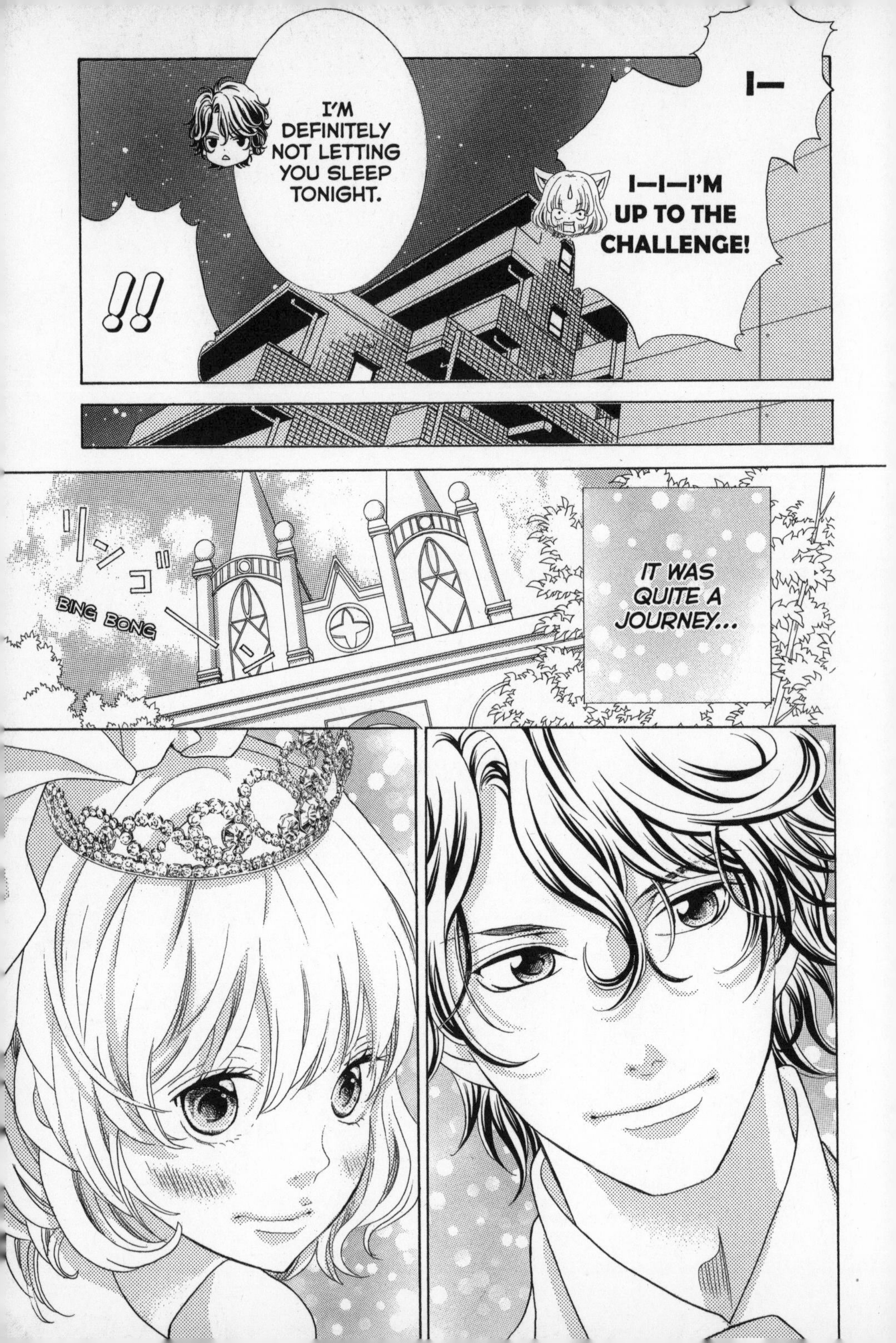
I—
I'M DEFINITELY NOT LETTING YOU SLEEP TONIGHT.
I—I—I'M UP TO THE CHALLENGE!
!!
IT WAS QUITE A JOURNEY...
BING BONG

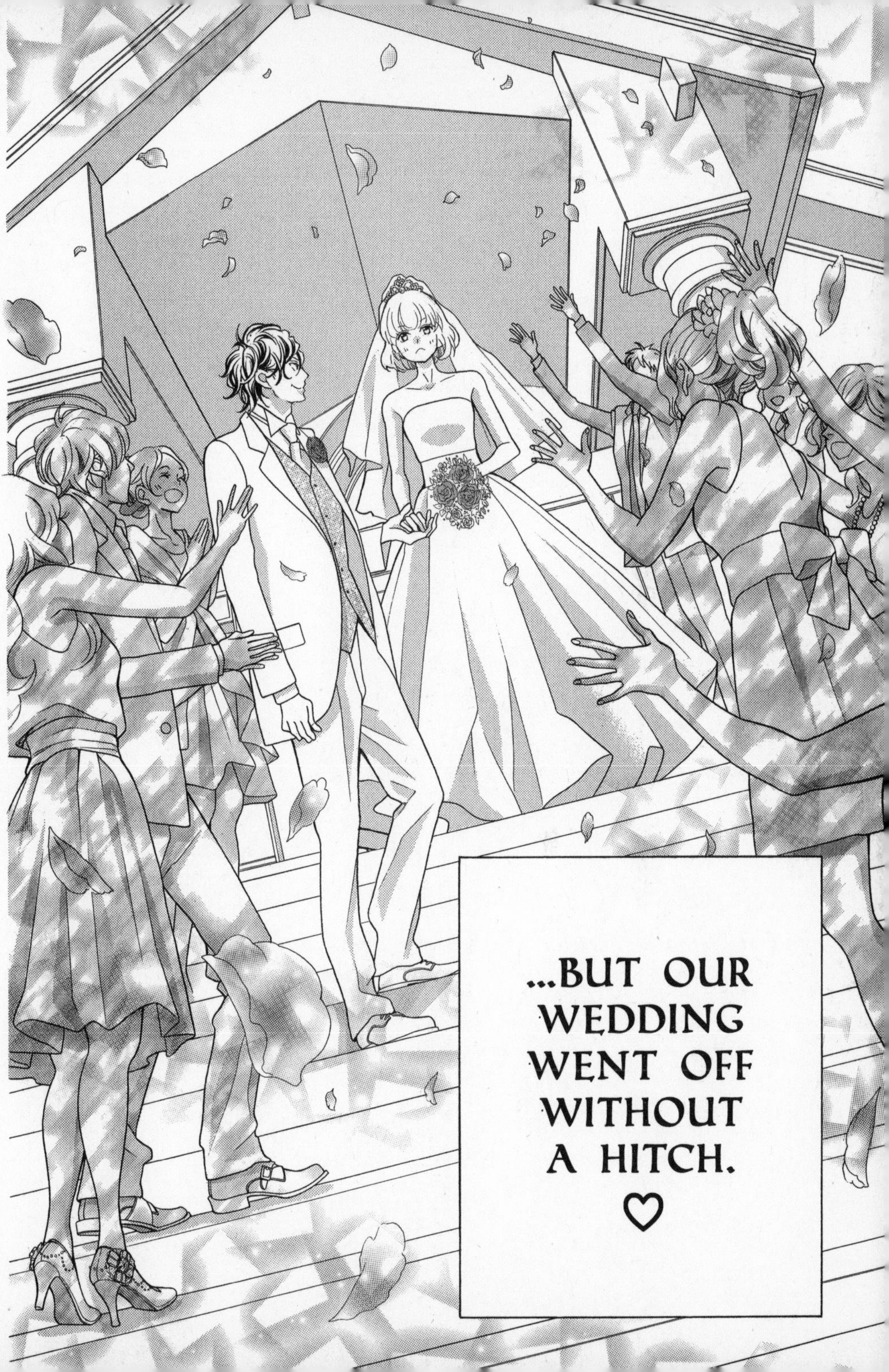
...BUT OUR WEDDING WENT OFF WITHOUT A HITCH. ♡

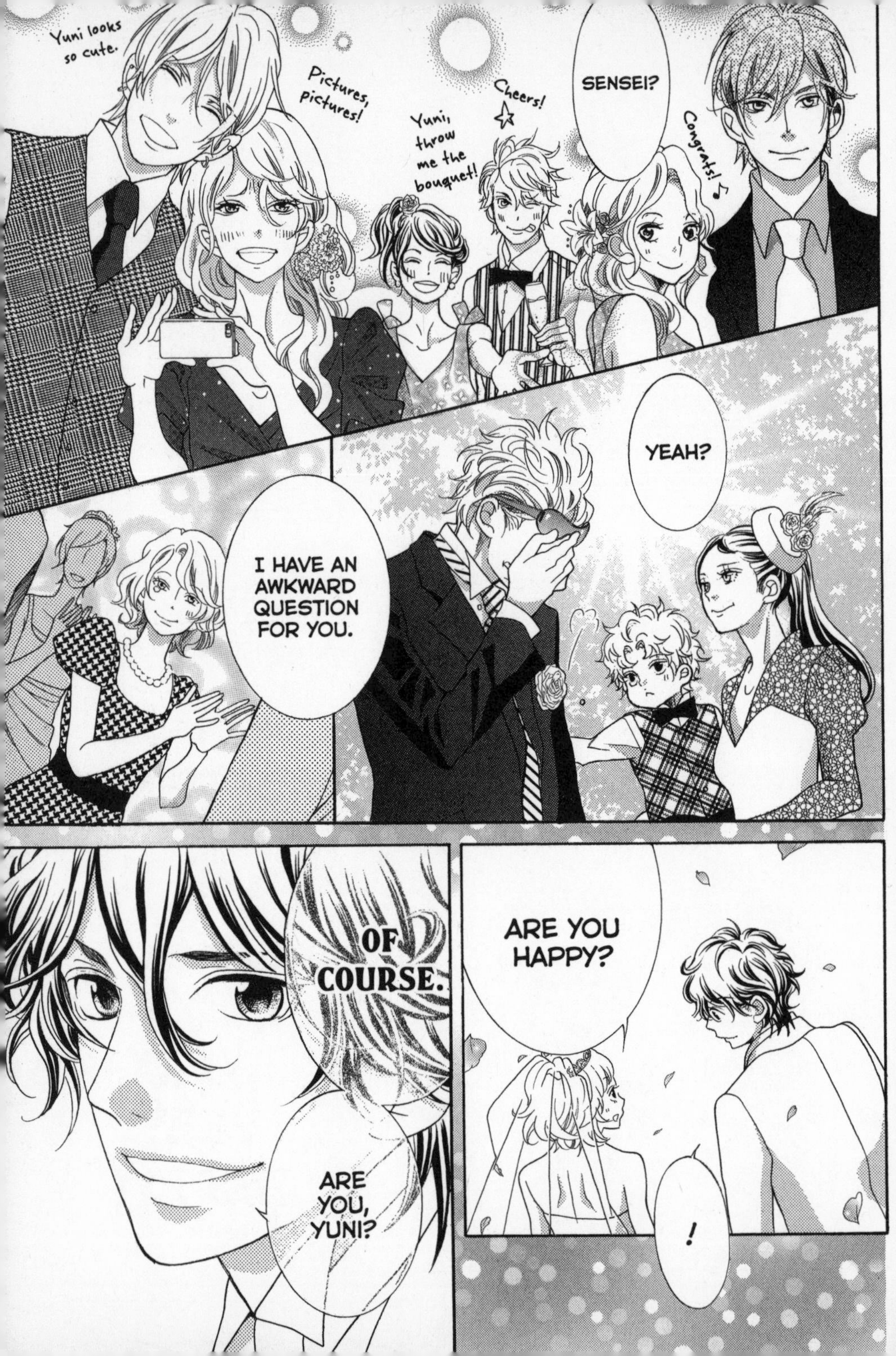
SENSEI?
Congrats!
Cheers!
Yuni, throw me the bouquet!
Pictures, pictures!
Yuni looks so cute.
YEAH?
I HAVE AN AWKWARD QUESTION FOR YOU.
ARE YOU HAPPY?
!
OF COURSE.
ARE YOU, YUNI?

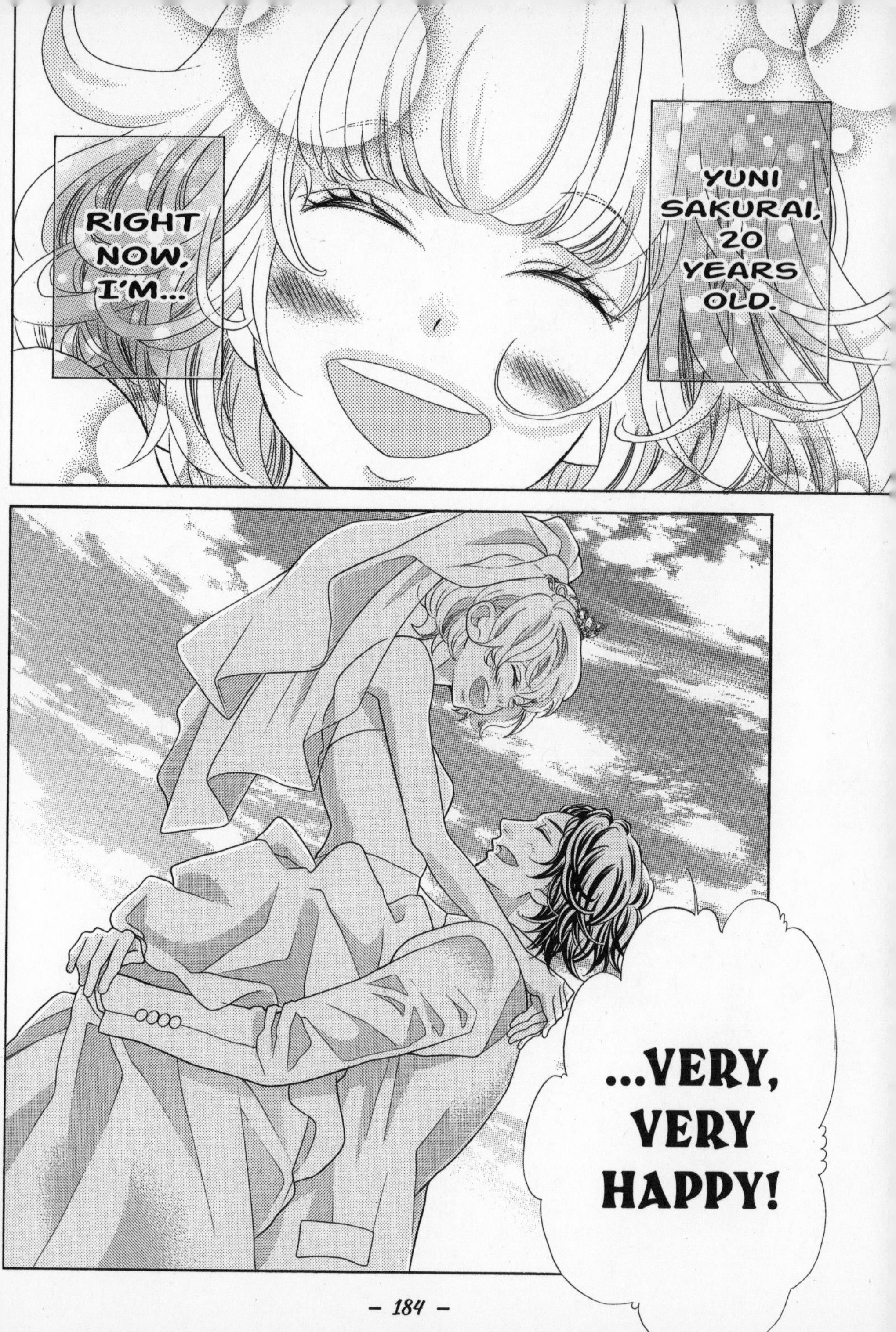
YUNI SAKURAI, 20 YEARS OLD.
RIGHT NOW, I'M...
...VERY, VERY HAPPY!

E Π D

LOVE'S REACH

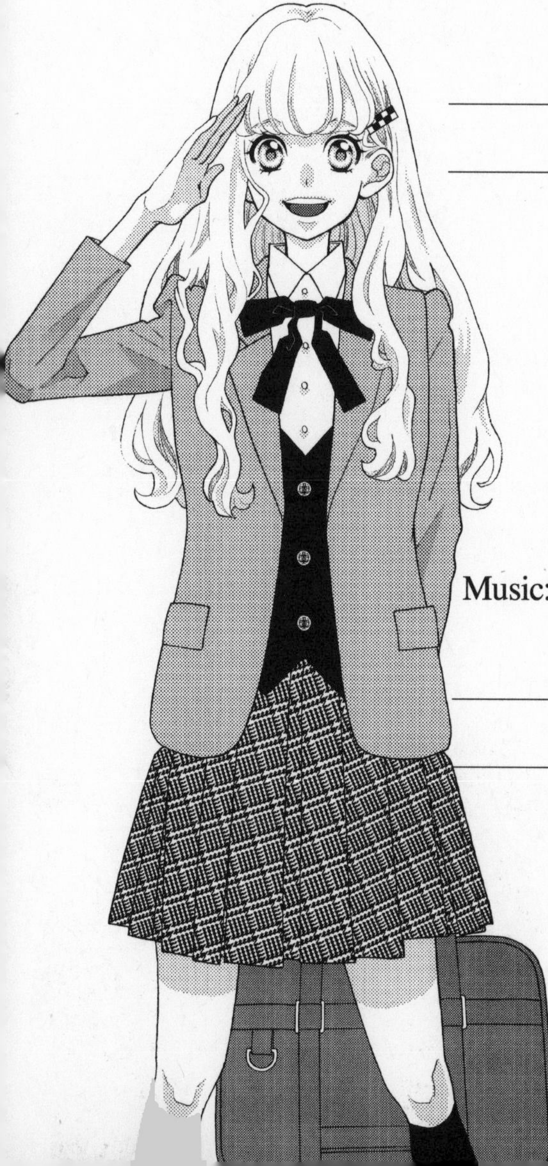

Hinana Hanazawa (16)

Nickname: Nana, Closet Pervert
Height, Weight: 160cm, 45kg
Blood Type: A
Hobbies: Movies, playing with her little sister
Obsession: Collecting barrettes

FAVORITE

Color: White, blue
Food: Udon noodles, okra
Animal: Cats, rabbits
Fashion style: Casual, girly
Celeb: Kaede Ayase
Book: Yellow Eye Fish by Takako Sato, fairy tales
Music: Perfume, Carly Rae Jepsen
Movie: Disney, Pixar

If I could have one wish...

I would want to wear a Cinderella dress!

Kaede Ayase (24)

Nickname: Ayase-san, Butt Alien

Height, Weight: 183cm, 63 kg

Blood Type: O

Hobbies: Movies, reading

Obsession: Collecting Panty Flash figures

FAVORITE

Color: Red, black

Food: Meat, cheese

Animal: Dogs

Fashion style: Streetwear

Celeb: Ogiyahagi (the comedy duo)

Book: Kanako Nishi's works

Music: Western music, Gen Hoshino, ONE OK ROCK

Movie: De Niro's works

If I could have one wish…

I would want to play around outside without worry!

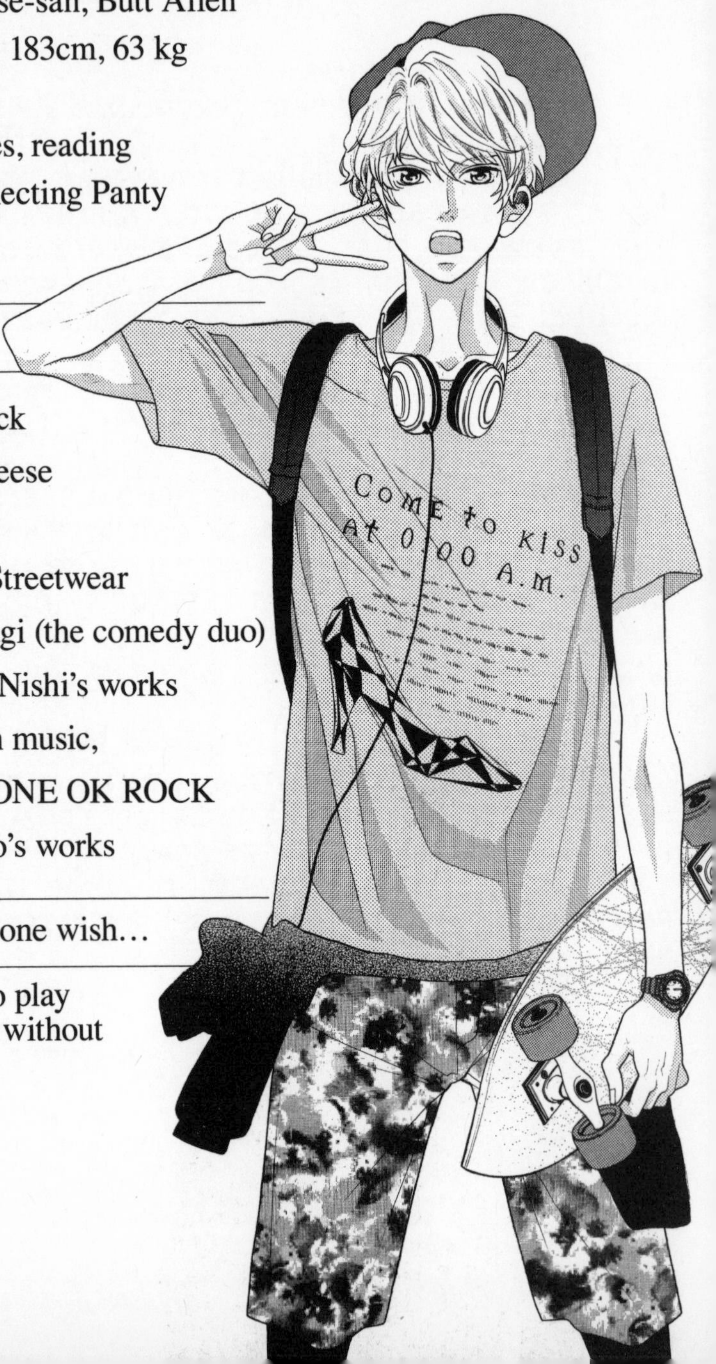
COME to KISS
AT 0:00 A.M.

AFTERWORD

HELLO, EVERYONE.
THANK YOU FOR READING VOLUME 3.
DID YOU ENJOY IT?
THERE'S AN OMNIBUS THAT CAME OUT AT THE
SAME TIME CALLED "HE'S AN IDOL" AND I'M MANAGING
THE COVERS FOR THAT. THERE ARE *STROKE OF MIDNIGHT*
INTERVIEW-TYPE THINGS AND FIRST DRAFTS AND STUFF
INCLUDED IN IT. THE STORY USED TO BE PRETTY DIFFERENT
FROM WHAT IT IS NOW; THERE ARE SOME WEIRD PLOTS AND
SETTINGS. NOW THAT I THINK ABOUT IT, I'M GLAD I DIDN'T
INCLUDE THAT FIGURE. IF YOU'RE INTERESTED, PLEASE DO
CHECK IT OUT!

THIS TIME AROUND, I INCLUDED A SPECIAL CHAPTER
OF *LOVE'S REACH*, BUT BECAUSE OF THIS, THE *STROKE OF
MIDNIGHT* CONTENT WAS 1 CHAPTER SHORT—I'M SORRY! I
WANTED TO AVOID THAT, BUT VARIOUS THINGS HAPPENED,
AND IT FOUND ITS WAY IN. (FOR THOSE OF YOU WHO WERE
LOOKING FORWARD TO *LOVE'S REACH* IN THIS, THANKS SO
MUCH! ♡)

AND FINALLY, ONTO VOLUME 4! THAT'S THE KIND OF
GUSTO I'M AIMING TO MAINTAIN FOR THE NEXT VOLUME.
IT'S GONNA BE NICE AND RISQUÉ RIGHT FROM THE START!
AH-CHAN'S GONNA HAVE MORE SCREEN TIME, AND THE GIRL
FROM THE LAST PAGE WILL ALSO SHOW UP! IT'S GOING TO
BE REALLY FUN, SO PLEASE LOOK FORWARD TO THE NEXT
BOOK!

3.2016   —RIN MIKIMOTO
                           TWITTER : @RINMIKIRIN

Special thanx

S.sato

H.saijyo

M.kawai

M.takayashiki

K.kaneko

Every one of the staff

Everyone in the editorial department

Horiuchi-sama

Morita-san

Saiki-san

arcoinc Kusume-sama

&U

I LOVE YOU

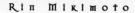

I imagine Scarlet to be big,
white, and fluffy. Shige-chan
usually takes her on her walks
since he's kind of a freeloader,
(haha). Also, when I think about
it, all my serialized works have
had animals in them—a cat, a
bird, a dog. I love animals!
Enjoy Volume 3!

Rin Mikimoto

HAPPINESS

——ハピネス——

By Shuzo Oshimi

From the creator of *The Flowers of Evil*

Nothing interesting is happening in Makoto Ozaki's first year of high school. His life is a series of quiet humiliations: low-grade bullies, unreliable friends, and the constant frustration of his adolescent lust. But one night, a pale, thin girl knocks him to the ground in an alley and offers him a choice. Now everything is different. Daylight is searingly bright. Food tastes awful. And worse than anything is the terrible, consuming thirst...

Praise for Shuzo Oshimi's *The Flowers of Evil*

"A shockingly readable story that vividly—one might even say queasily—evokes the fear and confusion of discovering one's own sexuality. Recommended." —The Manga Critic

"A page-turning tale of sordid middle school blackmail." —Otaku USA Magazine

"A stunning new horror manga." —Third Eye Comics

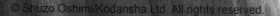

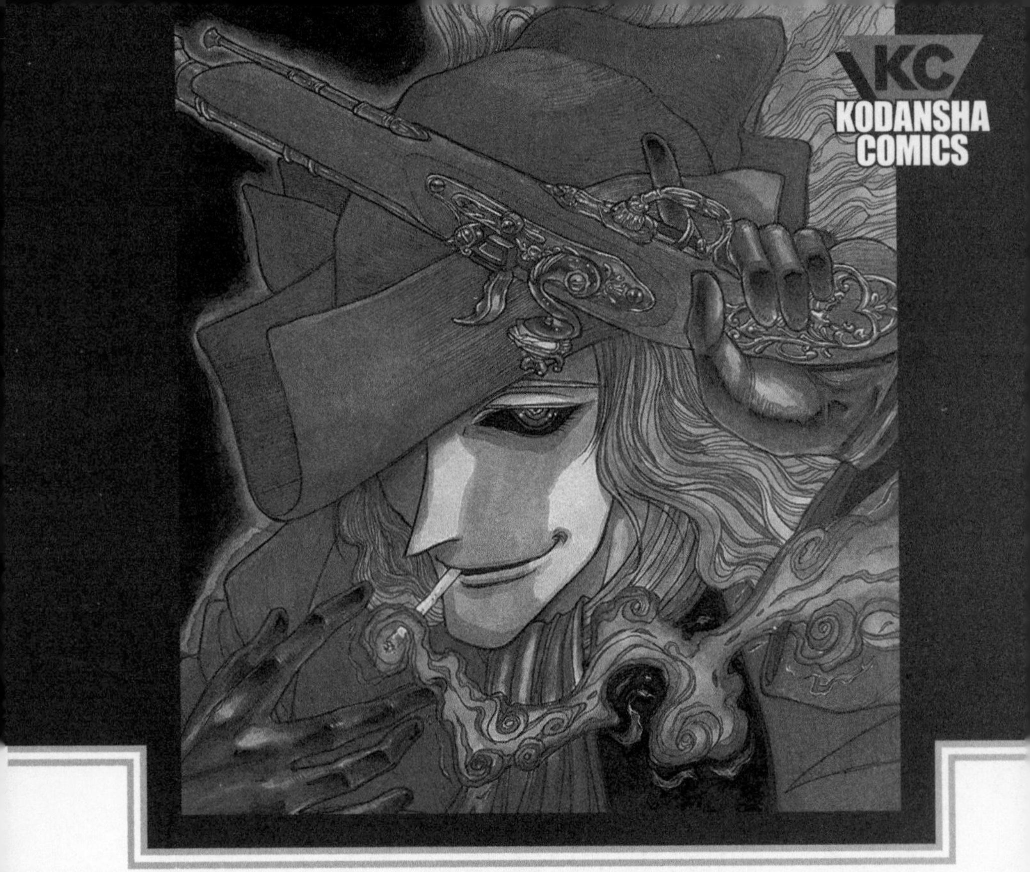
KC
KODANSHA
COMICS

The Black Museum: The Ghost and the Lady

By Kazuhiro Fujita

Deep in Scotland Yard in London sits an evidence room dedicated to the greatest mysteries of British history. In this "Black Museum" sits a misshapen hunk of lead—two bullets fused together—the key to a wartime encounter between Florence Nightingale, the mother of modern nursing, and a supernatural Man in Grey. This story is unknown to most scholars of history, but a special guest of the museum will tell the tale of The Ghost and the Lady...

Praise for Kazuhiro Fujita's *Ushio and Tora*

"A charming revival that combines a classic look with modern depth and pacing... **Essential viewing both for curmudgeons and new fans alike.**" — Anime News Network

"**GREAT!** The first episode of Ushio and Tora captures the essence of '90s anime." — IGN

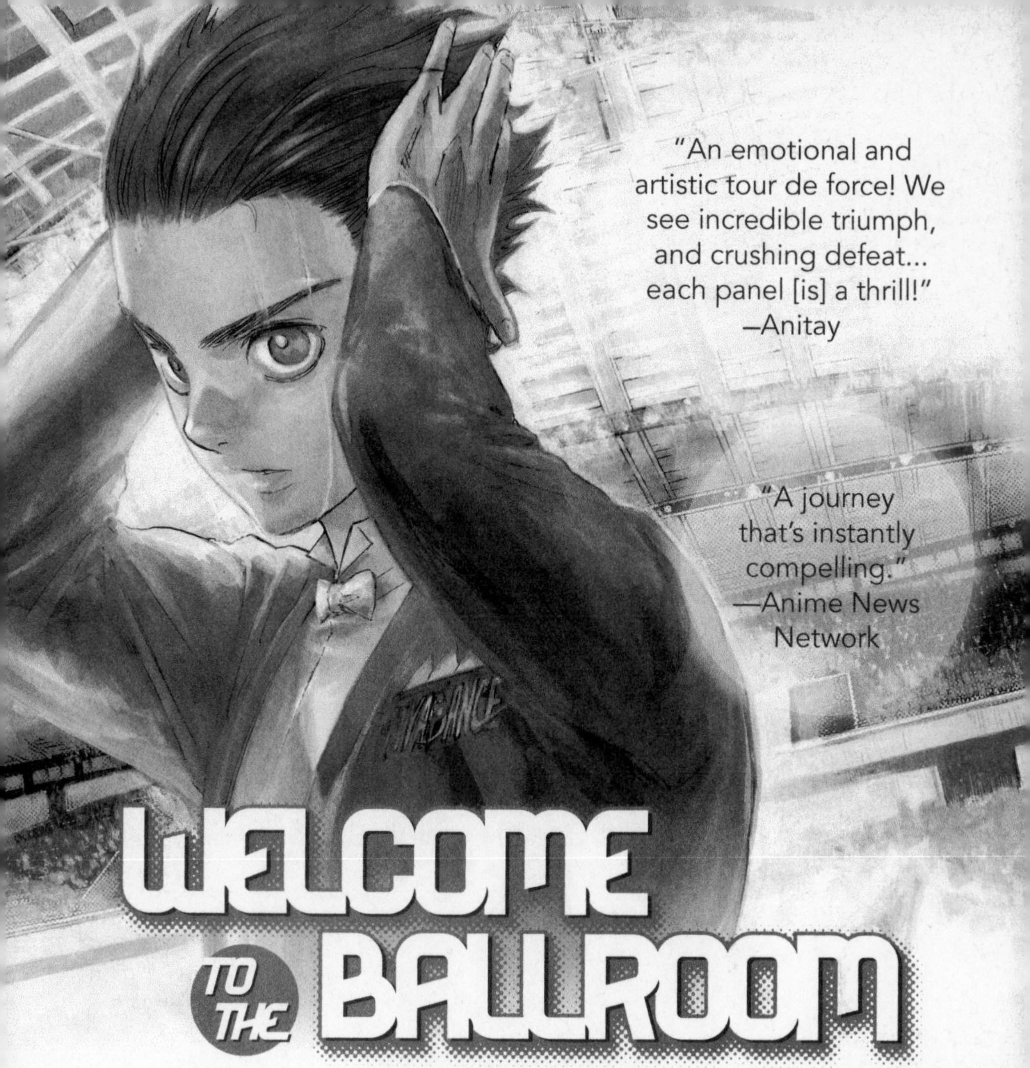

"An emotional and artistic tour de force! We see incredible triumph, and crushing defeat... each panel [is] a thrill!"
—Anitay

"A journey that's instantly compelling."
—Anime News Network

WELCOME TO THE BALLROOM

By Tomo Takeuchi

Feckless high school student Tatara Fujita wants to be good at something—anything. Unfortunately, he's about as average as a slouchy teen can be. The local bullies know this, and make it a habit to hit him up for cash, but all that changes when the debonair Kaname Sengoku sends them packing. Sengoku's not the neighborhood watch, though. He's a professional ballroom dancer. And once Tatara Fujita gets pulled into the world of ballroom, his life will never be the same.

KC KODANSHA COMICS

Based on the critically acclaimed classic horror manga

The first new *Parasyte* manga in over 20 years!

NEO PARASYTE f

BY ASUMIKO NAKAMURA, EMA TOYAMA, MIKI RINNO, LALAKO KOJIMA, KAORI YUKI, BANKO KUZE, YUUKI OBATA, KASHIO, YUI KUROE, ASIA WATANABE, MIKIMAKI, HIKARU SURUGA, HAJIME SHINJO, RENJURO KINDAICHI, AND YURI NARUSHIMA

A collection of chilling new *Parasyte* stories from Japan's top shojo artists!

Parasites: shape-shifting aliens whose only purpose is to assimilate with and consume the human race... but do these monsters have a different side? A parasite becomes a prince to save his romance-obsessed female host from a dangerous stalker. Another hosts a cooking show, in which the real monsters are revealed. These and 13 more stories, from some of the greatest shojo manga artists alive today, together make up a chilling, funny, and entertaining tribute to one of manga's horror classics!

KC
KODANSHA COMICS

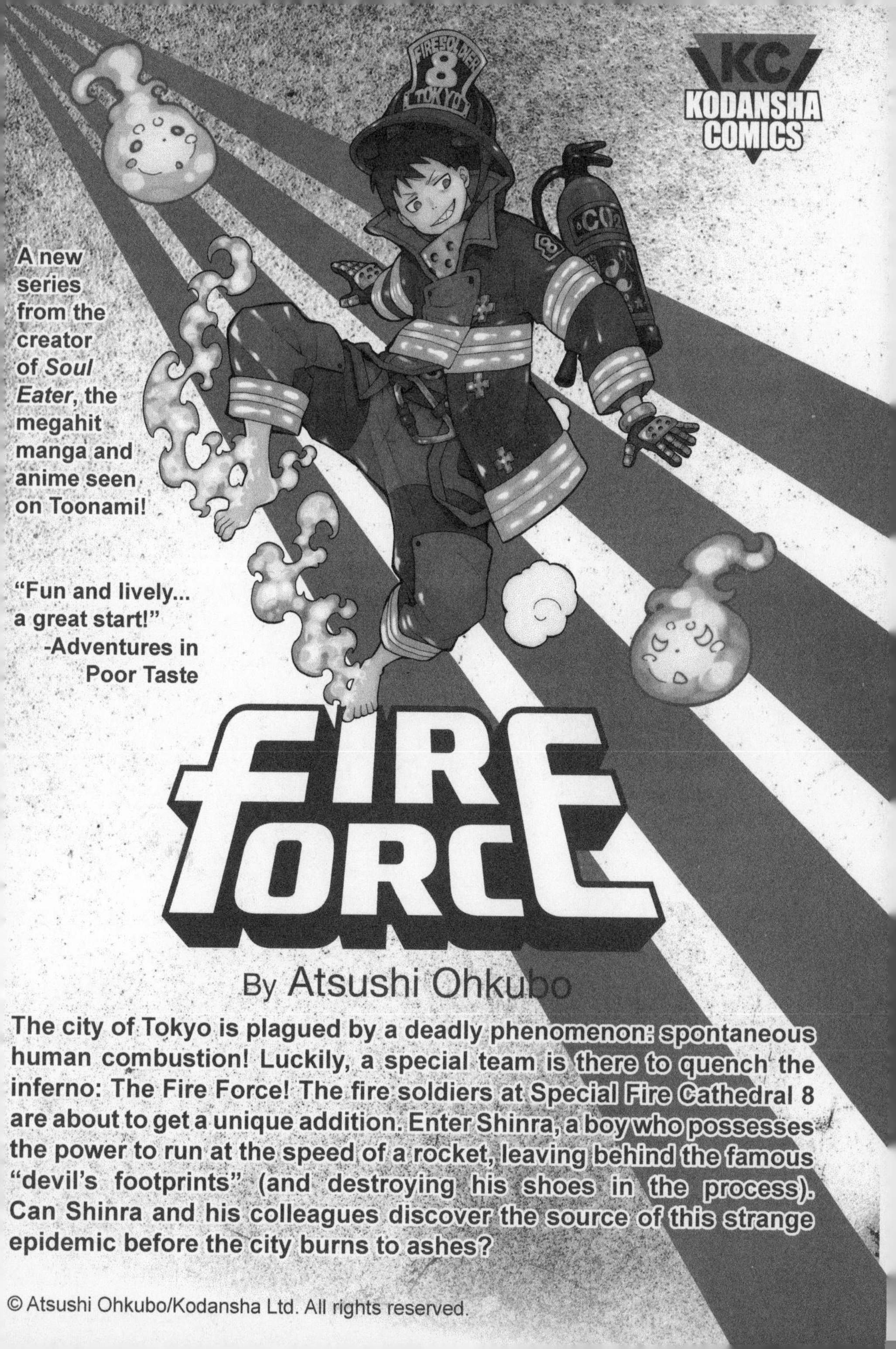

A new series from the creator of *Soul Eater*, the megahit manga and anime seen on Toonami!

"Fun and lively... a great start!"
-Adventures in Poor Taste

FIRE FORCE

By Atsushi Ohkubo

The city of Tokyo is plagued by a deadly phenomenon: spontaneous human combustion! Luckily, a special team is there to quench the inferno: The Fire Force! The fire soldiers at Special Fire Cathedral 8 are about to get a unique addition. Enter Shinra, a boy who possesses the power to run at the speed of a rocket, leaving behind the famous "devil's footprints" (and destroying his shoes in the process). Can Shinra and his colleagues discover the source of this strange epidemic before the city burns to ashes?

The award-winning manga about what happens inside you!

"Far more entertaining than it ought to be... what kid doesn't want to think that every time they sneeze a torpedo shoots out their nose?"
—Anime News Network

Strep throat! Hay fever! Influenza! The world is a dangerous place for a red blood cell just trying to get her deliveries finished. Fortunately, she's not alone…she's got a whole human body's worth of cells ready to help out! The mysterious white blood cells, the buff and brash killer T cells, even the cute little platelets—everyone's got to come together if they want to keep you healthy!

Cells at Work!

By Akane Shimizu

Kiss Me at the Stroke of Midnight volume 3 is a work of fiction. Names, characters, places, and incidents are the products of the author's imagination or are used fictitiously. Any resemblance to actual events, locales, or persons, living or dead, is entirely coincidental.

A Kodansha Comics Trade Paperback Original.

Published in the United States by Kodansha Comics,
an imprint of Kodansha USA Publishing, LLC, New York.

Publication rights for this English edition arranged through Kodansha Ltd., Tokyo.

First published in Japan in 2016 by Kodansha Ltd., Tokyo,
as *Gozen Reiji, Kiss Shi ni Kiteyo* volume 3.

Cover Design: Tomohiro Kusume (arcoinc)

ISBN 978-1-63236-496-8

Printed in the United States of America.

www.kodanshacomics.com

9 8 7 6 5 4 3 2 1

Translation: Melissa Goldberg
Lettering: Bunny To, Scott O. Brown
Editing: Haruko Hashimoto, Dawne Law
Editorial Assistance: YKS Services LLC/SKY Japan, INC.
Kodansha Comics Edition Cover Design: Phil Balsman